TRICKLE UP POVERTY

ALSO BY MICHAEL SAVAGE

Banned in Britain
Psychological Nudity
The Political Zoo
Liberalism Is a Mental Disorder
The Enemy Within
The Savage Nation
The Death of the White Male

TRICKLE UP POVERTY

Stopping Obama's Attack

on Our Borders,

Economy, and Security

MICHAEL SAVAGE

HARPER

NEW YORK • LONDON • TORONTO • SYDNEY

HARPER

A hardcover edition of this book was published in 2010 by William Morrow, an imprint of HarperCollins Publishers.

HarperCollins books may be purchased for educational, business, or sales promotional use. For information please write: Special Markets Department, HarperCollins Publishers, 10 East 53rd Street, New York, NY 10022.

FIRST HARPER PAPERBACK PUBLISHED 2011.

Library of Congress Cataloging-in-Publication Data is available upon request.

ISBN 978-0-06-201098-8 (pbk.)

11   12   13   14   15   DIX/RRD   10   9   8   7   6   5   4   3   2   1

*This is dedicated to all of the men who gave their lives
that we may have the freedom to write and read as we please*

CONTENTS

AUTHOR'S NOTE

President Obama is like a destructive child who takes apart a priceless watch that was carefully passed down to him. Without regard for the value of what he holds, he recklessly scatters the pieces on the floor and then can't put them back together again. Failing to learn from his mistakes, this destructive child moves on to another room where he finds another watch to take apart. Once again, he cannot put the pieces back together. That doesn't stop him from tearing apart yet another costly timepiece until all that's left are the pieces of discarded, functionless watches lying at his feet.

What's worse is that nobody steps in to stop him before he destroys again.

I've been watching in stunned amazement as Obama the Destroyer systematically takes apart America, piece by piece, while the complicit fifth-column government media complex and the lapdog political leaders remain silent. Barack Hussein Obama is tearing down everything that was built before this man was even born. Look no further than the fundamental requirement to preserve America's borders and national security. Despite the massive opposition to illegal immigration, and despite the new Arizona law, which mimics federal law to stem the flood of lawbreakers entering this country under the cover of darkness, on May 19, 2010, Obama the Destroyer made this astonishing statement to the President of Mexico:

> In the 21st century, we are defined **not** by our borders but by our bonds.[1]

Did you see what this petty dictator has done? With those fifteen words, the Traitor-in-Chief effectively erased our borders and compromised our sovereignty. Didn't Obama take an oath to uphold our laws? Didn't he take an oath to defend our borders against all enemies, both domestic and foreign? Without clearly defined borders, anyone can waltz right into America—including those who would kill us while we sleep.

Without borders, there's no country!

Wouldn't such a statement amount to an act of treason? What's more there's talk in Washington D.C. that Obama may use various executive actions to unilaterally grant mass amnesty to millions of illegal aliens if he can't get the Senate to pass a mass amnesty measure.

But Obama the Destroyer isn't satisfied.

There's so much more to demolish and so little time to do it.

He has taken apart the car industry, placing it under federal control. He has driven a knife into the heart of the best healthcare system in the world and replaced it with socialized medicine. He has desecrated the honor of America by apologizing to the world for a country he hates. He has set his sights on dismantling the military and our national security by slashing the comprehensive missile defense system. He is trying to destroy our nuclear capability with a foolish treaty with the Russians just when Iran, North Korea, and China are working overtime to build nuclear weapons.

Obama the Space Cadet is grounding the superior NASA space program with all of its technological advances and, instead, buying tickets to space on inferior Russian-made rockets. He is tearing apart our financial security by saddling future generations with trillions of dollars in new debt while at the same time allowing hedge fund, short-selling raiders to ravish the market, as they are accused of doing on May 6, 2010. What more do you need to know about this enemy within?

And yet, there *is* more.

Mark my words: History will show that Obama the Destroyer-in-Chief is impoverishing the middle class with taxation, regulation, and a desecration of our cherished freedoms. Moreover, as I will demonstrate in this book, Barack Obama is a naked Marxist-Leninist whose sole ambition in life is to transform America into the USSA: The United Socialist States of America.

You might be thinking, "Ah, come on, Michael, you're way off the mark here. Obama is just a regular guy with a wife, two kids, and a dog, who wants to make things better for the poor. He's no socialist. He's just doing the best he can for the country." You're wrong. While Obama's Robin Hood persona is the popular view, it's inaccurate, as I will demonstrate.

Look no further than where the money has actually gone from your pockets. Unlike the legendary medieval outlaw lurking in Sherwood Forest, a man whose mission was the betterment of the poor, President Obama has *robbed from the middle class to give to the rich*. You may want to read that again. Contrary to how it's been sold, there's no money falling down from the rich to the bottom, to the poverty-stricken.

Don't take my word for it. The evidence is everywhere. Millions of families in the middle class have lost their homes either to foreclosure or a short sale because they could no longer make their mortgage payments. Foreclosures and mortgage delinquency in the United States are at the highest levels since 1972.[2] Likewise, both business and personal bankruptcy filings are on the rise, with 2009 ranking as one of the highest on record.[3]

Obama wanted you to believe the stimulus money would be used to head off another Depression by creating millions of new jobs. Weeks before taking office, President Obama started campaigning for his bloated stimulus measure, which he claimed would "save or create 3 to 4 million jobs." What does he know about the topic? Is he a businessman? Has he ever owned a pizza shop or had to meet the payroll of a corporation of any size? Answer: No. What does he know about job creation? Nothing. In spite of his lack of experience or knowledge on the subject of job creation, Obama projected: "Ninety percent of these jobs will be created in the private sector. The remaining 10 percent are mainly public sector jobs we save, like the teachers, police officers, firefighters and others who provide vital services in our communities."[4]

It sounded good on paper. But he's wrong. He hasn't created new jobs. The opposite is true. Just look at where we are one year after rushing through the passage of the $819 billion "porkulus bill." Rather than alleviating the plight of millions of Americans, we're witnessing record levels of unemployed people on welfare or receiving unemployment benefits. Those are the facts, as the Washington Times story entitled, "American reliance on government at all-time high," reports: "The so-called 'Great Recession' has left Americans depending on the government dole like never before . . . moreover, for the first time since the Great Depression, Americans took more aid from the government than they paid in taxes."[5]

The middle class is getting poorer—not richer.

I'd like to chalk up this disturbing trend as nothing more than ineptness on his part. It's not. Let's be clear: *the trickle up poverty and the meltdown of our economy is quite by design.* More on that in the next chapter. The sooner you accept that fact, the greater the chance we have of saving this country. You see, Obama is trying to pass a systemic revolution in the United States of America. What do I mean by that? He is shrinking the middle class in order to create the socialist utopia of a two-class society, the ruling elite— meaning the bureaucrats—and the workers.

In other words, President Robin Hood has orchestrated an elaborate Ponzi scheme to scam the middle class. You've been taken. In spite of his speeches about looking out for the little guy, you are *not* the targeted ben- eficiary of his actions. He's just playing another game of Two-Card Monte. Forget what he's told you. It's all fraudulent. As I've always said, "Follow the money." Tell me, where has Obama's stimulus money gone?

Did you get any of it?

So, again, where's the money going? I'll explore that answer in greater detail in a subsequent chapter, but, in short, he's taking money from the middle class to give to his progressive cronies, big businesses, and the cabal of special interest groups who put Obama in power. Oh, sure, he's "spread- ing the wealth around"—just not in the way you originally thought. The question remains:

If he's not Robin Hood, who *is* he?

Barack Obama is a Reverse Robin Hood—a modern twist on the myth- ical character, packaged and sold to the sheeple he is exploiting. Make no mistake about it, unlike previous presidents who consulted with Congress seeking its cooperation to implement new initiatives, this president op- erates as if his wishes are the law of the land. As you'll see in this book, Barack Obama uses any means necessary—including circumventing the Constitution—to get his way. Why? He's living in a dream world acting as if his wishes are the sole determinant for the future of America.

Do these words sound extreme to modern ears? Perhaps.

But then again, I have a bias.

I was born in another time and come from another generation.

I come from a time in our history where all politicians, regardless of their political stripe, drew a line in the sand when it came to issues of national security. None of them intentionally engaged in policies that would leave the country naked and vulnerable to those who would harm us. If they did advance such views, they either remained unelected or were thrown out of office.

What a different world it is today.

So much has happened in just two generations.

America has gone from EISENHOWER to OBAMA in two generations. From BEN CASEY to NURSE JACKIE in two generations. From MUTUAL ASSURED DESTRUCTION to ASSURED NATIONAL DESTRUCTION in two generations. From JOHN WAYNE to LADY GAGA in two generations. From I SPY to I CRY in two generations. From I LOVE LUCY to I LOVE LOOSELY.

From AL EINSTEIN to AL GORE.

From I HAVE A DREAM to I HAVE A SCHEME.

From CATCHER IN THE RYE to KETCHUP ON THE FLY. From STARLETS to HARLOTS. PREACHERS to BREACHERS. ATHLETES to SEXLETES. BOY SCOUTS to TOY SCOUTS. GIRL SCOUTS to TWIRL SCOUTS. From LSD to ADD. CARDIGANS to PARTYKINS. From ASPIRIN to OXYCONTIN. From LADY JANE to LET'S GET INSANE. From SCI-ENCE to LIE-ENCE. From ACORN THE TREE, to ACORN THE SPREE.

From LASSIE to SASSY. From RELIGION to PIGEONS.

From EONS to PEONS. From RAPISTS to OFFENDERS.

From CAP AND GOWN to CAP-AND-TRADE. From STICKBALL to SPEEDBALLS.

In two generations.

That's the story of AMERICA THE GREAT . . . to AMERICA THAT GRATES.

I wrote *Trickle Up Poverty* for those who voted *against* Barack Obama, and those Obamanics who voted *for* Obama but now realize they were tricked and fear where he's taking America in the generations ahead. I clearly blame the Republican Party for Obama's ascension to power. They had every opportunity during the campaign to stop Obama. But every time they had the chance, John "McShame" McCain either refused to do so or outright shot himself in the foot.

Let me give you an example. On the day of the last presidential debate, I went on the air and said the following:

> John McCain, your handlers refuse to let you come on my show. They've told you that you should not speak to the Savage Nation. They told you that we are not your audience. They told you that my vast audience with undecided voters didn't matter. And you listened to them.
>
> Even though you wouldn't speak to my audience, I will give you one line that you could use to defeat Senator Obama during tonight's final debate. Here's what you do. Listen to Mr. Obama present his policies, smile as he talks in a Reaganesque way, and then say, "Senator Obama, that all sounds very nice. But we've heard this before. What you're proposing is **trickle up poverty.**"

That would have been the end of it. John McCain could have defeated Obama with that one line if he had introduced it that night and then hammered it home right up to the election. But his handlers, who, in my opinion, were stealth Democrats, didn't want him to win the election. Why? Because the Republicans had raped Lady Liberty for the previous eight years. We all know the way this game is played. The Republican establishment knew they had to give the power to a Democrat in order to take the spotlight off their own failure and excess—no matter how dangerous Obama might be once in power. They knew they had wrecked things so badly by running up the largest deficits in history and expanding the size of government—all under George Bush. They reasoned, "Let's give it to a Democrat so the country can blame him for the worst four years in American history, and then we'll come back triumphant with another Republicrat who will continue to hoodwink the sheeple."

That is how the established two party system works. Which begs the question: Are either of them the *American* party? Do they stand for the

American people? Do they represent the will of the people? Do they have America's best interest at heart? Answer: No. Thankfully, there's a third party emerging, the American party. You know it as the Tea Party. Granted, it's in its infancy. But it has a shape now; it's a thriving embryo.

However, the powerful forces on the other side believe in abortion. They have no qualms about aborting life in the womb and they're just as quick to abort life in the womb of politics. They want to abort this grassroots American party of patriots because they recognize it is the honest party—unlike themselves. Which is why they're trying every trick and poison known to the political process to discredit the movement.

That said, *Trickle Up Poverty* is for those who were either taken in by John McCain or voted for him reluctantly knowing that he was just Bush II. And it's for those who are stunned at the great lengths Obama has gone to wreak havoc on the country. In that respect, *Trickle Up Poverty* documents the rise of Barack Obama: how it happened, why it happened, and how to defeat him in the next election.

These pages contain invaluable information to win in the 2010 midterm election and, more important, to rescue the White House in 2012 when President Obama seeks another four years of destruction and desecration. Let it never be forgotten who this man is: *a diehard Marxist-Leninist committed to a socialist makeover of America*. This is the best treatise to date documenting Barack Obama's Marxist-Leninist roots and all the action points a reader will need to argue with neighbors, friends, and co-workers to make certain Barack is sent back!

Obama does not limit his megalomaniacal Marxist-Leninist views to America. He has set his sights on regulating the world, which is why I call him a "pan-Leninist."

As you'll see in this book, Obama and his radical fellow travelers view him as the world's leading *regulator*—witness his grovel tours of 2009, his friendship with dictators, and his desire to align U.S. policies with other countries around the world. He dreams of becoming the leader—not of the *free world*, but of the *regulated world*. From speech to heath care to energy, Obama envisions them all controlled by a world government which he leads.

That is pan-Leninism.

That is yet another reason he must be stopped.

Granted, there have been a number of books written about President Obama's ties to radical socialists and outright communists. This book is different. How? In it, I show you specifically and in detail the numerous ways that Obama's policies affect *you*, the individual reader, your family, and the nation. Moreover, I go beyond pointing out the problems he's creating and offer a hard set of solutions. In a very real sense, if you were running the government, these practical solutions are what you would do to preserve America's borders, language, culture, economics, and, yes, her future.

Let me put it to you this way. *Trickle Up Poverty* is not only about the past and what went wrong, but about how to prevent it from happening again in 2012. This book is a must for every independent voter who, in turn, should pass it around among friends and family all the way up to the 2012 election cycle until every thinking person knows the truth. And for those who doubt my assertions about this destructive administration, remember this key rule of science:

"ABSENCE OF EVIDENCE IS NOT EVIDENCE OF ABSENCE."

TRICKLE UP POVERTY

INTRODUCTION TO THE PAPERBACK EDITION

The Invisible Marxist Presidency

In April 2010, Barack Obama announced that he was shutting down America's space exploration program and would be making drastic cuts to NASA's budget. Less than a year later, our last space shuttle flew its final mission. The script is playing out just as I predicted in *Trickle Up Poverty*.

I tried to warn you.

Were you paying attention?

I said that Obama would relegate us to the position of having to hitch rides on Russian rockets when we want to send our astronauts to the International Space Station. The only difference is that since the first edition of *Trickle Up Poverty* was published, Russia has raised the ante. They've decided that since our president is naive enough to close down the U.S. space program, he's probably naive enough to think the Russians won't gouge us when we ask them to take our astronauts into space.

They were right.

The original estimate was $56 million per trip. The Russians recently informed us they'd be charging $63 million instead.[1]

I don't think they'll stop there. The Russians know a sucker when they see one. They know that a president who backed down from installing missile defense systems in Eastern Europe[2] isn't about to quibble over a $7 million price hike for a ride into space.

Less than two years into Obama's presidency, a majority of Americans had seen through the imposter in the White House. They recognized him for the tyrant he is. And they sent a strong message in the 2010 mid-term elections.

They voted to reverse the "trickle up poverty" that continues to erode the middle class.

Republicans picked up sixty-three seats in the House of Representatives,[3] giving them a forty-nine-seat advantage over Democrats. In state governments, the results were even more decisive: There are now Republican governors in twenty-nine of the fifty states,[4] and Republicans overthrew Democrats in another twenty state legislatures.[5]

What did our ever-arrogant president do in response?

Did he listen to voters and change course?

He did what you'd expect a leftist dictator to do. He doubled down on the policies that are weakening the country and driving the United States further toward bankruptcy.

More than a year after he put thousands of Americans out of work by ordering an unnecessary moratorium on deepwater oil drilling in the Gulf of Mexico,[6] Obama still hadn't allowed production to resume. That caused Federal Judge Martin Feldman to order the administration to lift the drilling moratorium. When it failed to do so, Judge Feldman found the administration in contempt of court[7] for acting with "determined disregard"[8] in refusing to obey his order.

In other words, the election results didn't change a thing.

Lisa Jackson, a radical environmentalist, is still overseeing the Obama administration's energy policy. She's the head of the Environmental Protection Agency (EPA), and she promotes "environmental justice." That's based on the idea that U.S. environmental policy disproportionately affects people of color, and we've got to shut down our energy industry so that minorities won't be further harmed by pollution. Jackson's idea of energy policy is to promote government-subsidized "green jobs" so she can create "environmentalists for life." For her, the EPA is synonymous with the environmental movement, and she makes it clear that she will do whatever it takes to implement policies that significantly impede the expansion of our energy industry.[9]

When the Senate refused to pass the cap-and-tax legislation that the House had approved in 2008, Obama simply transferred the power to regulate America's energy industry to Jackson and the EPA. This allowed him to continue his assault on America's energy production, weakening our economy and our national security.

Are you starting to get the picture?

Obama's continuing assault on America's position as the most powerful nation on earth doesn't stop with energy policy.

When the Middle East began to implode in February 2011, Obama wasted time and put human lives at risk while he tried to make up his mind about what to do. As uprisings against dictatorial regimes in the Middle East spread following the ouster of Hosni Mubarak in Egypt, Obama stood back and watched, unable to decide whom to support.

What you might not know is that Obama himself played a part in triggering the uprising against Mubarak in the first place.

Did you find it curious that Egyptian military leaders were in conference in Washington, D.C., when the rioting broke out? Did it occur to you that the meeting might have been scheduled that way so that Egypt's military response to the demonstrators would be delayed?

The United States knew as early as December 2008 that groups opposed to the Mubarak regime were developing a plan to overthrow the Egyptian government. They received the information from a young dissident who the United States had sponsored to attend a meeting for international political activists that took place in New York City. In addition, according to documents exposed by WikiLeaks, U.S. Ambassador to Egypt Margaret Scobey was aware of the plans of the Mubarak opposition group. Leaked documents also show that while the United States publicly supported the Mubarak government, U.S. embassy officials continued to communicate with the activist in question throughout 2008 and 2009.[10]

The International Crisis Group (ICG), founded and funded by none other than presidential puppetmaster George Soros and several other international leftist agitators, also had a hand in the Egyptian uprisings. The man most likely to become the next president of Egypt, Mohamed ElBaradei, was an ICG director and was handpicked by the group to step in after the ouster of Mubarak. ElBaradei is the former head of the International Atomic Energy Agency. He's the guy who kept assuring us that Iran had no intention of developing nuclear weapons. He's also received full backing from the radical Muslim Brotherhood.[11]

The president's own team of foreign policy advisors went along with the planned overthrow of Mubarak based on their stated creed: "[I]n a world in which power has diffused, our interests are best protected and advanced when others step up and at times lead alongside and even ahead of us."[12]

Do you understand that our president has relinquished our country's leadership role in the world?

Do you realize how much damage the shrinking violet in the White House is doing by his unwillingness to lead?

By the time the revolts in the Middle East reached Libya, Obama declared that "Qaddafi must go," then refused to provide any help to the rebels trying to overthrow the Libyan tyrant.[13] In an unprecedented move, the twenty-two-nation Arab League called for the establishment of a no-fly zone over Libya. They knew that the United States would have to establish the no-fly zone, and they were sending an unmistakable message that Obama needed to step in. They were emphasizing just how damaging the president's indecision was to Arab and U.S. interests in the region.[14]

Obama's response to criticism of his ambivalent approach in the Middle East? Who are the "rebels"? Why are we supporting them when they may be worse than Qaddafi?

He decided to hold a press conference. In it he explained that he had organized "a series of conversations about the situation."[15] In the meantime, Qaddafi was killing his own people with tanks and fighter jets, largely because Obama had frittered away any chance there was to help Libyan rebels.

The response to the unrest in the Middle East also pointed up the fact that our weak-willed leftist president has no idea how to effectively deploy America's military assets.

Obama sent a small rented ferry boat to rescue Americans from the dangerous situation in Libya while China and Great Britain sent warships to evacuate their citizens from the war-torn dictatorship.[16] Obama decided not to deploy warships to the Middle East as chaos threatened our oil supply. Then, only a month later, he sent two aircraft carriers to Japan to deliver food and water in response to the earthquake and tsunami that devastated that country.[17]

Obama's Middle East indecision had other consequences, among them rising oil prices. In the same press conference where he revealed he was having "conversations" about Libya, Obama addressed the oil issue.

Or should I say he seized the occasion to lie about our energy resources?

He made the false claim that the United States controls only 2 percent of the world's oil. The Energy Information Administration (EIA) estimate on which this claim is based doesn't take into account proven resources of nearly a trillion barrels of oil offshore on the U.S. Outer Continental Shelf, in the Arctic National Wildlife Refuge, and in shale deposits in Wyoming, Utah, and Colorado.

What Obama failed to mention is that the reason the EIA doesn't include these reserves in its estimate is because his own administration continues to ban oil production in those areas.

The oil is there; we just can't include it.[18]

Obama also claimed that in 2011 America's oil production had reached "its highest level in seven years." In fact, the EIA says there will be "a decline in production of 220,000 barrels of domestic oil per day in 2011," and next year production will decline by 150,000 barrels a day.[19]

I don't have to tell you that these declines are primarily the result of Obama's Gulf drilling moratorium.

The imposter in the White House continues to lie in support of his energy policies—policies he himself admits will cause energy prices to "necessarily skyrocket."[20] It's one more way he continues to inflict "trickle up poverty" on America.[21]

Domestically, the administration's agenda of undermining American values and refusing to carry out its sworn duty to uphold the Constitution continues unchecked.

You remember the Defense of Marriage Act, right? The 1996 law that declares that marriage is between a man and a woman? The law that passed with a 342–67 majority in the House and by an 85–14 margin in the Senate?[22]

Obama directed the Justice Department to stop defending DOMA in court on the grounds that, as Attorney General Eric Holder wrote in a letter to Congress, "as applied to same-sex couples legally married under state law," the act is unconstitutional.[23]

Obama's decision wasn't based on a voter referendum or court decisions. It was an executive decision that one former senator says represents "an affront to the will of the American people"[24] because it defied legislation that had passed with overwhelming majorities in both the House and the Senate.

The Obama administration's domestic policy affronts didn't stop there.

It wasn't enough that Nancy Pelosi and Harry Reid rammed through Obamacare legislation without a single Republican vote and against the will of a great majority of the American people. The administration continues the practice of buying support that enabled them to get the legislation passed in the first place.

Department of Health and Human Services (HHS) Secretary Kathleen Sebelius—who once said, like a true Marxist, that Americans need "reeducation on the Obama healthcare law"—granted more than 1,000 waivers to large corporations, health insurance companies, and labor unions so they don't have to comply with ObamaCare regulations. The waivers were given because without them, many Americans would simply lose their jobs and their insurance.

That's how poorly written and destructive ObamaCare legislation is.

The problem is that there's no provision in the healthcare bill that gives anyone the authority to grant waivers.

Is this one more example of Barack Obama simply ignoring the Constitution and federal law and ruling by executive decree?

My answer is "yes."

He's determined to bypass the legislature and the judiciary altogether if necessary. He's willing to do anything he can to short-circuit all of the constitutional checks and balances that are indispensable to American democracy in order to advance his subversive agenda.

The administration also continues to advance that agenda through its immigration policy. Several thousand acres along the Mexican border, including parts of a national wildlife refuge, have been declared off-limits for Americans because of the danger they'll be attacked by drug smugglers and human traffickers who now control much of the area.[25]

Homeland Security Secretary Janet Napolitano's response to this increasingly dangerous situation?

She now requires border patrol agents to use beanbag ammunition when they have to confront enemy intruders. This policy led directly to the death of U.S. border patrol agent Brian Terry, who was under orders to first fire "non-lethal" beanbag ammo at invaders before using live rounds. The invaders were firing live ammo from their AK47s.[26]

With 63 percent of Americans saying that control of our border with Mexico is the top immigration priority,[27] the administration continues to ignore the midterm election results. In the meantime, it's looking more and more like Obama wants to eliminate our southern border altogether and allow unlimited illegal immigration into the country.

Our southern border is where *Trickle Up Poverty* becomes *Trickle Up Murder*, and Napolitano should be tried for crimes against America.

Still not convinced?

With the economy still teetering on the brink of a double-dip recession, Obama submitted a federal budget for fiscal year 2012 that adds deficits totaling $1.5 trillion to a national debt that already stands at $14 trillion, equal to the entire U.S. annual economic output.[28] Adding insult to injury, Obama has the gall to tell Americans they need to tighten their belts, while at the same time he's throwing lavish White House parties[29] and sending his family on $75,000-a-day vacations at taxpayer expense.[30]

It doesn't stop there.

With the crises in the Middle East escalating, our "frat boy" president managed to tape the NCAA men's basketball tournament selections so he could fill out his brackets and pick the winner. While Japan was overwhelmed by a disastrous earthquake, tsunami, and nuclear meltdowns, he managed to squeeze in a round of golf, the sixty-first since he took the oath of office. That same week, he welcomed the 2009–10 National Hockey League champions, the Chicago Blackhawks, to the White House.[31]

He's the invisible Marxist in the White House. He orders his henchmen to loot our treasury, stifle our energy production, and trample on our freedoms, then he disappears when a strong leader is needed most.

Can you remember a single time you saw him on television during the crises in Libya and Japan?

And don't tell me the networks would deny him air time.

During his first year in office, he made more than 400 TV appearances, 52 of them to promote his healthcare takeover alone. You couldn't turn on a television set without seeing him chatting affably with an interviewer or leading a pep rally for his followers in one of the fifty-eight cities and thirty states he visited.[32] But with the world in flames, all he could manage was a single TV appearance where he talked about bullying. After that, he scheduled a trip to South America to promote American jobs and see the sights with his family.[33]

When strong and decisive presidential leadership was needed, Barack Obama retreated. His disappearance in this time of crisis—unprecedented in recent memory—will define his presidency as one characterized by cowardice and indecision.

Do you find this president's total lack of focus and leadership as disturbing as I do?

Do you understand how dangerous it is for our president to behave like a college sophomore while chaos erupts around the world?

I won't go so far as to say that Barack Obama's lack of leadership is *causing* the international meltdown we're experiencing.

I will say this, though: Without the anchor of a militarily assertive United States presided over by a strong president, the world is starting to fall apart. Barack Obama seems determined to carry on Jimmy Carter's traitorous legacy of encouraging Islamist dictatorships and putting shackles on our military and on our energy and economic policies.

We're paying the price for our leftist president's irresponsible policies. Obama continues to ignore the will of the American people, squandering taxpayer money and misrepresenting facts while the world goes up in flames and our economy faces bankruptcy.

You'd think this would provide the perfect opportunity for Republicans to continue their election success in 2012, right?

Wrong.

There's a problem here.

Republican leadership didn't listen to the American people any more than the Democrats did. They have the chance in 2012 to finish what they started when they won the House in 2010, but they're hobbled by stale policies and weak leadership.

Republicans boasted about their plan to cut $4 billion from the federal budget every two weeks through continuing resolutions until a budget was passed, but they remained oblivious to the fact that $4 billion barely covers what we spend every day just to pay the interest on the national debt. At the same time, they ignored Minnesota congresswoman Michelle Bachmann when she urged them to rescind $105 billion in hidden appropriations for funding ObamaCare that Nancy Pelosi and Harry Reid snuck into that legislation.[34]

They still don't get it.

There's little vision and no passionate leadership on the Republican side. They're setting us up to lose. The only strategy they seem capable of pursuing is giving in to the Democrats' calls for compromise.

Here's something they need to hear.

Trickle Up Poverty is still the most important political book to be published in the last decade. It's still the only book that documents exactly how dangerous this radical leftist president and his comrades are to our way of life, to the unparalleled opportunities and freedoms Americans enjoy.

It should be required reading for every Republican lawmaker and presidential candidate. Maybe it would open their eyes to the real danger we face. Maybe it would make them understand that it isn't just a political battle we're fighting, it's a battle for the survival of democracy in the world.

CHAPTER 1

A Revolution Is Brewing

Many years ago while I was in graduate school in Hawaii, a near death boating experience on the high seas taught me a life lesson that directly relates to the problems we're having with President Obama. Do you know what it's like for a kid from New York City to wind up in Hawaii? I'd never been to a place as remarkable as Hawaii. It was like walking into heaven itself. When you land in heaven, you think you can do anything.

Almost overnight, you have hubris.

Hubris is a sense of excessive self-confidence that only children and the mad should have. But when a grown-up has hubris, it becomes very dangerous and, in my case, that was true. So I get to the islands and it's a magical time. I never saw sunsets like this. They can break your heart. And the flowers—the plumeria blossoms—are beyond description.

I used to bicycle up to the University and I would see plumeria blossoms lying on the sidewalk. I'd stop the bicycle and pick up the plumeria blossoms for a closer look and, of course, to smell them. I'd never seen anything like them. Sure, we had rose petals on the fence back in the Bronx when I was a little kid. They were soft and beautiful in their own way. But this was something unique. The perfumed scent of the plumeria was unlike anything on the mainland.

There I am, surrounded by such incredible beauty—the yellow hibiscus,

the golden sunsets, the colorful rainforest birds in the back of the valley that
I'd never known existed—and before long, I start to get tuned into my own
body in a way I've never been tuned in.

Here's how the Hawaiian transformation works.

Even if you've never lived in the tropics, you instinctively start shedding
clothing. It's off with the long sleeves, the shoes, and leather. You put it
all away and now you're in flip-flops and shorts. At night, the breeze zips
through your sleeves and you start to become alive in a new way. You're
drawn to the ocean. With the migratory seagulls soaring overhead, you start
to feel like the original man.

In that magical state of mind, you decide to buy a sailboat. I bought
the Taranga—a sloop-rigged sailing vessel, about 22' long, made primarily
of white oak. It had been built in Oregon and sailed out by somebody to
Hawaii. I bought it for next to nothing. Although she was in perfect shape,
she had no engine. I kept her in the Ala Wai marina and quickly learned
most people who owned boats mainly used them to drink on and just hang
out. Me? I was foolish enough to actually want to *sail* the boat, even though
I knew nothing about sailing.

What's more, I decided to take her out without an engine.

I figured it would be easy to get out because the wind was prevailing
westward out of the harbor. A few of my new friends released the lines, cast
me off, and pushed me backward for my maiden voyage. There I was sailing
down the Ala Wai channel and then out into the ocean by myself. I zipped
along with the sail wide open, heading further out to sea.

I was thinking, "This is unreal. I can do anything."

It wasn't long before I realized I had miscalculated the situation.

Simply put, I didn't know how to get back. Suddenly my mind was racing for answers. You know, "How do I turn this thing around if the wind is
blowing out to sea?" I had no idea. Not a clue. The sloop didn't come with
an owner's manual. I hadn't paid for lessons. So I'm thinking I had better
figure out what to do because, at the rate I was going, I'd soon be in the
middle of the Pacific Ocean with no way back at all.

What's worse, I had no flares, no radio, no engine, and no provisions.

I don't think I even had a life preserver.

I know that sounds crazy. But remember, I was an inexperienced operator. I didn't know what I didn't know. Besides, the late sixties was an age when many people had total madness about what they could do and accomplish—whether or not it had a basis in reality. I admit, all I had was hubris.

My first move? I resorted to common sense.

I dropped the sails because that, of course, would cut the motion of the boat. With the sails secured, I tried using the tiller to turn the boat around. You know, flip-flop, flip-flop, until I got the boat pointing back toward land. Then, I figured if the wind is blowing against me, there must be way to go into a prevailing wind and still move against it. I've seen other people do it. And, little by little, lo and behold, I was able to return to the harbor. I still don't know whether it was pure luck, a strong undercurrent, or God's hand pushing me to safety. I quickly learned that sailing is not for the amateur.

Here's the connection to President Obama.

America is the boat. Whoever is at the helm determines her destination. If he's experienced, if he's wise, if understands the fundamentals of boating, then all is well. She'll remain safe and strong, able to sail again for generations to come. If not, apart from a lucky break or God's direct intervention, she'll drift further out into dangerous waters without a prayer of survival.

It all comes down to the heart, soul, and experience of the sailor.

Does the sailor have a healthy respect for the laws of boating on the high seas? Or, does he ignore them and do as he pleases, putting himself and the boat in mortal peril? Is he wise enough to recognize the danger signs on the horizon and quickly change course? Or, in the face of certain disaster, is he too arrogant and reckless to make the necessary adjustments while there's still time?

We're living in dangerous times.

We have a political novice in America's wheelhouse.

Moreover, the president is propelled only by a dangerous hyper-dosage of hubris. Is that an overstatement? We all know the former junior senator from Illinois had about a five-minute political career before campaigning for the highest office of the land. In other words, Obama has no governing experience. He doesn't know how to lead. Worse, he has been indoctrinated by Marxist professors. He's convinced that the failed ideas of Marxism and socialism will suddenly work now that *he's* in charge of the ship. However, the navigational chart he's relying on to steer the country from capitalism to socialism is fatally flawed. And now he's lost and over his head.

Obama has taken a hammer and sickle to our economy, saddling us with a national debt we can never repay. He's exercising ultra-tolerance with Islamic terrorists, rendering America vulnerable. What's more, there's not a scintilla of bipartisan consensus in Congress as Obama had promised. It's gridlocked while the middle class is shell-shocked.

Let me put it to you this way.

Obama never ran a state before he became the Head of State.

Which brings me back to the point of this story. All Barack Obama has is hubris. That said, here's what makes Barack Hussein Obama so dangerous—his hubris is based on nothing more than the failed Sugarplum Fairy fantasies of Leninism and Marxism dancing around in his head. Since the president has no governing experience, since he has rejected the fundamentals upon which this country has been built, he relies on the fanciful notions of utopia colorfully painted by his communist professors, his Mao-infatuated inner circle of presidential advisors, and his Leninist-loving close personal confidantes.

I refuse to sit idly by and allow this man to take America out for a joy-ride into deep waters. He may be the captain, but I can tell there's a mutiny on board the ship. Just look at how the middle class is taking matters into its own hands. Thousands are speaking up for the first time in town hall meetings, millions of mothers with strollers are attending local tea parties from coast to coast, tens of millions more are listening to conservative talk radio, and the invisible pajama army is carving out spots all along the information superhighway offering fellow travelers news and insight they can find nowhere else.

Yes, there is a revolution brewing.

The middle class sees the naked reality of what's going down and they're bracing to fight the enemy within. That's why the Tea Party movement is growing so strong. That's why so many patriots have pinned the flag of American exceptionalism to the mast. No one in his right mind wants to sail headlong into the coming perfect storm. And that's exactly where America is headed unless we reverse this president whose roots, as you'll see in the next chapter, are firmly planted in the poisoned soil of Marxism and Leninism.

Tea for Two Parties

Americans are boiling mad.

They understand that the future of America hangs in the balance like a loose tooth. They're furious over the way Congress and this Marxist-Leninist–oriented president are manipulating the current economic crisis to nationalize businesses. They're steamed over the fraud science used to support global warming and view it as nothing more than a gigantic Ponzi scheme. Middle-class Americans are watching their life savings evaporate while the president saddles them with $3.8 trillion in new debt. And they're frightened because other countries are losing faith in the long-term financial viability of America and the dollar.

This trend toward the impoverishment of the middle class is more than just an economic issue. The policies of President Obama are creating a poverty of the body, mind, and spirit of all Americans. How? As I demonstrate throughout this book, Obama is impoverishing how we *think, feel, and view ourselves* as a people while robbing our personal freedoms and bankrupting our clout as the leader of the world.

The middle class isn't just mad about these developments; they're asking hard questions about the guy at the helm—something that should have been done more thoroughly by the lame-stream press before he took command of the deck. And so the middle class is wondering: Why are we as a nation sinking so fast? Why has America strayed off course so quickly? Why aren't sensible corrective measures being taken? How long can we continue to plunge recklessly into deep waters and survive? As even the Obamanics are finding out, there's a junior officer at the wheel—not a captain with sufficient experience.

Yes, a political revolution is at hand.

After years of my calling George W. Bush a "fiscal socialist" and my railing against a "one party system with two faces," someone in the midstream media finally exploded. In February, 2009, CNBC financial analyst Rick Santelli railed against President Obama's irresponsible mortgage bailout plan. It was an unforgettable, spontaneous moment in broadcasting with repercussions that are still rocking America's political infrastructure.

Reporting live from the trading floor of the Chicago Board of Trade,

Santelli had the courage to stand up to President Obama, saying, "the government is promoting bad behavior" and then asked, "This is America! How many of you people want to pay for your neighbor's mortgage that has an extra bathroom and can't pay their bills?" [1]

Cheers erupted across the land—except in the halls of power. Obama's spokesmouth and press secretary Robert Gibbs fired back at this broadcaster with a rant of his own: "It's tremendously important . . . for people who rant on cable television to be responsible and understand what it is they're talking about. I feel assured that Mr. Santelli doesn't know what he's talking about." [2]

Is that so?

Contrary to what Gibbs believes on his Fantasy Island, this frustration clearly represented the growing rage and fury of the middle class who don't believe the government is entitled to their earnings. This outburst resonated with people who already felt squeezed to the point of suffocation by shrinking paychecks and shriveling retirement funds. His words connected with families angry over losing their jobs and their homes. I'm sure that broadcaster had no idea that his next statement would, like a hot spark on dry tinder ignite a national movement: "We're thinking of having a Chicago Tea Party in July. All of you capitalists that want to show up at Lake Michigan, I'm gonna start organizing."

The rest was history.

From Maine to New Mexico, millions of moms and dads, primarily from the middle class, took to the streets to stage angry, but peaceful, protests known as Tea Parties. At first, the media ignored them while politicians offered a collective yawn. Not anymore. As I write these pages, thirty citywide Tea Party protests hosted around the country are being closely scrutinized by those in power. You see, Washington still hasn't fully come to terms with what the Tea Party movement is really about. Instead, they wonder: *What's all the fuss?*

Let me break it down for them.

It's pretty much what I've been saying for sixteen years: You have been dismantling my country. You have tried to rip my freedoms into shreds. You have caused the social order to degenerate. You have broken my borders. You have disrespected my traditions. You have burned my flags. You have spat upon my warriors. And if you don't like what we have to say, it's too damn bad. No, the Tea Party movement isn't a publicity stunt dreamed up because Americans have nothing better to do.

Far from it.

Real people are really angry.

They're armed with a real knowledge of what the hell is going on in Washington, D.C. What's more, they've been betrayed by their government and they refuse to take it anymore. They know the political parasites are having a party on our dime and it's killing the host. These patriots know they're in a battle to save the land they love. They're participating actively and passionately in a revolution based on a return to the core principles found in the Constitution.

This fight is between radicalism and constitutionalism.

They understand the radical left led by President Obama is dedicated to socialist values that are, by definition, destructive to America. Moreover, the middle class doesn't want Obama's trickle up poverty. They want less government and more freedom. They want wasteful spending to stop—*now*. They've put the politicians in Washington on notice: It's time to start reading the tea leaves.

The Savage States of America are rising up.

Perhaps nothing best typifies the "irresponsible behavior" in Washington behind this trickle up poverty than the following examples of abuse of power, government waste, and intrusion into our freedoms.

Power Corrupts, Absolute Power Corrupts Absolutely

We all know Speaker of the House Nancy Pelosi is a bit off.

This woman is so intoxicated with her own power that she runs around Washington like a despot. Don't get me wrong. My intention isn't to tarnish Madame Pelosi's reputation. She's already done a first-class job of that. Her behavior speaks for itself. Take, for example, the matter of her commandeering military jets for her family's use in which she flew her daughter, son-in-law, and grandson to a private event. Okay, if that had happened one time because there weren't seats left on a Southwest flight, fine.

But it wasn't once.

Not twice.

Not three times.

Amazingly, in just a two-year period, Pelosi's family flew on military jets *thirty-one times!* Details of this corruption are staggering. According to records obtained by the Judicial Watch organization, Nancy Pelosi was repeatedly misusing U.S. Air Force aircraft for personal use to the tune of $2,100,744.59 in just two years.[3] That price tag includes $101,429.00 for in-flight expenses such as food and alcoholic beverages. You might want to read that again. This autocrat is running an open bar in the sky—at your expense.

One particularly outrageous trip happened on May 15–20, 2008, in which Madame Pelosi and friends flew from Washington, D.C., to Baghdad via Tel Aviv. Just look at the beverages Pelosi, several members of Congress and their spouses ordered: Johnny Walker Red scotch, Grey Goose vodka, E&J brandy, Bailey's Irish Crème, Maker's Mark whiskey, Courvoisier cognac, Bacardi Light rum, Jim Beam whiskey, Beefeater gin, Dewar's scotch, Bombay Sapphire gin, Jack Daniels whiskey, Corona beer, and several bottles of wine.[4] What the hell was she throwing?

A Mardi Gras party?

Judicial Watch reported that this trip cost American taxpayers $17,931 *per hour*—and that was just for the aircraft. Are you beginning to get the picture?

Not only does Madame Pelosi expect the sheeple to pick up the tab for her exorbitant, wasteful, and improper spending, which is dishonorable enough, but let's not forget that members of the U.S. Air Force were being forced to serve as personal escorts for her and her kin instead of engaging the enemy! They should be flying reconnaissance missions over Teheran instead of flying babysitting missions over Akron.

Isn't the country at war with Muslim fascists who want to convert us or kill us? People understand this. Not Pelosi. She's cavorting in the skies in military jets without regard for the troops on the ground in Afghanistan. Tell me that's not the epitome of elitism.

Somewhere a marine dies while Pelosi flies.

The people are angered by her sheer arrogance.

When it comes to health care, as you'll see in chapter five, Pelosi's prescription was to ram a government plan down our throats whether the American people wanted it or not. The fact of the matter is that the majority of Americans—a full 61 percent—think Obama's plan should be scrapped, you know, dumped into the Potomac River.[5] There's a number of reasons why they want Congress to go back to square one. They want lawyers stopped with caps on medical lawsuits.

They don't want the feds telling them which doctors to use.

They don't want the feds nosing around in their medical files.

They don't want the feds telling them which medical procedures to have.

They don't want illegal aliens getting free medical care.

And they most certainly don't want to be fined for noncompliance. And yet, the voice of the people has fallen on deaf ears where Madame Pelosi is concerned. Listen to how this harridan thinks:

> We will go through the gate. If the gate is closed, we will go over the fence. If the fence is too high, we will pole vault in. If that doesn't work, we will parachute in. But we are going to get health care reform passed for the American people for their own personal health and economic security and for the important role that it will play in reducing the deficit.[6]

If Pelosi had as much passion for killing al-Qaeda as she has for killing our freedom of choice with her healthcare bill, the Democrat's approval rating would have soared 30 percent overnight. Her passion is misplaced. It's backfiring. Her zeal to pass socialized medicine has awakened the middle class who see healthcare premiums rising 20 percent or more and the destruction of the finest doctors and hospitals in the world!

Do you see why people are seething at the abuse of power by their elected officials? According to a liberal CBS/*New York Times* poll, a paltry 8 percent of Americans think members of Congress should be reelected.[7] They can't take this anymore. In fact, 75 percent disapprove of the job these false "representatives" are doing. Furthermore, in what was the lowest assessment of congressional incumbents in eighteen years, the survey found that 81 percent of those surveyed said, "it's time to give new people a chance" to represent them in Congress.

The more we learn about the way Pelosi is running Congress, the more we see we're living in an oligarchy, not a democracy. This is why the Tea Party movement is ready to throw the bums out. They know the local undertaker could do a better job representing them than Madame Pelosi, a monarch in her own mind, who's hell-bent on passing a socialist agenda that doesn't resemble the America they know.

The America they love.

The America they must now fight to defend.

From J.Crew to Screw You

When Michelle Obama was on the campaign trail with her husband, the press fawned over her thrifty, budget-conscious attire. Much was written about her contentment with a J.Crew wardrobe and the fact that her husband Barack wore suits right off the rack—as if they were an average American couple watching every nickel to make ends meet. You know, the kind of frugal people just living paycheck to paycheck who'd clean up the pork in Washington.

What's more, Michelle gave us the "I'm-no-different-than-you-I-wasn't-born-with-a-silver-spoon-in-my-mouth" speech when she told a crowd on the campaign trail, "There's a lot of people talking about elitism and all of that. But let me tell you who Barack and me are, so that you are not confused. Yeah, I went to Princeton and Harvard, but the lens through which I see the world is the lens that I grew up with. I am the product of a working-class upbringing."[8]

That charade lasted maybe five minutes after Michelle's husband landed in the White House.

Virtually overnight, as if she were suddenly royalty, Michelle was sporting a handmade Naeem Khan dress and a pair of Bochic earrings valued at more than $5,000. Five grand for earrings? My first car cost less than that. And, what does the Empress of America spend on a staff of twenty-six personal assistants?! The First Lady wasn't elected and has no official duties, and yet she certainly enjoys the trappings of royalty; or should I say the life of a Czarina?

Let's set aside the cost of her full-time personal makeup artist and hairdresser. If she feels the need for some help in that department, fine. But let's look at the list of servants: there's Michelle's Chief of Staff who, at $172,200 a year, makes more than some bank presidents. Add to that a Director of Policy and Projects for the First Lady at $140,000, a Director of Communications at $102,000, a Deputy Chief of Staff to the First Lady at $90,000, and a Director and Press Secretary to the First Lady who makes $84,000.

Should I go on?

How about $75,000 for a Director of Scheduling, $70,000 for a Deputy Director of Policy and Projects (since when is the First Lady involved in making policy decisions?), another $65,000 for a Deputy Director/Deputy Social Secretary—she's got two of them, $62,000 for someone to coordinate her events, $60,000 for a trip director—again, she's got two of them probably because she's planning lots of trips at your expense—and that's just a partial list.

When taken together, Czarina Michelle's twenty-six-person staff costs taxpayers $1.75 million dollars, excluding the cost of their elite benefits package.[9] You might wonder what benefit you're getting for that. But wait, there's more. Much more. That figure doesn't include the necessary Secret Service detail or the White House staff of servants who must cater to her every whim—whether she's serving wagyu steak valued at $100/pound at a White House cocktail party,[10] or motoring around Paris in a twenty-car caravan with her daughters for a weeklong European vacation while visiting all the "must-see" sites.[11]

I imagine she's proud for the first time in her life to be an American tourist.

Look, I understand how things work. Laura Bush was no penny-pincher, either. She had a sizable staff as well, although not as large and her tab was about $700,000 less than what Michelle is dropping. But both are out of line to spend taxpayer money to that extent while the economy is in a tailspin, that's all. As one commentator pointed out, "Mary Lincoln was taken to task for purchasing china for the White House during the Civil War. And Mamie Eisenhower had to shell out the salary for her personal secretary."[12]

Where's the fiscal restraint from our First Lady?

Why aren't the Obamas leading by example?

Whatever happened to president-elect Obama's call to Americans to make personal sacrifices? While on national television, Obama proclaimed, "Everybody's going to have to give. Everybody's going to have to have some skin in the game." [13] Remember that one? Or, how about this: President Obama, having just tripled our national debt, had the audacity to say, "After a decade of profligacy, the American people are tired of politicians who talk the talk but don't walk the walk when it comes to fiscal responsibility. It's easy to get up in front of the cameras and rant about exploding deficits. What's hard is getting deficits under control—but that's what *we must do*." [14]

We must do?

"We" who?

We—not he, obviously.

Of course, this nice little teleprompted speech begs the difficult question: If the Spender in Chief can't get the First Lady to pare down her bloated budget, how can the man be taken seriously when he claims he wants to cut wasteful government spending? What happened to walking the walk? He's lecturing us about fiscal responsibility while tripling the federal budget deficit and increasing our national debt by $1.9 trillion. In fact, according to the Economics Editor of the United Kingdom *Telegraph* newspapers, Edmund Conway, "under the Obama administration's current fiscal plans, the national debt in the US (on a gross basis) will climb to above 100pc of GDP by 2015—a far steeper increase than almost any other country." [15]

But there's a much more insidious dimension to all of this.

I'm talking about Michelle Obama's vision of the future, which, no doubt, has been shaped by the man she married—along with the indoctrination of her leftist professors at Harvard and Princeton. As I'll document in the next chapter, Barack Obama is a Red Diaper Doper Baby (RDDB); a full-fledged Marxist-Leninist. As such, he and Michelle are moving us toward a two-class society common in socialist nations: *the ruling class* and *the workers*. This explains why Michelle will never cut her staff or spending. As a newly arrived member of the ruling class, she believes she's entitled to it.

Her extravagance and hypocrisy haven't gone unnoticed by the people. America is breaking under the weight of one of the deepest recessions in our history and they wonder how Michelle can take a pleasure jaunt to the Eiffel Tower. How can she have the audacity to take a million-dollar vacation when people all across America are losing their jobs and their homes? In the end, this, too, will backfire. The taxpayers don't like seeing their hard-earned money being wasted.

The taxpayers don't consider themselves second-class.

The taxpayers don't like being lied to.

The taxpayers don't want a First Lady who fashions herself as Czarina.

This Land is His Land

As I write, Obama's czars are eyeing one of the largest federal land-grabs in history. Their target? That depends. A confidential internal government document stamped "NOT FOR RELEASE" somehow found the light of day. In it, Obama's henchmen identified fourteen sites in nine states spanning millions of acres primarily in the west. With the stroke of a pen, bypassing both public and congressional consent, Obama plans to designate thousands of square miles as "National Monuments." This Soviet-style mandate by fiat would prohibit any development of millions of acres rich in timber, clean coal, gold, minerals, natural gas, and other vital resources.

Translation: States and local communities will lose jobs and tax revenues.

Can Obama do that?

Can Barack the Buccaneer use the powers of government to shutdown the natural resources of individual states? Technically speaking, yes. Hiding behind the Antiquities Act, this president—who promised an open and transparent government—can use his executive power to hijack and yank the land out from underneath a state and turn it into a national monument in the name of "*conservaaaaation.*"

As you well know, this seizure of property deprives ranchers, miners, and others in the energy development business the opportunity to make a living. How will they support themselves when energy production, ranching, and mining grind to a halt? What does Comrade Obama think they'll do for work?

Become community organizers?

The pirating of public land has been done before, most notably by Bill Clinton in 1996. President Clinton took a break from getting a Lewinsky in the Oval Office long enough to place 1.3 million acres in southern Utah in a federal lockbox, permanently making the land off-limits to current or future exploration and development. Almost a decade later, the people of Utah are still furious and, upon hearing about Obama's plans, have further reason to distrust and fear their government. Gary Wilcox, a resident of Utah, remembers what went down the last time around: "I keep thinking about what President Clinton did to us . . . came in here, snuck in here, did the land-grab. I can see that happening right now."[16]

Obama's land-grab by the feds is another example of what he must have been thinking when he announced, "We are going to roll up our sleeves and we are going to remake this country, block by block, neighborhood by neighborhood, county by county, state by state."[17] Remake the country? By the looks of how he's operating, Obama's real agenda is to "take over the country" acre by acre.

Some two hundred years ago, James Madison, the fourth President of the United States, warned about the kind of intrusion on freedom and liberty currently "under review" by the forty-fourth president. Madison said: "Since the general civilization of mankind, I believe there are more instances of the abridgment of the freedom of the people by gradual and silent encroachments of those in power, than by violent and sudden usurpations."[18]

Isn't that precisely what Obama's Leninist-like behavior is doing? Behind closed doors, out of public scrutiny, he is orchestrating another "silent encroachment" against the people of this republic. He's been very careful to do his dirty work behind the scenes rather than resort to the violence Madison mentioned—at least for now. But one has to wonder what the true purpose of Obama's proposed militia may ultimately be. Or didn't you hear about that one? Unless you were listening to my show at the time, you're probably be in the dark. Maybe two newspapers reported his statement.

Here's what this Lenin-wannabe said in the early days at a campaign stop in Colorado Springs, Colorado:

> We cannot continue to rely on our military in order to achieve the national security objectives we've set. We've got to have a **civilian national security force** that's just as powerful, just as strong, just as well-funded[19] [emphasis added].

Don't we already have a National Guard? Don't we already have the FBI, DEA, TSA, park rangers, state troopers, sheriffs, and local cops in all fifty states? What's the man talking about? Is he working toward the creation of a police state? The fact of the matter is that Obama's plan to create some sort of domestic army that is "just as powerful" as our military is reminiscent of a certain German in the 1930s who had his own brownshirts. Or have you forgotten that world leaders down through the ages have created their version of a "national security force"?

Remember the KGB, the Gestapo, or the Praetorian Guard?

Look, I know this might sound far-fetched. But wasn't it Obama's pal and handpicked czar, Ron Bloom, who said, "We kinda agree with Mao Zedong that power comes largely from the barrel of a gun"?[20] There you have it. What more do you need? This Leninist-Marxist administration turns to Chairman Mao, the butcher of China—an evil dictator responsible for the deaths of more than sixty million people—for inspiration. The more we learn about Obama, the more we see he envisions an oligarchy, not a democracy.

This land-grab by the feds is causing the people to brace for tyranny.

They know only the people can stop it.

I'm afraid there's very little time left.

The People Speak Up

As I wrote in my bestseller, *Liberalism is a Mental Disorder*, the sheeple will not walk around forever with a zipper on their mouths while the left systematically dismantles our great nation and everything that gave rise to this shining enterprise of freedom. The middle class has awakened. They see clearly what is happening to them and they don't like it.

They resent the arrogance of their leaders.

They are livid over the intrusion into their personal freedoms.

Their wallets are on life-support.

They detest illegal aliens getting free medical care and other social "services." And the last thing they want is for the country to end up like Greece—bankrupt! What's more, they understand America is embroiled in a crisis that threatens democracy. They know what must be done. Which is why they're turning up in record numbers to elect constitutionalists—or run against incumbents for office.

The elections in New Jersey, Virginia, and Massachusetts have sent a tsunami shock of voter outrage right to the doorsteps of Washington, D.C. The politicians on both sides of the aisle are saying they hear us—there's something going on in the land that they cannot control. Even after Obama descended from his throne to campaign heavily in these three states for the Democratic candidate, the trio of Democrats lost.

It was a stunning trifecta of defeat.

Meanwhile, history was made on Long Island, New York, where the citizens handed their State Assembly seat to forty-five-year-old Dean Murray, a local businessman and Tea Party organizer. Murray is the first Tea Party supporter to take office since the movement began. Reflecting on his victory, Murray said, "What this movement is about is ordinary citizens, taxpayers, hard working people who have just had enough . . . we want fiscal responsibility. We want accountability from our political leaders, and we want personal responsibility." [21]

I think it's safe to say Murray won't be joyriding on Air Force aircraft.

He's not the only Tea Partier jumping into politics at the local level for the first time. As Fox News reports, "A plethora of Tea Party followers are now running in Republican primaries across the country, either for open seats or challenging incumbents in Alabama, California, Illinois, Michigan, Mississippi, Ohio, Texas, Utah and elsewhere." [22] Moreover, a number of those currently in power are quitting or changing parties rather than face certain unemployment.

Arlen Specter comes to mind.

As a Republican turncoat, Specter voted in favor of Obama's reckless $800 billion stimulus package. That didn't sit well with the people of Pennsylvania. Faced with a crushing primary challenge by Pat Toomey, a former business owner who, at one point, held a twenty-point lead in a race for Specter's seat, Specter ducked and ran for cover, switching his party affiliation to Demoncat.

It's encouraging to see the Tea Party holding conservative candidates accountable when, for example, they unseated a three-term RINO (Republican In Name Only) in Utah, Republican Bob Bennett. By the time this book rolls off the press, no doubt there will be others who will be given a much-needed boot from office. In other words, the Tea Party is working. How? By holding Washington elites accountable for their fiscal irresponsibility with the threat of unemployment. As a WorldNetDaily commentator points out, "tea partiers now play the role of Red Army commissars who sat at machine guns behind their own troops to shoot down any soldier who retreated or ran. Republicans who sign on to tax hikes cannot go home again."[23]

I say more power to them.

The Mad-Hatter's Tea Party

Even a blind man can see that the Tea Party movement has changed the political landscape of the country. The evolution of the Tea Party movement has probably been the most important political development in the last two years. Much of its initial success has to do with the purity of the party. By that, I mean it's neither a Republican nor Democrat movement. It's organic. It's autonomous. It's of the people. And it transcends traditional labels or party affiliations.

The movement gained strength because, at its heart, this is a center-right country. Regardless of prior political party affiliation, the middle class has joined hands to stop the left-wing onslaught by the most powerful, most dictatorial president this country has ever seen. But I want to help you see what's going on. I want you to see how the Tea Party movement is being co-opted and gobbled up primarily by the Republican Party, the beltway boys, the neo-conservatives, and the old boys in checked pants.

Take Republican National Committee Chairman Michael Steele. Much like the snake in the Garden of Eden who tempted Adam and Eve to go over to the dark side, which they did and now we're paying for that lapse of judgment, Steele has made a number of tempting overtures to various leaders of the Tea Party movement in order to co-opt it.

Oh, sure, Steele talks a good game. After inviting and meeting with fifty or so Tea Party leaders deep within the belly of the RNC Headquarters, Steele said, "We share a common purpose in stopping President Obama's agenda and standing up for principles such as smaller government, lower taxes, free enterprise, and the Constitution."[24] Sounds good on paper.

Don't be deceived.

Don't let this Republican charmer trick you.

What Steele and the old guard within the GOP fears most is that the Tea Party movement will, as Senator Orrin Hatch—another Republican RINO—put it, "fractionalize the Republican Party." [25] I say it's time to pull out the Savage Decoder Ring. What Steele and Hatch really care about is maintaining their power and control of the GOP. They're scared because of the emerging conservative versus establishment split. They're looking over their shoulders at the Tea Party movement fearful that true conservative candidates will emerge and unseat their more moderate buddies in office.

Then there's Sarah Palin.

I personally think she's a good woman. I think her heart is in the right place when it comes to this country. But she's dead wrong about the Tea Party movement. She fails to see that this is a movement made up of people driven by core principles, principles valued above any party affiliation. Am I being unfair? Here's what the former Governor of Alaska told a crowd in Little Rock, Arkansas: "Now the smart thing will be for independents who are such a part of this Tea Party movement to, I guess, kind of start picking a party."

Really? Why?

In Sarah's view it's "Because the Tea Party movement is not a party, and we have a two-party system, they're going to have to pick a party and run one or the other: 'R' or 'D'." [26] What's this? The mainstream conservative voter believes she's an outsider and yet she had the audacity to say you'll have to vote "R" or "D" so make a choice. Is Sarah Palin the chair of the co-option league? I realize this will be seen as a personal attack on her. False. She is unelectable at the executive level for several reasons, including her attempts to drive Independents back to the "K Street" Republican establishment.

She's wrong on this. I'm not the only one saying so, either.

Listen to Dale Robertson, president of TeaParty.org. He's one of the early founders of the movement. Dale's retired from the military, married, and has five children. In other words, he's not a political hack. He loves and fought for his country and, like millions of us in the middle class, just wants to make sure his children inherit an America that is both free and great. On the heels of Sarah's appearance in Little Rock, Robertson observed:

I am deeply concerned the Tea Party is becoming nothing more than a wholly owned subsidiary of the Republican Party . . . Sarah Palin's well delivered speech and her attractive demeanor is little more than a veneer for her less than attractive political philosophy . . . [she] is not dense or erroneous in her view of the Tea Party, just the opposite. She represents a growing **insider's attack** to the **heart** of the **Tea Party,** very much like a wolf in sheep's clothing entering the gate as an ally, but for all intents and purposes there to seize and capture, not only one or two stray sheep, but the whole flock![27] [emphasis added]

Can you blame him for fearing Palin's sole purpose is to capture what has been a populist movement? As Robertson went on to point out, "What Republican wouldn't want 10 million angry voters marching in the streets shouting, God Bless the Republican Party, where a few months before the same voices sang, God Bless America!"[28] The last thing Robertson or any of us should want is for patriotism to be supplanted by party-ism.

Just like those of us in conservative talk radio, the Tea Party must remain an independent voice, free from the entanglements of any party. But how, you may ask? While I disagree with former Bush strategist Karl Rove on many points, he's right when he says the pro-life and pro-gun movements give us a road map of how the Tea Party movement can and should stay independent from the GOP. Rove said, "These [movements] have been powerful because they have allies in both parties, not because they've been co-opted and have become an appendage of one party only."[29]

So, no, you don't have to pick a team.

Actually, it's suicide if you do.

Another attempt to hijack the Tea Party movement and to get them to pick a side happened in February, 2010, at the annual gathering of GOP cheerleaders in Washington, D.C., hosted by the Conservative Political Action Conference (CPAC). Organizers peppered the podium with just enough faces of the real Tea Party patriots to satisfy the crowd, then paraded out the Republican dinosaurs who've been haunting Washington since the Stone Age: the John Boehners, the Newt Gingriches, and the Bob Barrs. How does their presence fit into the Tea Party movement?

Think about this one. During the CPAC love-in, Newt Gingrich threw his weight behind Republican Senator Robert Bennett of Utah, a man running for reelection who supports TARP and the mandated purchase of health insurance.[30] If CPAC were serious about listening to the heart and soul of the Tea Party movement, these men should have been backstage carrying water for the new breed of patriots. Instead, the RINOs took center stage where they peddled more of the same old rhetoric. It's as if the old guard was saying to the middle class, "You've done a nice job, sonny, now vote Republican—vote for one of us."

I say shame on the leadership of CPAC.

Did they forget that Bob Barr, the former Republican Congressman from Georgia, went to work for the American Civil Liberties Union (ACLU)? How could a man with those values ever be taken seriously? Let's be clear. When it comes to anti-American activities, the ACLU is the head of the snake, as I've carefully documented in my other bestselling books. I guess given the fact that Bob Barr was there, we shouldn't be surprised that CPAC allowed the ACLU to have an exhibit at the convention![31] I believe it's guys like Bob Barr who are the type of fifth columnist trying to destroy the Tea Party movement from within.

Which brings me to shine the Savage spotlight on Dick Armey, the former Republican House Majority Leader. He's another fake; a pseudo-tea partier. Bet you didn't know this quisling worked for the ACLU, did you? Pretending to don the garb of the Tea Party movement, he's the co-founder of a supposedly Tea Party–oriented organization known as "Freedom-Works." I'm not sure what Armey has in common with the true Tea Party movement, besides the fact that he might drink Earl Grey.

As I write, Dick Armey is circulating a position paper, a manifesto of sorts, billed as the "Contract From America." We're told more than 100,000 Americans submitted ideas that, after debate by who knows who within Armey's organization, were pared down to a list of twenty-two proposed, grassroots-inspired solutions. These solutions include stopping tax hikes, demanding a balanced budget, protecting the Constitution, rejecting cap-and-trade legislation, protecting freedom of the press, passing real healthcare reform, and limiting the size of government, among others.

In fairness, every one of them is a good statement, something the government ought to do. I have no problem with that. But after studying their proposal, something stood out in bold caps to me. There's not one mention of *illegal immigrants*, not one mention about the need to defend our *borders*, there's not one mention about *language*—English-only—or ballot reform to make sure dead people and illegal aliens don't vote. Moreover, there isn't any mention of ways to deal with our crumbling *culture*, nothing about prayer, or abortion, or gun rights, or traditional marriage, or the corrupting influence of pornography.

That's when I started to smell a rat.

I dug deeper.

One lackey, who worked on the project, a man whose name is unimportant, said, "The goal of this document is to create the biggest tent around economic conservatism as possible. This is a bottom-up document. It is from the people, and that is a very powerful idea."[32] Pause there for a moment. The first problem is that they've focused only on "economic conservatism." Of course, the middle class cares deeply about that topic. But what does it matter if the economy is thriving if we've lost personal freedoms, our borders remain open to anybody with a dirty bomb in their backpack, and our kids are told they should "learn Muslim prayers and dress as Muslims"[33] in public school?

No, this "Contract From America" is flawed. It's just another way the Republican Party hopes to co-opt the Tea Party movement by crafting proposed solutions simply to get themselves reelected without alienating the huge block of people who are pro-abortion, pro-open borders, pro-same-sex marriage, or who are otherwise uncomfortable with our Judeo-Christian heritage. They're pretending they are the real patriots.

I don't buy it for one second.

What's more, virtually all movements that begin strong, that are based on core principles, are co-opted by wolves wearing sheepskin. How? They get seduced by those in the center of power. Right now it's the Tea Party movement that's being courted by the same dunces that got us into the mess we're in. Watch out for those who put "Tea Party" in their name but in fact are nothing more than front groups for other interests.

Beware Republicans bearing grifts.

Tempest in the Teapot

So, there's a counter-revolution going on.

The people have thrown incumbents out in several places already: Virginia, New Jersey, and Massachusetts. Nobody expected Scott Brown, a political unknown, to be the first Republican to capture the seat previously held for fifty years by a Democrat, most notably by the now-deceased Chappaquiddick Survivor. Turns out Scott Brown was Judas with a shave and a haircut. I warned you not to trust the guy. I told you not to Obamalize him. I was the only conservative to stem the euphoria two days after the Brown victory in Massachusetts. After all, Brown is only a politician. Maybe I've watched too many episodes of the *Brotherhood* on Showtime, but I expected he'd compromise—and he did.

As we've seen, the Republican establishment wants to co-opt the party. When a beast is cornered, it always strikes back. We know this. There's no way the GOP elephant is going to roll over and die. But what's the reaction in other quarters in Washington? How are the Demoncats responding? Are they pleased to see Mr. and Mrs. America showing up at their carefully orchestrated town hall meetings asking tough questions? Are they happy that a sea of regular citizens, most of whom want to toss them out, are engaging in the political process? Hardly. If they're not pleased by these developments, are the Democrats looking for ways to either leverage or co-opt the Tea Party movement?

The answer would be a resounding "No."

The Demoncat leadership wants to destroy it.

Right now, they're planning a vicious counterattack. They've recruited the cheeseburger eater, Bill Clinton, to strategize the assault. What's Clinton's first move? He installed a fresh set of batteries in his giant smear machine, that's number one. He rallied his political operatives in a scheme targeting maybe a dozen leaders within the Tea Party movement. With James "Pit Bull" Carville doing the heavy lifting, the old Clinton army is looking for ways to drag them through the mud. To discredit them. To assail their character. It's a page right out of the old Clinton playbook. Remember the FBI files in Clinton's possession?

Different day, same drill.

Team Clinton plans to do to the Tea Party leadership the same thing that was done to me by the George Soros funded group that took sound bites out of context and sent them to the socialist government in England. Those very same "compassionate" liberals who, I might add, are losing their own country to the invasion from Pakistan and elsewhere, had the audacity to blacklist and ban me from visiting Britain. I am the only member of the U.S. media to receive such treatment.

But that's another story.

The Democrats see the handwriting on the wall. They know they face political annihilation in 2010 and beyond. Their precious majority status in both houses of Congress has been threatened by a movement that many of them originally viewed with a scornful eye. If their fears are realized and they lose control of Congress, guess what else is in jeopardy?

Redistricting.

That's the golden door prize of the decade.

I won't bore you with the technical details of how redistricting works. Suffice it to say that the redistricting process in 2011 will have a direct bearing on the political makeup of the country. Redistricting ultimately determines the number of congressional seats each party can have. Big Democrat losses at the ballot box in 2010 could set back the so-called progressive movement for a decade.

From my perspective, that's a good thing.

While the libs derided and dismissed the Tea Party movement at first, they're now desperately digging around for dirt to besmirch its leadership with an eye on bringing down several of the larger tea parties. Will their heavy-handed thuggery work? Hard to say. The movement is sure to recognize any attempt by the Clinton-Obama machine to take down one of its own. And unlike traditional politics, the Tea Party movement isn't quick to throw its kind under the bus.

As of this writing, Clinton has come up empty-handed.

Before leaving this matter regarding the concerted effort to co-opt or destroy the Tea Party, I must touch briefly on the media. As you well know, an entire book could be written about media bias and the fifth column, those enemies of freedom embedded inside newsrooms and television studios. I will say, however, that to their credit the media have done a "B-minus" job reporting the story thus far. This is really quite good news considering how they usually trash anything resembling conservatism.

That said, I couldn't help but notice how Pinchy Sulzberger and the *Old York Times* jumped at the first chance to subvert this populist movement. This formerly great newspaper went on the attack, seizing on a completely unrelated story to malign the movement.

The headline says it all: "The First Tea-Party Terrorist?"

The writer of this trash journalism—whose name doesn't matter—

attempted to link a lone lunatic, Joseph Stack, with the Tea Party for obvious reasons. I'm not surprised. The *Old York Times* is nothing more than a government organ of the House of Obama. On February 18, 2010, Stack flew his small airplane into an IRS office building in Austin, Texas, and left behind a rambling screed about this and that.

However, there was not one word in his missive about the Tea Party!

This reality didn't prevent this yellow journalist from yapping, "Given the apparent momentum of the Tea Party movement, it would be nice to know if Slack's kamikaze mission was a not-all-that-shocking emanation from it—whether, as some claim, more than a few Tea Partiers are unhinged." There's absolutely no basis for such a connection in the facts. None.

Yet the writer goes on to say, "a person with Stack's fuzzy ideology wouldn't feel terribly alone at a big Tea Party."[34] Which sounds strikingly similar to what an apparatchik of the editorial board for the *Washington ComPost* wrote, "I am struck by how his alienation is similar to that we're hearing from the extreme elements of the Tea Party movement."[35]

Even before the *Old York Times* and the *Washington ComPost* ran their groundless hit pieces, I had predicted this would happen. I warned my radio audience in *The Savage Nation* to expect such wild-eyed attacks. That warning still stands. The stronger the Tea Party becomes, the more the old left-wing guard and the government media complex will do to shut it down, even using lies, half truths, wild allegations, and character assassination to paint the movement as little more than an extension of the John Birch Society.[36] They'll do whatever it takes to reduce the Tea Party to dried, spent leaves.

My Cup of Tea

We've seen what the counterfeit Tea Party plan has to offer. Now take a close look at the real deal by a real Tea Party organizer and patriot, Dale Robertson. I want you to see what he's calling for and how different it is from the fake proposal we've already examined. You'll see it just so happens to emphasize the same things I've been talking about for sixteen years on radio: borders, language, and culture.

Dale begins outlining what he calls "the non-negotiable core beliefs" of the Tea Party movement by asking, "What shall we do next? Turn a blind eye to the 20 million or more illegal aliens who demand citizenship because they believe they have earned it by nefariously entering our beloved nation and who continue to break the law by staying here? The Republican elite say 'Yes to amnesty!' But I believe the Tea Party will not reward law breakers, especially with our most sacred commodity—Citizenship in our beloved nation."

It's clear Dale understands the Tea Party isn't a picnic. It's a showdown.

There's more. Dale asks the movement to do more soul-searching as they prepare to codify their core ideals. He asks: "Has the Tea Party forgotten the tax hikes poised and ready to crush the American people? How can we fail to remember the unrelenting line of gun grabbing legislation continually snaking its way through Congress? Yet, where is the outrage? . . . I say NO and HELL NO! We are non-negotiable in our stand against dumbed-down politics spun by deadhead Republican political hacks dreaming of emasculating the greatest thing going since 1773."[37]

Even before getting to his list of core beliefs, you can see the passion brewing behind this patriot. Here, then are his list of fifteen core beliefs:

1. Illegal Aliens are illegal.
2. Pro-Domestic Employment is indispensable.
3. Stronger Military is essential.
4. Gun ownership is sacred.
5. Government must be downsized.
6. National Budget must be balanced.
7. Deficit Spending will end.
8. Bailout and Stimulus Plans are illegal.
9. Reduce Personal Income Taxes a must.
10. Reduce Business Income Taxes is mandatory.
11. Intrusive Government Stopped.
12. English only is required.
13. Traditional Family Values are encouraged.
14. Common Sense Constitutional Conservative Self-Governance is our mode of operation.
15. And, yes, we are a Christian Nation!

Are you beginning to get the picture? These are the kinds of themes we must be talking about in our town halls, on talk radio, and in our meeting places on the Internet. And, without question, these are the core principles we must adhere to when we step inside the voting booth. For far too long, America has had a bumper crop of idiots and traitors running the show.

Is Healthcare Reform Really Reparations by Another Name?

For years, Marxist huckster Louis Farrakhan has been pushing for reparations for slavery. He won't rest until the government makes amends for what he views as the irreversible and lasting damage done to the African-American community. Nothing will satisfy him until Washington ponies up with some sort of an acceptable apology—and piles of cash. The fact of the matter is that slavery ended in the United States something like 140 years ago and there isn't a white American living today who ever owned a slave.

This means nothing to him.

In his twisted view, there's no statute of limitations on such matters. In fact, he believes innocent people should suffer. Speaking to a small gathering on the tenth anniversary of the Million Man March, Farrakhan said:

> We want more than an apology for slavery. We want more than a monument. We want America to acknowledge her wickedness to the indigenous people of this hemisphere; acknowledge the wickedness of slavery and the trans-Atlantic slave trade; acknowledge what you did in robbing our fathers of their names, their language, their culture, their religion.[38]

Farrakhan was panhandling for reparations then and he's still calling for it today. At a speech in February, 2010, Farrakhan said President Obama had to do more on behalf of the black community to improve their lot in life. Directing his words to the president, this Obamanic said, "Your people are suffering . . . put some money on back of us."[39] Farrakhan then blasted the "white right" who he believes is conspiring to ensure President Obama doesn't serve more than one term. What's does this have to do with reparations?

You'll have to follow the bouncing ball on this.

Healthcare reform is one of Obama's top agenda items. We all know the reform Team Obama is promoting is nothing short of socialized medicine with loads of freebies for illegal aliens and ostensibly for those who aren't able to afford coverage. That's where Farrakhan comes in. He views the healthcare bill as one way Obama can do his part to ease the plight of black America. It's a giant entitlement in his view. So, in the end, Obama is a stealth enactor-enforcer of the reparations package Farrakhan seeks.

Real People, Really Angry

The other night after a long day on the radio talking about Obama's assaults on the middle class, I had had enough. My mind couldn't take it anymore. I mean, you can only take so much of the insanity. Your heart just breaks watching working families become poorer in spite of their best efforts to get ahead. After supper, I figured I'd watch some TV to unwind. I love watching nature shows. Always have. That probably goes back to my research into exotic plants years ago.

So I'm sitting with Teddy, the dog, on my lap watching the Science Channel when the cameraman suddenly took a dive, plunging us six thousand feet below the ocean surface. Next thing I know I'm looking at sea creatures I never knew existed. Teddy was probably looking at the fish swimming around dreaming about dinner. Me? I marveled at God's incredible handiwork buried like hidden treasure deep within the water.

The announcer was going on about this fish and that mollusk when a new thought struck me. Each of those living creatures knows they must do two things in order to survive: *hunt for food* and *hide from the predators* who want to eat them. Every one of those deep-sea creatures is either prey or predator.

That got me thinking. Just like their aquatic fellow travelers, virtually every animal on earth *works* to both protect itself and to find its own food. There's one exception: man. Man may be the only living being on earth that will rely upon others to feed it—and gives nothing to others in return!

On second thought, there *is* a parallel in the animal kingdom: the parasite—the original freeloader. A parasite attaches itself to the host body, exploits it, and gives nothing back. They don't create anything original. They don't contribute to the general good. What's more, there isn't anything beautiful or beneficial about a parasite—whether it's a leech, tick, or louse.

Now my mind was whirling. It's no wonder why the middle class is resentful of a government that is more concerned about the welfare and "benefits" of the freeloaders than about those of us who provide the income for the freeloaders. It's no wonder Tea Partiers are boiling mad at the way their hard-earned money is being taken from them.

If you think this is all hot air and rhetoric, you are mistaken. Did you know that 60 percent of Americans are operating like parasites? How? According to the Tax Foundation, they receive more in benefits from the government than they pay in taxes. You might want to read that again.

Of course, when we talk about the government giving benefits, the "government" produces *nothing* and has *nothing* to give these "takers"—unless it first reaches into the pockets of the sheeple. So, it would be more accurate to say "60 percent of Americans receive more in benefits from the taxes paid by hard-working fellow Americans than they themselves put into the hat."

Put another way, 40 percent of Americans are picking up the tab for 60 percent of the leeches. That is an unsustainable economic model. What happens when 60 percent becomes 70 percent? What happens if the "makers" get tired of underwriting the lifestyle of the "takers" and stop working so hard to generate income?

The whole country goes bust, that's what.

Isn't that what we're seeing now?

Why should we support able-bodied people who refuse to work? Why should we educate and provide medical care for illegal aliens and their children? Why should prisoners be given such gold-plated treatment in prison where it costs $50,000 or more *per year* to give them everything under the sun: special religious meals, books, cable TV, dental cleanings, even porno. I'm not saying we should turn the prisons into Devil's Island. But I would say something is wrong with a country that is so led by the liberal left that we are bled until there's nothing left for us to give.

Like many people my age, I was raised to work and to work hard. Freeloading was out of the question. I'm not saying I was beaten with a rubber hose if I didn't work. I'm saying my father and mother presented a view of work that was honorable. My father made me work hard with him polishing bronzes in the basement with acid, like a scene out of Dickens. And my parents showed respect to those who worked hard, too.

I can still picture Momma Savage sitting at the kitchen table with the plastic table cover, you know, talking while moving the bread crumbs around with a knife, sifting them. If she were to talk about someone in the building where we lived in the Bronx, she would say things like, "You know Paul the painter is a *hard worker*." She'd say "hard worker" in almost a whispered tone as if looking up to him. It didn't matter what the guy did, my parents had a respect for someone who worked to provide for his family. That was an important thing in my development as a child.

Look, my parents weren't putting on a show for my benefit. They weren't thinking, "Let's show young Michael how to grow up." They had respect for those who labored and contempt for the leeches—although there wasn't a soul living in our building who didn't put in long hours. Everybody we knew worked hard to provide for their family. The children were all well fed, although most of us were poor. We just didn't know it. What's more, each family did its part to keep the apartment building clean.

Nobody was a freeloader.

Nobody was looking for a handout.

Long after we left the neighborhood, another generation moved in from a different country of origin. It became clear they didn't have the same appreciation for work. Frankly, most of them were on welfare. They had an entitlement mentality that was so ingrained they burnt their mattresses and threw them out onto the streets if they weren't being fed—sort of like what you might see at a zoo on a Monday.

And you wonder why there's anger in this country?

You're surprised at the rage building against those who think everyone owes them a living. How did this happen? How did a nation of hardworking people get taken over by a nation of leeches? What happened to working toward a common good, not a common handout? What kind of government caters to the leeches and not to the hardworking people who work to give their money to those who work the system?

It's unnatural. It's insane.

It's destroying my country.

As you will see in the next chapter, this trend is not happening by accident. Unlike trickle down *affluence*, which thrived under the free and open
market philosophy of President Reagan's administration, what we have now
is *trickle up poverty* because of Obama's Leninist-socialist economics. While
some degree of socialist economics has been at work for a number of years
under various presidents, it has reached new heights under this socialist-
Marxist administration. I predict the middle class will continue to be impoverished unless this trend is reversed.

CHAPTER 2

Obama's Marxist-Leninist Roots

I chose my friends carefully . . . **the Marxist professors**
and structural feminists.

—President Barack Obama

When I was a little boy, maybe between the ages of six to nine, I'd go on long rides with my father across the bridges into Manhattan to work in his antique store. His shop was on the Lower East Side of New York where he sold clocks and figurines, mainly 19th-century French bronzes. That was his specialty. I learned a lot about art because Dad put me to work cleaning off the patina. The nouveau's who were buying them wanted them to look shiny, like gold.

So down in the musty basement I'd work long hours, scrubbing off the brown or black patina. After they were ready, I'd bring up the figurines to the store for my father to sell. Glad to be out of that dark basement for a few minutes, I'd smile and linger before I headed back to the dungeon. I'd watch the customers coming in and out of the store looking at this and that.

They'd see something they liked, ask my father the price and he'd tell them. Sometimes they'd pay it. Sometimes they winced as if biting down on a bit of raw garlic. They'd shake their heads and say they couldn't afford his price. Whether they could afford it or were just trying to work my Dad over, I didn't know. I took it at face value that they didn't have enough money.

On the long ride home, I had time to think about many things including the exchange between my father and the customers. That's when a new idea struck me. I thought how nice the world would be if the vegetable man could give me his vegetables and I could give him some of my father's merchandise in exchange. Or how the butcher could give me meat to take home to my mother, and in exchange I'd give him a lamp from my father's store. Or how the butcher might give the vegetable man a lamb chop and the vegetable man gave him some cucumbers.

I started to wonder, "Why wouldn't such a system work? Then we wouldn't need any money and everybody would be happy." But then again, I was a child.

Awakening from my reflections on the ride home, I came to understand that not all people want to work, and not all people will work as hard as their neighbor to get that lamb chop. Some will refuse to work yet still expect something for nothing. And that's the essence of communism, of socialism. Millions of people living in this country right now do not work and yet still gain an awful lot for nothing on the backs of the taxpayers.

Yes, they're gaming the system with the help of the government.

As I grew older, I watched in disbelief as the handout crowd swelled in size during the mid-sixties under the light socialist revolution of Lyndon B. Johnson and his creation of the "Great Society." I'm sure President Johnson's intentions to end poverty were good. I can't say for sure. I never met the man. But codifying socialized medicine for welfare recipients, known as Medicaid, continues to be a fiasco.

His dalliance with socialism forever changed America.

And not for the better.

Due to President Johnson's socialist experiment to end poverty, American taxpayers have been forced to pick up the tab, spending trillions of their hard-earned dollars over the decades. In effect, Lyndon Johnson took from the middle class to give to the poor. Did his bailout program to end poverty work? Hardly. If anything can be said, the cycle of poverty in America has grown worse.

Which leads me to Barack Obama.

Here's a man who, like President Johnson, is represented as a modern-day Robin Hood figure. You know, the Great Equalizer—taking from the rich to give to the poor. That's the popular image of him, prepackaged and sold with a slick, Madison Avenue–style marketing to the masses. Obama got into office claiming he wanted to spread the wealth around. He flew into Washington like Superman as if he were the ultimate Righter of Wrongs and Champion of the Downtrodden.

And the sheeple bought the cartoon version based upon their first impressions. Who can forget the excitable ejaculation by one enraptured supporter who, after listening to Obama, bubbled, "I never thought this day would ever happen. I won't have to worry about putting gas in my car! I won't have to worry about paying my mortgage! . . . if I help Obama, he's gonna help me." [1]

There you have it. She speaks for millions who were taken in by this fable.

But during the 2008 election cycle, I wasn't buying Obama's grandiose rhetoric of "hope and change." I dug deeper. I pulled back the curtain to see what kind of change Obama was envisioning. I studied how he was educated. I saw what was important to him. I focused on the people he associated with—in short, I did my homework. Which is why I knew Obama was no Robin Hood. The opposite is true.

I warned you Barack Obama was a stealth candidate.

I saw through him.

I saw the red flags of socialism.

Is Obama a Marxist-educated Mole?

I maintain that Barack Hussein Obama is a naked Marxist.

More than that, he's a Marxist with a Leninist complex. Does that sound far-fetched? Why would I make such a provocative claim? What evidence, if any, exists to back me up? Plenty. I realize that the mainstream media laugh off my assertion because most of them are so far gone down that road they're unaware of their own conversion.

These phonies don't know socialism from sausage.

The fact of the matter is that Obama's indoctrination began in 1970 at the impressionable age of 10. [2] That's when his maternal grandfather, Stanley Dunham, introduced young Obama to radical activist, Frank Marshall Davis, in Hawaii. I'm not sure why Grandpa Dunham thought that it would be a good idea to connect his grandson with a communist, but he did. I would have thought a grandfather would have protected his grand-child from such a radical influence, someone whose sympathies didn't line up with America's best interests.

Obama's half sister, Maya Soetoro-Ng, explained, "Our grandfather thought [Mr. Davis] was a point of connection, a bridge if you will, to the larger African-American experience for my brother."[3] If anything, Davis appears to be a different kind of bridge—a bridge to the dangerous doctrines of communism.

For his part, Frank Marshall Davis, who had migrated to the islands from Chicago, was a black poet, journalist, and a member of the Communist Party USA (CPUSA).[4] By his own admission in a weekly column of the *Honolulu Record*, Frank served on the national executive board of the Civil Rights Congress, which, at the time, had been identified by the Attorney General of the United States as a Communist subversive organization.[5]

There can be no doubt that Frank Davis embraced communist views. The FBI had assembled a thick file on Frank Davis' participation in, writings about, and speeches regarding his interest in communism dating back to 1931.[6] According to one FBI report, Davis "has been active in affairs of the Hawaii Civil Liberties, a Communist front, and occupies the position of Chairman of the Legal Action Committee of this organization."[7] Robert Kempa, a communist party-member-turned-FBI-informant, recalled collecting CPUSA dues from Davis and discussing their mutual interest in communism:

Late in the fall of 1950, I started contacting Frank Marshall Davis in connection with Communist Party matters, and relaying to him information received from my superior contact in the Communist Party, either James Freeman or [redacted].

During a portion of 1950, 1951 and part of 1952, I continued contacting Frank Marshall Davis and also transmitted dues for the Communist Party received from him to my contact above. During the period of my contacts with Frank Marshall Davis, he advised me that his wife, Helen was a member of Group #10. . . . During a portion of 1951 [redacted] took over contacts with the Davis group but

I resumed contacting Davis in 1952 and continued meeting him on Communist Party matters until I left the Party in June of that year.[8]

There's more. Dr. Kathryn Takara, a professor at the University of Hawaii at Manoa knew Frank Marshall Davis personally for fifteen years. She called him a "socialist realist" and noted that Davis "espoused freedom, radicalism, solidarity, labor unions, due process, peace, affirmative action, civil rights, Negro History week, and true Democracy to fight imperialism, colonialism, and white supremacy."[9]

Why does any of this matter?

In his memoir, *Dreams from My Father*, Barack Obama shares fond memories of developing a close relationship with Frank Marshall Davis, who treated the young Obama "almost like a son."[10] He'd spend hours listening to Davis' poetry and seeking his advice regarding his college and career choices. In other words, Obama sought out a Communist to be his mentor. Let's not forget the fact that Karl Marx was co-author of *The Communist Manifesto* upon which the ideology of communism and socialism are based.

As I've said, Barack Obama is a naked Marxist, a classic Red Diaper Doper Baby. Which is why in the pages ahead we'll explore the poisoned seeds of socialism planted in Obama's education and philosophy. We'll examine Obama's affiliations, his choice of czars and inner circle, and put his strategy and actions under the Savage microscope. Along the way, you'll discover that, for decades, Obama has had "friendly associations with communists and terrorists, ranging from Communist Party USA member Frank Marshall Davis in his youth in Hawaii to communist terrorists Bill Ayers and Bernardine Dohrn in Chicago when he was doing community organizing and running for political office."[11]

These associations and his conversion to their way of thinking are clearly seen in all the czars that he has appointed. One after another, by their own admission, is a Maoist, Marxist, Leninist, or socialist. That's an absurd claim, you say? It's not absurd—it's alarming. And in a moment, we'll take a look at what these czars believe, including Manufacturing Czar Ron Bloom, Pay Czar Kenneth Feinberg, Science Czar John Holdren, Climate Czar Carol Browner, Regulatory Czar Cass Sunstein, former Green

Jobs Czar Van Jones, and former White House Communications Director Anita Dunn.

Let's start with Barack's own admission about his pursuit of Marxism. In his memoir, *Dreams from My Father*, Obama freely admits that he sought out Marxist professors in college: "To avoid being mistaken for a sellout, I chose my friends carefully. The more politically active black students. The foreign students. The Chicanos. The Marxist professors and structural feminists."[12]

What are we to make of this personal disclosure?

Was his interest in Marxism a casual thing? Perhaps nothing more than a passing flirtation with liberal ideals? Did he study it to impress the liberal girls on campus, you know, like some sort of genius spouting heady Marxisms? Or, was the young, impressionable Obama aligning himself with Marxist ideology? Did he become a disciple of Marxist-Leninist philosophies? And, more important, is he functioning in the White House as a closet Marxist revolutionary?

Pause there for a moment.

Many of us have changed in our beliefs in adulthood from the days of our youth. I am one of them. When I was young and inexperienced, I was once a liberal—never a Marxist or follower of Lenin, but I was admittedly a liberal. There's an old adage that says, "Those who are not a Marxist at 20 have no heart, and those who are still one at 40 have no mind." Obama is at the age of enlightenment in that he's over the age of forty. We can only assume that his politics have changed somewhat—but we really don't know how far they may have changed from his early enchantments with Karl Marx, Vladimir Lenin, and Leon Trotsky, the fathers of communism.

Back to my original question:

Is Barack Obama a casual or a serious disciple of Karl Marx?

Dr. John Drew, a contemporary of young Barack at Occidental College, witnessed Obama's total immersion and participation in Marxism. To understand the significance of this, you must know a few basics about John Drew. While a student at Oxy, John wrote his senior honors paper on Marxist economics and, by his own admission, was a dyed-in-the-wool Marxist and founder of the only Marxist student association on campus. What's more, he was well aware of the grave implications of being a "Marxist revolutionary." He explains:

I did not take my status of Marxist revolutionary lightly in the fall of 1980. To me it was a serious business. It meant that I was an enemy, in a sense, of the U.S. government. It meant that I was an enemy of the wealthy people who were ruling the country. And it meant that I was willing to take whatever sacrifices . . . to confront that power structure. So for me, being a Marxist college student wasn't sort of a light-hearted walk in the park. It was a dead-serious statement that was impacting my career, my relationships, and my studies.

In other words, he had a serious Marxist BS detector.

After being introduced to Obama who, he was told, "was one of us," John spent long hours discussing their mutual interest in Marxist theories. He came to view Obama as a "blood brother" and a "member of this revolutionary elite that was going to turn around our country when the revolution hit." There's another firsthand observation of Obama the Marxist student worth noting. John recalls:

He wasn't an idle explorer of intellectual Marxism. I know this is kind of incendiary, but he was basically a Marxist-Leninist. He believed that there was a revolutionary class that was going to turn around our whole nation, redistribute wealth, change control over private property.[13]

Are you starting to get the picture?

Is it any surprise, then, that candidate Obama spoke of "spreading the wealth around"? That's Marxism Economics 101. Or, that after a hundred days in office masterminding the nationalization of America's largest automobile company, General Motors, President Obama said, "We've begun the work of remaking America . . . I'm pleased with the progress we've made, but I'm not satisfied."[14]

He's not "satisfied" because he's only getting started with his Grand Marxist–Leninist Makeover of America. Obama hasn't completed his long march toward nationalizing (that's code word for a Leninist-style government takeover of private industry) the banks, the mortgage industry, and the healthcare system. Along the way, he's engaging in massive federal land-grabs in the western states. It's all about chaos, command, and control. Obama's radical actions and beliefs are 100 consistent with the teachings of Marx.

Evidently, Barack Obama must have been an "A" student.

We, of course, don't know since his grades are sealed and nobody's seen the paperwork. Which is ironic in light of this statement found on the official White House Blog: "President Obama has committed to making his administration the most open and transparent in history, and WhiteHouse.gov will play a major role in delivering on that promise."[15] Well, then, maybe we should ask the blogmeister to start by releasing Obama's college transcripts from Occidental College, Columbia University, and Harvard Law School—all of which remained sealed as of this printing.

As one reporter noted, "the shroud surrounding his experience at Columbia contrasts with that of other major party nominees since 2000, all whom have eventually released information about their college performance or seen it leaked to the public."[16] Obama's secrecy about his college work would be appropriate if we were talking about classified nuclear missile plans. We're not. Then again, maybe there's something explosive to be learned about the kind of classes he was taking if the truth were unveiled.

One thing about the President of Uncertain Grades is that he learned his Marxist lessons well.

God Damn America!

Obama's indoctrination into the ways of Marx and Lenin and socialism continued well after college. For two decades, these anti-capitalist, anti-American radical views were further mentored at church by his anti-Semitic pastor, the America-hating Reverend Jeremiah Wright. Again, this was no casual relationship. We can only guess that Obama—as he did with his Marxist professors—chose his pastor carefully upon moving to Chicago. Theirs was a close-knit friendship; Reverend Wright married Barack and Michelle, baptized his daughters, and, in turn, Obama "loved him like a father."[17]

As we all know, Reverend Wright's contempt for this country has been well documented. In case you missed it, one of the alphabet news channels reviewed dozens of Wright's sermons and reported finding "repeated denunciations" of the United States.[18] So bitterly hostile to America is Reverend Wright that, just five days after the head cutters in dirty nightshirts slammed two airplanes into the Twin Towers, he took to the pulpit and, rather than denounce this act of terrorism, had the audacity to blame America for the 9/11 attacks.

He thundered, "America's chickens are coming home to roost!"[19]

Remember that one?

But did you also know that Obama's pastor studied Karl Marx?

On September 17, 2009, at the sixtieth anniversary celebration of a socialist magazine, Reverend Wright shared how Marxism shaped his personal philosophy. Taking the stage to lend his praise and endorsement of the *Monthly Review*, after blasting America as the "land of the greed and home of the slave," he said:

> My work with liberation theology, with Latin American theologians, with the Black Theology Project and with the Cuban Council of Churches taught me thirty years ago the importance of Marx and the Marxist analysis of the social realities of the vulnerable and the oppressed who were trying desperately to break free of the political economics undergirded by this country that were choking them and cutting off any hope of a possible future where all of the people would benefit.[20]

We shouldn't be surprised that Reverend Wright called for a "New World Socialist Order" before leaving the stage.[21] Since these comments represent his decades-old personal philosophy, it's safe to surmise that his pro-Marx, pro-socialist views were frequent themes in the pulpit. Without rehashing all Reverend Wright's political radicalism and outright contempt for the country that, let's not forget, allows a buffoon like Wright the freedom to speak his mind, four examples will help crystallize the picture of Barack Obama's pastor:

1. "America is still the No. 1 killer in the world."[22]
2. "The government lied about inventing the HIV virus as a means of genocide against people of color."[23]
3. "[They will] attack you if you try to point out what's going on in *white America*—the U.S. of KKK A."[24]
4. "The government gives [African-Americans] the drugs, builds bigger prisons, passes a three-strike law and then wants us to sing 'God Bless America.' No, no, no, God *damn* America!"[25]

Tell me that's not the mindset of an America hater.

When asked about his attendance at Trinity United Church of Christ where Reverend Wright delivers his fiery rhetoric, Obama said, "I don't think my church is particularly controversial."[26] Really? Where was he when Reverend Wright was spewing his hate-filled sermons? Are we to believe Obama was asleep in the pew for twenty years and none of this America-bashing rubbish rubbed off? Or, did the tirades of the America-loathing Reverend Wright and the teachings of Obama's Marxist professors fuel Obama's socialist agenda to remake America?

I think the evidence speaks for itself.

How else do we explain President Obama's "American Apology Tour"? Within the first six months of becoming the Head of State, President Obama traveled extensively both here and abroad apologizing to the world for what he saw as America's wrongful past behavior. That was Job One for this guy. Even as awful as Jimmy Carter was as a president, he didn't stoop that low during his pitiful four years at the helm. Niles Gardiner at the Heritage Foundation put together the Top 10 Obama Apologies.[27] Here are several of them:

1. **Apology to Europe: Speech in Strasbourg, France, 4/3/2009.** "In America, there's a failure to appreciate Europe's leading role in the world . . . there have been times where America has shown arrogance and been dismissive, even derisive."

2. **Apology to the Muslim world: Interview with Al Arabiya, 1/27/2009.** "My job to the Muslim world is to communicate that Americans are not your enemy. We sometimes make mistakes. We have not been perfect."

3. Apology to the Summit of the Americas: Address to the Summit of the Americas, Port of Spain, Trinidad and Tobago, 5/17/2009. "While the United States has done much to promote peace and prosperity in the hemisphere, we have at times been disengaged, and at times we sought to dictate our terms."

4. Apology for Guantanamo: Speech in Washington, D.C., 5/21/2009. "There is also no question that Guantanamo set back the moral authority that is America's strongest currency in the world."

I've never seen anything like this in my lifetime. Have you?

Who asked BO to offer a mea culpa on our behalf?

President Obama's incessant public apologies serve to undermine America's standing in the world. Clearly, Obama is embarrassed by the fact that we're the world's lone superpower. At the core, he's conflicted because he's been brainwashed by certified America haters. While Obama eats international humble pie, we at home are starving for a president who affirms the greatness of our industries and accomplishments, who celebrates our generosity and sacrifices on behalf of those who are suffering around the world, and who is quick to commend our exceptional servicemen and women fighting for freedom.

Yes, a leader who inspires our patriotism not berates us into pauperism.

Instead, we get a limp-wristed, quisling of a president who bows to other world leaders. Remember Obama's embarrassing bowing down before King Abdullah of Saudi Arabia—an Islamic monarch, and, on a second occasion, Japanese Emperor Akihito? How about the bowing before Chinese President Hu Jintao, this time in the nation's capital as world leaders gathered for the Nuclear Security Summit? Obama couldn't have picked a more inappropriate time or place in which to genuflect before a communist leader.

For an American president to bow is beyond bad decorum; it reveals his agenda to quicken America's decline as a world superpower. This usurper is fixated on making us the laughing stock in every corner of the world. Make no mistake, Obama's unlimited faultfinding with America impoverishes all Americans and weakens the American spirit.

Evidently, the words of Reverend Wright stuck.

It's not "God bless America"; it's "God damn America."

Indeed, Barack Obama is doing a first-class job remaking America into a turd-world nation, but he isn't pulling off his radical, socialist transformation by himself. He's getting a little help from his Marxist friends. For years, Barack Obama, Bill Ayers, and Louis Farrakhan all lived within two blocks of one another in the Hyde Park suburb of Chicago. It appears this cozy proximity with fellow agitators served as a leftist incubator of sorts, although Obama is dismissive about the fact that they were neighbors.

On that topic, much has been written about Obama's close personal association with the unrepentant domestic terrorist Bill Ayers. As you know, Bill Ayers was one of the founders of the Weather Underground—a radical group of terrorists who were responsible for about 30 bombings, including the 1970 bombing of the New York City Police headquarters, the 1971 bombing of the Capitol, and bombing the Pentagon in 1972.

When Ayers released his memoir *Fugitive Days* in 2001, he fondly recalled the day when his terrorist group set off explosives at the Pentagon. He wrote: "Everything was absolutely ideal on the day I bombed the Pentagon . . . the sky was blue. The birds were singing. And the bastards were finally going to get what was coming to them."[28] No remorse. No regrets. No apologies. Just a vindictive, anti-America vermin who, in a 2001 interview, said, "I don't regret setting bombs. I feel we didn't do enough."[29]

According to Ayers, the Weather Underground was "an American Red Army." Their goal? Ayers characterized the Weatherman philosophy as: "Kill all the rich people. Break up their cars and apartments. Bring the revolution home. Kill your parents."[30] By the way, Bill Ayers is now a professor at one of the institutions of lower learning in Chicago. From an ideological perspective, it's clear why Obama would gravitate toward someone like Ayers; they were two birds of the same Marxist feathers. In 2002, Ayers described himself this way:

> I considered myself partly an anarchist then and I consider myself partly an anarchist now. I mean I'm as much an anarchist as I am a Marxist which is to say, you know, I find a lot of the ideas in anarchism, you know, appealing . . . and I'm very open about what I think.[31]

Let's connect the dots. Bill Ayers was open about his convictions as an anarchist and Marxist, that's number one. He lived around the corner from Barack Obama for many years. And, number three, the two men are friends—in spite of the fact Obama has tried to create the illusion that he was just "a guy who lives in my neighborhood." [32] For example, in 1997, while serving as an Illinois State Senator, Obama took time out of his schedule to endorse *A Kind and Just Parent: The Children of Juvenile Court* written by none other than Bill Ayers.

Question: Are we really supposed to believe Obama and Ayers never talked shop with each other? You mean to tell me they never spoke about their mutual interest in Marxism or bantered around Obama's ideas about a revolutionary class and the redistribution of wealth? That would be like having dinner with Babe Ruth but never talking about a mutual interest in baseball.

Are things starting to come into focus for you?

Obama sought out Marxist professors and chummed around with fellow Marxist students during college. A number of years later, he's the neighbor and friend of a Marxist-loving, domestic terrorist. What's more, he was being tutored in church by an America-bashing, Marxist-loving pastor. Now that he's president, what's the next step in his long march toward a Marxist-socialist takeover of America? Simple.

He's assembling an inner circle of advisors who share his agenda.

Obama's Marxist-Leninist Czars and Czarinas

They got the call. They packed their bags. They headed to Washington.

Without so much as a five-minute congressional hearing, public input, or FBI background check, Barack Obama handpicked and placed into power men and women who share his Marxist-Leninist convictions. Some of Obama's czars and czarinas admire, quote, and are inspired by Mao Zedong—the butcher of humanity with the blood of sixty to seventy million on his hands. I'm not making this up. We are being ruled by a new class of czars, the likes of which haven't been seen since the last days of the Romanov Dynasty in Russia.

These appointments are of people with extraordinary powers over our lives, many of whom, by their own admission, their writings, and their speeches are enamored with Lenin, Marx, and Mao. What's more, they're sitting in the center of power under President Obama. His entire administration is infested with socialists running through the place like termites gnawing on the foundations of America. Let's go down the list.

Take Van Jones, President Obama's former Green Jobs Czar. Jones started his career as an anti-police street thug and rabble-rouser in the San Francisco Bay area. He was arrested during a riot in Los Angeles and, once in jail, started running with a string of anarchists and communists. Upon his release, he found a new con game: shaking down people under the guise of environmentalism. Did I mention that Van Jones was one of the founders of Standing Together to Organize a Revolutionary Movement (STORM)? This, naturally, qualified him to be appointed by Obama to be his top eco-fascist storm trooper . . . that is, until America learned the truth.

Here's Van Jones' résumé as he presented it:

> [In jail] I met all these young radical people of color—I mean really radical, communists and anarchists. And it was, like, 'This is what I need to be a part of . . . I spent the next ten years of my life working with a lot of those people I met in jail, trying to be a revolutionary . . . I was a rowdy nationalist on April 28th, and then the verdicts came down on April 29th. By August, I was a communist.[33]

Sounds like the perfect kind of guy we want advising the president, right?

Obama seemed to think so.

Okay, I understand you might think that Van Jones probably reformed his extremist views somewhere along the way, right? I mean, what kind of American president would knowingly bring a communist to come and work in the White House? If you think that, you'd be mistaken. Van Jones never abandoned his revolutionary delusions and diehard conviction of radically reshaping America. On the cusp of being appointed special advisor to President Obama, listen to the heartbeat of the man:

> No, we're going to change the whole system. We're going to change the whole thing. We're not going to put a new battery in a broken system. We want a new system![34]

If anything, Van Jones was saying all the right things as far as Obama was concerned. What else did you think Obama meant when this pan-Leninist said, "We are five days away from fundamentally transforming the United States of America?"[35] The two of them were peas in a pod; both have grand plans to "change the whole system." Thanks, but no thanks. Keep your change. I happen to like our Constitution. I happen to believe in the ideals set forth by our Founding Fathers. The last thing this country needs is a pack of socialist sycophants raping Lady Liberty.

Let's set aside the fact that Van Jones displayed a complete lack of civility when he called Republicans "assholes." And let's not focus on the fact Jones was one of the nut jobs who, in 2004, signed a petition in support of the bizarre claim that the Bush administration was somehow behind the 9/11 terrorist attack.[36] The fact of the matter is that the public learned the truth. They saw what a skunk this guy was and immediately demanded he be kicked out. All we heard from Obama was a chorus of crickets when he should have fired him on the spot.

Then again, Obama should never have hired him in the first place!

It took enormous public pressure from people like me in talk radio and on television hammering away his ties to communism before Van Jones resigned. None of that mattered to Howard Dean, former Democratic National Committee Chairman. Dean said the resignation of Van Jones was a "loss for the country."[37] In a similar display of insanity, the National Association for the Advancement of Colored People (NAACP) proudly presented Van Jones one of their Lilliputian awards while calling him an "American treasure."[38] In other words, the NAACP honored a stonehearted, unrepentant communist and ex-con, street thug in a suit.

While America dodged a bullet on that one, Van Jones wasn't an aberration. Quite the opposite. He's just one in a long line of unvetted socialist radicals. Several examples will suffice:

1. **Manufacturing Czar Ron Bloom:** "We know that the free market is nonsense. We know that the whole point is to game the system. We kinda agree with Mao Zedong that power comes largely from the barrel of a gun."[39]

2. **Pay Czar Kenneth Feinberg:** "Here's what I've said publicly in

my pay determination—*nobody* should receive more than a base cash salary of $500,000 maximum."[40]

3. Science Czar John Holdren: "The rate of growth of material consumption is going to have to come down. And there is going to have to be a degree of redistribution."[41] And, "Redistribution of wealth both within and among nations is absolutely essential, if a decent life is to be provided for every human being."[42]

4. Former White House Communications Director Anita Dunn: "My two favorite political philosophers: Mao Zedong and Mother Theresa—not often coupled with each other, but the two people I turn to most . . ."[43] And, "Very rarely did we communicate through the press anything that we didn't absolutely control."[44]

Do you see the common thread weaving Obama's czars and social-ist co-conspirators together? They speak of controlling what the press can know. They support the redistribution of wealth. They're working to place limits on your freedom to make as much money as you want. And, they engage in a shameless approval of Mao's strong-arm approach to governing through force if necessary.

Should I go on?

How about Obama's Climate Czar Carol Browner who worked as a commissioner for the Socialist International's Commission for a Sustainable World Society. The *Washington Times* reports that the Socialist International is an "umbrella group for many of the world's social democratic political parties" which just so happens to support "socialism and is harshly critical of U.S. policies."[45] The Socialist International's agenda is well known and it involves "gaining and exercising government power based on socialist concepts."[46]

Just what we needed, another socialist environmental radical.

Of course, the moment Browner was appointed by Obama, out came the big airbrush. Almost overnight, her photo and bio were scrubbed from the Socialist International's website.[47] You might ask why is she attempting to hide her past service for a socialist organization, but then again we all know why. These vermin are stealth creatures of the night. Why deny it? Why not just say she's a socialist and let the people debate it.

What is she trying to conceal?

Then there's Obama's Regulatory Czar Cass Sunstein, a real piece of work and a die-hard animal rights zealot. I'm not sure where he had his brains twisted, but Sunstein believes that animals—livestock, pets, and just about all forms of wildlife—ought to have "rights" so they can sue people in court.[48] How? Last time I checked animals couldn't talk. Sunstein proposes using private citizens acting as their representatives! This "bleating" heart lib wants to ensure that animals get a fair shake in court if they're not being properly treated.

And you thought I was joking when I said liberalism is a mental disorder?

But there's more.

In his 2004 book, *The Second Bill of Rights*, Sunstein slips into cheerleader mode, rooting for socialism, and is frustrated that "In a variety of ways, subtle and less subtle, public and private actions have made it most difficult for socialism to have any traction in the United States."[49] But he is ever hopeful that socialism will take hold through, of all things, the farce known as climate change. He writes, "It is even possible that desirable redistribution is more likely to occur through climate change policy."[50]

Let's not forget that John Holdren, Obama's science czar, sat on the board of editors of the *Bulletin of the Atomic Scientists*, which was little more than a left-wing propaganda rag. In that capacity, he edited or wrote for the same propaganda sheet as these communist sympathizers. Why am I not entirely surprised to learn that the magazine's co-founders, Leo Szilard and Robert Oppenheimer, were "accused of passing information from the Manhattan Project to the Soviets"?[51] According to one report, "In 1994, Pavel Sudoplatov, a former major-general in Soviet intelligence, named Szilard and Oppenheimer as key sources of crucial atomic information to the Soviet Union."[52]

In other words, they're traitors!

With regard to smuggling U.S. atom bomb secrets to the former Soviet Union, Sudoplatov explains, "The most vital information for developing the first Soviet atomic bomb came from scientists engaged in the Manhattan Project to build the American atomic bomb—Robert Oppenheimer, Enrico Fermi and Leo Szilard."[53] And the man Obama picked to be his science czar worked for the same publication as these communist sympathizers. Either Obama is totally incompetent to have made such a blunder, or he knew full well what he was doing.

Both options are unacceptable.

This begs the question: Why did Obama pick *socialist* czars?

Did he pick any patriots?

Did he pick any fans of George Washington or Thomas Jefferson or Ronald Reagan? No. Instead, he picked outright Marxists and lovers of Lenin. Two of them are thankfully gone—Van Jones and Anita Dunn—because they were exposed for who they really are, not because Obama wanted them gone. Can't you see that the kind of people Obama is picking as his czars speaks volumes about what he believes and who he really is?

Czar by czar, Barack has put into place a far left infrastructure.

You may ask why there's so much divisiveness in America. You don't have to look any further than Obama and his czars. They're the ones who brought this division to America. If Mr. Lenin-lite was merely a Democrat trying to push liberal reforms and doing it in a legitimate way, yeah, there'd be disagreement, but there wouldn't be this much rancor. There's a real counter-revolution going on against the Leninist-Marxist revolution coming out of the Obama administration. That's why the Tea Party movement is picking up steam. And that's why even the left is starting to ask questions.

Against the backdrop of this parade of socialist czars, a *New York Times* reporter—who suffered from a brief moment of clarity—who was flying aboard Air Force One, asked President Obama a direct question: "Are you a socialist as some people have suggested?" Obama, stunned, stammered, "You know, let's take a look at the budget . . ." and then, almost as an afterthought, added, "the answer would be no."[54]

We all know that's baloney.

If it walks like a socialist . . . it's a socialist.

If it talks like a socialist . . . it's a socialist.

Apparently his own statement didn't sit too well with Obama either. Which is why the president called the reporter afterward from the Oval Office and said, "It was hard for me to believe that you were entirely serious about that socialist question."[55] Really? Why is it so difficult to believe the reporter wasn't serious? How many more socialist-Marxist czars does Obama have to appoint before we're allowed to ask the question?

In September, 2009, North Carolina Representative Patrick McHenry called for a congressional review of Obama's czars. McHenry said, "If the czars have high-level, decision-making authority as their titles would indicate, then it is my concern that their appointment without Senate approval represents a circumvention of our Constitutionally-mandated confirmation process." Speaking of Van Jones, he added, "His ability to slip into a position of power without due Congressional diligence only further underscores the necessity for a confirmation process."[56]

We're still waiting for those hearings to begin.

And while we wait, Obama continues to stack the government with more Marxists. In May, 2010, Team Obama named Ben Scott to be a Policy Advisor for Innovation at the State Department. While it's unknown what an "advisor for innovation" does, we do know something about Ben Scott and the communist organization where he was working at the time of his appointment.

Scott was the Policy Director of Free Press—a Marxist-founded outfit reportedly funded by George Soros.[57] It's the same radical firm from which Obama hired his former "green jobs" czar Van Jones, who was a board member of that organization. We know that their name—Free Press—is misleading. As one reporter pointed out: "Free Press is a well-known advocate of government intervention in the Internet."[58] In other words, they want *more* government control, not a free press.

This view held by Free Press is consistent with something Vladimir Lenin has said:

> We Bolsheviki have always said that when we reached a position of power we would close the bourgeois press. To tolerate the bourgeois newspapers would mean to cease being a Socialist. When one makes a Revolution, one cannot mark time; one must always go forward—or go back. He who now talks about the 'freedom of the press' goes backward, and halts our headlong course toward Socialism.[59]

This begs the question: Why did Obama handpick a fellow traveler like Ben Scott? Answer: I predict Obama will seek to curtail freedom of the press as Hugo Chávez has done.

We also know that Scott's writings included a book entitled, "The Future of Media" co-edited by Robert McChesney, founder of Free Press. Why does that matter? In February, 2009, McChesney, the former editor of a Marxist-oriented magazine, wrote: "In the end, there is no real answer but to remove brick-by-brick the capitalist system itself, rebuilding the entire society on socialist principles." You might want to read that again.

What more do you need to know? Ben Scott worked for a Marxist organization and collaborated on a book with a diehard Marxist who wants to dismantle capitalism and replace it with the failed system of socialism. Just what America needs—another Marxist mole inside the State Department.

Obama's Judgmental Non-Judge Picked for Supreme Court

Barack Obama has appointed another socialist, Elena Kagan.

Of all the highly qualified candidates he could have picked to be the next justice on the U.S. Supreme Court, this time he picked a real prize. What do we know about Kagan? For starters, she tried to kick the military off the Harvard campus when she was Dean of the Law School because she didn't like their "Don't ask, don't tell" policy. She took money from Goldman Sachs just as her boss, Obama, has done. And the empty skirts in the media are saying that Kagan doesn't have much of a "paper trail" that would reveal her views on various issues that may come to the high court.

The fact of the matter is we do know something about her viewpoints. Look no further than her senior thesis at Princeton, which was entitled, "To the Final Conflict: Socialism in New York City, 1900–1933." Kagan laments, "In our own times, a coherent socialist movement is nowhere to be found in the United States. Americans are more likely to speak of a golden past than of a golden future, of capitalism's glories than of socialism's greatness." [60]

In other words, she's a New York City radical Marxist lawyer through and through. In spite of her Marxist background, we know that Obama is replacing a liberal with another liberal. No surprise there. Her presence on the Supreme Court will not change the ideological balance.

The deeper issue, however, is that Kagan is completely inexperienced.

Not only does she lack meaningful judicial experience, she lacks *any* experience!

Kagan has never been a judge. She is a judicial nonentity. Judge Judy on television has tried more cases than this judicial wannabe. If you think I'm being unfair to bring this up, you're wrong. I pointed out the same thing of Harriet Miers, whose nomination by George W. Bush in 2005 I also opposed. In fact, it was because of the *Savage Nation* that conservative voices raised their anger and made known to the White House they opposed that nominee. Miers' nomination was withdrawn.

Kagan could and should suffer the same fate.

Of course, if it's up to the weak-kneed Republicans in the Senate, Kagan will probably sail through. Lugar, Kyl, and Coburn, supposedly all solid conservatives, all voted in favor of her nomination as Solicitor General. They were joined by RINOs Gregg, Collins, and Snowe. So don't count on the Republican Party to save you from Kagan or even put up a meager fight.

As I searched for a reason why Obama would make such a choice—aside from the fact that Kagan is just another Marxist hack he can control—I concluded that Obama views her lack of judicial experience as a plus. Being a judicial nonentity makes her a "well rounded" nominee. That's the backward logic of the mental disorder of liberalism. However, Obama already has Christina Rohmer, Sonya Sotomayor, and Janet Napolitano. I'd say Team Obama is already "well rounded" with enough incompetent people. America doesn't need another imbecile in a robe rubber-stamping whatever the hell this president wants to do.

From Churchill to No Will

Winston Churchill is one of the greatest champions of freedom the world has ever known. After Churchill led England to victory over Nazi Germany in World War II, he faced an election in Britain. Keep in mind that socialists and communists were on the opposite end of the political spectrum from the Nazi enemy they'd just helped to conquer. As such, socialism was seen by some as a legitimate political philosophy. You know, many of the sheeple viewed it as just another valid political antidote to Nazi tyranny.

However, the opposite was true. Churchill was among the few who real-

ized it. Churchill saw the menace that socialism represented for free people everywhere, which is why he used his radio broadcasts to expose what
would happen if socialists came to power. Listen to Churchill's words and
tell me they're not equally important to Americans today as we battle the
forces of totalitarianism under the presidency of Barack Obama:

> My friends, I must tell you that a Socialist policy is abhorrent to the . . .
> idea of freedom. Although it is now put forward in the main by peo-
> ple who have a good grounding in the liberalism and radicalism of
> the early part of this century, there can be no doubt that socialism is
> inseparably interwoven with totalitarianism and the abject worship of
> the state. It is not alone that property, in all its forms, is struck at, but
> that liberty, in all its forms, is challenged by the fundamental concep-
> tions of socialism.
>
> Look how even today they hunger for controls of every kind, as if
> these were delectable foods instead of war-time inflictions and mon-
> strosities. There is to be one state to which all are to be obedient in
> every act of their lives. This state is to be the arch-employer, the arch-
> planner, the arch-administrator and ruler, and the arch-caucus boss.
>
> [N]o socialist system can be established without a political po-
> lice. Many of those who are advocating socialism or voting socialist
> today will be horrified at this idea. That is because they are short-
> sighted, that is because they do not see where their theories are lead-
> ing them.
>
> No socialist government conducting the entire life and industry
> of the country could afford to allow free, sharp, or violently-worded
> expressions of public discontent. They would have to fall back on
> some form of Gestapo.[61]

More than sixty years after Churchill spoke these words, they describe
exactly what is happening under our socialist president today. I should point
out that Churchill's opponent in that election, Clement Attlee, was the
leader of the socialist Labor Party. Among the issues that Attlee was promoting were a national healthcare system and a birth-to-death welfare state.
That's precisely Barack Obama's agenda.

Does that sound unfair?

Didn't President Obama use every trick in the book to ram through socialized health care? (I'll document more on that in a subsequent chapter.) Without question, Obama and his minions are out to do nothing less than imprison us in a totalitarian socialist system in which the federal government usurps our God-given right to make decisions for ourselves. That's what his socialist redistribution of our earnings through confiscatory tax policies and legislative initiatives is all about. He's assuring that trickle up poverty becomes institutionalized in America.

That will be the Obama legacy.

In the years immediately following World War II in America, although our country didn't face quite so direct a confrontation with our socialist-communist enemies as did Great Britain, the process leading to the totalitarian-wannabe regime that is now in power in the White House was nonetheless steadily advanced. The gradual implementation of socialist policies in the United States was furthered by the efforts of a pair of radical socialist Columbia University professors, Richard Andrew Cloward (rhymes with "coward") and Frances Fox Piven (rhymes with "driven"). This husband and wife duo were lifelong members of the Democratic Socialists of America. The Cloward-Piven strategy they advanced in their writings and teachings centered on leveraging a *manufactured crisis* to advance the socialist agenda in America along with the redistribution of wealth.

Remember what Obama's radical Chief of Staff, Rahm Emanuel, said? "You never want a serious crisis to go to waste."[62] That's right out of the Cloward-Piven playbook. That's why Team Obama thrives on creating or leveraging crises by demanding quick action, which is a vehicle for socialist change. That is what the Cloward-Piven strategy is all about. In short, in order to usher in socialist change, Cloward-Piven taught:

- Make a crisis
- Make it publicly visible
- Make sure it involves disrupting some institutional or societal sector
- Capitalize on the social unrest it produces

Here's a perfect example. In the middle of the healthcare cyclone, when the national debate had reached a fevered pitch, Obama started talking about the illegal immigration issue. Why? He wanted to create a thunderstorm to go along with the healthcare cyclone in order to really rock the boat and knock the opponents of his socialist healthcare plan off their feet. What did Obama propose? The granting of amnesty to twenty million illegal aliens. He did that to overwhelm the system along the lines of the Piven strategy—flood the system with more unrest in order to break it down.

Let me remind you that Columbia University, Obama's alma mater, is where Cloward taught! I think it's very likely Obama took his courses, given his leftist background at Occidental. If you recall, Obama said he sought out the Marxist professors. Of course, we don't know who his professors were at Occidental, Columbia, or Harvard because, as a WorldNetDaily columnist quipped, "The Obama camp guards those scores, like his SAT scores, more tightly than Iran does its nuclear secrets."[63]

What's more, there's a virtual blackout on all of Obama's personal records—from his adoption, baptism, and passport information to his files when he was a senator of Illinois. Tell me why we are not permitted to see his kindergarten school records? What could possibly be so explosive from seeing his grades during his time at Punahou elementary school? If he's as brilliant as some have claimed, why aren't we permitted to read any of his scholarly writings at Harvard Law or the University of Chicago? Is there a reason why his Columbia thesis is being kept from the public eye? Why are we not allowed to see his Occidental College or Columbia University grades? Most presidents release that information.

Why the secrecy? Might it reveal something about the roots of his pan-Leninism?

While we don't know with certainty if Obama studied under Cloward at Columbia, we do know that Obama's childhood mentor, Frank Marshall Davis, was a member of the Communist party. We know that Obama admits attending socialist conferences. We know that Obama admits reading Marxist literature. We know that Obama became a "community organizer" and came into contact with the Democratic Socialists of America, who endorsed his campaign for Illinois state Senate seat. And we know that Obama became friends with William Ayers, a member of the Socialist Group "Students for a Democratic Society." And yet, in spite of these facts about his radical associations and Marxist mentoring, Barack Obama has infiltrated government bureaucracy at the highest level of all!

We now know that Barack Obama, in his days as a community organizer, employed tactics espoused by these leftist enemies of America. We
also know he's using them to define and implement his legislative agenda
today. In fact, one of the ways to understand how insidious the leftist
agenda is to look at its priorities:

1. Confiscating money from taxpayers and consumers, as has been
   done with the passage of stimulus and healthcare legislation;
2. Making a killing in financial dealings by taking advantage of the
   so-called "priority," as John Paulson and Goldman Sachs did in taking advantage of the 2008 financial meltdown; and
3. Distracting the public from a real or important issue that they don't
   want to deal with for fear of hurting the cause of an enemy of America, as the Obama administration has done by, among other things,
   soft-pedaling the federal government's refusal to enforce existing
   immigration laws.

Make no mistake about it: The primary reason for the existence of the
left, including Obama and all the principal players in his administration,
is to bring about the downfall of western capitalist democracies. Remember, our Socialist-in-Chief Obama has said that he's committed to "fundamentally transforming the United States of America."[64] Just look below the
glossy surface of every one of Obama's legislative initiatives. In each case,
you'll find evidence that he either wants to overwhelm the capitalist system
and bring it to its knees, or he wants to take direct control of a significant
segment of the American economy in order to weaken our country and advance the cause of our totalitarian enemies.

Unfortunately, those totalitarian enemies now include—along with such
rogue nations as Iran, Venezuela, and North Korea—the United States itself. If we allow the Obama administration to continue to advance its nefarious agenda, America will continue on the path toward becoming an
enemy of free speech and religious choice, of individual initiative and the
creation of wealth. Under this president, we're on the way to becoming our
own worst enemy.

Barack Obama and his radical czars are out to do nothing less than reduce

America to second-rate nation status. Which explains their delusional desire to leverage the nonissue of global warming to control businesses, their intentional subversion of our national defense, while both causing and then taking advantage of the recent financial crisis, and their unlawful support of encouraging aliens to enter this country illegally—as you'll see in the coming pages.

If Obama and his czars are allowed to succeed, they will cause global economic and military chaos the like of which we have not witnessed since Winston Churchill led Britons in the war against totalitarianism at the middle of the last century. What's more, if Obama succeeds, we'll go from the USSR to the USSA—the United Socialist States of America—in one generation. America's last hope can be found in the true conservative patriots working with the Tea Party movement to stop this socialist revolution in its tracks.

I, for one, am committed to that fight.

You Say You Want a Revolution

You may wonder why Barack Obama's associations are such a big deal. You know, what's so bad about Marxism? Was communism such a bad thing? What's wrong with socialism? Let's start there. After all, according to a January, 2010, Gallup poll, more than half (53 percent) of Democrats and a third (36 percent) of all Americans have a *favorable view of socialism*.[65] Do these people hold a wrong understanding of this political and economic theory? Or, are they correct in their belief that socialism is praiseworthy?

What's more, if there's nothing fundamentally wrong with socialism, Marxism, Leninism, and all the other "isms," if they're just another acceptable approach to governing a nation, then the fact that Barack Obama is an ardent follower of Lenin and Marx, and pals around with avowed communists, would be of little consequence. If he's right that redistributive change really does benefit the American middle class (as he has claimed, saying, "I think when you spread the wealth around it's good for everybody"[66]), then shouldn't we welcome socialism along with the horde of Obamanics who have already bought into it? Or, if the worst thing that could be said of socialism is that it's benign, we might just agree to disagree and move on.

No harm, no foul, right?

If, however, socialism in its various forms has a long track record of enslaving the hearts, minds, and souls of the people subjected to it, then we sure as hell had better wake up and put the brakes on this man before he does any more damage to the country. So which is it? Is socialism a friend or foe of the people? Should we embrace it or erase it?

As you'll see in chapter three, the despotic Soviet Union enslaved the people and killed tens of millions in slave labor camps—all in the name of economic freedom under a very different economic system than ours. What you may not understand is that Leninism, Marxism, and Trotskyism—all the "isms" of the Soviet Union—are not quite dead. In fact, their followers have taken center stage. Take President Obama. He's not a "NEO-CON," but what I call a "NEO-COM." He's a neo-communist.

What do I mean by that?

Traditionally, in communist countries such as Cuba, North Korea, and the former Soviet Union, communism brought with it complete state control of the culture and the economy. Today, however, communist nations such as China are operating a little differently. They have hybridized their state control of the economy, for example, by permitting limited levels of capitalistic freedom.

That's why you can go to McDonald's on the mainland.

But don't let the presence of a few Big Macs fool you.

The People's Republic of China is still ruled by the Communist Party of China and *not* the people, in spite of what notions "People's Republic" may bring to mind. As such, there's zero tolerance for freedom of speech. You say or write the wrong thing—*boom*—you're suddenly locked away in a hellhole for years. Likewise, there's no freedom of religion, no freedom of thought. So while their brand of communism isn't identical to the iron heel of Lenin, it's still a form of communism, thus, neo-communism.

Like its cousin in China, Obama is pursuing more of a neo-communism or "soft" socialist-communist approach. In a way, he's using a "tri-brid" revolutionary plan: some Marxism, some Leninism, and some Trotskyism. While we don't have commissars in America as are found in communist countries, we do have czars and czarinas. This cadre of like-minded companions shapes the direction of the government without congressional oversight or approval and is only accountable to Comrade Obama.

Any European with reasonable political knowledge knows what's going on here in America. I'm afraid, however, that the American voter is terminally naïve. How else can we explain 64.6 million sheeple voting him into office? They were willing to give Obama the benefit of the doubt in spite of the evidence, that's how. I bet they'd refuse to believe what I'm saying about Barack Obama even if they were to see him with their own two eyes marching around the White House under a Lenin banner wearing a Che Guevara shirt and red beret.

If you care about your future, if you love your country as much as I do, you owe it to yourself to listen carefully as Doc Savage lays this out for you in plain English. Better brace yourself. The next chapter provides the crash course on socialism they never taught you in school. And, in the end, I promise the scales of liberalism will fall from your eyes. You'll see I'm right when I say that Barack Obama is a naked Marxist. You'll understand how and why Obama intends to use trickle up poverty in order to garner even more power and control for the multicultural, ruling elite.

Are you ready for the Savage truth?

Then read on.

CHAPTER 3

Spending Other People's Money

Those who cannot remember the past are condemned to repeat it.
—George Santayana[1]

The other day I was watching a movie on television about Rocky Graziano, a great middleweight Italian boxer from New York. You might say he was the original Rocky. This guy was one of the greatest knockout fighters in the history of boxing. I think he ranked in the top twenty or so. Doesn't matter. What really caught my eye were the street scenes from New York City. It was a different time. I was fascinated to see kids gliding down the sidewalks on homemade scooters because I had one.

As I watched, I remembered making a wooden scooter with my father out of scraps of wood. Since we couldn't afford to buy one, we took whatever was lying around, and made it work. About all I could scrounge up was a six-foot length of a 2x4, one roller skate, an orange cart, some handles from who knows what, and a few rusty nails. If you were creative, it was enough.

Dad took the board and, on one end, we attached the front wheels of the roller skate. On the opposite end, we hammered on the back set of wheels from the skate. We nailed those wheels on as you put a horseshoe on a horse. With that done, we took the wooden orange crate and fastened it to the front end of the board. We nailed two handles on top of the orange crate.

Presto! I had an instant scooter.

Some kids would build a go-cart out of wood using the wheels from a baby carriage. They were inventive and, while these toys weren't necessarily beautiful in the traditional sense of the word, we loved them because we had made them ourselves. The point of the story is that I come from a time in America when kids made toys because they didn't have the money to buy them. They made them out of scraps of wood, nails, a hammer, and sweat.

What a different time it was.

If we wanted something but couldn't afford it, we knew we had to make it ourselves, work to buy it, or learn to do without it. Which is why I have serious problems with Barack Obama's entitlement and redistributing of wealth scheme. I don't care what Marx the Slacker preached. No man, woman, or child is entitled to benefit from the fruit of another man's labor—unless that worker decides to be charitable.

Why do naked Marxist-Leninist politicians like Obama ostensibly take from the middle class to give to the rich and poor? Because they understand the power of a well-placed handout to buy off the people and to further their real socialist agenda—a cycle of dependency on the government from cradle to grave and to diminish the "bourgeoisie," the middle class. Make no mistake. This Marxist-Leninist president is converting America into a socialist nation step by step, the same way Mao Zedong did it on the Long March in China.

I've said this president is a revolutionary socialist.

I've said he's a naked Marxist-Leninist.

I've said these things because I know what I'm talking about.

My interest in this topic of Marxism, Leninism, and socialism goes back to my own heritage. I am the son of an immigrant. My grandfather fled Communism, Marxism, and the Red Revolution. He came to New York right after 1917 to find a new life for himself in a free society. Thanks to him, I was steeped in anti-communist philosophy from the earliest age. I was taught to cherish the freedom of the American experience. I was told how sacred and fragile liberty is and how I should always work to protect it.

Taking advantage of his newfound freedom, my grandfather opened a little tailor shop of his own and was proud of the suits he designed and made for his customers. He died young of a heart attack because he worked with a passion seven days a week. Naturally, I wanted to know why this man traveled thousands of miles away from his home, family, and friends to start over here in America. Which is why I've studied Marx, Engels, Lenin, Stalin, Mao, and Pol Pot—all of them, since I was eighteen years old.

I didn't read them because I worshipped them or saw them as possessing the answer. I studied them because I was a college student who didn't want to repeat the mistakes of history. It's not as though I just started reading this stuff yesterday so I could be on Fox News with a blackboard lecturing everyone. I've studied revolutions for over forty years. I know what's going on with this president and Americans would, too, if they had not been inculcated with socialism in America's public schools.

That said, a few questions are in order.

Do the Tea Party movement and the middle class have any basis to be suspicious that President Obama's true agenda is to spearhead a socialist revolution? Or, are these fears nothing more than unfounded rumors raised by rabble-rousers? Is Barack Obama operating within the grand traditions of America? Or, is he philosophically aligned with the traditions of the European socialist theories of Marxism-Leninism, as many suspect? Is Obama simply an idealist and not an ideologue? Or is he a "Manchurian candidate"?

I think we have to approach these questions almost clinically.

Before we get started, I must warn you of something. I have no gray zone when it comes to this topic of Marxism-Leninism. This discussion is going to disturb the old sixties hippies who still cling to their Leninist illusions. The same goes for the unenlightened leftists who have been in therapy for twenty years, the Woody Allen types hooked on Marx and medical marijuana.

The Head of the Snake

Entire books have been written about Karl Marx, Vladimir Lenin, and Joseph Stalin, the Three Stooges of Communism. These men thought they had invented a better economic and philosophical system upon which to build a nation. All three couldn't have been more mistaken. Like their TV and film counterparts, Marx, Lenin, and Stalin were always working on a new angle to pull the wool over the sheeple's eyes—although their results were far from a laughing matter.

My purpose here is not to rehash in detail what we know of these dangerous radicals, whose beliefs led to the enslavement and deaths of tens of millions of people wherever communism has been tried. No, this is a simple crash course in Marxism-Leninism, upon which communist socialism was built. This brief examination will include how it's being marketed today by our Marxist-Leninist president who, as we established in the last chapter, studied Marxism in college.

We begin with the granddaddy of communist thought, Karl Marx.

In an odd way, it could be argued that Karl Marx was the original hippie.

Why do I say that? Like the hippies in the sixties, Marx was a counterculture-type who sought a cultural and political revolution in his native Prussia. While he may never have worn flowers in his scruffy hair, Marx spent countless hours drinking and smoking his pipe in contemplation and the pursuit of enlightenment—and a benefactor who'd support him. He found one in Friedrich Engels, the son of a successful business owner in Prussia who, for the better part of twenty years, did what he could to subsidize Marx.

You see, although Marx was born into an educated family—his father, Heinrich Marx, was a lawyer—Karl Marx turned out to be a negligent bum of the lowest order. His was a hand-to-mouth existence. He detested manual labor, preferring to dream up ideas about mooching from others and spreading their wealth around.

Does that sound harsh?

How's this for harsh: His own family was evicted from their apartment in London and faced extreme hunger from their impoverished state because Marx apparently cared more for his lofty ideas than his obligation as a father and husband to provide.[2] One historian, whose name is unimportant, described the pitiful conditions of his home life:

> . . . his family bore a burden of poverty far heavier and more
> unbearable than the one carried by the average proletarian family in those days. There were days in the Marx household when
> the stove was cold, the frost biting, the pantry empty and hunger upon the bill of fare; when the impatient landlord stormed

and threatened, and the children's starved faces and beseeching glances seemed to accusingly form themselves into a veritable indictment against their father.[3]

Marx was so driven in the pursuit of his fledgling communist theories, so consumed by his interaction with fellow intellectuals while collaborating with Engels on *The Communist Manifesto*, that he neglected the needs of his own family. He lost sight of the fact that his primary responsibility was to provide food and shelter for his children.

But there's more.

His obsession led to a personal tragedy glossed over by the fawning professors of Marxism; namely, that with a diet primarily of bread and potatoes, three of his seven children died before age ten and one died in infancy before he had been named.[4] In other words, they were malnourished and "literally starved to death."[5] Marx was so destitute he couldn't afford medical care for his children when they fell sick and was unable to scrape together enough money to purchase a small coffin for one of his daughters.[6] When his one-year-old son Guido died, Marx told his friend and financier, Friedrich Engels, co-author of the *Communist Manifesto*, that little Guido was "a sacrifice to bourgeois misery."[7]

A sacrifice? I told you liberalism is a mental disorder.

What kind of father would place the pursuit of his fanciful musings over the welfare of his own flesh and blood? What kind of dad wouldn't put his kids first? Why didn't Marx get a job as a professor of philosophy and provide for his household as any man would do? After all, Marx obtained his Doctorate of Philosophy at Berlin University, which means at the very least he was qualified to teach gym class at the local elementary school.

In 1852, a police agent from Prussia was dispatched to spy on the Marx family who were, at the time, living in a cramped, two-room flat in one of the worst sections of London. Although Marx's wife, Jenny von Westphalen, was the sister of the Prussian Minister, the agent wasn't sent because he wanted to know how Jenny was doing. Rather, the background information was sought because Marx was "the moving and active spirit, the real soul of the [Communist] Party."[8] According to the report filed by this agent, the thirty-four-year-old Marx could have easily passed as a homeless bum:

In his private life he is a highly disorderly, cynical human being and a bad manager. He lives the life of a gypsy, of an intellectual Bohemian; washing, combing and changing his linen are things he does rarely, he likes to get drunk. He is often idle for days on end. . . . There is not one clean and solid piece of furniture to be found in the whole apartment: everything is broken, tattered and torn . . . in one word everything is topsy turvy. . . . When you enter Marx's room, smoke and tobacco fumes make your eyes water so badly, that you think for a moment that you are groping about in a cave. . . . Everything is dirty and covered with dust. It is positively dangerous to sit down. One chair has only three legs. On another chair, which happens to be whole, the children are playing at cooking.[9]

Look, I'm not saying that just because Marx was eccentric, his political theories should be discounted. By all accounts, Albert Einstein was eccentric, too. At least Einstein's theories actually worked when put into practice. The same cannot be said of the things Marx dreamed up at the expense of his family.

Not to be too cynical, his actions were consistent with his advocacy. As he wrote, "The theory of Communism may be summed up in one sentence: Abolish all private property." I'd say he did a pretty good job of that one with his own family. What's more, history has shown that his ignoble theories impoverished millions of families around the world. I have no idea how anyone can call him the "creator of the most important political movement of the 20th Century."[10]

Marx believed the reason poverty exists is because wealthy fat cats (the bourgeoisie) are giving the working class (the proletariat) a raw deal. We can only assume he was referring to the working class who actually held down a regular, full-time job, something he never did. The rich are the oppressors, while the poor are the victims of oppression. That's number one. Then, in the interest of *fairness*, Marx believed the only solution to the problem was to redistribute the wealth (socialism).

It's the classic "makers versus the takers" mind-set.

The rich have something the poor want—primarily money and possessions. Rather than work harder to realize his dreams, as my grandfather did, Marx's behavior demonstrates he preferred to look for a handout. Not surprising, he believed it's the government's job to redistribute the wealth and end the inequality between the classes—which, in a nutshell, is Marxist thinking at the core. In the end, Karl Marx died a pauper.

If only his dangerous ideas had died with him.

If they had, the people in the Marxist-Leninist country of Cuba wouldn't be in such misery. Due to Cuba's "disastrous state-run agriculture industry,"[11] widespread shortages of food and food rationing abound forcing Cuba to import 80 percent of its food.[12] What's more, inadequate housing and deteriorating living conditions are the norm,[13] and Cubans are not permitted to switch jobs unless the government grants them permission.[14]

Other failures of Marxism-Leninism were the formation of the Socialist Federal Republic of Yugoslavia, which dissolved as a socialist state after less than fifty years in 1992; the People's Republic of Poland, a centrally planned socialist state with a failed economy, widespread impoverishment, food rationing, and martial law; and the Socialist People's Republic of Albania, which collapsed in less than fifty years when, in 1992, the communists were booted from power in a national election.

Are you starting to get the picture?

There are twenty-seven examples where a nation was built specifically upon the principles of Marxism-Leninism, yet ended up on the ash heap of history. Of the five countries still operating with an allegiance to the principles of Marxism-Leninism, namely, China, North Korea, Laos, Vietnam, and the aforementioned Cuba, personal freedoms are restricted, poverty abounds as the typical worker makes less than a dollar a day, and access to modern consumer goods is outside of the reach of the majority of the citizenry.

Only Hollywood idiots such as actor Sean Penn dream of living there.

A Better Marxist Mousetrap?

The teachings of Karl Marx, known as Marxism, formed the basis of communism and socialism. Marx, however, was more of an armchair quarterback, waxing eloquent about how the system should be changed yet never doing any of the heavy lifting. He never held a political office or position of leadership from which to implement his notions. By contrast, Russian revolutionary and avowed atheist, Vladimir Lenin, was a hands-on kind of guy.

True, Lenin loved to theorize about Marx's ideas with the other thinkers of his day, but he was far more pragmatic. Lenin quickly moved from the theoretical to the practical. And, he was quite a persuasive orator.

Given his ability to talk a good game and persuade others about his socialist ideas, Lenin was elected Chairman of the Council of the People's Commissars. In that capacity, Lenin wasn't above the use of propaganda and the manipulation of the press to sell his new Marxist-Leninist communist program, saying, "The press should be not only a collective propagandist and a collective agitator, but also a collective organizer of the masses."[15]

To sell his ideas to the peasants, Lenin modified Marx's order of economics over politics, enabling him to usher in his concept of a socialist economic system while solidifying the Soviet Union. In other words, he leveraged the lofty ideals of socialism—"From each, according to his abilities; to each, according to his needs"—to promote communism that, in theory, delivered a classless society through force, centralized planning, and control by an authoritarian government.

Lenin wasn't above twisting a few arms or breaking a few necks along the way, having signed execution lists to weed out at least twenty-five czars. I'm not suggesting that he was paranoid; he just backed his rhetoric with a rifle. As Lenin has said, "One man with a gun can control 100 without one." In 1918, Lenin authorized the execution of the Russian Royal Family and the deaths of another 765 insurrectionists.[16] No wonder there were two assassination attempts on his life. Regarding the application of socialism, in spite of his best efforts, Lenin only scratched the surface.

Which brings us to Joseph Stalin, the first General Secretary of the Communist Party of the Soviet Union. Stalin was heavily influenced by the writings of both Marx and Lenin. No doubt he was familiar with Lenin's opinion that "The enemies of the workers are the capitalists of all countries."[17] So, what's one of the first things Stalin did when he came to power? He thought it would be a great idea to topple the capitalists in various industries and replace them with a more efficient and fair state-controlled ownership.

Did his idea work?

Let's consider what happened to the farm industry in Russia.

Prior to Stalin's tinkering with the system, the farms in the Soviet Union were individually owned and operated by small family farmers, much as you might have in parts of this country today. These farmers, known as kulaks or individual landowners, were the backbone of the agriculture industry for the Soviets, having worked the soil for generations. Before Stalin intervened, the kulaks were quite productive and the people were eating fairly well.

That wasn't good enough for Stalin. Why? Because he had embraced Marx and Lenin's view that evil capitalists were the antithesis of socialism. For socialism to work, the capitalists had to be weeded out. And, as Marx had taught, "The theory of Communism may be summed up in a single sentence: Abolition of private property." Since the farmers were landowners who sometimes employed a handful of others, that made them a threat to communism and, as such, Stalin said they had to go.

At the barrel of a gun if necessary.

What's more, Stalin was of the opinion that the government, with the help of a centralized game plan, could run the farms *better* than the farmers. He figured he'd eliminate the profit motive of these greedy individual farmers and, by nationalizing the agriculture business, make it more efficient, increase productivity, and expand farmland output. Or so the man thought.

In that respect, Stalin's behavior is no different from Barack Obama's imposition of a socialist revolution here in America. From the moment Obama came to power, he leveraged the power of the government to nationalize major portions of the economy and private industries. Few sectors of American life haven't been impacted by the far-reaching arm of this president.

From the auto industry, the banks, and various financial institutions, to Obama's plan to snatch expansive tracts of land depriving the middle class of mining, farming, and cattle-raising opportunities, and commandeering the energy industry through his green socialism scheme of cap-and-trade, Obama is hell-bent on crippling capitalism through massive taxes and his bureaucratic state. His unswerving commitment to nationalize health care is nothing short of a power grab in which he hopes to co-opt and destroy one-sixth of the economy by any means possible, legal or otherwise.

This should come as no surprise given the fact that Barack Obama is a dedicated disciple of Saul Alinsky, the Chicago Marxist and community organizer of choice for leftist revolutionaries. Alinsky was an ultra-liberal and "communist/Marxist fellow-traveler," one writer, a former communist, asserts. This writer further explains that Alinsky "helped establish the dual political tactics of confrontation and infiltration that characterized the 1960s and have remained central to all subsequent revolutionary movements in the United States."[18]

Alinsky codified his America-hating strategies of confrontation and infiltration in his book, *Rules for Radicals*, which he dedicated to Lucifer.[19] You might say that gives new meaning to the idea that the devil is in the details. What's more, Alinsky's model for an anti-American revolution is built upon "the strategy of working within the system until you can accumulate enough power to destroy, it was what sixties radicals called 'boring from within.' . . . Like termites, they set about to eat away at the foundations of the building in expectation that one day they could cause it to collapse."[20]

These Alinsky-inspired tactics and actions by President Obama and his czars are guaranteed to cause trickle up poverty for the American middle class, which is the same thing Stalin caused, as you'll see, when he nationalized the agriculture business in Soviet Russia.

Let's not dwell on the fact that Stalin never planted a turnip and had no idea what was involved in running a farm. For whatever reason, Stalin placed his faith in the brilliant government bureaucrats in Moscow, believing they could do a better job than the kulaks who actually had dirt under their fingernails. Almost overnight, Stalin's regime swung into action, enforcing the collectivization of agriculture.

It was the way of "The Man of Steel" (Stalin), or the feel of his crushing heel.

In the early 1930s, Stalin proceeded to steal the land from the people—ordinary men and women like you and me—arresting those who refused to go along with the program. Millions of kulaks were exiled to distant corners of Russia.[21] Many landed in Stalin's Gulag labor camps, and more than twenty thousand who resisted were executed. Yes, there was widespread resistance because, in simple terms, as musician Frank Zappa once quipped, "Communism doesn't work because people like to own stuff."[22] What was the fruit of Stalin's takeover of the farming industry?

Russia experienced widespread famine of biblical proportions.

An estimated *ten million* Russians died from starvation because Stalin's promise of government efficiency and increased output turned out to be nothing more than fiction, a product of Stalin's fertile yet warped thinking. In fact, "the people who grew the grain were dying at a rate of 25,000 a day."[23]

Prior to 1917, Russia had always been a significant exporter of grain. In fact, Russia was the "most important grain exporting country"[24] in the world. After Stalin's communist takeover and the practice of a state-controlled agricultural industry, Russia's grain export business ground to a halt. In fact, in order to meet its own needs, years later Russia was forced to *import* upwards of six million tons of grain annually. This embarrassing situation continued until 1994 when Russian farmers were finally able to begin modest exports of grain.[25]

Let's not lose sight of the fact that this loss of productivity and massive, unnecessary loss of life occurred because Stalin put socialism into practice, bringing it out of the theoretical realm in ways that neither Lenin nor Marx himself had ever tried on such a large scale. What's more, this dictator and disciple of Marxism-Leninism became one of the worst mass-murderers in history.

This isn't an isolated example of the failure of nationalization.

History continues to repeat itself.

We see this happening just about anywhere the government takes over a private industry in any country down through the ages. If you look at government-run industries around the world, very few of them are profitable. Take Airbus. It's run by a joint consortium—France and Germany and several other European countries—and it's still dependent on government aid. These governments must keep pumping more money into the company to keep it airborne. One report pegs total government subsidies at more than $200 billion over the last four decades.[26]

Airbus, by the way, competes with our Boeing company, which has no such benefits as government subsidies. Boeing just produces a better airplane for a lower price, which, of course, customers want to buy. Because Boeing is profitable, the employees have jobs, the economy grows, and the country benefits. That's the fundamental difference between socialism and capitalism.

The More Power They Have, The Less You Have

When it comes to government control, I don't care which topic we're talking about—be it nationalizing private business, introducing socialized health care, crippling the military through sensitivity training, or redefining marriage in the name of tolerance—every time the government seizes control of your rights and starts meddling with your choices, a part of your freedom dies. Let me put it to you this way: *the more power they have, the less you have*. It's a simple principle of life and yet so many sheeple don't seem to know this.

In Barack Obama's case, he *does* know this.

That's the whole point.

He's been brainwashed by the myth of Marxism-Leninism and, in spite of the overwhelming evidence that socialism impoverishes the people, leads to oppression, robs individual freedom, and bankrupts nations, Obama is committed to transforming America into a socialist state. As President Ronald Reagan has said, "How do you tell a communist? Well, it's someone who *reads* Marx and Lenin. And how do you tell an anti-Communist? It's someone who *understands* Marx and Lenin." [27]

Obama has *read* them.

I *understand* them. Which is why I oppose him.

Let's look at the thread weaving the past to the present.

Karl Marx had an idea essentially born out of the fact that he suffered from a severe dose of class envy. Lenin put feet on Marx's theories and added a few of his ideas to the mix creating Marxism-Leninism. The result was a disaster for the people. The middle class suffered, not benefited. Along comes Stalin, a student of Marxism-Leninism, who tried his hand at it. The results? An even greater disaster for the middle class who were further impoverished.

Everywhere Marxism-Leninism has been tried, it has failed.

Along comes our neophyte president, captivated by Marx, who wants to turn America into the socialist state first envisioned by Marx. In addition to what Obama has said and done, one of the clearest signs of his creeping socialism can be found in Obama's inner circle who, as I've established, are fans of Mao Zedong, the brutal dictator of China. What you may not know is that Mao was yet another student of Marxism-Leninism whose regime created widespread economic and social mayhem for the people of China.

When I talk about President Obama moving America toward socialism, I'm not talking about a benign European socialism, which the media thinks Obama is engaging in. I am talking about the hard line Marxist-Leninist attitude that was most clearly described not only by Marx and by Lenin, but also by Mao Zedong in his little red book, *Quotations from Chairman Mao Zedong.* "With a Marxist-Leninist attitude," Mao wrote, "a person applies the theory and method of Marxism-Leninism to the systematic and thorough investigation and study of the environment. He did not work by enthusiasm alone. But as Stalin says combines revolutionary sweep with practical-ness."

What does that mean with regard to Obama?

Obama's a very practical man. He's studied the lay of the land—the "thorough investigation" Mao speaks of—and determined that the most practical way to accomplish his socialization of America was to co-opt and socialize one-sixth of the American economy. This power grab would be Obama's first building block on the road to a Marxist-Leninist state, which is why he spoke so often about the need to reform health care on the campaign trail and made it his top priority as president.

Mao goes on to write, "In order to guarantee that our party and country will not change their color, we must not only have a correct line and correct policies, but must train and bring up millions of successors who will carry on the cause of the proletarian revolution." Notice the emphasis on the word "correct." Do you hear the phrase "political correctness" in that? The PC crowd doesn't understand what they're saying when they argue in favor of political correctness. When they make concessions in terms of what qualifies as "correct" speech, they move the country toward an early phase of a communist dictatorship.

Mao develops this thought further, saying, "What are the requirements for worthy successors to the revolutionary cause of the proletariat? They must be genuine Marxist-Leninists and not revisionists wearing the cloak of Marxism-Leninism." That sounds like he's describing Obama's manufacturing czar Ron Bloom who agrees with Mao "that power comes largely from the barrel of a gun" and the Mao-loving former White House Communications Director Anita Dunn who turns to the mass murderer of China for inspiration. One other passage from Mao is in order. He writes:

> Our party organizations must be extended all over the country and must purposely train tens of thousands of cadres [who] maintain extensive, constant and close ties to the working people. This is a major measure of fundamental importance for a socialist system.

What are we talking about when we apply this advocacy of cadres—groups of people trained for a specific purpose—to Obama's America? Think ACORN (Association of Community Organizations for Reform Now). I'll explore ACORN's role in the remaking of America in chapter eight. But make no mistake about it. ACORN is one of the early cadres of the Marxism-Leninism that I've been warning you about.

Power to the People

If for some reason you're an Obamanic who still clings to the notion that socialism brings liberation to the people because it curbs the powers of an oppressive government, guess again. Former FBI Director J. Edgar Hoover, an expert in communist tactics, observed, "Communism means fewer and fewer rights for the private citizen, curtailment of freedom of speech and press and worship of God. The state becomes all-powerful, the absolute reverse of American tradition."[28]

Even the left-leaning *TIME* magazine agrees that the application of Marxist philosophy in the real world was a fiasco. In one of those rare brushes with reality, *TIME* reported:

> By any empirical standard, Marx's major prophecies—such as Communism's triumph over capitalism or the outbreak in industrialized societies of the workers' revolution—have proved false. No economy based on his teachings has approached the efficiency of a free-market system, and governments that tried

to enforce his Utopian views have been compelled to rely on totalitarian methods.[29]

In the face of such an indictment, you may wonder why Barack Obama doesn't abandon Karl Marx, the failed darling of the radical far left. It's a question I've given some thought to and believe the answer might surprise you. See if you agree with me on this. I'd say there's a striking similarity between Karl Marx and the young Barack Obama.

Just as Marx aligned himself with a wealthy patron who picked up the tab for his lifestyle, Obama did the same thing while a student pursuing his Marxist ideologies at Occidental College. In a moment, I'll explain why this is noteworthy. Let's begin with Obama's choice of a roommate, Mohammed Hasan Chandoo, a wealthy Pakistani student. John Drew, Obama's contemporary at Oxy, recalls:

> When Barack Obama was a young man at Occidental College his sophomore year, he had a very wealthy patron in Hasan Chandoo. They had a wonderful, big house where they threw lavish parties. Chandoo was throwing the money around. Obama was dressed in the nicest, slickest clothes . . . I thought they were both wealthy.[30]

Dr. Drew recalls going out to dinner with Obama and his roommate Chandoo in Chandoo's BMW while arguing for hours about the merits of Marxism and Leninism over drinks and cigarettes. He says:

> [Obama] was arguing a straightforward Marxist-Leninist class-struggle point of view, which anticipated that there would be a revolution of the working class, led by revolutionaries, who would overthrow the capitalist system and institute a new socialist government that would redistribute the wealth.[31]

Do you see the irony? On one hand Barack Obama—a student who comes from a broken home and with no visible means of support—was living high on the hog, compliments of his rich roommate. On the other hand,

Obama was arguing about the merits of redistributing the wealth to end class struggle. Doesn't that strike you as bizarre, if not downright hypocritical? He and Marx had a lot in common. Both suffered from a severe case of *class envy* coupled with an *entitlement mentality*.

Each wanted the good life.

Neither wanted to work for it.

Both were happy to sponge off someone else.

And so it should come as no surprise that when Obama's patron saint pulled out of town, that was his cue to move on to greener pastures to find another sugar daddy. Here's how Dr. Drew saw it:

> When Obama knew that Chandoo was going to leave Occidental College he knew that the money supply was gone, the big house was gone, the parties were done, and he thought it was better for him to get the heck out of there and go to Columbia. Because Chandoo wasn't financing his lifestyle anymore I don't believe Obama was ever able to create that same charismatic presence on the Columbia campus.[32]

Things didn't quite work out at Columbia as the budding Marxist Obama might have imagined. Upon arriving in New York, Obama sought out Sohale Siddiqi, a friend of Chandoo. Maybe he thought any friend of Chandoo would be able to offer him another gravy train to ride for a season. Turns out Siddiqi was no moneybags. "We were both very lost," he said. "We were both alienated, although [Obama] might not put it that way. He arrived disheveled and without a place to stay."[33]

Siddiqi says he and Obama ended up in "a slum of a place" on East 94th Street in a rough neighborhood infested with druggies, where gunshots were just part of the backdrop. Siddiqi admits, "it wasn't a comfortable existence. We were slumming it."[34] Why is this important? What does this have to do with Obama's socialist views? I'm no psychologist, but I do know how people with an entitlement mind-set, like Obama, see the world. I understand the subtext to their twisted convictions.

After his free ride in California, Obama may have resented his poverty-stricken circumstances on the streets of New York City. I don't blame him. Who wants to live in a rat hole? Especially after tasting the benefits of the good life, the parties, the fancy house and car, compliments of his college roommate at Oxy. Having lived in two vastly different worlds—one characterized by wealth, one marked by poverty—Barack the student couldn't reconcile the dichotomy these experiences presented.

That's where he went wrong.

Rather than see economic and individual freedom, entrepreneurialism, capitalism, and self-determination as the best engine to drive people out of poverty, Obama filled the vacuum in his head with the failed theories of Marx he had been studying in school. What's more, those classes were supplemented with what he learned from his childhood mentor and communist friend, Frank Marshall Davis.

I've been opposed to communism all my life because I see the devastation that is wrought around the world everywhere it's been tried. The worker has never benefited from a Communist Revolution. Never. The worker has always been sold the nonsense that after the Revolution, after nationalizing (transferring private businesses to state ownership and abolishing class distinctions) the bourgeoisie (those allegedly greedy capitalists) would be strung up and their property distributed to the poor (the working class).

That has never happened.

The worker was supposed to be the king.

Instead, their property and wealth were always redistributed to the ruling elite, to the bureaucrats. Look at Cuba, that communist state where the workers have been crushed, for fifty years, under the thumb of Fidel Castro, and remain so to this very day. Likewise, the middle class under Venezuela's Hugo Chávez remains oppressed. Have the workers benefited? Of course not. Only Castro's and Chávez's inner circle have been enriched. How can this be? Didn't Marx say, "Workers of the World, Unite. You have nothing to lose but your chains!"

He was dead wrong.

This phenomenon is a reversal of the Marxist-Leninist theories that Obama was programmed to believe. What's more, time and again, the elimination of private enterprise created widespread trickle up poverty instead of ushering in the promised efficiency and collective profitability that would benefit everyone. Under communism and socialism, *the poor got poorer* because Marxism-Leninism *inherently* enslaves people—body, mind, and spirit.

You might want to read that again.

Contrary to what Marx taught and Obama believes, spreading the wealth around impoverishes us. This really isn't so difficult to understand. Taking money from you and me to give to someone who is looking only for a handout, a bailout, or a way out, removes our incentive to excel, to grow, to risk investments, to invent, and to dream big dreams.

Why work so hard to underwrite another man's slothfulness?

Lessons from a Tuna Fish Sandwich

When I was between the ages of eight and nine, I was a typical kid living, at the time, in Queens, New York. I remember it was a warm Saturday morning late one June. School was out and summer was in full swing. Most of my friends were sleeping late or goofing off. Me? I'm wearing the dungarees, polo shirt, and sneakers, working for my father in his Manhattan antique store since dawn. I'm not complaining, mind you. My father gave me a hard work ethic most kids today can't comprehend. Everything's been handed to them on a silver platter—with a remote control and a cell phone.

As noon approached, Dad called down the stairs and told me to go buy some lunch for us. While I was glad to be out of the basement, my heart started to race when it became clear he wasn't going with me. I hated the thought of facing the mean streets alone, dodging the rats, the garbage, and the thugs hanging out on the street corners.

I think my father saw my hesitation, but he insisted that I face those horrible streets alone. Sending me out into the byways of Manhattan was how he wanted to toughen me up. My father thought I might be too soft, you know, growing up in a safer neighborhood as we did. So, off I go in search of lunch.

Several blocks away was a restaurant that served no meat, just salads, tuna fish sandwiches, and such. I ordered the tuna, paid the man behind the counter, and a few minutes later headed back to the store. When I gave my father the sandwich, he opened it up and saw a huge dead fly in it. I'll never forget his reaction. His face turned red, his eyes went wide as twin saucers, and the veins along both sides of his neck bulged. He looked as if he were ready to erupt like Mount St. Helens.

Dad was infuriated that someone would take advantage of his son like that. He assumed they did it on purpose—just to be spiteful. They probably did, but what did I know? Now, my father wasn't necessarily a violent man, but, in that moment, he looked as if he could have strangled a bear with his bare hands. He was incensed by the sheer wrongness of what he had discovered.

So, my father grabbed me by the hand and dragged me up the street back to that lousy luncheonette. He opens the door with a bang and looks around. The sleepy customers glance up from their menus with interest at this new development. Dad spots the owner coming out of the kitchen wearing a smirk and an apron as if nothing was wrong. My father unloaded with both barrels, yelling, "How *dare* you give my son a sandwich with a fly in it!"

The deli man said, "Don't worry, I didn't charge you for it."

I learned a valuable lesson that day.

I learned that there are bad people in the world who will do bad things for whatever reason and that remaining silent when faced with wrongdoing isn't an option. It might be unpopular to take a stand. It might turn a few heads. But my father taught me to speak up in the face of adversity. Which brings us to Obama's socialist revolution, which is far worse than planting a fly in a tuna sandwich. Which is all the more reason you and I have an obligation to speak against the destruction he's planning of this once great country.

Make no mistake. The storm of trickle up poverty is about to hit the middle class with the force of a tsunami. Everyone of us has to start pulling on the oars, whichever way we can in order to steer the ship out of its path. For me, that's driving home the message everyday on my radio show, *The Savage Nation*. But you don't have to have the third largest radio talk show in the country to make a difference. You don't have to be the author of numerous *New York Times* bestsellers, as I am, before you can speak up.

Everyone has a part to play.

"But Michael," you may think, "I'm just a homemaker trying to stay afloat with the Herculean job of raising kids and managing the household. What can I do to lend a hand?" Or maybe you're a small business owner working far too many hours already just to keep food on the table. It doesn't matter where you are in life, there's a simple strategy that you can employ to turn this ship around while there's still time. As J. Edgar Hoover once said, "If our government is to remain free, it needs the help of every patriotic man, woman, and child."[35]

Let's get practical for a moment.

Let's look at how you can start to shape public opinion even in the supermarket line. I'm not suggesting that you should jump on a soapbox and start screaming, "Obama is a closet communist!" If you try that stunt, the men in white jackets will come and put you into a nuthouse. Instead, you use the methods of the quiet cultural revolution and turn it back on the left to defeat them with their own tactics.

The next time you're standing in a supermarket line, look at the magazine rack. Pick one that features President Obama or Michelle smiling on the cover and then just casually say to the checkout clerk while others in line hear you, "You know I voted for him and he turned out to be such a liar and such a phony. Look what he's done to this country." Or maybe, "Obama might be spreading the wealth around, but I haven't seen any, have you?" Or even, "He sounded like Robin Hood, but he's taxing me into poverty."

That's all you have to say.

Don't sound angry or engage in a discussion or launch into a five-minute diatribe. Just make the statement. And if there's a Tea Party scheduled near your town, why not plug it? Why not say, "I've decided enough is enough. I'm going to check out the Tea Party this weekend." Throw that pebble into the quiet lake and you'll see the ripples go across America. Why? There's tremendous power when you challenge the status quo.

There's even more power when we who are patriots collectively speak our minds. Imagine the impact if the ten million weekly listeners of *The Savage Nation* said something each week at the supermarket about Obama wrecking the country, or that he studied Marxism, or that he surrounds himself with those who embrace communism. You'll create a quiet revolution in the country. Who cares what the people in the checkout line may think about you. The truth you speak will resonate with the Liberty Bell when it first sounded out its message of independence in 1776.

It's a sound the sheeple have long forgotten.

It's a sound rarely heard.

It's a sound that must awaken us if the American Dream is to survive.

CHAPTER 4

Nightmare on Wall Street

We know that **the free market is nonsense,** we know
that the whole point is to game the system . . .
—Ron Bloom, Obama's Manufacturing Czar, 2/27/2008

When I was eleven years old, I had my first bank account at Bankers Trust Company on Union Turnpike in Queens, New York. Each week I would deposit the money I earned from the local candy store where I worked after school as a soda jerk. I felt like the richest kid on the planet when the account grew to something like $618.08 after one year. One night, while reviewing my account, I discovered something startling. I looked at the balance and discovered that, while I had only deposited six hundred dollars, there was $18 more than I had actually put in.

I went to my father and, holding my savings summary for him to see, said, "Dad, the bank made a mistake. They deposited more money than I put in. Should I return it to them?"

He said, "Michael, that's your interest."

"Dad," I said, "What's interest?"

He said, "Well, they take your money and invest it and then they give you back a little bit of what they make on their investment. That's called interest—and you get to keep it." That was the day I became a capitalist. That's the day when I first understood the value of saving and investing. Over the years, I grew in my understanding of building wealth through savings and investments, as well as the risks and rewards associated with placing funds in the stock market. I imagine you may have had a similar experience when you were young. And, if you are like many in the middle class, you probably opened an Individual Retirement Account or employer-based 401k retirement savings plan maybe in addition to modest investments in the stock market.

While you and I played by the rules and trusted Wall Street with our monies, others, behind the scenes, manipulated America's leading financial institutions for their own personal gain. That gain wasn't just measured in lining their pockets. In some instances, as you'll see in a moment, it was to advance an agenda. Case in point.

In 2007, Christopher Cox, then Chairman of the Securities and Exchange Commission (SEC), under pressure from lobbyists did not prevent the change of two regulations that allowed hedge fund pirates to plunder the U.S. financial markets. This change in policy was responsible for driving down the value of America's assets by more than $10 trillion in 2008. Let's be clear. There was an agenda lurking behind the shadowy dealings. Is it a coincidence that this happened right before the presidential election? Hardly.

Where did those dollars go?

They ended up in the hands of a relatively small number of people and companies whose purpose was far more nefarious than merely making profits: The raiders who trashed our markets sought nothing less than to use the control they had gained over our financial system to put a wet-behind-the-ears leftist president in office. Moreover, they leveraged that power to create a government run on socialist principles but controlled by a small group of wealthy investors who dictate policy to the puppet president they elected. In effect, they pushed us further along the path to a socialist oligarchy.[1]

Another player in the financial meltdown is leftist financier George Soros, WHO SOME BELIEVE, has been trying for decades to manipulate American politics to the advantage of the Marxists with whom he is in league. It seems to me that Soros tried to rig the 2004 presidential election in favor of John Kerry. How? By pouring tens of millions of dollars into Kerry's campaign coffers and into building anti-capitalist, anti-democratic organizations such as MoveOn.org.

In spite of that massive investment, Soros was unsuccessful.

Did he give up? Far from it.

During the next few years, the Managed Funds Association (MFA), a group of hedge fund investors with whom Soros is affiliated, lobbied SEC Chairman Cox to have the rules changed. Why? So they could engineer a raid on U.S. markets to trigger a financial crisis that they foresaw could turn the election in favor of their 2008 candidate, Barack Obama. This time, the strategy worked. In the end,end, some believe that George Soros and similarly minded financiers benefited in an extraordinary way while moving the country dangerously toward control by leftists.[2]

Despite this alleged manipulation of the marketplace, Soros is free and active today. While he's still denying his involvement in one of the greatest scandals in American history, that is, when he's not crowing that he had "a very good crisis,"[3] I'm wondering why there isn't an investigation into this matter.

Hundreds upon hundreds of minor players were involved in this fraud as well. Another member of the MFA is John Paulson (no relation to former Treasury Secretary Henry Paulson, one of the architects of the TARP bailout). Paulson saw the value of his hedge fund firm rise exponentially in 2007, thanks to the rule changes that the MFA lobbied for. While he predicted the crash and the demise of Lehman Brothers and Wachovia, the real reasons he was able to realize huge profits from the financial meltdown were the rule changes that he took advantage of to line his pockets. Paulson, like Cox and Soros, is still plying his trade—in his case as a hedge fund trader. He's still enjoying the billions of dollars in profits he made personally from participating in the attack on the American economy.[4]

The Threat of Nationalization

Make no mistake about it: American businesses are under attack.

The threat comes from a Marxist president with his drive to nationalize many aspects of the private sector—from General Motors and insurance giant AIG, to our lending institutions and health care. Some argue this is Obama's move toward a Bolivarian socialist revolution like the one Hugo Chávez has created in Venezuela. Obama is putting rank amateurs in charge of businesses that they did not create, that they did not build, and that they do not know how to run.

Take, for example, Peter Orszag, Chairman of the Office of Management and Budget. Under this man, our national debt crisis has exploded into a systemic problem characterized by unrelenting governmental and corporate greed at the top of the economic food chain and unsupportable mortgage and credit card debt at the bottom. This should come as no surprise. Orszag is one of the guys who was advising the Russian government during the time when Russian businessmen absconded with billions of rubles in the economic chaos after the fall of the Soviet Union in the early '90s. He also advised the nation of Iceland during the time just before the country went bankrupt. He's another empty suit at a time when the country needs real leaders with solid credentials.

All of this will lead to total disaster and failure! Never in American history has one man—in this case, Obama—been in such a position of power to destroy personal freedoms, individual ownership, and the cycle of risk and reward inherent within market capitalism. The American middle class is especially vulnerable.

In fact, if you're a member of the middle class, you're one of the hundred million-plus people Obama has singled out to be brought to your knees. That's because you're one of the people who have made America the great nation that it is. You're raising your family, working at your job or running the business you created, contributing to investment and retirement accounts, attending church or temple, and, now, you're asking yourself what you've done to deserve Obama's attack on your wealth and freedoms. The answer is unsettling.

To leftists and pan-Leninists like Obama, you are not simply "middle class," you're part of the bourgeoisie—that's the group most despised by Marxists like Obama and so many members of his inner circle and czars. The savage truth is that you're part of the group Obama has singled out to feel the pain of trickle up poverty.

The Puppet Masters

Those who conspired to create the financial meltdown have something in common. They're either affiliated with, or in the hip pocket of, the Managed Fund Association (MFA). The MFA consists of hundreds of financial firms and private investors who run hedge funds. Hedge funds are not bound by the rules that govern most stock and mutual fund trading. They thrive on such practices as short selling (selling a stock that you don't own in the hope that its value will decrease, and then buying it at a lower price, thus making a profit) and trading derivatives (financial instruments based on such things as bonds and mortgages that are designed to reduce the risk associated with owning the underlying securities).

I believe Soros and hundreds of other hedge fund traders, most of them MFA members, manipulated the system using, primarily, changes in two rules that enabled them to raid the financial markets, generating huge profits for themselves, causing the financial crash of 2008, and enabling Barack Obama to be elected. In other words, it appears they engineered the fraud that ushered in the era of the socialist oligarchy in the United States. If so, they were successful in accomplishing their objectives in the 2008 election because they managed to have two of the primary safeguards to investors—the "uptick rule" and conventional accounting standards—removed in 2007.

During Christopher Cox's term at the SEC the uptick rule was eliminated on July 6, 2007.

The rule, initially adopted in 1938, was one of the primary reasons we were able to recover from the Great Depression. This uptick rule limited short sales to stocks whose last trade was higher than the previous one. The uptick rule meant that traders who sell short could not cause the market price of a stock to drop continuously at a precipitous rate. Once the rule was removed, "naked" short selling was enabled, and the circumstances were ripe for a raid such as the one that occurred in 2008.

Mark-to-market accounting standards were implemented on November 15, 2007. Prior to the implementation of mark-to-market accounting standards, the value of assets held by banks and other financial institutions was based on the price at which they were acquired. After mark-to-market was instituted, those assets had to be valued at the prices at which they could be sold at the present time. That meant that, even if a given asset had long-term value and might eventually be sold for a profit, if its present value was very low, that current low market value was the value banks must carry on their books.

One of the effects of mark-to-market accounting was that banks and other financial institutions were required to revalue their assets at the end of every trading day. This led to a dramatic rise in day trading of securities, often including unchecked short selling, which put enormous pressure on the issues traded. It resulted in the value of many financial institution stocks plummeting, because under mark-to-market rules, if asset values decline, the holder of the assets must produce cash to offset the decline. It meant that banks had to find cash in order to make up for the lost asset value that the new accounting rules generated. The result was a liquidity crisis that led ultimately to the Troubled Asset Relief Program (TARP), a $700-billion bailout of America's financial institutions whose very existence had been jeopardized by the change in accounting rules, and the so-called "stimulus" legislation.

By November, 2008, just prior to the presidential election, the elimination of the uptick rule had begun to have its desired effect. Short sellers raided the market, triggering the panic that changed the election's outcome in favor of Barack Obama. The value of shares of major financial institutions dropped precipitously, and Americans were rapidly cheated out of some $10 trillion in their 401K and other investment and retirement accounts. Who could forget that one?

The result was the election of a leftist president, Barack Obama. No doubt Soros recognized that Obama was utterly ignorant of how capital markets work, and he knew that the new president could be led around by the nose by him and his associates. That, coupled with Obama's leftist upbringing and education, made him the perfect stooge for the financial saboteurs with designs, not just on our economy, but on our very way of life.[5]

This situation is exacerbated by Mary Schapiro, who replaced Christopher Cox when he resigned from the chairmanship of the SEC in 2009. Schapiro, along with Treasury Secretary Timothy Geithner, has long been a supporter of mark-to-market accounting practices. Investors in the stock market fear the potential for the same risks that severely damaged the market in 2008, and are reluctant to get back into the market as fully as they might. Banks are reluctant to assume the risk of lending to businesses, especially small businesses, because of the risk that Schapiro will reinstitute some form of mark-to-market rules for banks and other financial firms, again causing them to mark down their assets and precipitating another liquidity crisis like that of 2008.

The result was what appeared to be an economic stalemate until early May, 2010.

On the afternoon of May 6, the Dow Jones Industrial Average plummeted 998.50 points in a matter of minutes, the largest intra-day drop in the history of the Dow. As usual, commentators and analysts missed the mark completely when trying to unravel what had happened. Some speculated that a trader had mistakenly added too many zeroes to the number of shares he was selling and triggered the fall; others blamed the Greek debt crisis and the underlying weakness in the Euro and in the EU's approach to the financial woes of several of their member nations for launching panic selling; still others blamed the rise in electronic trading for causing the drop. While there is certainly some validity in the last two, in fact, the immediate trigger of the sudden sell-off was very likely a raid by short sellers on the stock market.

First, the precipitous drop occurred shortly after 2:30 in the afternoon.

That should have been a clue to those trying to figure out what had happened.

As Nelson D. Schwartz and Louise Story explain:

> Some circuit breakers do exist, a legacy of the reforms made following the 1987 stock market crash, but they only kick in after a huge drop—and only at certain hours. Before 2 p.m., a 10 percent drop in the Dow causes New York Stock Exchange to halt trading for one hour. Between 2 p.m. and 2:30 p.m., the pause shrinks to a half-hour and after 2:30, there is no halt in trading.[6]

The time of day is significant. Why? If the drop had occurred before that time, the size of the drop would have triggered a halt in trading. Any further potential damage that the continuation of such a drop might have caused could have been contained. Since it occurred immediately after that time, no protections were in place.

That in itself points the finger directly at short sellers.

In fact, the May 6 drop was the quite possibly the work of hedge fund traders raiding the market with the intent to send a message that they could still do whatever they wanted, despite the fact that only days earlier a new, "alternative" uptick rule had been put in place. They demonstrated clearly that the new rule had no teeth whatsoever; that traders who staged the raid were free to do what they would for the remainder of the afternoon.

In fact, before it closed for the day, the market had gained back more than half of what it had lost. Short sellers first drove down the price of many stocks dramatically; what's more, the value of a number of issues dropped to a penny a share, making them worthless. The raiders then bought them back, driving the market back up, although not before they pocketed somewhere in the neighborhood of half a trillion to a trillion dollars. Short sellers had what they sought: significant profits and a trial run to prove that they were still in control of the market, despite the new rule supposedly protecting investors from precisely the kind of raid that had just been staged.

The "alternative" uptick rule, just implemented, halts the trading of a stock whose price declines by 10 percent in a single day, but after 2:30 in the afternoon, the rule doesn't apply. The incident demonstrates that the SEC is essentially still a toothless entity headed by someone who's in the bag for hedge fund traders. It may well mean that things haven't changed significantly, that the market is still at the mercy of the MFA.

In an important sense, the hedge fund traders of the MFA hold power over the economy. Until they determine again that there's a need for them to step in and resume control of the economy and political policy by staging yet another raid of the capital markets, the uncertainty that accompanies this threat is likely to stall a return to a full economic recovery at pre-2008 levels. Banks will continue to be wary about lending to businesses and homeowners, fearing sudden policy changes like a resumption of mark to market accounting that might again jeopardize their balance sheets. And middle Americans' investment portfolios will once again be hog-tied by what may well be a shadow government.

This is un-American on the face of it.

What has occurred over the past several years is a power grab of epic proportions, and no one in Congress is even close to understanding what happened and what a dangerous position we're in. From a high of more than fourteen thousand in October, 2007, the Dow Jones Average had lost *nearly half* of its value by the time of the 2008 election.[7] Much of the lost money went into the pockets of the hedge fund raiders who, thanks to changes permitted by the SEC, were able to sell short with no limits, further driving down asset values. SEC's giving in to those lobbying on behalf of the MFA cost millions of average Americans invested in the stock market and in money market funds through their 401K plans as much as half the value of the assets they had planned to retire on. The raid made Bernie Madoff look like a piker. By the way, SEC also looked the other way where Madoff was concerned.

By the time John McCain correctly called for Cox's resignation as part of his bumbling response to the financial meltdown that cost him the election, it was already too late. In his response to McCain, Cox disingenuously said, "we have no tolerance for naked short selling," despite the fact that under his leadership, that's precisely what the SEC enabled.[8] The uptick rule was reinstated (February, 2010) and the mark-to-market accounting relaxed (March, 2009) only after potentially irreparable damage to the economy and to millions of Americans' savings and retirement accounts had been done.

But there's another disturbing layer of alleged treachery behind this story. There are those who have claimed that the financial meltdown—ostensibly engineered by the MFA—may well be a part of an even larger movement to both manipulate and reduce the United States (as well as other powerful world economies) into mere pawns of a shadow world government. Some assert that is the goal of the Bilderberg Group. You may wonder, What's that? After all, most people don't know the difference between Bilderberg and Pittsburgh.

The Bilderberg Group is a secretive organization whose activities, from its inception in 1954, remain hidden from both press and public scrutiny. While little is known about their inner workings, we do know that the Bilderberg Group is an international consortium of politically and economically powerful people who envision a New World Order—with them at the top pulling the strings. They're dyed-in-the-wool pan-Leninists. They're egotists of the lowest order who want to effectively erase national boundaries and control the world economy.

And they have the connections to pull if off.

After all, the Bilderberg Group isn't a bunch of average blue collar guys working the night shift at a bowling alley. Far from it. The membership list from past attendees reads like a Who's Who of United States and international politics, finance, and communications, including former U.S. President Bill Clinton; Fox News owner and media mogul Rupert Murdoch; George Soros; U.S. Treasury Secretary Timothy Geithner; Richard Holbrooke, U.S. Special Envoy to Pakistan; EU Bank President Jean-Claude Trichet; Fed Chairman Ben Bernanke; and U.S. Senators Chris Dodd and Dianne Feinstein, among others.

Those attending from the U.S. in 2010 included Roger Altman, Chairman, Evercore Partners; Sonia Arrison, Author and policy analyst; Timothy C. Collins, Senior Managing Director and CEO, Ripplewood Holdings; Martin Feldstein, George Baker Professor of Economics, Harvard University; Niall Ferguson, Laurence A. Tisch Professor of History, Harvard University; William Gates, Co-chair, Bill & Linda Gates Foundation and Chairman, Microsoft Corporation; Philip H. Gordon, Assistant Secretary of State for European and Eurasian Affairs; Donald Graham, Chairman and CEO, The Washington Post; Richard Holbrooke, Special Representative for Afghanistan and Pakistan; Robert Hormats, Under Secretary for Economic, Energy and Agricultural Affairs; James Johnson, Vice Chairman, Perseus; John Keane, Senior Partner, SCP Partners; Henry Kissinger, Chairman, Kissinger Associates; Klaus Kleinfeld, Chairman and CEO, Alcoa; Henry Kravis, Kohlberg Kravis Roberts & Co.; Marie-Josée Kravis, Senior Fellow, Hudson Institute; Eric Lander, President and Director, Broad Institute of Harvard and MIT; Jessica Mathews, President, Carnegie Endowment for International Peace; Craig Mundie, Chief Research and Strategy Officer, Microsoft Corporation; Moisés Naím, Editor-in-Chief, Foreign Policy; Peter Orszag, Director, Office of Management and Budget; Sean Parker, Managing Partner, Founders Fund; Frank Pearl, Chairman and CEO, Perseus; Richard Perle, Resident Fellow, American Enterprise Institute for Public Policy Research; Charlie Rose, Rose Communications; Robert Rubin, Co-Chairman, Council on Foreign Relations, Former Secretary of the Treasury; Eric Schmidt, CEO and Chairman of the Board, Google; James Steinberg, Deputy Secretary of State; Lawrence Summers, Director,

National Economic Council; Peter Thiel, President Clarium Capital Management; Christine Varney, Assistant Attorney General for Antitrust; Paul Volcker, Chairman, Economic Recovery Advisory Board; F.J. Bing West, Author; and James Wolfensohn, Chairman, Wolfensohn & Company.

That's just a list of those who are coming from the U.S. that we know of. Many who attend choose to be anonymous and, as such, are not included in this list. We also know that the annual meeting of these elitists is a heavily guarded affair—complete with armed sentinels. Why the secrecy? What are these heads of states, financial tycoons, and world leaders saying and doing behind closed doors? Let's be clear. I'm not a conspiracy thrill seeker. The fact of the matter is that where there's smoke there's fire. Once in a while a picture of their aspirations for world control emerges.

Take, for example, this statement made by Bilderberg member David Rockefeller. In his 2002 book entitled, *Memoirs*, Rockefeller wrote:

> Some even believe we are part of a secret cabal working against the best interests of the United States, characterizing my family and me as 'internationalists' and of conspiring with others around the world to build a more integrated global political and economic structure—one world, if you will. If that's the charge, I stand guilty, and I am proud of it.[9]

One investigative reporter described the group's charter as coming to an "agreement on questions of policy, economics, and strategy in jointly ruling the world."[10] And Former NATO Secretary-General, Willy Claes, who attended the Bilderberg meetings twice thus far, made this astonishing disclosure during a radio interview following the 2010 meeting. He explained each participant is given ten minutes to speak to the group. These comments are summarized and form the basis for a report. In turn, Claes went on, according to this translation of the interview, to state: "The participants are then obviously considered to use this report in setting their policies in the environments in which they affect."[11] In other words, he's admitting that the Bilderbergers set global policy based upon the exchange of views shared in secret and, in turn, return to their sphere of influence to carry out the plan.

Another pundit claims the Bilderberg Group's overall objective is the elimination of the middle class and the creation of a world order comprised only of "rulers and servants," and using such tactics as the establishment of such instruments as "green taxes" (including "cap and trade" legislation) in order to control the world energy market and to subjugate the world's citizens in the interest of combating the now proven-fraudulent notion of man-made global warming.[12]

What does all of this have to do with the financial crisis that sent Wall Street reeling out of control? Plenty. It validates the idea that the run on the American economy was ultimately a conspiracy designed to elect a leftist, globalist president of the United States. How else do you explain the actions of Barack Obama and Hillary Clinton in June, 2008, during the campaign, when they ditched members of the press and disappeared?

According to one report, during their absence the two candidates were meeting secretly with members of the Bilderberg Group in a northern Virginia hotel to discuss Obama's and Clinton's involvement with the group after the election. It is also reported that powerful businessman James A. Johnson, a Bilderberg Group member, selected Obama's running mate after the Democratic primary.[13]

Which is why investigating the abuses on Wall Street is the furthest thing from Barack Obama's mind. In my opinion, Mr. Obama would rather conspire with the members of the Bilderberg Group to control the world. And, what better way could Obama endear himself to this inner circle of globalists than to keep Wall Street vulnerable to outside manipulation in the future?

The Housing Crisis and TARP Bailouts

Two thousand eight marked a perfect leftist storm of financial conditions ensuring that the shadow government would be able to engineer the election of Barack Obama through their raid on U.S. markets. Among the most important contributors to the financial meltdown was a housing bubble that began in the 1990s, during the Clinton administration, as part of the left's entitlement mentality.

Using taxpayer-funded mortgage guarantees through two quasi-governmental organizations, the Federal National Mortgage Association (FNMA), better known as Fannie Mae, and the Federal Home Loan Mortgage Corporation (FHLMC), better known as Freddie Mac, policies were enacted that federally guaranteed home loans and encouraged giving mortgages to people who were unqualified to receive them. This, of course, perpetuated the left's strategy of expanding entitlements in order to create widespread dependency.

One of the leaders of this expansion of entitlements was über-leftist Massachusetts Soviet-Democratic Congressman Barney Frank. Although Democrats, with the collusion of the mainstream media, managed to convince Americans that the financial crisis was overwhelmingly the result of "capitalist greed," the fact is that the triggers for the crisis included both anti-capitalist hedge fund short sellers and corrupt Democratic policy-driven governmental agencies Fannie Mae and Freddie Mac. In fact, Allan H. Meltzer, writing in the *Wall Street Journal*, declared that "without the policies followed by Fannie Mae and Freddie Mac—and the destructive changes in housing and mortgage policies, like authorizing sub-prime and Alt-A mortgages for impecunious borrowers—the crisis would not have happened."[14]

Corruption surrounding Fannie and Freddie was rife.

In the late '90s, Barney Frank seems to have "been in bed" with Fannie Mae's Director of Project Development, Herb Moses, as he (Frank) made decisions that benefited Fannie and its principals enormously. During that period, for instance, Clinton crony and Fannie Mae CEO Franklin Raines absconded with $90 million in "bonuses." At the same time, directives from Democrats to loosen the standards on mortgages so that people previously unable to obtain them meant that the system was overweighted with bad credit risks. When the subsequent over-leveraging of the mortgage market through highly suspect mortgage-backed securities came home to roost, the rout was on.

Among many other things, the rout led to the failure of Lehman Brothers, the largest financial institution failure in American history. In addition to its extensive sub-prime mortgage holdings and its inability to meet demands for collateral against loans it was seeking to help it avoid bankruptcy, the 158-year-old company hid some $50 billion in distressed assets just before its collapse.[15] Richard S. "Dick" Fuld, then Lehman CEO, had guided the company deep into the business of making sub-prime loans and then repackaging them and reselling the resulting bonds.

Fuld was just getting started.

He then approved hiding these and other toxic assets from public scrutiny, all while raking in more than $500 million in compensation.[16] Fuld, having sold his $13 million mansion in Florida to his wife for $100,[17] remains a free man, although he is being sued for fraud and misrepresentation. He's currently working for (what else?) a New York–based hedge fund firm, Matrix Associates.[18]

Mike Whitney, a virulent, unrepentant leftist whose work appears on a number of blogs, actually got something right when he wrote, "Lehman was a planned demolition (most likely) concocted by ex-Goldman Sachs CEO [and then Secretary of the Treasury] Henry Paulson, who wanted to create a financial 9/11 to scare Congress into complying with his demands for $700 billion in emergency funding (TARP) for underwater U.S. banking behemoths."[19]

Even without the TARP legislation, there were strategies in place, including the Fed's guaranteeing the "commercial paper" Lehman was trying to sell to raise cash, which could have saved the distressed company. But Paulson and Fed Chairman Ben Bernanke chose not to use them. By doing this, Bernanke (he's a former Goldman Sachs associate also) "blackmail[ed] congress" to achieve his and Paulson's goal of pushing through the TARP legislation and using the money to save AIG, Bear Stearns, and Goldman Sachs, all of which would now likely be dead without Federal Reserve and U.S. Treasury intervention.[20]

Within a week of the passage of TARP legislation, the Fed created "a special lending facility to buy commercial paper,"[21] precisely the strategy that was already available and could have been used to save Lehman, and without putting Americans $700 billion further in debt. The U.S. Court of Appeals in Manhattan has ruled that the Fed must release the names of the institutions that received TARP money after the Lehman collapse and the amounts of money they received, something those involved have strenuously resisted because it might reveal the extent of the criminal collusion involved in their actions.[22]

Lehman's bankruptcy announcement had the effect of causing a run on other financial institutions by investors wanting to withdraw their money, creating the panic that enabled Paulson and Bernanke to get TARP pushed through Congress, committing U.S. taxpayers to bail out an entire industry of too-big-to-fail financial behemoths through a legislative initiative that, like so many others since late 2008, was unnecessary and unwise. In fact, as many commentators have pointed out, the passage of TARP was simply not needed to "save" the financial industry.

All that would have been required was a federal guarantee of the commercial paper financial companies needed to sell in order to stop the run on their funds and quiet investors' fears. Congress eventually capitulated and passed TARP legislation, after rejecting it once, and Paulson and Bernanke had fortified their financial fiefdoms against further assault by grabbing a stranglehold on three quarters of a trillion taxpayer dollars. Talk about the ultimate spreading the wealth around scheme.

What happened to the money is typical of what happens in cases where federal bureaucrats get their hands on money that confers power. It went right into the hands of the institutions that contributed campaign money. Connecticut Democratic Senator Chris Dodd, Chairman of the Committee on Banking, Housing, and Urban Affairs, received nearly $900,000 in campaign contributions from financial institutions receiving TARP bailout money. President Obama did even better, garnering more than $4 million in contributions for his war chest from the same group.[23]

We can only imagine what the retiring Dodd received from the Mohegan Indian tribe in his state which was awarded an astonishing $54 million in federal stimulus dollars. While techically a low-interest loan from the Department of Agriculture which must be repaid, it's not as if the Mohegan tribe is cash-starved. Far from it. After all, they own the Mohegan Sun casino—which scored more than $1.3 *billion* in gross revenues in 2009. Talk about hitting the jackpot. Those funds were supposed to help rural communities with fewer than 20,000 people struggling to "obtain other credit at reasonable rates and terms and are unable to finance the proposed project from their own resources."[24]

Tell me how the owners of a cash-rich casino fit the bill? This is nothing but an abuse of power and taxpayer money by Chris Dodd.

That said, much of the rest of the TARP money was used to purchase newly issued stock in banks, thus replenishing their capital and, presumably, encouraging them to resume lending at normal rates. The problem is that banks haven't ramped up lending. Neil M. Barofsky, appointed by President Bush as the Special Inspector General for the Troubled Assets Relief Program, attests to this. SIGTARP, as the position is known, released its report on the uses of TARP funds in October, 2009.

The report revealed that "Treasury and the TARP program lost credibility when lending at those institutions [the nine banks that were the recipients of the initial $300 billion in TARP funds] did not in fact increase and when subsequent events—the further assistance needed by Citigroup and Bank of America being the most significant examples—demonstrated that at least some of those institutions were not in fact healthy." [25] The fact that this strongly worded conclusion was drawn by a government agency emphasizes just how crooked, ineffective, and unnecessary the TARP legislation was.

TARP also provided Barack Obama with fuel for a further assault on capitalism in the form of his opposition to high levels of executive compensation, especially for TARP fund recipients, but for other financial industry executives as well. "This is America," the president declared at the White House. "We don't disparage wealth. We don't begrudge anybody for achieving success. And we believe success should be rewarded. But what gets people upset—and rightfully so—are executives being rewarded for failure, especially when those rewards are subsidized by U.S. taxpayers." [26]

The problem is that this isn't really "America" anymore.

Barack Obama *does* begrudge anybody who achieves success.

He supports forced bailouts of financial institutions, then declares $500,000 annual limits on compensation of executives who take bailout money. He also places restrictions on such expenditures as "golden parachutes" and "luxury spending" on extras like corporate jets and office remodeling, decisions that should be the responsibility of Boards of Directors and shareholders. The *Wall Street Journal* called the president's actions and pronouncements "the most aggressive assault on executive pay by federal officials." [27]

Interestingly, no one bothered to tell Goldman Sachs about Obama's restrictions on executive pay. The company's Chairman and CEO, Lloyd Blankfein, received nearly $10 million in compensation in 2009, including "a $600,000 annual salary, $9 million in restricted stock awards and about $262,000 in other compensation."[28] Compensation for other financial industry executives was equally lucrative. JPMorgan Chase CEO Jamie Dimon received $15.5 million, and American International Group head Robert Benmosche will receive $7 million in salary alone in 2010. AIG is the giant insurance company that has received more than $182 billion in TARP funds.

The website OMBWatch.org provides this assessment:

> The Special Inspector General for TARP . . . estimates that taxpayers will lose almost $30 billion on [the government's investment] in AIG, in large part because of bad choices the government made when bailing out the company. Instead of forcing AIG creditors to take a loss, Treasury insisted that they be paid in full.[29]

The reason for the government's paying full value for AIG's troubled assets has everything to do with Goldman Sachs alums Paulson and Geithner bailing out their buddies, at taxpayer expense. Both the government and the financial institutions are fending for themselves, very likely in collusion against American taxpayers.

What you may not know is that Goldman Sachs is the former home of many of the Obama administration's top financial advisors, including Neel Kashkari, who headed the TARP bailout; Mark Patterson, Chief of Staff for Treasury Secretary Timothy Geithner; Gary Gensler, a top executive at the Commodity Futures Trading Commission; Goldman Sachs lobbyist Michael Paese, placed as a top aide to Massachusetts Democratic Congressman Barney Frank, chair of the House Financial Services Committee;[30] and Adam Storch, a Goldman Sachs Vice President, Chief Operating Officer of SEC Enforcement.[31]

Are you beginning to get the picture? It's a recurring theme, the association of Goldman Sachs with the financial meltdown and ongoing corruption in the financial industry.

In April, 2010, Congress opened hearings into SEC allegations that Goldman Sachs had created, in league with hedge fund trader John Paulson, a financial instrument based on mortgage-backed securities that was designed to fail and that, like Paulson, Goldman Sachs actually helped insure its failure by having their own traders sell it short while not advising their investors that there was a virtual guarantee that the instrument would fail. This caused Goldman Sachs clients to lose significant amounts of money as a result of their having followed the advice of their investment counselors at the financial giant, advice the counselors themselves were betting against.

Am I the only one who has a problem with Congress holding their sham hearings on Goldman Sachs? It's a classic case of the fox guarding the henhouse. Why do I say that? Aren't the members of Congress to be trusted? Let me put it to you this way: One of the key players in the hearing, Senate Banking Committee Chairman Democrat Chris Dodd, is up to his ears in financial misdeeds himself. Dodd profited through being a preferred customer of Angelo Mozillo's now discredited Countrywide Financial, receiving low-interest loans that saved him tens of thousands of dollars in interest charges.

But it gets worse. Other recipients of favored treatment from Mozillo included Democratic Senator Kent Conrad of North Dakota, former Clinton Secretary of Health and Human Services Donna Shalala, and Obama advisor James Johnson, who resigned from Obama's campaign after his involvement with Mozillo was made public.[32] Add the nonexistent Congressional "oversight" responsibilities with regard to Fannie Mae and Freddie Mac, and you have the makings of a multi-pronged scandal that involves, not only corrupt financial institutions and hedge fund traders on Wall Street, but rampant corruption among those in Congress charged with protecting the public's interest. In fact, when he had a chance to make sure Fannie and Freddie were appropriately regulated in 2006, Dodd cast a "no" vote as the legislation failed.

President Obama campaigned hard for the financial reform bill. His underhanded tactics included having Michigan Democratic Senator Carl Levin order the release of internal Goldman Sachs e-mails that documented the fact that the company had sold short securities they advised their own clients to buy. Goldman, for its part, refused to release financial information that showed the profits it made from shorting the housing market while emphasizing the losses it sustained in that same market.

The financial regulation reform legislation whose passage the Goldman Sachs fraud hearings were designed to assure in fact does very little to "regulate" the financial industry—especially given the fact that the current oversight bodies have proven woefully inadequate to do the job. The fact of the matter is that neither the Congress nor their partners in crime, the financial players, can be trusted to act in the public interest.

Why? Once again, you must follow the money trail.

According to a report by the Associated Press, during the last 20 years the barons on Wall Street have enriched the coffers of federal politicians to the tune of $2.3 billion.[33] Don't think for one minute that those deep pockets aren't having an enormous sway over what gets passed in Washington. Money talks. Any bill that Congress passes into law will likely do next to nothing to muzzle those who would devour the little guy's savings for their personal gain.

The bill further consolidates the rapidly expanding power of the central government, authorizing it to interfere broadly with the financial markets. As Treasury Secretary Timothy Geithner, speaking about financial institutions in an MSNBC interview, put it, if financial firms do get into trouble, "we get to put them out of their misery, unwind them, you know, organize the elegant funeral for them."[34]

Let me put it to you this way.

Geithner and his confederates are judge and jury.

First, they decide *who* gets closed down. Then they'll close them down.

Tell me that's not a formula for abuse by government hacks.

The legislation gives regulators the power to break up banks and other financial entities that they deem have grown too big for their own good, but those regulators are still paid by the banks. Talk about letting the fox stay in the henhouse! Not much incentive for the regulators to do the job they're supposed to. The legislation empowers the consumer protection agency, also under the control of the Federal Reserve Board, to set rules that are intended to curb unfair consumer loan and credit card practices.

What's more, the legislation contains a provision that requires banks, hedge funds, and other institutions to go through clearinghouses in an effort to make many trades more transparent. The problem is, though, that the legislation includes "loopholes and gaps that weaken their impact," because many types of traders are exempt from this monitoring, including some hedge fund traders, those trading in the foreign exchange markets, and many financial institutions trading derivatives to reduce their risk.[35]

In addition, the same regulators who allowed the 2008 financial crisis to happen are in charge of the same institutions that caused it. You might want to read that again. Instead of being hauled up on charges for allowing the meltdown in 2008 that destroyed the retirement savings of the middle class, these regulators get to keep their job of not doing their job. And the new law "does little to prevent big banks from getting bigger, meaning taxpayers might have to intervene again."[36]

To add insult to injury, the bill does nothing to regulate Fannie Mae and Freddie Mac. We, the taxpayers, are still on the hook for hundreds of billions of dollars—which may become trillions in the future—the result of continuing mismanagement by the people running these quasi-governmental financial sinkholes. As the *Wall Street Journal* has noted, it virtually "guarantees bailouts as far as the eye can see."[37]

There is also the possibility that the bill will drive an entire segment of the financial industry into unregulated territory. One of the things the bill does is prohibit banks from being in both the business of trading securities and the business of loaning money. This might force banks to sell off their trading businesses to other financial institutions, or to spin them off into separate businesses. In either case, that could mean that those businesses do not fall under the control of the regulatory agencies created by the financial regulation bill. They're precisely the components of the banking industry that the bill seeks to regulate, and they're precisely the components that will slip from regulators' oversight with passage of the bill.

Under the new financial regulation legislation, hedge funds, the engines of the financial manipulation that triggered the 2008 meltdown, are subject to somewhat greater regulation. Those funds managing over $100 million will be required to register with the SEC, and the SEC will be required to report to Congress how investors have been protected from risks posed by short sellers.[38] There are questions about whether these provisions will effectively prevent short sellers from once again raiding the markets and caus-ing another crash, though. In fact, only a ban on short selling will protect legitimate investors from returning to the market without risking having their investments devalued by hedge fund raiders. Rasmussen Reports sums up the likelihood that Congress is really addressing the root causes of the current economic situation with this headline: "72% Are Not Confident Congress Knows What It's Doing When It Comes to The Economy."[39]

Don't count on the Federal Government to start listening any time soon. Writing in *Rolling Stone* magazine, Matt Taibbi sums up the situation:

> Some parts of the new reforms border on insanity, threaten-ing to vastly amplify Wall Street's political power by institu-tionalizing the taxpayer's role as a welfare provider for the financial-services industry. At one point in the debate, Obama's top economic advisors demanded the power to award future bailouts without even going to Congress for approval—and without providing taxpayers a single dime in equity on the deals.[40]

In the most sensible solution yet proposed for the AIG bailout, the web-site DotPenn.com envisions a scenario in which a Samurai is brought in to train AIG executives to commit seppuku, Japanese ritual suicide, because, as the Samurai explains to his audience, "you have dishonored your fami-lies, your company, and your nation."[41]

Put the Brakes on Auto Bailouts

TARP funds were also used to prop up failing automakers General Mo-tors and Chrysler. The Bush administration released $17.4 billion to the two automakers in December, 2008.[42] A year later, GM and Chrysler had gone through more than $40 billion in additional TARP funds.[43] In taking over the two auto giants, the Obama administration ignored the law and awarded huge stakes in the companies to the auto unions, offering stock-holders pennies on the dollar while reducing them to minority status. The United Auto Workers (UAW) labor union now owns about 40 percent of

GM and 55 percent of Chrysler and effectively controls both companies, something Karl Marx himself would have applauded!

The General Motors bailout is a perfect example of what this corrupt Obama regime considers fair: Unions got a hundred cents on the dollar, primary shareholders, who should have been first in line, were forced by government fiat to settle for twenty cents on the dollar. Illegal, unconstitutional, done deal. But the corruption and inequity don't stop there. You might be familiar with the commercials that aired in the spring of 2010 in which the then-new president of General Motors, Ed Whitacre, an Obama appointee who is paid nearly $10 million annually, brags about how his company is paying back the bailout funds it received.

In a turn of events typical of this administration's perverted notion of fairness, General Motors robbed Peter to pay . . . Peter. The former automotive giant "paid back" the federal bailout money given to it by taking money from another chunk of government bailout money that it had sitting in an escrow account. GM lost billions of dollars in its first year as a ward of the state, and so it was little wonder that eyebrows were raised when it "paid back" some of the "loan" from taxpayers.

Of course, as it turned out, GM didn't pay it back at all. We're still on the hook for a company none of us would likely have bought stock in the first place, if we hadn't been forced to by the Obama administration. By the way, the Ford Motor Company, which refused federal bailout money, announced a $2.1 billion profit for the first quarter of 2010. The company also announced that it was adding employees and expanding production. That means nothing to Obama, who thinks Washington is the answer to the questions Detroit faces.

The crisis that faced America's big three auto manufacturers before the government bailed out GM and Chrysler arguably had a single source: legacy costs resulting from union contracts negotiated half a century ago. The financial burden thus incurred weighed down their balance sheets to such a degree that, even if the industry in which they compete had been thriving, it would have been extremely difficult for them to maintain long-term profitability.

As automobile manufacturing became a global industry, the foreign manufacturers that expanded their operations into the United States flourished. But while Toyota and Honda, along with relative latecomers Hyundai and Kia, have a significant manufacturing and sales presence in the United States, they don't have the staggering labor-related financial obligations under which GM, Chrysler, and Ford are struggling.

GM, for instance, has some 450,000 retirees. That's more than three times the number of its current full-time employees, to whom GM pays pensions and for whom it provides medical care. By some estimates, medical costs for retirees alone add more than $1,500 to the average cost of each GM automobile.[44] Need I point out the obvious? The higher sticker price to cover these perks contribute to stalled sales. What's more, the company faces an unfunded liability of more than $80 billion, about half its annual pre-downturn gross sales, for future healthcare costs for employees and retirees and their dependents.[45]

Without the balance-sheet-killing albatross resulting from union contracts, foreign manufacturers have been doing very well in the United States. When Obama bailed out the auto industry by nationalizing GM and Chrysler, he put the burden of saving the industry from the consequences of union contracts negotiated by his leftist political forbears squarely on the shoulders of American taxpayers. In doing so, he virtually assured that these companies would either sink into oblivion or become permanent corporate wards of the state, with American taxpayers footing the bill.[46]

Unions have been losing members and influence in the private sector for years. Unfortunately, in the public sector, their presence has continued to grow. Andy Stern, president of the 2.2 million-member Service Employees International Union (SEIU), has logged more visits to the Obama White House than any other outsider. Stern is what conservative commentator Kimberly Morin describes as a "progressive, anti-business, anti-American left wing extremist who deserves no place in the White House."[47] The SEIU contributed more than $60 million to Obama's presidential campaign.

Like Hitler's brownshirts, Obama's purple-shirted SEIU-member supporters, who seem to appear everywhere he speaks, are his equivalent of union storm troopers. They've showed up in several cities to "drown out" the voices of town hall meeting attendees protesting Obama's policies. They turned out in Massachusetts in support of Martha Coakley in her unsuccessful campaign against Scott Brown for the Senate seat vacated by Teddy

Kennedy. They assaulted Kenneth Gladney, one Tea Party protestor, beating him badly in order to intimidate him and prevent him from selling "Don't Tread On Me" flags.[48]

Union membership is declining dramatically in the private sector. In 2009, there were more unionized employees in government (7.9 million) than in the private sector (7.4 million). By this year, union membership had dropped to 12.3 percent of wage and salary workers from more than 20 percent in 1983, with 37.4 percent of public sector workers unionized while only 7.4 percent of private sector workers are. It means that private industry in our free market has discovered that unions are budget-busters and done something about it. It also means that, being a Marxist president who was ushered into office in no small part because of union support, Barack Obama is going to do anything he can to reward those supporters.

That, in turn, plays out as support for such policies as "card check," the elimination of the secret ballot for workers faced with voting for or against unionizing their shops. And it means that every industry the president is able to nationalize will soon become a unionized industry, helping the president and his union thug allies consolidate their power and gain ever-increasing control over our lives and our jobs. The fact that Obama is clearly using his relationship with the SEIU to further union interests in the United States attests to his ongoing push to bring labor unions back to an unearned and undeserved position of prominence in America.[49]

When Obama "rescued" GM and Chrysler, he committed American taxpayers to underwriting the leftist agenda of the past half century, as manifested in labor agreements antithetical to capitalism. That it's taken so long for this leftist tactic, in tandem with the current exacerbating financial crisis, to finally bring the American auto industry to its knees is a testament to the resilience of capitalism. That Obama's "solution" to this crisis might spell the end of American automobile manufacturing should not be lost on those of us who will have to bear the financial burden of "saving" it.

For all the manipulation and downright fraud that went into the passage of TARP legislation, one of the most egregious aspects of the law is that it creates a permanent debit on our balance sheet. When banks do pay back their TARP loans, guess what? The money doesn't go back to the taxpayers who are underwriting the government borrowing that made it possible. It is treated as part of the general revenue of the federal government, to be spent by our elected and appointed officials on whatever they decide they want to spend it on. All repayment of TARP money does is give the government license to increase its TARP spending.[50]

And so, Barack Obama "inherited" a situation any leftist would love.

Left leaning hedge fund managers and their cronies appear to have engineered a financial crisis that they could blame on the "capitalist pigs" and, in turn, elect one of their own on the grounds that the capitalists themselves had undermined the very foundations on which they built their empires. Obama used this phony leverage to enact, *less than a month* after his inauguration, a nearly 1,000-page "stimulus" bill that requires the government to borrow upwards of $800 billion. This added to the national debt and tying up capital that would otherwise be available to fund private sector expansion that might actually create jobs.

The bill, which Mike Huckabee named the Congressional Relief Action Program (CRAP), was designed to "create" or "save"—as if saving jobs can be measured—more than three million jobs, according to it supporters. After a year, the White House's own website declares that 1.2 million jobs have been "funded." It appears as though the administration has given up trying to claim that any jobs were actually created or saved.

The primary things funded by the bill include expanded unemployment benefits, food stamps, healthcare subsidies for those out of work, and aid to states. The "aid to states" category is where most of the jobs have been funded.[51] It also proposed to fund "shovel ready" local, state, and federal construction projects, although there were almost no such projects ready to be funded, thanks in no small part to the difficult process of satisfying all the leftist environmental-interest-group-related paperwork required to initiate such projects. A year after its passage, the bill has had little effect, except to contribute to international credit ratings agency Moody's threat to downgrade the U.S. credit rating.

Meanwhile, the unions are far from losing power in the Obama administration.

Approximately eleven seconds after the last member of Congress left Washington at the beginning of the 2010 Easter Break, President Obama made fifteen recess appointments of administration officials. When President

George W. Bush exercised this constitutional right given to our presidents, the *Old York Times* reported approvingly on the fact that Congressional Democrats were livid at Bush's malfeasance and had vowed to make sure Bush's constitutional rights were denied if they could find a way.[52]

Their reasons centered on the fact that Bush, in appointing Charles W. Pickering and William H. Pryor, Jr., wasn't choosing judges who were willing to ignore the constitution when they rendered their decisions in important cases. Speaking for Democrats, former Senator Tom Daschle, who was himself voted out of office in 2004 and subsequently forced to withdraw his name from consideration for an appointment as Health and Human Services Secretary in the Obama administration for tax evasion, insisted that the president promise to "no longer abuse the [recess appointment] process."[53]

Barack Obama, on the other hand, merely appointed Craig Becker to the National Labor Relations Board (NLRB) after Becker's appointment had failed to get the requisite sixty Senate votes to be approved by the Senate. Rather than savage Obama after his recess appointments, as Democrats did Bush, forty-one Republican Senators chose to send a letter to Obama prior to the appointment strongly recommending that he not appoint Becker to the NLRB. Becker is an Andy Stern–Service Employees International Union (SEIU) lapdog, and his appointment represents Obama's paying back the labor unions that spent hundreds of millions of dollars to help get him elected. Becker had been the associate general counsel for the SEIU, and his appointment gives labor the advantage it's long been seeking at the NLRB.[54]

The NLRB is charged with supervising union elections and interpreting the National Labor Relations Act, and Becker's appointment gives the organization another leftist voice that will likely tip the balance of the agency further in the president's favor, meaning that Obama can again bypass the legislative process and rely on the NLRB to implement such affronts to democracy as "card check." The so-called "Employee Free Choice Act," is exactly the opposite of what its name implies. Among other things, card check eliminates the secret ballot in union elections, meaning that every employee's vote will be known by union organizers. It's a strong deterrent to free elections, one that Becker favors.

Becker has also argued, in an article published in the *Minnesota Law Review*, that "traditional notions of democracy should not apply in union elections."[55] Becker, associate general counsel for the SEIU, is also a strong defender of ignoring immigration law. In a 2001 speech, Becker admitted that the "SEIU and other large unions have a very, very progressive position on immigration and immigration reform."[56] With Becker's appointment, another avenue of assault on our democratic institutions can't be far behind.

The Fallout: An Ongoing Takeover

On December 24, 2009, the same day the Senate passed its version of the budget-crippling Obama healthcare legislation, the Treasury Department, following the directive in an executive order issued by the president, and after already having allocated some $900 billion in special loan and rescue funds, announced that there would be no limits on the loan guarantees it would provide to Fannie Mae and Freddie Mac for the next three years. This came in the face of tens of billions of dollars in losses during the year by the two agencies and with the likelihood that those losses could mount well into the trillions before the bleeding was stopped.[57]

That same week, Fannie and Freddie revealed compensation packages for their executives. Fannie CEO Michael Williams and Freddie CEO Charles Haldeman Jr. will each receive as much as $6 million in annual salary and bonuses. This announcement came during the time when Obama had been mounting a furious attack on the pay packages of the officers of banks and brokerage houses.

I thought Obama wanted to end the practice of "rewarding failure."

The government seized control of Fannie and Freddie in September, 2008, and has yet to produce a plan to divest itself of them. Barack Obama, Congress, and the Treasury Department are on their way to doing what would have once been thought impossible: overspending budgets that are now, for all practical purposes, unlimited.

The housing crisis that was such an important factor in the economic collapse of 2008 isn't getting much better. The value of the roughly 75 million owner-occupied homes in America has declined by nearly $5 trillion since then, and more than 10 million homeowners are "underwater," with their mortgages being greater than the value of their homes.[58] One of Obama's "solutions" to the collapse of the housing market that left tens of millions of homeowners underwater on their loans was to institute a $75-billion mortgage relief program called Making Home Affordable. The program was designed to enable lenders to modify the terms of loans so that homeowners could stay in their houses.

Of course, the program, which eliminates the market's ability to fore-close on houses that their owners really can't afford and shouldn't have been able to purchase in the first place, is essentially delaying and making more difficult a real housing recovery. It was supposed to enable as many as four million people to restructure their loans, but it's helped only about 66,000 homeowners while nearly three million home foreclosures were made.[59] It's another of the misguided leftist policies that Obama has insti-tuted in order to further the government's ability to worm its way into our lives, to convince us that we can't solve our problems without the interven-tion of the federal government.

Like so many of Obama's programs and trickle up poverty policies, it rewards bad behavior on the part of both lenders and those paying on their mortgages. And like all Obama's bailouts, it's we, the American taxpayers who do behave responsibly and who do pay taxes, who bear the burden of the government's ill-advised and irresponsible largesse. Obama essentially confiscates our money in order to undermine the very economic system that we've helped to build and to which we contribute.

It doesn't stop there, though.

Barney Frank seems hell-bent on creating a repeat of the Fannie-Freddie disaster to which he contributed so heavily in the late 1990s. Once again, Frank is vowing to force those agencies to write sub-prime loans, pretty much guaranteeing a delay in the housing market recovery. The good news is that the American people seem to be catching on to the utter economic and social devastation the Soviet-Democrats' policies promise to cause.

Obama Tilts the Playing Field . . . To the Left

Capital markets function effectively because they allow investors to assume the risk and reap the rewards (or the failure) associated with buying and selling stocks and other assets. When the playing field is not level, when the government steps in and guarantees loans and dictates the terms under which the markets can operate, those risks and rewards are dramatically skewed in the direction of those making the rules. Allowing hedge fund traders to steal trillions of dollars from Americans who invested in good faith in the companies that were raided by the short sellers is a prime example of how this administration manipulates capital markets. When it changes the rules, when it grants small groups of people the ability to manipulate capital markets, it's the everyday investor who suffers.

In October, 2008, less than a month before the election, then-candidate Barack Obama made Joe "The Plumber" Wurzelbacher a household name. As you well know, when responding to his question, Obama said, "Right now everybody's so pinched that business is bad for everybody and I think when you spread the wealth around, it's good for everybody." [60] As is his practice, Obama was lying to Wurzelbacher, as he has lied to the American people since he appeared on the national stage. He and his confederates are implementing a plan to do nothing less than steal from middle America and redistribute the wealth to their powerful cronies, exactly the opposite of what they would have you believe they stand for.

Among the ways the Obama administration seems determined to steal from the middle class and spread the money to the poor and the wealthy is through increasingly confiscatory tax policies, many of which target the middle class. As early as June, 2008, during the presidential campaign, Obama's team released an economic plan that included not renewing the Bush tax cuts (effectively raising the highest marginal tax rate from 35 percent to 39.6 percent), phasing out personal exemptions and deductions and removing the $102,000 cap on paying social security taxes for those with incomes over $250,000 annually. [61]

And the alternative minimum tax will, in 2010, be applicable to people whose annual incomes are as low as $47,000. In fact, his administration's new legislative and policy initiatives threaten to raise taxes even beyond the 56 percent rate increases proposed during the campaign.

As its spending has spiraled further and further out of control, the Obama administration has been forced to find even more ways to raise revenue through increased taxation. Cutting spending seems never to have been an option. In February, 2010, an eighteen-member blue ribbon panel, headed by former Republican Senator Alan Simpson and former Clinton White House official Erskine Bowles, was commissioned by the president to explore ways to reduce the deficits this administration was amassing. Within weeks, former Treasury Secretary Paul Volcker was floating the idea of implementing a Value Added Tax (VAT) similar to the ones that are so effectively limiting growth in many European countries. The intention behind Volcker's floating the idea of a U.S. VAT was clearly to pave the way for the panel to propose that as a way to reduce deficits.

VAT taxes in many European countries are as high as 20 percent, and because they are a stealth tax, added on incrementally at every stage from acquisition of raw materials to manufacture to wholesale and retail distribution of a product or the provision of a service, they end up substantially increasing the cost of many goods and services to the consumer. In many countries, the VAT adds as much as 20 percent to the costs paid by consumers, with low- and middle-income families being hit the hardest.

Another of Obama's tactics for advancing his socialist vision for America is to bring more and more people under the umbrella of government employment and away from the private sector. One way of doing this is to pay public employees significantly higher wages and provide them greater benefits than their private sector counterparts. In fact, that's exactly what has happened. In December, 2009, the average compensation of those working in private industry was $27.42 an hour, including $19.41 per hour in wages and $8 per hour in benefits. Government workers earned an astonishing $12.18 per hour *more* than those in the private sector, with an average hourly wage compensation of $26.11 and an additional $13.49 in benefits, for total compensation of $39.60 per hour.

That's 44 percent higher than the private sector average.[62]

But it's not only workers who profit so handsomely from being employed in the public sector. According to *USA Today*, at the beginning of the recession, "the Transportation Department had only one person earning a salary of $170,000 or more. Eighteen months later, 1,690 employees had salaries above $170,000," at a cost to taxpayers of nearly $300 million. There was, in fact, an increase of more than 400 percent of government employees making over $150,000 annually during that time, from 1,868 to more than 10,000. This explosion of high salaries has boosted the pay of the average federal worker to $71,206 annually, while the private sector equivalent is $40,331.[63] So much for the myth of people sacrificing earning power to work for the federal government.

With nearly 40 percent of public sector workers unionized, as opposed to less than 10 percent of private sector workers, and with the number of public sector employees increasing while the private sector struggles to correct a loss of more than 7.3 million jobs and a stubborn unemployment rate that stays around 10 percent, we're witnessing another component of the socialist takeover of labor by the Obama administration. More workers are hired for public sector jobs as the bureaucracy grows by leaps and bounds, and they're better compensated, thanks in no small part to the fact that more of them are unionized.

Under Obama's Thumb

In March, 2010, as Pelosi, Reid, and Obama were hammering through their socialized medicine scheme to bring another 15 percent of the American economy under Barack Obama's control, Florida Democratic Representative Alcee Hastings explained the process: "There ain't no rules around here—we're trying to accomplish something. And therefore, when the deal goes down, all this talk about rules, we make 'em up as we go along."[64] In other words, with the Obama administration, we're being treated to raw Chicago-style politics, where threats, intimidation, arm-twisting, and outright lies are used to coerce legislators into getting with the program, and laws and the Constitution be damned.

None of this bothers the Obamanics who are convinced this president can do no wrong.

In every major area where he's trying to remake the economy and bring it under federal control, Barack Obama has resorted to using underhanded (and often illegal) strategies to make it happen. Where he can't advance his agenda through passing federal law, he resorts to executive order or to using other means, such as tapping the EPA to administer energy policy and calling on the FCC to try to implement so-called "net neutrality," to get his way, even if he can't force these egregious affronts to America through the legislative process.

In fact, Obama himself is playing the revolutionary role to perfection as he trots out his deadly proposals to remake the U.S. economy into something that resembles a third world tyrant's dream. In short, Obama doesn't like individual freedom very much, and he will do anything he can to reduce your power and your control over your life to the point where the central government makes every important decision for you.

Assuming control over the economy is one of the ways he plans to do this.

Assuming control over Wall Street is another.

Assuming control over the auto industry is yet another power grab.

Since he took office, President Obama has led the biggest takeover of the American economy by the government since the administration of Franklin Delano Roosevelt. And he's done it with money confiscated from middle-class Americans.

And their children.

And their grandchildren.

And their grandchildren's children.

With government entitlement programs such as Social Security, Medicare, and Medicaid facing bankruptcy, this president has decided to go ahead and break the bank. The so-called stimulus legislation and bailouts of the financial and auto industries, government institutions like Fannie Mae and Freddie Mac, and individuals who exercised or were lured into bad judgment by government policies designed to institutionalize irresponsible financial behavior are not affordable, sustainable, or wise governing.

The title of Michael J. Boskin's March 6, 2010, *Wall Street Journal* op-ed piece proposes, "Obama's Radicalism Is Killing the Dow." It's worth asking, *Is that, in fact, the President's intention?* When we watch the bumbling and thus far ineffective responses of the Obama administration to the financial downturn, it's difficult to come up with an explanation as to why they've been unwilling to address the root causes of our economic problems. The president veers dramatically from calling it a crisis that's about to turn into a catastrophe to uttering soothing words of encouragement about better economic times ahead. In light of this, the further question becomes, "What's at the bottom of the administration's apparent ineptitude?"

Those of us who have at least a rudimentary understanding of capitalism often can't comprehend the liberal mentality. On the one hand, Obama presents himself as something of an economic rube. And, being a very left-leaning Democrat, the president may simply not understand how a market economy works. The president has referred to the Dow Jones Industrial Average as a "poll," comparing the Dow, it appears, to political opinion surveys that he and his advisors use to triangulate their political positions, or to *People Magazine* questionnaires that try to determine which celebrity is the most popular.

His remark seems to indicate that he simply doesn't realize that the DJIA is connected in a very real way to a market that collectively renders its judgment, on a moment-to-moment basis, about the state of the economy, and that it does this by tracking a representative sampling of the worth of thousands of companies whose stock is traded publicly. The president, in his ignorance about how capital markets work, seems unaware that such averages as the DJIA are in reality much more than simply "opinion polls," that in fact there are dozens of other such polls in the form of capital markets around the world that actually provide measures of economic activity on which the global economy depends to function.

Virtually every economic policy of the new administration, from plans to increase taxes on income and capital gains to proposed cap and trade legislation to a significant increase in the money supply, promises to have a negative effect on the markets. And yet there's another perhaps more disturbing component of the Obama economic policy, namely, that the president genuinely distrusts America, especially its middle class. He distrusts what it stands for.

Barack Obama is arguably ideologically blinded by his enmity toward America, which he learned in church under his America-hating pastor. His willful misapprehension of how a capitalist market economy works leads him to think that if he finds ways to take money from "the rich" and redistribute it to the rich and the poor, the only consequences will be that the middle class shrinks. That and the ushering in of the Soviet model of a two-class society. He may simply not understand that the creators of wealth, the capitalist businessmen and women so many of whom are members of the middle class, cannot function without the markets.

If the markets' function is crippled, there will be no wealth to redistribute.

He'd know this if he had any experience running a business.

Among the many problems with what historian Amity Shlaes has called "state capitalism" is that it tends to produce, again in Shlaes' words, "junk GDP."[65] With government dictating what technologies must be pursued and developed, and providing billions of dollars in incentives for their pursuit, we lose the trial-and-error resilience of a free market, the small projects, privately funded, that actually develop the technologies that work and that make our lives better and more efficient.

From such disastrous mandates as the development of ethanol fuel to the new emphasis on developing "green" technologies that defy what the market has already demonstrated, such government-mandated businesses always have unintended consequences. These consequences are damaging to the people in the middle class who have to live with them long after Obama leaves office.

Our national debt ceiling has been raised to more than $14 trillion. According to the 2009 Social Security and Medicare Trustees Reports, the unfunded liabilities for these two governmental entitlements are more than $107 trillion, more than seven times the annual GDP of the United States.[66] Our monthly deficits have reached more than $200 billion. We've mortgaged our and generations of our descendants' futures to create a nation of dependents, people who no longer are taught to pay their own way nor have the desire to do so. Leftists, Marxists, progressives . . . whatever you want to call them, they're perilously close to realizing their aim of total control over our lives and every important decision we make, and to bankrupting the country in the bargain.

Obama's popularity is plunging precipitously, as is support for more untenable spending by the current congress. Both the Office of Management and Budget (OMB) and the Congressional Budget Office (CBO) have issued projections of drastic revenue shortfalls, and those who are taking the time to read the healthcare bill are discovering the virtual disappearance of healthcare options for seniors, not to mention the collapse of private insurance, that they contain. The fact that the president has been able to pass that disastrous bill, even as the financial consequences of the bill were beginning to be comprehended by the American people, indicates just how unimportant what we think is to the current administration. Nothing

Obama does, not one single policy or legislative initiative, has anything to do with the will of the people or what might benefit the people.

Even Iowa Republican Senator Charles Grassley, not someone known for standing up for the American people's interests, seems to understand what's going on here. In comments about then-pending healthcare legislation, Grassley told Fox News, "For every family that gets some benefit from this program, in other words, a premium subsidy, three families are going to get a tax increase and those three families obviously include the bulk of people you'd call middle class America."[67] You might want to read that again.

Seventy-nine percent of people polled in a March, 2010, Fox News survey believe that the U.S. economy might collapse. What's more, they think that our politicians have no clue as to how to prevent a collapse from happening.[68] Part of the reason they believe that might be the president's own willful misunderstanding of how a capitalist economy works. In offhand remarks during a speech, Obama made it clear how he feels about hard work and the marketplace:

> I want to be clear, we're not trying to push financial reform because we begrudge success that's fairly earned. I mean, I do think at a certain point you've made enough money.[69]

That leftist watchword, "fairly," tells us all we need to know about our leader's economic inclinations. He's quick to tell everyone exactly how income should be "fairly" earned. And he's ready to set limits on all of us, as he's trying to do with financial industry executives, on just how much is "enough" when it comes to our earnings.

There's a wisp of good news in all of this.

Day by day, the president's agenda is being exposed to be what it really is, namely, a massive political coup designed to turn the United States into a socialist state. Yes, the citizens of the United States are starting to understand that the world Obama envisions is one in which the central government confiscates its citizens' money and transfers it to his political comrades. This is yet another reason why the Tea Party movement is attracting unprecedented crowds.

The people are livid.

They cannot take another minute of this madness.

They are no longer willing to sit idly by as their personal savings and financial security are transferred to the pockets of hedge fund pirates. Nor should they. Indeed, if America's patriots will turn out in droves for the 2010 mid-term elections, they can oust the enemy within. They can purge the scum from the system. They can put a stop to those who are wrecking our economy and subjugating us to their political will. And maybe, just maybe, the new leadership will have the courage to bring those who have betrayed us on Wall Street to justice.

CHAPTER 5

The Health Scare Fraud: What's Really in the Bill

The American public overwhelmingly voted for socialism
when they elected President Obama.
—Al Sharpton[1]

It takes a long time to . . . put the legislation together
to control the people.
—Representative John Dingell[2]

When I was fourteen, I took a job in a local drug store in Queens, New York. It had nothing in common with the big, name brand drugstores found in just about every neighborhood these days. This was a simple mom-and-pop affair. I'll never forget the first time I met Doc the Pharmacist. Doc was an Italian immigrant from the old country who probably lived in a small apartment over the shop. He was a thickset man with an oversized shoe on his right foot. The heel must have been eight inches high to compensate for his short leg.

Unlike the sterile-looking pharmacies today with their harsh overhead lighting designed to give you a migraine so you buy more aspirin, I don't think there was a fluorescent light bulb in the place. Doc's store had wooden shelves sagging under the weight of tonics and lotions, and glass display cases with rows of first aid supplies and sundries.

It even *smelled* different.

To this day, I still remember the distinctively pleasing aroma greeting me the moment I'd walk through the door of Doc's drugstore. I'll put it to you this way. It was as if the mahogany counters and floor had been scrubbed down with Old Spice and Lysol with a hint of leather. Whatever happened to that incredible smell? I should have bottled it. These days, drugstores smell like nothing. And nobody knows your name. With Doc, you felt like family.

Let's set aside the fact he was paying me fifty cents an hour below minimum wage to save a few bucks. I had a paying job on the weekends and after school, that's all. I was glad for the work and looked forward to going there. At lunch, Doc's wife treated him like a king. She'd bring in a big tray with a top to keep the veal parmigiana or other homemade feasts warm. He'd sit at his desk for the better part of an hour savoring every bite. Preferring to eat his meal in peace, he'd make me the "pharmacist."

I mean, how hard was it to fill out the prescriptions?

All I had to do was read "Penicillin, 250 mg," find the right jar that said "Penicillin," and then count out a dozen pills. I didn't need medical training to count to twelve. The only time things got a bit dicey was on the rare occasion when some doctor wanted a blend of drugs ground together. You know, he'd ask for two milligrams of sulfur powder and half a gram of phosphorous plus other ingredients. These, Doc would compound himself. All I did was count pills—like today's college educated pharmacists.

One afternoon, I'm doing my job, counting out pills, minding my own business while Doc was wiping the sauce from the edges of his mouth. In walked a guy in a dark suit and a receding hairline. He looked a lot like Robert Duvall as Tom Hagen in *The Godfather*. I glanced up as he approached the counter. I never saw the man before and had no idea what he wanted. He studied me like a hawk, watching me filling out the prescriptions and then, with a fake smile, said, "Hi, how are you, son?"

"Fine," I said. While I didn't know at the time why he was scoping out the place, something about him made me instinctively wary. "Can I help you, Mister?"

"No, no, just looking," he said. He raised an eyebrow like an IRS agent who just found an unreported nickel during an audit. His eyes, darting around the drugstore, zeroed in on Doc sitting beside me eating the last few bites of his veal parmigiana. The next minute, he marches behind the counter to Doc, pulls out his ID and says, "I got real bad news for you, Doc."

I later learned he was a city government inspector.

That afternoon Doc got hit with a fine—and I lost my job.

It was a watershed moment in my life.

Looking back, there have been two life-changing outcomes from those experiences working in the pharmacy. I came away with a profound interest in medicine and, years later, went on to write several bestselling books on the topic, including *Earth Medicine, Maximum Immunity, Healing Children Naturally*, and *Reducing the Risk of Alzheimer's*. That's number one. Second, I grew to be leery of government intervention, particularly when a bureaucrat flashes a fake smile and pretends he or she is there for my benefit. Can you blame me?

Back then, I lost my job when the government stepped in.

Today, I'm losing the best healthcare system in the world because the government seized this industry and now controls one-sixth of the economy![3]

On March 23, 2010, with the stroke of a pen, our Naked Emperor signed the death certificate on what was once the greatest healthcare system in history and the envy of the world. He did so even after the overwhelming majority of Americans—a full 61 percent—opposed it saying, "Congress should scrap that plan and start all over again."[4] As the deadline for passage approached, an estimated 100,000 calls an hour from irate voters bombarded Congress.[5]

None of that mattered to Barack Obama, Nancy Pelosi, or Harry Reid.

In order to usher in socialized medicine, these Demoncats shackled the middle class with $2 trillion in new debt[6]—not the $940 billion figure touted by Team Obama to get the measure passed. That, according to the Congressional Budget Office (CBO), is the *real* cost of the bill's first-decade. As the *Weekly Standard* points out, the CBO says "we need to start the clock when the costs would actually start in any meaningful way: in 2014."[7]

In other words, ObamaCare is a ticking time bomb. It's set to explode *after* Obama leaves office saddling us with skyrocketing debt, reduced care, and unprecedented invasion of privacy. The painful side effects caused by this bill will be lethal to the physical and financial health of Americans. As soon as 2019, ObamaCare has provisions designed to soak the middle class with a $3.9 billion tax increase![8] Likewise, young adults seeking health insurance will, according to the Associated Press, "carry a heavier burden of the medical costs of older Americans—a shift expected to raise insurance premiums for young people" by an estimated 17 percent.[9] Other estimates place the figure of increased premiums as high as 30 to 50 percent for young people.[10]

And, as you'll see in a moment, there's a "death panel" that may just deny you the coverage you need in the name of "medical rationing" . . . especially if you're a senior citizen—the very death panels the Obama tricksters denied existed before the vote. Indeed, ObamaCare creates trickle up poverty for the middle class. What did Congress pass under the cloak of darkness while America slept?

Buried within more than 2,000 pages of complex regulations, Obama's Demoncats have granted massive new—and dangerously expansive—powers to the IRS costing $10 billion over the next decade primarily to hire 16,500 additional IRS agents and examiners.[11] What purpose does this *Healthstapo* serve? President Obama knows his healthcare bill will be so wildly unpopular once the provisions kick in, he's preparing to marshal an army of mean-faced IRS agents to enforce full compliance. If you fail to comply by purchasing the "minimum essential coverage" mandated by ObamaCare, the IRS has the authority to fine you up to 2 percent of your income.[12]

Thanks to Barack Obama, you *must* buy a healthcare policy.

Unless, of course, you're an illegal alien.[13]

That's right. Those who are here illegally are exempt from these fines.

And, while the ObamaCare bill excludes extending coverage for illegal aliens, which some say was the price of securing the vote from conservative Democrats, that omission won't prevent illegals from continuing to sponge off the taxpayers pocketbooks. As one illegal immigrant said, "My daughter is six. She was born here. The state pays for her to go to [the] hospital. If I get sick, I do what all the Mexicans do: I go and sit in the emergency room where they cannot turn you away."[14] You and I must pay for coverage and then stand in line behind someone else who hasn't paid a dime and doesn't belong in the country in the first place.

Tell me that isn't upside-down logic.

What's more, isn't it comforting to know that ObamaCare has made the IRS the government's chief enforcer of the new socialized medicine program? Make no mistake: there's no grace where the IRS is concerned. Before the bill was signed into law, Dave Camp (R-MI), Ranking Member of the Committee on Ways and Means, and Charles Boustany (R-LA), Ranking Member on the Subcommittee on Oversight, warned about the consequences if your coverage were to lapse for even one month:

> Disturbingly, the IRS [is now] in charge of verifying that every American taxpayer has obtained acceptable health coverage for every month of the year. If the IRS determines that a taxpayer lacks acceptable insurance for even a single month, then the IRS would impose a new tax on that taxpayer, even auditing the taxpayer and could assess interest and penalties on top of the tax.[15]

In other words, as Camp and Boustany explain, the IRS now must track the "monthly health insurance status of roughly 300 million Americans." To help the IRS with that task, your insurance carrier must rat on you by providing the IRS with personal "information about the taxpayer"— including your name, address, phone number, tax identification number, and employer[16]—and the "type of coverage, including the portion of premiums paid by the employer."[17]

Who said Big Brother wasn't watching us?

A Bad Prescription for America

As if expanding the IRS—the most feared arm of the federal government known for its fascist-like enforcement tactics—wasn't bad enough, ObamaCare created "159 new government offices and programs."[18] One of those programs is beefing up the U.S. Public Health Service "Commissioned Corps." Most people have never heard of the Commissioned Corps, which has been around for years. The government describes the Corps as "an elite team of more than 6,000 full-time, well-trained, highly qualified public health professionals dedicated to delivering the nation's public health promotion and disease prevention programs and advancing public health science."[19]

Maybe we need six thousand health czars in the case of a national emergency. Fine. Personally, I think if we have the funds for an "elite team" of six thousand "well-trained" professionals, the country would be better served if they were trained and used to screen the hordes of illegal aliens flooding into this country for diseases. The larger point is this: Obama-Care expands the existing Commissioned Corps with the creation of a "Ready Reserve Corps" to be mobilized "for service in time of national emergency."[20]

Who's to say what qualifies as a "national emergency"?

President Obama?

The bill doesn't specify that detail, so draw your own conclusions.

What's more, Fidel Obama has set himself up as the one who handpicks the officers of this Ready Reserve Corps! This is unbelievable. Section 203 (3) of HR 3590 states: "Commissioned officers of the Ready Reserve Corps **shall be appointed by the President**" [emphasis added]. It gets worse. This new arm of the government includes "Warrant Officers," and Section 203 goes on to state that members of the Ready Reserve Corps must "be available and ready for **involuntary calls to active duty** during national emergencies and public health crises, similar to the uniformed service reserve personnel [emphasis added]."

You might want to read that again.

President Obama appoints officers for this new "Ready Reserve Corps," whose membership may be *involuntarily* called into duty, for a yet-to-be defined "national emergency." To be redundant, we already have the military, the FBI, the Secret Service, State Troopers, and county and local police forces. What's this "Ready Reserve Corps" *really* about? Let's connect the dots. As I documented in chapter one, on July 2, 2008, in Colorado Springs, Colorado, then–presidential wannabe Obama said something alarming, which was completely ignored by most of the major media. He proclaimed:

We cannot continue to rely on our military in order to achieve the national security objectives that we've set. We've got to have a civilian national security force that's just as powerful, just as strong, just as well-funded.

I must ask the difficult question: Is the formation of a Ready Reserve Corps the first step in the establishment of Obama's private national security force? It certainly appears as though Obama laid the groundwork for his version of the brownshirts. Where's the outcry from the civil libertarians? Why does the un-American Civil Liberties Union remain silent? I thought they opposed layers of government regulation and bureaucracy meddling in our personal affairs.

Maybe the ACLU is too busy defending—*pro bono*—Muslims sought by the FBI for Homeland Security–related questioning.[21] Maybe the ACLU is too busy calling on the president to grant the 9/11 terrorists *civilian* trials rather than, more appropriate, face a military commission.[22] Then again, going to the core of their ideology, maybe the ACLU resonates with Obama when he promised to begin "fundamentally transforming the United States of America."[23]

Their silence on this potential threat is deafening.

Obama's Death Panel from Hell

You have to hand it to Nancy "Stalin in High Heels" Pelosi. She did a remarkable job preventing Congress from knowing what the hell they were about to vote on. She kept the public equally in the dark. Just days before calling for a vote, she had the audacity to say, "We have to pass the bill so that you can find out what is in it."[24] That time has come. We're now finding that what we feared about ObamaCare was just the beginning.

Case in point. Another one of President Obama's controversial and dangerous "transformations" of the United States found in Section 1899A of the ObamaCare bill is the establishment of an "Independent Medicare Advisory Board" (IMAB)—often referred to as a "death panel" by critics. Advocates of the IMAB say the board is necessary and will have nothing to do with end-of-life decisions.

Which position is true?

Using innocuous sounding language, the bill explains that the IMAB exists to "reduce the per capita rate of growth in Medicare spending." Translation: the IMAB is supposed to find ways to cut costs through the practice of medical rationing. While not specifically tasked with end-of-life decisions, the fact is that the IMAB is nothing more than a government-controlled panel that, in its quest to cut costs, will establish policies discouraging or prohibiting certain medical procedures. Or, conversely, it will give doctors "incentives" to withhold treatment in certain instances. Either way, coverage of certain life-enhancing, life-extending procedures will be killed.

In practical terms, here's how the IMAB will work.

Let's say you're seventy-two years old and need a heart transplant. With it, you'd be able to enjoy another fifteen or more years of life. The IMAB could set forth a policy denying seniors heart transplants in the name of *faaaairness*—since there's only so much money to go around and medical rationing is a reality in light of supposedly finite resources. Instead, they'll give the heart to a thirty-three-year-old since he's a "productive" member of society and the elderly, in their view, will have outlived their usefulness.

Don't think for one minute that this is a far-fetched scenario.

On June 13, 2009, in his weekly radio address, Barack Obama talked specifically about giving doctors "incentives" to "avoid unnecessary hospital stays, treatments and tests that drive up costs."[25] Two days later, speaking to the American Medical Association (AMA), Obama said, "Make no mistake: the cost of our health care is a threat to our economy. It is a ticking time bomb for the federal budget." So far I agree with him. Just because I oppose ObamaCare doesn't mean I think we shouldn't work to make reforms.

I believe in tort reform, for example, which is something this bill fails to address. Tort reform would make it more difficult for people to bring frivolous lawsuits for alleged harm or wrongdoing during medical treatment. Likewise, the size of the financial awards for damages in a medical malpractice suit must be capped, as it has been done successfully in California. Another cost-saving solution would be to close emergency rooms to noncitizens. That would go a long way to save the healthcare system. Again, this bill doesn't address that option.

So what's Obama's cost-cutting solution?

That depends on which speech the man gives, but most often he and his advisors speak in terms of slashing 30 percent from the Medicare-Medicaid budget.[26] As WorldNetDaily columnist Richard Poe points out, "A 30% annual cut is going to take a big bite out of somebody's health care. The only question is whose. The numbers make clear that most of these cuts will have to come at the expense of those who need health care the most—the elderly, the disabled and the gravely ill."[27] Which is only logical. In fact, that's what Obama implied while speaking to the AMA: "Older, sicker societies pay more on health care than younger, healthier ones."[28] In other words, the older you get, the more you cost society.

Now, when you understand that 5 percent of the public—those over age sixty-five—are the beneficiaries of 50 percent of all spending on health care, you realize that's where Obama must surgically trim healthcare expenses— butcher expenses is more like it. Richard Poe puts it this way, "Obama will not meet his cost-cutting targets by reducing care to healthy young people. They are already spending next to nothing. It is the old, the dying and the chronically ill whose health care he will cut. The numbers make this clear."[29]

Even a reporter for the über-leftwing *Los Angeles Times* picked up on this cold, hard reality of ObamaCare. He writes, "President Obama suggested at a town hall event Wednesday night that one way to trim medical costs is to stop expensive and ultimately futile procedures performed on people who are about to die and don't stand to gain from the extra care."[30] Indeed, Obama said, "Maybe you're better off not having the surgery, but taking the painkiller."[31]

How's that for compassion?

Ironically, Obama cited his own grandmother, Madelyn Dunham, as an example of this need to make tough choices about "ultimately futile procedures." You see, Obama's grandmother had terminal cancer. The doctors had given her six to nine months to live. Complicating her situation was a fall in which she broke her hip. Regarding grandma's hip surgery—in what was one of those Bill Clinton "I feel your pain" moments—Obama told his town hall audience, "and the question was, does she get hip replacement surgery, even though she was fragile enough they were not sure how long she would last?"[32]

So, did she, or didn't she get the surgery?

Obama never answered the question for them.

Why not? Because the president wanted to lead his audience to believe that denying coverage in such a case would be *the right thing to do*. You know, take the painkiller instead of having surgery. In reality, Obama's grandmother *did* get a hip replacement.[33] Of course, it's unclear whether she would still have had that option now that ObamaCare has passed. As Barack Obama told the *Old York Times*, "you get into some very difficult moral issues" when deciding "to give my grandmother, or everybody else's aging grandparents or parents, a hip replacement when they're terminally ill as a sustainable model, is a very difficult question."[34]

Who does Obama think should answer these issues?

You? Your doctor?

Wrong, and wrong again.

Obama says, "There's always going to be an asymmetry of information between patient and provider. And part of what I think government can do effectively is to be an honest broker in assessing and evaluating treatment options."[35] Once again, government knows best. The government should be the ultimate referee because the self-serving American public knows nothing. Instead, we're supposed to bow before this "honest broker" with our most intimate medical issues and trust them to do the right thing.

Doesn't this president understand that the public's distrust of Congress is at an all-time high? Does he really think the sheeple will go along with such a plan when, in March, 2010, a Rasmussen poll found 41 percent of voters "think most members of Congress are corrupt"! Furthermore, 64 percent of voters say Congress is doing a "poor job."[36] If they're botching their job in Congress, why should they be entrusted with our individual health and welfare? No, Obama wants you to trust the feds instead of a doctor by your hospital bed.

Where does the Constitution grant such powers to the government?

Actually, that's just the start of Obama's intrusion into the patient-doctor relationship. Like a good social engineer, Obama wants to use other "experts" to help us shape those pesky "moral issues":

> I think that there is going to have to be a conversation that is **guided by doctors, scientists, ethicists.** And then there is going to have to be a very difficult democratic conversation that takes place. It is very difficult to imagine the country making those decisions just through the normal political channels.[37] [Emphasis added].

Which scientists? Which ethicists?

If Obama has any say in the matter, and if his track record on the appointment of czars tells us anything, we can expect the worst of the worst. Do we really want someone like Princeton University's im-moralist professor, Peter Singer, making these sorts of decisions and policies? Singer, who is ideologically akin to Hitler, believes in infanticide—which is a belief consistent with Obama. Singer has said, "Very often it is not wrong at all to kill a child once it has left the womb. Simply killing an infant is never equivalent to killing a person."[38]

Just what America needs. More psychos like this Red Diaper Doper Baby determining who gets to live and die in Obama's grand dream of integrating "ethicists" into his plan to cut costs. Soylent Green, anyone? Make no mistake, Obama *is* eyeing the elderly as the prime target audience for making cuts. He's on record saying as much: "When it comes to Medicare and Medicaid, where the taxpayers are footing the bill . . . we have an obligation to get those costs under control."[39] If that's not clear enough, Obama pointed that "the chronically ill and those toward the end of their lives are accounting for potentially 80% of the total health care bill out here."[40]

If they're 80 percent of the bill, then that's where the savings are to be found.

Are you starting to get the picture? He's targeting the most vulnerable portion of the population! That's exactly the opposite of the liberal propaganda.

This is why Obama created the Independent Medicare Advisory Board.

As you might expect, all this talk of a "death panel" was repeatedly mocked by Paul Krugman, a radical leftist and illogical Nobel laureate who writes a column in the *Old York Times* that few outside of the media take seriously. Krugman said the idea of a death panel in ObamaCare was "a complete fabrication"[41] and blasted the concept as an invention of "the crazy right, the tea party and death panel people—a lunatic fringe that is no longer a fringe but has moved into the heart of the Republican Party."[42] Really? Watch how this ignoramus talks out of both sides of his forked tongue.

While participating in a roundtable discussion on ABC's *This Week*, Krugman sneered at those who believe the newly passed ObamaCare bill will lead to something resembling a death panel:

> **Paul Krugman:** Think about people on the right. They're simultaneously screaming, "They're going to send all of the old people to death panels" and "It's not going to save any money." That's a contradictory point of view.

> **Jake Tapper (host):** Death panels would save money, theoretically.

> **Paul Krugman:** The advisory path has the ability to make more or less binding judgments on saying this particular expensive treatment actually doesn't do any good medically and so we're not going to pay for it. That is actually going to save quite a lot of money. We don't know how much yet. The CBO gives it very little credit. But most of the health care economists I talk to think it's going to be a really major cost saving.[43]

So which is it, Mr. Krugman?

One moment you're mocking the concept, the next moment you're praising it as a means to "save quite a lot of money." Let's face facts. Even if the sun stood still and hell froze over, there's no way Krugman or Obama would publicly admit that medical rationing via the IMAB is an essential tool to provide universal healthcare coverage for tens of millions of uninsured Americans—who may or may not want the coverage in the first place.

Whether they acknowledge it or not, socialized medicine comes with a hefty price tag: *increased taxation and medical rationing.* Period. Dr. Miguel Faria Jr., a Clinical Professor of Surgery (neurosurgery) at Mercer University School of Medicine, isn't wearing Obama's rose-colored glasses. With regard to higher taxes and dwindling coverage, he sees clearly the handwriting on the wall:

> To reach the goal of universal coverage and capture those elusive 30–45 million Americans, who remain uninsured and, inconveniently for government planners, refuse to buy coverage, the rest of America will be saddled with socialized Obama-Care, more taxes and less coverage, as in Canada and the United Kingdom.[44]

You see, Obama has a problem. His healthcare bill saddles the American taxpayer with at least a $2 trillion tab over the next decade, according to figures released by the Congressional Budget Office (CBO). We all know that government cost projections are rarely accurate and often end up costing the middle class significantly more than the original estimate. Case in point.

When President Lyndon Johnson signed the Social Security Act of 1965, he set into motion the first step toward government-run, socialized medicine. It was sold to the public as a necessary and relatively inexpensive benefit. As we all know, Medicare is now teetering on insolvency. That said, look how far off the government estimates were regarding the projected cost of this program:

> At its start, in 1966, Medicare cost $3 billion. The House Ways and Means Committee estimated that Medicare would cost only about $12 billion by 1990 (a figure that included an allowance for inflation). This was a supposedly 'conservative' estimate. But in 1990 Medicare actually cost $107 billion.[45]

Put another way, the government microcephalics at the CBO and the bureaucrat hacks missed their Medicare projections by nine-fold! Nobody in the real world would get away with such a flagrant mismanagement of cost projections. Most businesses would fire such incompetent accountants and economists on the spot.

Imagine if you owned your own contracting business. Imagine that you had a customer who needed a new office building. What would happen if you told your client that his new building would cost $1 million to construct, but the final cost was $9 million? He'd laugh in your face and tell you to go to hell. And yet, the CBO wants us to trust its figures.

They want us to believe that ObamaCare will cost $2 trillion.

I don't think it comes close to the total tab the middle class must pick up.

Even if, for the sake of argument, that figure proved to be an accurate cost projection, the president and Congress have told future generations of Americans to drop dead. Their tax burden will be, out of necessity, so disproportional, our productive children and their children can forget about saving, building personal wealth, or enjoying many of the things you and I take for granted. It will take everything in their power just to keep feeding the beastly ObamaCare monster.

Your Pain, His Gain

If you're a senior citizen, hold on to your pacemaker.

There's plenty more bad news in this bill targeting you.

In an attempt to assuage the justified fears of seniors, who smelled a rat every time the president tried to sell them on his bill, Obama told the elderly at an AARP-hosted forum: "Nobody is talking about reducing Medicare benefits. Medicare benefits are there because people contributed into a system. It works. We don't want to change it."[46] Guess what? As I documented a moment ago, it was just another one of this president's boldfaced lies.

With Obama, you must ignore what he says and watch what he does.

The plan Obama signed into law *slashes* $500 billion from Medicare,[47] which is guaranteed to hurt the coverage that seniors over age sixty-five receive. After paying into the system their entire lives, seniors will spend their sunset years with shrinking coverage—although "Democratic leaders," who never mislead us on anything, "have promised the reductions will not affect service to Medicare recipients."[48]

Tell me, how is that possible?

How do you cut *half of a trillion dollars* from a program and not impact coverage? What world do they live in? Why can't the Obamanics see this economic reality? What more proof do you need that liberalism is a mental disorder? The Democrats demonstrate a complete lack of understanding of how supply and demand works. Even Obama's CBO Director Doug Elmendorf disagreed with the president's rosy assessment. Testifying before the Senate Finance Committee, Elmendorf stated that any Medicare cuts "would reduce the extra benefits that would be made available to beneficiaries through Medicare Advantage plans." [49]

Which begs the question: how many seniors will be affected?

According to U.S. Representative Paul Ryan (R), *millions* of senior citizens will be impacted by Obama's cuts. "As a practical result of this legislation," says Ryan, "an estimated six million current Medicare Advantage beneficiaries no longer would be able to afford their current plans or would lose access altogether." [50] Six million? Let's put that figure into perspective. That's the equivalent of terminating the health benefits for every senior sixty-five or older living in the states of Florida and New York combined! [51]

I thought nobody was talking about reducing Medicare benefits.

What's more, did you know your government intentionally worked to silence such information from becoming public? That's right. Obama's promise of conducting his administration as "the most open and transparent in history" just stuffed a rag in the mouths of his critics. [52] According to Representative Ryan, a gag order was put into place to prevent insurance companies from warning their customers about the serious nature of the cuts should ObamaCare be passed. Representative Ryan said:

> The Centers for Medicare and Medicaid Services (CMS), a division of the U.S. Department of Health and Human Services, recently placed a gag order on Medicare Advantage providers to prevent them from sharing information with their enrollees about pending changes to their plans. Disregarding private health care plans' right to inform their enrollees about consequential legislation, CMS has launched an investigation against Humana for mailing a factually verified warning about proposed cuts. [53]

Do you see how these gangster thugs in the Obama administration work?

First, they silenced the opposition and violate their free speech rights.

Then, when Humana had the nerve to inform its clients about the downside of ObamaCare, a pack of ravenous government hounds was immediately dispatched to make Humana's life hell on earth. Representative Ryan rightly concludes, "The administration's actions open an array of troubling questions about both the appropriateness and legality of such political intimidation."[54] If, however, you think that the Attorney General will look into this violation of free speech, guess again.

Which brings us to Dr. Donald Berwick, Obama's radical choice nominated to run Medicare and Medicaid. If confirmed, Berwick would bring his far leftist ideas to these government programs—which is especially bad news for the elderly. I'm not the only one who sees problems with this pick. The *New York Post* describes Obama's choice as "A fervent ideologue" who "puts social engineering ahead of the individual patient's needs" because in his Triple Aim plan, Berwick "laments that US health care is 'designed to focus on the acute needs of individual patients' He argues for a different focus, social justice." What's more, Obama's nominee has praised the British National Health Service (which is a disaster of the highest order) for its "central planning, frugality, wealth redistribution and rationing."[55]

The last thing America needs is a doctor like this in the house.

Too Damn Bad

Not only will ObamaCare create widespread trickle up poverty within the middle class, it is designed—yes, *designed*—to take away your freedom of choice. Not one or two freedoms, but dozens of them. The Doctor of Truth is in and I'll break down several of them for you this way. Let's say you're a young person, you're healthy, you jog, eat right, take vitamins, drink plenty of water, and don't feel the need or want to pay for health insurance at your stage in life.

Too damn bad.

Section 5000A of ObamaCare requires you to maintain minimum essential coverage or pay a $750 fine or 2 percent of your income—whichever is greater.

Here's one for the single guys. Let's say you have no plans to get married any time soon. Let's say you're 28, 48, or 88, and have no projected need for pediatric services. So you're in the market to buy a health coverage plan without an option to insure children in order to enjoy lower premiums.

Too damn bad.

Let's say you're a woman and you're medically incapable of having children. Furthermore, you have no plans to pursue adoption so you want a lower-cost policy without maternity or newborn care.

Too damn bad.

Section 1302 forces you to cover it anyway.

What if you prefer to go to a physician-owned hospital because they feel more personal, especially in the doctor-patient decision making process—rather than the larger, more bureaucratic, corporate-owned hospitals?

Too damn bad.

While the current limited supply of physician-owned facilities will be allowed to exist, new physician-owned projects will not be able to receive reimbursement for Medicare and Medicaid patients under Section 6001. Without those payments, it will be difficult for a hospital to be financially viable. In short, ObamaCare bans the development of new physician-owned hospitals while throwing roadblocks in the way of expanding old ones.[56]

Prior to ObamaCare, one of the "perks" of employment was an employer-sponsored "gold plated" insurance plan, which represents about the top 20 percent of health plans enjoyed by millions of Americans. In the past, employees were not taxed on that benefit. If you were happy with that arrangement and you would like to keep it that way, guess again.

It's too damn bad.

Section 4980I now imposes a 40 percent excise tax on "gold plated" plans—whether your employer pays for the coverage, or whether you, as a self-employed person, pay for it out of pocket. Obama is saying it's a sin to provide a generous healthcare plan for your family. Is it any wonder why the Dems in Massachusetts lost their seat in the Senate? We know the election of Scott Brown was as if a tsunami hit the White House. But the reasons why Brown won aren't necessarily obvious on the surface. It takes insight to break it down. Here's what was really going on.

The people of Massachusetts already have the sort of socialized medicine championed by Obama. They got stuck with it from Mitt Romney. At the time Romney's administration proposed it, it sounded like a good idea. The people voted for it—and now they've watched their premiums soar through the roof while service decreased. As *FORTUNE* magazine has documented, Massachusetts now faces a number of undesirable side effects after launching Romney's health care reform program. Topping the list is the ever-increasing price tag. According to this report:

> When Massachusetts launched its reform program in 2006, it already had the highest medical costs in the nation. Today, the burden is still rising far faster than wages or inflation, from those already lofty levels . . . Costs are rising relentlessly both for families and for the state government.[57]

What accounts for the spike in costs and premiums in The Bay State?

Two primary reasons: the adoption of "guaranteed issue" (a law requiring insurance companies to offer coverage regardless of the medical condition of the applicant) and "community rating" (the practice of charging everyone a comparable premiums regardless of the actual cost associated with their risk factors). These factors create a perfect storm for rising costs, as the *FORTUNE* report points out:

> The result is that prices rise steeply for young, healthy customers, who must pay far more than their actual costs. It also give them a strong incentive to drop insurance; then they can "game the system" by signing up any time they need surgery or get diabetes.[58]

Even though "guaranteed issue" and "community rating" are driving the costs of health care through the roof, both are features of ObamaCare.

Another reason the people of Massachusetts are sick over their new health care plan is because "low-to-medium earning families often suffer financially if they get a raise, work overtime, move to a higher paying job—or if a spouse rejoins the workforce." Why do they "suffer financially" if they earn *more* money? For starters, a family making less than $33,000 can get health coverage through Commonwealth Care for free. But, let's say they're a growing family and have more financial needs. If they work harder or longer hours and bring home $46,000, the state requires them to pay approximately $2,400 in health care premiums. As this report points out, "That's an effective tax rate of 18.5% on that $13,000 raise. A pay increase of $44,000 to $46,000 is mostly erased by higher premiums alone." [59]

The "free" care actually encourages workers to earn less, not more.

Once again, ObamaCare offers a similar disincentive to work harder and prosper due to higher health care taxes. *FORTUNE* points out the scenario in which "a $55,000 earner contributes $4,400 a year towards insurance. At $65,000, the bill is $6300; so the family is paying a 'tax' of $1,900 or 19% on that $10,000 raise. After payroll taxes, those Americans would face a marginal rate of around 35%, a number that's heretofore been the territory strictly for high-earners." [60]

Did I mention that illegal aliens also receive free health care in Romney's state? This, of course, is what happens when the government imposes socialized medicine. So the people, angered by this reality, voted their first Republican Senator into office in fifty years. What happened in Massachusetts with high premiums and inferior coverage is about to happen in all fifty states.

There's more bad news buried within the bill. For you parents whose kids have finally left the house and who thought you would no longer have to underwrite their expenses, guess again. President Obama has redefined when childhood ends (previously considered to end at age 18 or 19 depending on the state) and gives parents the "option" to pay for health care coverage of "dependent children" through age 26 (Section 2714).

While the law calls this an optional feature, it doesn't specify what will happen if you refuse to pay for your twenty-six-year-old slacker who insists that you cover him even though, by any reasonable definition, he is old enough to provide for a family of his own. No doubt the IRS *Healthstapo* will come knocking.

If you recall, one of the much-touted accomplishments of ObamaCare was to be the end of the "pre-existing conditions" clause for children. If that's what you think happened, guess what? It isn't in there. The Associated Press reports, "Under the new law, insurance companies still would be able to refuse new coverage to children because of a pre-existing medical problem, said Karen Lightfoot, spokeswoman for the House Energy and Commerce Committee, one of the main congressional panels that wrote the bill Obama signed into law."[61]

There's plenty of bad news for business owners, too.

In the past, large employers (those with at least 101 employees on the payroll) had a choice of how to compensate and provide for their workers. On one hand, they could elect to offer health coverage as an incentive to attract employees. Or, they might decide against that because their business model wouldn't sustain such a costly outlay. It's their business, their choice, right?

Wrong.

Employers with as few as fifty employees must provide healthcare coverage or pay a fine *per employee*. According to House Minority Leader, John Boehner, "The new law imposes a tax of $2,000 per employee on employers with more than 50 employees that do not provide health insurance. These new taxes on employers are sure to be passed on to workers in the form of lower wages or reduced hours, and will undermine job creation as well."[62]

If you believed the president when he pledged not to raise taxes on the middle class—"not one dime"—for those making less than $200,000 if single, and $250,000 if married, your faith was misplaced and it's too damn bad. Dave Camp, Ranking Member of the Committee on Ways & Means Republicans, cites a dozen ways Obama has raised your taxes indirectly or directly, several of which I've touched on:

1. A "Cadillac tax" on high-cost plans
2. An individual mandate tax on Americans who do not purchase government-approved health insurance
3. An increase in the 7.5 percent AGI floor for medical expense deductions to 10 percent
4. Limits on Flexible Spending Accounts in cafeteria plans
5. Increased penalties for nonqualified HSA distributions
6. Other restrictions on Health Savings Accounts, Health Reimbursement Accounts, and Flexible Spending Accounts
7. A tax on tanning services
8. An employer mandate tax
9. A sales tax on medical devices

10. A tax on health insurance premiums
11. A tax on prescription drugs
12. A tax on insured and self-insured health plans[63]

There's yet another downside to this boondoggle of a bill. David Hogberg of *Investor's Business Daily* says ObamaCare will result in "physicians leaving the field in droves, making it harder to afford and find medical care." Why such a dire prediction? Here are two of Hogberg's compelling reasons:

• If you are a physician owner and you want to expand your hospital? Well, you can't (Section 6001 (i)(1)(B)). Unless, it is located in a county where, over the last five years, population growth has been 150% of what it has been in the state (Section 6501 (i)(3)(E)). And then you cannot increase your capacity by more than 200% (Section 6001 (i)(3)(C)).

• If you are a physician and you don't want the government looking over your shoulder? Tough. The Secretary of Health and Human Services is authorized to use your claims data to issue you reports that measure the resources you use, provide information on the quality of care you provide, and compare the resources you use to those used by other physicians. Of course, this will all be just for informational purposes. It's not like the government will ever use it to intervene in your practice and patients' care. Of course not. (Section 3003(i)).[64]

What's more, analysts warn that there are simply not enough doctors and nurses to treat the tens of millions of newly insured patients. The Association of American Medical Colleges (AAMC) reports, "at current graduation and training rates, the nation could face a shortage of as many as 150,000 doctors in the next 15 years."[65] This translates into limited access, longer waits, and inferior service as doctors are stretched thin to handle the influx of new patients. How long will this bleak picture last? The AAMC's chief advocacy officer, Atul Grover, predicts "It will probably take 10 years to even make a dent into the number of doctors that we need out there."[66]

Are you beginning to get the picture?

You're losing your freedoms.

You're losing your choice.

You're losing your access to the best healthcare system in the world.

Of course, the ever-arrogant Barack Obama dismisses all such talk. One week after ObamaCare passed, Obama publicly chided journalists for citing polls demonstrating that America is bitterly divided over what just went down. Obama wagged his finger in the face of his critics, saying:

> Every single day since I signed the reform law, there's been another poll or headline that said, 'Nation still divided on health care reform.' It just happened last week! It's only been a week! Can you imagine if some of these reporters were working on a farm and you planted some seeds and they came out next day and they looked—'Nothing's happened! There's no crop! We're going to starve! Oh no! It's a disaster!' It's been a week, folks.[67]

In one respect, Obama is right. The economic damage and the trickle up poverty that will come once his wrecking ball hits the healthcare industry will take some time to bear its ugly fruit. The full force won't be felt overnight. Why? Many of the draconian measures don't kick in until 2014 and beyond. Even so, plenty of weeds are sprouting in Obama's garden of healthcare paradise. Within a week of its passage, three hundred companies screamed bloody murder. Among them, 3M Corporation, AK Steel, AT&T, Caterpillar, Deere & Company, Valero Energy, and Verizon said the new law "will make it far more expensive to provide prescription drug coverage to their retired employees."[68]

AT&T screamed the loudest. The company announced its plan to take a $1 billion charge against their earnings due to the new tax provisions in ObamaCare. Likewise, the executives at "Deere & Company announced a $150 million charge, Caterpillar a $100 million charge, and 3M a $90 million charge."[69] The result for these and numerous other companies is to stop providing prescription drug coverage altogether.

This wasn't supposed to happen.

ObamaCare was going to improve medical benefits not harm business.

Which is why Linda Douglass, Communications Director for the White House Health Reform Office, remains in denial. She said of these cuts, "We're confident that the benefits are going to accrue and strengthen business's bottom line."[70] What does she or Obama or Pelosi or Reid or any of the Obamacrats on the hill know about running an international corporation? Nothing.

They don't live in the real world. They never even ran a hotdog stand.

Of course, the rapid negative response by corporate America to Obama-Care makes Henry Waxman angry. As Chairman of the House Committee on Energy and Commerce, Waxman issued a decree from this Lilliputian throne summoning executives from these evil, money-hungry corporations to appear before him in Washington, D.C. Why? Waxman refuses to believe these companies are just doing their best to survive after being sucker-punched by their own government. Waxman wrote:

> The new law is designed to expand coverage and bring down costs, so your assertions are a matter of concern . . . To assist the Committee with its preparation for the hearing, we request that you provide the following documents from January 1, 2009, through the present.[71]

Waxman went on to demand a far-reaching list of confidential, internal documents, e-mails, accounting methods, and other company correspondence in what is clearly a heavy-handed act of government intimidation. Representative Michael Burgess, of the Energy and Commerce Committee, questions Waxman's tactics:

> The timing of the letters and the hearing and the scope of information requested looks an awful lot like an attempt to intimidate and silence opponents of the Democrats' flawed health care reform legislation.[72]

And so the battle over health care heats up.

Barack Obama and Nancy "The Hammer" Pelosi may be gloating today, but the passage of socialized medicine in America is a blunder of major proportions. Businesses will have to reduce or cut benefits to remain solvent—or move jobs abroad. Period. We're already seeing businesses making changes in order to survive the spike in additional health care costs. In fact, three short months after ObamaCare passed, the White House "outlined broad new rules designed to prevent employers from dropping health insurance benefits for their workers or shifting huge new costs onto them."[73] Yes, ObamaCare is a blunder—and the worst is yet to come. All that Pelosi and Obama have accomplished is artificially to increase the "demand" for health insurance by forcing everyone to be covered or suffer financial penalties. What they fail to see is this simple equation:

High demand + limited supply = higher prices.

That's Economics 101, which Obama must have missed while studying Marxism 401. The consequences of ObamaCare might not hit middle-class earners overnight, but very soon there will be little relief from the rate hikes we're all about to receive.

Obama has won. Your pain has just begun.

Seizing Control

Rather than be a pragmatic centrist, as the compliant media insists on portraying him, Obama is an ideologue. His actions during his first year and a half in office demonstrate that he is hell-bent on turning America into a socialist land with an impoverished citizenry dependent on the government. Regarding the passage of ObamaCare, he pursued his agenda with an almost maniacal flare—even at the risk of badly damaging the Democratic Party. And, while Obama was the front man, Nancy "Mussolini in a Skirt" Pelosi was the fixer. The most hated woman in America has pushed this country to the brink of communism.

It wasn't easy. It was an impressive act of chicanery.

First, she had to design a bewildering, convoluted bill spanning 2,074 pages because she wanted to make sure even a speed-reader wouldn't have time to go through all of it—nor fully understand it if they did. Second, she chose the end of the week to release the details of the bill because she knew that this would prevent the handful of media members who weren't already on the side of socialized medicine the barest minimum of time to find out what was in it or, in turn, have time to tell the public about it.

What's more, Pelosi scheduled the vote for a Sunday. Why?

So that the real America that she scorns, the loyal patriots who hate this bill and don't want the government shackling them with mandatory insurance, would be in church, praising God while Congress desecrated God by voting for ObamaCare on a Sunday. What's more, Pelosi suddenly got that good time religion when she said on the Sunday morning of the vote, "Today is the feast of St. Joseph the worker, particularly significant to Italian-Americans. It's a day when we remember and pray to St. Joseph to benefit the workers of America." [74]

Let's set aside the fact that Saint Pelosi was factually wrong. The feast of Saint Joseph the Worker is May 1 while the date she referred to was really the Solemnity of Saint Joseph. So she flubbed her religious history. Fine. I'm not one to take issue with someone's personal beliefs. But this smacks of religious pandering of the worst order. Imagine the outcry if a Republican Speaker of the House were to have said they were praying to a saint to help get a highly controversial, much-hated bill passed.

Not a word from the government media complex taking her to task for integrating church and state.

Beyond pandering to the Catholic voters, Madam Pelosi had to threaten and whip Congress into going along with Obama's American-style socialism. She whipped the right so the Blue Dogs would go along. She whipped the left so the Kuciniches would go along. And now America is about to be whipped by Pelosi's lash. Indeed, Pelosi had to take out her opponents one by one, dangling sweetheart deals to secure key votes with payoffs, paybacks, and plenty of pork.

After the bill passed, House Minority Leader John Boehner said, "Look at how this bill was written. Can you say it was done openly? With transparency and accountability? Without back room deals that were struck behind closed doors? Hell no you can't!" [75] With regard to Pelosi's Pork, it's a well-known fact that, for example, Nebraska Senator Ben Nelson was promised millions in additional Medicaid cash for his state, a controversy known as the "Cornhusker Kickback." Only after the terms of that deal saw the light of day and after the ensuing public outcry was that provision later extended to all fifty states. [76]

For her part, Louisiana Senator Mary Landrieu got $300 million in pork funding and became the sixtieth vote to bring the bill to the Senate floor. As a pundit on *Good Morning America* whom I've never heard of said, "The people of Louisiana sent her to Washington to get as much sausage as they could, you know, she could." On the same show, George Stephanopoulos called the kickback a bargain for the Demoncats: "But I think Democrats are saying it's a pretty cheap vote. $300 million. Without Senator Landrieu's vote yesterday, this bill would have died, would have been very difficult to put it back together."[77]

I guess we have Senator Landrieu to thank for this nightmare.

Pelosi wasn't the only member of the administration strong-arming the rank and file into compliance. Rahm Emanuel accosted one uncooperative representative, Eric Massa, in the shower. Remember that one? Afterward, Massa described the White House Chief of Staff as "an individual who would sell his mother to get a vote. He would strap his children to the front end of a steam locomotive." Regarding Emanuel's confrontation, Massa said, "I am showering, naked as a jay bird, and here comes Rahm Emanuel, not even with a towel wrapped around his tush, poking his finger in my chest, yelling at me."[78] Let's set aside the question whether or not the guy was engaged in extra-marital relations. The fact of the matter is that, in the end, the administration destroyed Massa's reputation with crypto-gay smears, forcing him to resign.

That's just what has been made public. Who knows how many threats Rahm Emanuel made that we'll never hear about. Who knows how many backroom meetings were held by this pit bull, or the number of other naked encounters he made in the showers. In 1965, Malcolm X declared that civil rights must be achieved by "any means necessary."[79] In 2010, that's clearly the Obama view.

And then there's Ohio's Representative Dennis Kucinich, the Whore who sold out to Obama after getting a ride on Air Force One. This communist congressman from Cleveland betrayed his own far-left principles in order to appease Chairman Obama. At first, Kucinich wasn't going to vote to pass ObamaCare—because he didn't think it went far enough! After his joyride with the president, Kucinich the Whore acknowledged that the vote would be "quite close" and decided to vote "not on the bill as I would like to see it, but as it is."[80]

What was his original problem with Obama's bill?

Kucinich opposed it because it didn't "protect states that want to create a single-payer system" and was miffed because he saw it, wrongly, as a "step toward privatization."[81] As communistic as his position might be, I would have had a modicum of respect for him if he had stuck to his guns, been true to what he really believed, and voted against the bill. Instead, he fell in lockstep with his power-hungry comrades whose main concern is not principle but power.

If he and Obama would have come out and said, "We want to take over the health care industry and turn America into a socialist nation," then at least we could admire them for their honesty. At that point, Americans could have had an open and honest debate about whether democracy or communism was the better way to go. But these backstabbers know that America is a fundamentally center-right nation.

They knew they'd lose if they were upfront about their goals.

Instead, they minced words and danced around the edges, essentially saying, "ObamaCare isn't socialist. We're just nice guys trying to make sure everyone has access to health care." But when you examine the fundamentals of this bill—the mandatory nature of the insurance, the extreme government regulation of the private sector, the layer after layer of bureaucracy—you find that it is, in fact, socialist pure and simple.

In an attempt to sell his healthcare bill to the half-asleep American public, the president told an audience in Glenside, Pennsylvania:

> On one side of the spectrum, there were those at the beginning of this process who wanted to scrap our system of private insurance and replace it with a government-run health-care system like they have in some other countries. Look, it works. It works in places like Canada, but I didn't think it was going to be practical and realistic to do it here.[82]

You have to read between the lines to understand what Obama is *really* saying. Since I'm the best analyst in the business, let me unlock what he's trying to hide. When this usurper says, "there were those . . . who wanted to scrap our system . . . and replace it with a government-run" program, Obama is one of "those" of whom he speaks. He wants a government-run system. He wants total control. That's what dictators like this Socialist-in-Chief ultimately hope to accomplish.

Furthermore, when Obama says, "I didn't think it was going to be practical and realistic to do it here," he left off the most important word in the sentence: "yet." It's all about taking baby steps to hoodwink the American public into accepting a single-payer, socialist-style, government system, which is precisely why he's been vilifying the private insurance sector. As one Canadian paper put it:

> U.S. President Barack Obama cast America's private health insurance companies Monday as the **premium-hiking villains** in the nation's health-care crisis and hailed Canada's publicly funded Medicare as a system that "works"[83] [emphasis added].

If Obama thinks the Canadian healthcare system is so good, why did the Premier of Newfoundland, Danny Williams, travel to America for heart surgery? Williams was unapologetic about his decision to fly to Miami for treatment. He said, "This was my heart, my choice and my health. I did not sign away my right to get the best possible health care for myself when I entered politics."[84] Likewise, former prime minister of Canada, Jean Chretien, flew on Canadian government jets—at Canadian taxpayer expense—to the United States to go to the Mayo Clinic.[85] So, if America offers the best treatment, why would we want to have socialized medicine as they have in Canada?

Or, is it possible, that ObamaCare isn't just about socialized medicine?

If you look closely, you'll find it's really about the redistribution of wealth.

Yes, now that ObamaCare has passed, the sheeple, who were previously too busy grazing in the colorful fields of Sports-Land or were glued to their iPhones, are beginning to comprehend this nasty reality: the Democrats circled the wagons around our Socialist Medicine Man because many of them also believe in the redistribution of wealth—not in genuine health-care reform. You better read that again. ObamaCare *isn't* about health care, it's about the government stealing from the "makers" and giving it to the "takers."

Take, for example, Demoncat Senator Max Baucus who described ObamaCare as "an income shift" designed to help the poor. Speaking to the press after the bill passed, stumbling like a drunken man after an extended bender, Baucus made the following incongruous statement:

> Too often, much of late, the last couple three years, the mal-distribution of income in America is gone up way too much, the wealthy are getting way, way too wealthy and the middle income class is left behind. Wages have not kept up with increased income of the highest income in America. This legislation will have the effect of addressing that mal-distribution of income in America.[86]

Baucus's affinity for spreading the wealth was echoed by the former Democratic National Committee chairman, Howard Dean who, thank God, lost his bid for president. Because Dean is a classic Obamanic, he was likewise upbeat about the use of ObamaCare to redistribute the wealth:

> The question is, in a democracy, what is the right balance between those at the top . . . and those at the bottom? When it gets out of whack, as it did in the 1920s, and it has now, you need to do some redistribution. This is a form of redistribution.[87]

Upon passage of ObamaCare with its redistribution of wealth provisions, David Leonhardt, one of the many hard-left columnists at the *Old York Times*, was as giddy as a junior high school girl getting her first kiss. He wrote, "The bill that President Obama signed on Tuesday is the federal government's biggest attack on economic inequality since inequality began rising more than three decades ago."[88] Tell me, Mr. Leonhardt, where in the Constitution does it state that the role of the Congress is to redistribute the wealth? Where is it written that correcting economic inequities is the job of government?

Joining the socialist *faaaaaairness* squad is Vice President Joe Biden who said, "The top 1% of earners get 22% of all income made in the U.S.. Taxes have been lowered for the wealthy considerably over the years. It's about time we get a little tax equity here."[89] I must point out that the "earners" he is speaking of don't "get" wealth. Nobody hands it to them like candy at a parade. They work damn hard for it. I resent the notion that a hardworking American should be punished for being industrious. That's number one.

Second, while it's true that the top 1 percent *earn* 22 percent of income, Biden conveniently left out the deeper issue. As Curtis Dubay of the Heritage Foundation points out, these top performers "also pay more than 40% of all income taxes"![90] Or, put another way, as the Tax Foundation points out, "the share of the tax burden borne by the top 1% now exceeds the share paid by the bottom 95% of taxpayers combined."[91]

Look, while I disagree with Joe Biden on many issues, it's clear to me the man doesn't pay homage to a poster of Lenin at bedtime. And yet, regarding the charge that ObamaCare is a scheme to redistribute the wealth, the vice president is more comfortable mincing words and splitting hairs than admitting the truth of the matter:

> It's a simple proposition to us: Everyone is entitled to adequate medical health care. If you call that a "redistribution of income"—well, so be it. I don't call it that. I call it just being fair—giving the middle class taxpayers an even break that the wealthy have been getting.[92]

No, sir, everyone is *not* entitled to health care, or houses, or cars, or a college degree . . . not even a chicken in every pot. Nowhere in the Declaration of Independence are such things guaranteed. What it *does* say is that Americans are endowed by their Creator with certain unalienable rights: life, liberty, and the *pursuit* of happiness. Fairness isn't on the list.

This push by Obama for socialist medical care doesn't come as a surprise to me. After all, as a student of history, I know that Job #1 for any radical Marxist-Leninist like Obama is to seize control of health care. He wants to revolutionize everything from within and the seminal battle is health care. Why? Because it gives him total power over the people from cradle to grave. The government now has access to all your health and medical records, including your psychiatric or psychological records.

Doesn't anyone understand this?

Once you centralize medical control in the federal government, your medical records, including your psychiatric history—anything you shared with a therapist in privacy—will not be private but held in a government databank. It can be used against you by the government. It can be used against you by people who infiltrate the computer data.

It can be used against you by the bureaucrats who hold the data.

It can be used against you to manipulate and control you.

It's about power. It's about stealing the money from the middle class.

There are a few "winners" in the ObamaCare bill: the IRS, the unions, and the lazy, money-grubbing slackers who don't work and don't pay taxes and who live off the public dole. They are the biggest beneficiaries of this monstrosity. And, of course, the illegal aliens who will continue to get free coverage at their local hospital while you stand in line behind them.

Given the fines and penalties for the rest of us, I predict the number of people on Medicaid will explode. Think about it. Why should you bother to work if everything is handed to you on a silver platter? You'll actually be better off working "off the clock" and then claiming to be impoverished, rather than holding down a job and paying your share of the newly imposed taxes.

Doctor, My Eye

The other day after working long hours on this book, I bicycled down to the mall for some fresh air. In the distance, I happened to notice that the farmers' market was set up and open for business. Yes, even in San Fransicko the local farmers come and sell their fruits, vegetables, eggs, meats, and cheeses directly to the public right from the back of their trucks and car trunks. Some sell flowers or homemade baked goods. Many offer free samples in hopes of attracting customers. All of them are just trying to make a living selling their wares.

There's something very primal, very earthy about the whole affair. Everywhere you look there are crates and boxes piled high with fresh produce, mason jars of canned goods, and people milling about. In short, my kind of environment. I love to mingle with the merchants, talking about whatever, while buying a little of this and that to take home for supper. You can tell by their simple mannerisms and warm smiles that they're regular people, unlike the lunatics running the city. So, I pedal my bike over thinking I'll savor a few enjoyable moments in the open-air market.

That's when it all fell apart for me.

As I walked through the place, I couldn't help but notice the disgusting drifters and liberals eating for free from the poorest of the poor. Everywhere I turned, I'd see the pig liberals going from stand to stand sampling free food with tiny little forks like insects at a picnic. They'd smile at the farmers pretending they would buy something, all the while shoveling another freebee into their tubby faces.

I've seen this before, and it bothered me then.

This particular afternoon, I tried not to engage, but at one point I just couldn't remain silent. Twenty feet off to my left I spotted a large woman in her seventies, wearing a cotton moo-moo dress. She had a craw on her that could devour a school bus. She was knocking down as many free samples as she could, moving from booth to booth like a cow grazing in the field.

I'm watching her as she moved closer and closer until she almost collided with me in front of a meatball booth. She starts packing away the meatballs like a squirrel shoving nuts in its cheeks, stocking up for winter. One after another, she's chowing down as if she's at a bar mitzvah. It was disgusting. That's when I had to speak up. I said to the owner, but loud enough so others around me could hear, "Do you *sell* anything or do you only have these people eating for nothing?"

The cow in the moo-moo kept stuffing her face.

The owner said, "Oh, you've got to give samples in order for them to buy."

I said, "Yes, but do any of them actually buy, or do they just eat for free?"

At that point, the woman stopped eating like a hippopotamus with food hanging out of its mouth. She stopped long enough to give me a dirty look and then said, "Ah, he must be from *New York*."

I said, "Wherever I'm from, at least I pay for my food, unlike you." She was already shoveling in another meatball. Stunned at my directness, or stunned by the truth, she opened up her trap to say something smart. That's when half a meatball fell out of her mouth and onto her huge, Coney Island bosom. Here's the connection to what's wrong with health care in America.

If you want to know why America's health care is out of control, I'll tell you. And this will get a little touchy. I'm sure the seniors will get mad at me. But the fact is that we're in the mess with the healthcare industry because you have *too much* health care. You've never had it so good. You have far too much access to doctors. You have far too much access to high-tech procedures. You have far too much access to premium prescriptions. And, in many instances, it's been relatively "free" to binge on the care your plan affords.

Like the slob in the farmers' market, you graze from one doctor to another for every little ailment. You've been taught to call the doctor if you have a headache, stomach-ache, eye-ache, earache, foot ache, nose-ache, throat-ache, ankle-ache, toe-ache, behind-ache, or private-ache. Whatever bothers you, you call a doctor, see a specialist, and run up the bill. Whoever had doctors like this for nothing?

Do you really think a $20 co-pay covers the cost?

My mother used to say, "Treat yourself, Michael. Don't go to the doctor for every complaint. Don't go for every ache." Today, we have a totally different mind-set. You wake up with a touch of pain in the side of your ear, you run to an ear specialist when a $3 bottle of antihistamine or aspirin would probably have cleared things up. Every cringe, every soreness, creak and groan sends us to the doctor when much of it is just a part of normal living.

And there's fifty quacks lined up to bill the government.

If only you had practiced some self-control. If only you practiced dietary control. If only you integrated some level of exercise. If only you practiced holistic medicine, you wouldn't need as much of this expensive health care. Which is not to say it's not life saving when you really need it. It certainly is. But it only makes sense to save those trips to the doctor for when you need it, not for every little thing.

What's more, you have been encouraged by the drug industry through endless streams of TV ads, to take six painkillers a day if you play sports. You know, take six or eight of these liver-killing, kidney-killing painkillers all day long, every day of your life because it's good for the pharmaceutical companies. It's certainly not good for your liver or your kidneys.

Personally, I've always paid for my health care. Even when I was a student, I paid for my health care for my young children and myself. It was always very expensive. But I managed to get good health care when I needed it. I only bought healthcare plans for the catastrophic illness, which so far, thank God, never came. And, I've done my best to take care of myself rather than rely upon a pill. When I was in the emergency room last year for an accident, they asked me right away, "How many drugs are you on? What medications do you use?" They figured a man my age would be on five, six, maybe seven.

I said, "None."

The nurse looked up and said, "I said how many medications are you on?" I said, "None. I don't take medications. I don't need them." She about fainted. I was the one out of a million, maybe one out of ten million. Over-medication is part of the entire healthcare problem in this country. Americans have far too much health care and take far too many medications. If we're serious as a nation to rein in the costs, start by reining in the misuse of doctors and prescriptions.

Chickens to Chicken Little: The Schecter Brothers

For the better part of his first term in office, Barack Obama behaved like the central character in one of Aesop's Fables, *Chicken Little*. Remember that one? As the tale goes, an acorn fell on Chicken Little's head who, in turn, ran around like a chicken with its head cut off shouting: "The sky is fall-ing! The sky is falling!" Her big mistake was to misinterpret the acorn (no relationship to the infamous ACORN scandal) as an omen of bad things to come. She, in turn, created a wave of mass hysteria among her friends.

Things didn't end well for Chicken Little and company.

They all became dinner for Foxy Loxy.

In similar fashion, using a manufactured healthcare crisis, Obama spent a year whipping up the masses into a panic with his version of "The sky is falling." He manipulated those fears to shove socialized medicine down our throats. And while it's a bitter pill to swallow, it isn't the first time big gov-ernment has tried to force nonsensical, draconian regulations on the Ameri-can people. Nor will it be the last, especially given this Marxist-Leninist president's track record.

America saw the same sort of government intrusion in the 1930s under

President Franklin D. Roosevelt (FDR). Like Obama, FDR skillfully leveraged the crisis of the day to usher in a number of "New Deal" socialist programs. As one reporter puts it, "The New Deal was a heady mix of redistribution, regulation, and rhetoric."[93] The operative word there is *redistribution*. That's pure Marxist-socialism. Does the fact that FDR was Obama-lite surprise you? It shouldn't. You see, in the 1930s, centralized government control was appearing around the world.

Russia had Stalin.

Italy had Mussolini.

America had Roosevelt.

"But Mike," you may say, "FDR wasn't a fascist. He was a good guy."

I'm not suggesting Roosevelt was an outright fascist. I'm saying he was dabbling in the popular thought of the day; namely, that the government knows better than private business and the private sector about what's best for the people. If the prices are too high or too low, the government will fix it. If the people don't save enough for retirement, the government will force them to save à la Social Security, one of FDR's pet programs. What's more, if the sheeple don't go along with the plan, they end up with a stiff fine—which isn't hyperbole.

Remember, that's in Obama's health-scare bill.

That said, just as this isn't the first time Americans have been shackled with unfair, unconstitutional legislation, history demonstrates a legal way to fight back—and win. How? Let me set the stage by taking you back to the Great Depression when, in 1934, unemployment had reached 23 percent. Virtually one-in-four Americans were without work. The Dow Jones Industrial Average plummeted from its high point of 381 in 1929 to just 93 points. Against that backdrop, FDR went into a quasi-socialist overdrive by over regulating banks, railroads, farming, and private industries.

The people accepted it because they were desperate.

The people lost sight of the freedoms they'd give up in the exchange.

Using the heavy hand of government intervention—think Lenin, think Stalin—FDR instituted the National Recovery Administration (NRA). His goal? Under the guise of *fairrrrrrness*, FDR mandated a number of regulations or "codes of fair competition" in order to minimize what he thought were destructive competition practices. In reality, FDR was "systematically

vilifying businessmen whose leadership had brought goods to their customers, jobs to their workers, and profits to their shareholders."[94]

Why am I rehashing this history?

Because, as you'll see in a moment, buried in the dusty pages of history
lies the tool I believe Americans can use against the ObamaCare jugger-
naut. Yes, a legal maneuver has been used successfully when one of the three
branches of government overstepped its boundaries.

Here's the rest of the story.

It's the case of the Schecter Poultry Company in New York City, founded
by four Jewish brothers—the Schecter Brothers. These first generation immigrants migrated to America to open two kosher poultry slaughterhouses.
In Yiddish, their last name means "ritual butcher" and the value of their
service was based upon the fact that they butchered chickens to conform
to Jewish dietary law. In order to maintain a kosher operation, the Schecter
Brothers had to sort out and remove sickly or dangerously unhealthy chickens. That flew in the face of the new regulations handed down by FDR's
totalitarian mandate.

In short, the government said customers had to buy either an entire coop
of chickens or half a coop of chickens—but they were forbidden to pick out
particular birds in the transaction. In other words, the new law forced the
Schecter Brothers to sell unhealthy chickens to people who didn't want to
buy them. Somehow operating a "kosher" business that way made sense in
the upside-down world of liberalism. But from the Schecter Brother's viewpoint, this was nothing short of a violation of their religious freedom.

That meant nothing to the government, which cracked down on the
Schecter Brothers saying they couldn't sell chickens their way. They had to
sell them the government way—or go to jail. The brothers failed to comply.
Having run afoul of the Live Poultry Code of the NRA, they were arrested
and tried in court where they went head-to-head with the government
lawyers.

Let's not lose sight of the fact that these were uneducated men and had
no legal training. While they did have legal representation, they didn't have
deep pockets and couldn't hire some big-shot lawyer from a top law firm to
represent them. In fact, their command of English was broken and "their in-
tonation and syntax were the sort we today associate with a stand-up comic

from the Catskills." [95] In the end, the court found them guilty as charged, fined them a years' wage, and then sent them to prison.

But the story doesn't end there.

The Schecter Brothers appealed their case, which ended up in the U.S. Supreme Court. Against all odds, in *Schecter Poultry Corp v. United States*, the Supreme Court unanimously ruled in favor of the Schecter Brothers. The Supremes ruled that FDR's program was unconstitutional on several levels. Of primary concern was the way his NRA program sought to regulate intrastate commerce. Constitutionally speaking, intrastate law is governed by the *states* and not the feds.

Furthermore, the court said that FDR's regulations were a usurpation of congressional power. After the decision was handed down, Justice Louis Brandeis told a lawyer representing FDR's New Deal:

> This is the end of this business of centralization, and I want you to go back and tell the President that we're not going to let this government centralize everything. It's come to an end. [96]

Back then we had justices who could speak plain English and tell the plain truth. Imagine one of our Supremes drawing a line in the sand against this president in such a direct manner. This brings us to how Obama's Frankenstein healthcare bill can be repealed. After all, 58 percent of Americans want to see it repealed according to a Rasmussen poll taken three short weeks after ObamaCare passed. [97]

Keep in mind this is something *you* can do rather than wait around for the checked-pants Republicans to act. They've already signaled they won't go to the mat to repeal the unpopular measure. They're cowering before the ever-arrogant President Obama who welcomed that fight: "My attitude is, go for it. If these congressmen in Washington want to come here in Iowa and tell small-business owners that they plan to take away their tax credits and essentially raise their taxes, be my guest." [98]

Let's set aside that Obama's bill doesn't do small business any favors, as I've already documented. The strategy to undo this mess lies within the pages of the bill Congress passed. Did you know that Baby Dictator Obama's healthcare bill makes religious exceptions in several instances?

That's right. Buried within this 2,000+ page monstrosity is the Achilles' heel that can be used to fight back. Read it for yourself:

Exemptions From Individual Responsibility Requirements

In the case of an individual who is seeking an exemption certificate under section 1311(d)(4)(H) from any requirement or penalty imposed by section 5000A, the following information:

(A) In the case of an individual seeking exemption based on the individual's status as a **member of an exempt religious sect** or division, as a **member of a health care sharing ministry,** as an **Indian,** or as an individual eligible for a hardship exemption, such information as the Secretary shall prescribe [emphasis added].[99]

The three groups mentioned are "a member of exempt religious sect" of which the Amish or practitioners of Islam who view insurance as a form of gambling might be included, Indians, and members of a "health care sharing ministry"—which are non-profit, non-insurance, and typically faith-based organizations such as Samaritan Ministries International or MediShare whose members pool their funds and share in one another's medical expenses.

If you're a religious person—whether you're a member of the Christian Science Church, the Old Order Mennonites, or a member of another religion that does not believe in using modern medicine who, instead, believes in faith healing—you can follow the Schecter brothers. You can get yourself a top-flight lawyer and sue Obama once you are forced to buy a healthcare plan. It might take a few years to fight your way through the legal system, but, as we challenge this bill in court, the time will come when this entire centralized, socialist healthcare plan will tumble down around Obama's clay feet. Yes, he will be brought to his knees and exposed for being the dictator that he is.

What's more, the fact that "religious conscience" exemptions exist for some religious groups but not all could run contrary to the "equal protection clause" in the Constitution. Professor and lawyer Marci Hamilton of Yeshiva University's Benjamin N. Cardozo School of Law says, "If the government can tolerate a religious exemption, then it must do so evenhandedly among religious believers with the same beliefs. This is sheer favoritism for a certain class of religions, or even for one religion." [100]

Just as FDR's regulations turned out to be unfair to the Schecter Brothers, the Supreme Court found them to be an unconstitutional breach of power. Do you understand that? That's exactly what Obama's health insurance scam is going to turn out to be for you and me. What we're seeing is a repeat of history. Once again, the government has overreached. Nationalizing health care will be destructive to smaller insurance agencies.

It will be destructive to independent doctors.

It will be destructive to small hospitals.

Mark my words, it will destroy the entire medical infrastructure of the United States of America. Irrespective of whether you're a Democrat, Republican, or Independent, when the government forces one man to pay for another man's illnesses or to pay for another man's problems such as lack of medical coverage, what's that called? Obama smiles and calls it spreading the wealth around. I call that robbery. And I'm not smiling.

Obama is a liberty stealer.

Obama is a business killer.

Obama is a spreader of trickle up poverty.

If this man can get away with force-feeding us socialized medicine when the majority of American people do not want it, what's to stop him from doing anything else he may damn well please? Don't think for one minute that socialized medicine will be the last stop on the train bound for perdition. When the stooges in Washington follow the marching orders from Obama like Lemmings, and when they continue taking us down the road of socialism in the days ahead, don't think this benign joyride will end well. It is aimed at circumventing the Bill of Rights. It is aimed at robbing your freedoms.

It is aimed at destroying the middle class.

Only the American people can stop him.

I just showed you how. Use the religious freedom exemption. If four immigrant butchers could stop FDR, you might stop BO.

CHAPTER 6

The Late Great Climate Scam

This is not fiction. It is science.

—President Barack Obama, Copenhagen Climate Summit 2009 [1]

If you tell a lie long enough, it becomes the truth.

—Joseph Goebbels, Minister of Propaganda, Germany 1933 [2]

My mother told me never to talk about politics or religion or else I'd get into too many arguments. Since I now talk mainly about politics and religion, I thought I would add a third rail to her admonition—the weather. From the beginning of humankind, people have speculated about the weather. They've prayed to weather gods, made sacrifices for the rains to come so there would be bountiful crops. The Bible contains numerous references to the weather. Yet now, in this generation, we have seen complete madness overtake this ancient subject.

Al Gore, the huckster who I have not so affectionately called "Al Goreleoni"—head of the Goreleoni crime family—for years on my radio program, is the high priest of the voodoo-science called "Global Warming," which, owing to the cooling trend of the past decade, has been renamed "Climate Change." Goreleoni's disciples had to revise the name given the fact that the winter of 2009–2010 produced snowfall in every state in the union, including the mountaintops in Hawaii. [3]

And yet, as some in the press have reported, Al could "become the world's first carbon billionaire"[4] from this global warming panic, even though global warming has now been proven to be built upon a foundation of false, fabricated, and pseudo-science. They continue to promote this fraud despite all the contrary evidence, namely, that some of the "authoritative science" used to support global warming was nothing more than "data" gleaned from anecdotal evidence cobbled together by a geography student and ripped from the pages of a mountain climbing magazine.[5]

That's number one.

Stephen Schneider, climatologist, professor for Interdisciplinary Environmental Studies at Stanford University, and ardent global warming defender, has said this about what scientists need to do to convince people that global warming is real: "[W]e have to offer up scary scenarios, make simplified, dramatic statements, make little mention of any doubts we might have. This 'double ethical bind' we frequently find ourselves in cannot be solved by any formula. Each of us has to decide what the right balance is between being effective and being honest. I hope that means being both."[6]

"Scary scenarios" and "dramatic statements"?

I thought this was science.

Make no mistake. Global warming alarmists and environmental radicals have been lying about climate change for decades, as I will demonstrate in a moment. We'll touch on the history of this farce, the shifting sand upon which the "science" has been built, who pushed it, who stands to profit from it, and how the "cap-and-trade" legislation that Congress is considering will hammer every middle-class family with a tsunami of new taxes. Speaking about those new taxes, if cap-and-trade were to become law, here's how the Heritage Foundation quantifies the financial impact: "Six hundred hurricanes couldn't cause this much economic damage" to our country.[7]

You have Al Gore to thank for that.

After all, the history of this bogus phenomenon started with him.

Al Goreleoni, having failed in his bid for president in 2000 against George W. Bush, was a lost man. After twenty-four years in politics, this career politician faced an uncertain future. Unaccustomed to manual labor or a real job, Goreleoni roamed around the halls of his ten-thousand-square-foot mansion in the hills of Tennessee dreaming up his next move. Having been one of the early global warming alarmists and a strong advocate for the passage of the Kyoto Protocol, Al, the ultimate Hollow Man that T. S. Eliot wrote about, decided that saving the planet would be his next move.

His first step?

In 2006, Gore presented a global warming disaster scenario in his film, *An Inconvenient Truth*. With the skill of Freddy Krueger, Al butchered science on the big screen, bludgeoned the truth to a pulp, and scared the hell out of millions of unsuspecting dolts. His "gore-fest" included the release of a book based on the same junk science used in his movie. The Hollywood lapdogs ate it up, handing Al an Academy Award for this so-called documentary—a real piece of fiction if ever there was one.

His second step? Like a good con artist, Goreleoni invested heavily in a range of companies poised to benefit from the "carbon credits" scam that was sure to rise as mass hysteria mounted over the fate of the planet unless carbon emissions were capped. Responding to the ensuing public outcry over Al's end-of-the-world-we're-all-gonna-die-if-we-don't-act-now fear tactic, several of our not-so-brilliant politicians introduced so-called "cap-and-trade" legislation.

In short, the "cap" in cap-and-trade is a government-imposed limitation on the carbon emissions (also called greenhouse gases), which a business may legally emit. Each business under this plan would be issued a finite number of "permission slips" or carbon credits. Once they're gone, they either must buy more credits or suffer heavy fines.

In theory, this forces companies to find creative ways to pollute less. Less pollution, less impact on the environment and, in turn, less global warming. Or so the argument goes. The "trade" part of cap-and-trade is a government-created market that allows businesses to buy or sell their unused greenhouse gas credits. What's this got to do with you? More than you can imagine as you'll see momentarily.

What you should know is that global warming connivers like Al Gore are not so much saving our planet from the disastrous effects they disingenuously insist a few degrees rise in temperature might bring. Rather, their ultimate goal has everything to do with their thirst to exercise power and accumulate wealth they otherwise could only imagine. But before going into the details, as I write, there's a new twist emerging in the battle to pass cap-and-trade legislation. It's a move designed to deceive the public.

Here's what the *Old York Times* reports: Cap-and-trade is dead.

They cite a number of reasons why this "policy of choice" won't gain any traction in Congress. The *Times* points to a weak economy, the meltdown on Wall Street, and a polarizing name, but no mention of the fraud surrounding the junk science used to justify such far-reaching legislation. The *Times* says, "the concept is in wide disrepute, with opponents effectively branding it 'cap-and-tax' and Tea Party followers using it as a symbol of much of what they say is wrong with Washington." Furthermore, "the sponsors of a Senate climate bill likely to be introduced in April, now that Congress is moving past health care, dare not speak its name."[8] In other words, they'd like you to think that Congress will face far too much opposition to pursue a "cap-and-trade" bill.

Is that so?

Didn't Congress face a mountain of opposition to Obama's healthcare bill? Didn't the overwhelming majority of Americans reject socialized medicine? None of that stopped the leftist dictator from Chicago from putting the screws to our healthcare system. I predict you'll see the same thing with a new version of cap-and-trade.

What's more, the global warming eco-extremists aren't waiting around for Congress to enact cap-and-trade. They are convinced in their own minds that global warming is man-made and, as such, must be stopped by any means possible. Their new strategy? They're suing a wide range of companies whose carbon emissions or greenhouse gases, they claim, are largely responsible for the problem of global warming. Their angle? They're using "public nuisance" laws to extract hefty fines from those they think are responsible, on some level, for global warming, and they're seeking injunctions to reduce or prevent further offenses.

As of this writing, three such cases have already been filed:

1. Connecticut v. American Electric Power. Using "public nuisance" tort law, electric power producers are being sued by the global warmers to cap and then reduce their carbon emissions.

2. Corner v. Murphy Oil. The oil company is being sued for allegedly causing Hurricane Katrina! Those filing the suit even want compensation for the damages they suffered.

3. Kivalina v. Exxon. Alaska natives are suing oil, power, and coal companies claiming the emission of greenhouse gases threatens their very existence by provoking more global warming.[9] That case is pending appeal before the ninth Jerk-it Court of Schlemiels in San Fransicko.

Proving causation between an oil company's emissions and a hurricane is as absurd as it gets. It just goes to show how desperate these fools are to send our industries back to the Stone Age. A senior fellow at Chicago's Heartland Institute think tank evidently agrees with me that these are frivolous lawsuits. "The only public nuisance here," says James M. Taylor, "is liberal activists seeking to circumvent the democratic process by cherry-picking liberal courts and asking them to impose restrictions on the American people that our elected representatives are wise enough to reject."[10]

Whether there will be a flurry or a blizzard of such lawsuits is yet to be seen. What is clear is that the Obama enviro-Marxists are not suddenly abandoning their quest to seize control of the energy sector just because they encountered some resistance at first. After all, cap-and-trade is central to Obama's agenda. He made that clear on the campaign trail and he hasn't given up his push to—in his mind—slow global warming. He's committed to cutting emissions by 17 percent by 2020.[11] Don't underestimate the deviousness of this president or Nancy "The Hammer" Pelosi.

The Democrats are smart enough to realize their pet initiative has been tarnished as more people view it as "cap-and-TAX." That's why they're regrouping. They're still looking for ways to accomplish the same massive tax grab via an economic package sporting a new name. Senate Majority Leader Harry Reid gave his comrades clear marching orders to, as the *Washington Post* reports, "produce a bill as soon as possible to have any chance of passage in 2010" because, according to Reid's spokesmouth, Reid wants to "bring it up to the floor for a vote."[12]

Make no mistake. They haven't given up. Not by a long shot.

Here's how the *Wall Street Journal* puts it, "If this Democratic Washington has demonstrated anything, it's that ideology often trumps common sense. Egged on by the left, dug in to their position, Democrats might plow ahead [on cap-and-trade]. They'd be better off acknowledging that the only 'consensus' right now is that the world needs to start over on climate 'science.'"[13]

No question, the Demoncats have become emboldened by the passage of their socialized healthcare plan. They're drunk with their own power. As Obama's press secretary said, "[Obama] goes into these negotiations, and into these legislative battles, with a stronger hand because people understand that he's going to fight for what he *believes in*"[14] [emphasis added].

As I demonstrated in chapter one, this president "believes in" a makeover of the country. Which is why I believe he will ignore the will of the people once again and attempt to pass a clean energy bill with striking similarities to cap-and-trade.

It may have a new name, but it will be the same old game.

Need proof? Look no further than how Obama tried to grab even more power using the nation's greatest environmental crisis—the BP Gulf oil spill—to promote his pan-Leninist agenda. On June 15, 2010, in his first televised speech from the Oval Office, Obama blasted "our addiction to fossil fuels" and spoke of a need to "transition away from fossil fuels." In the spirit of never letting a crisis go to waste, Obama was quick to leverage the disaster in the Gulf to push what will be a disaster for the nation. He said, "Last year, the House of Representatives acted on these principles by passing a strong and comprehensive energy and climate bill."

That's code language for cap-and-trade.

Obama continued, "Now, there are costs associated with this transition [to clean energy]." Pause there. Better hold on to your wallet when this man tells you there's a price to be paid. He's a tax and spend president of the lowest order, and his taxes are impoverishing the middle class. Obama said, "And some believe we can't afford those costs right now." You got that right, Mr. Obama. People are out of work. They're losing their homes. What's more, those in the middle class fortunate enough to have a job are already shouldering the cost of *two* failed bailout schemes. These facts were ignored by this tone deaf president, who droned on: "I say we can't afford not to change how we produce and use energy—because the long-term costs to our economy, our national security, and our environment are far greater."[15]

As you might expect from a man with no executive leadership experience, Obama advanced ideas not in keeping with the problem at hand (i.e. the oil disaster). Rather, he advanced ideas about "clean energy" and "green jobs" in keeping with what you'd hear in a college faculty lounge filled with limited minds and unlimited tenure. This really isn't about Obama's desire to create a "green economy" so that America will never have to face another environmental catastrophe. Far from it.

Obama won't rest until he seizes yet another slice of the economy through cap-and-tax.

The BP oil spill just so happens to be putty in his hands.

Pay No Attention to the Man Behind the Curtain

Much like the Wizard of Oz, who used smoke and mirrors to stay in power and control the people of Oz, a not-so-hidden sinister agenda sits behind the curtain of this fraudulent global warming initiative. Radical environmentalists, through the promotion of cap-and-trade policies and legislation, hope to grab control of yet another significant segment of our economy and funnel untold billions of dollars into the hands of the leftists.

In the bargain, the government is about to weasel its way into our everyday lives, dictating everything from what kinds of light bulbs we can use to what kind of fuel we can put in our cars. And they're banking on the fact that you're too lazy to learn what's going on.

What really matters to environmentalists, and those on the left in general, is the promotion of an anti-capitalist agenda, specifically one that says industrial civilization is bad for the environment across the board, in the current instance because it tends to generate significant amounts of the gas carbon dioxide, which ostensibly contributes to the greenhouse effect, which in turn they say is going to lead, possibly within our children's lifetimes, to massive changes in the earth's climate that will render many regions of our planet uninhabitable and create unimaginable chaos in our descendants' lives.

So goes the fairy tale.

Al's original self-serving, fabricated notion of a warming earth crisis has snowballed and is promoted relentlessly by an international organization, the Intergovernmental Panel for Climate Change (IPCC), whose claims are backed by a group known as the Climatic Research Unit (CRU) of the University of East Anglia, Great Britain. It was revealed through e-mails made public in November, 2009, that the CRU systematically falsified data and generated fraudulent computer models to support their pro-global warming agenda.

Writing for *New American*, Rebecca Terrell and Ed Hiserodt discuss the role of climatologist Professor Phillip D. Jones of the University of East Anglia, who was among the "scientists" contributing to the now discredited IPCC Fourth Assessment Report of 2007 (AR4). Jones refused to produce the raw data on which his projections were based when he was requested to do so, and his e-mails are among the most damning of those released.

In them, he whiningly requested that several of his colleagues "delete any emails you may have had . . . re AR4." He promised to do likewise. Jones was also a leader in trying to get peer-reviewed articles that disputed the CRU and IPCC claims of global warming barred from publication. "I can't see either of these papers being in the next IPCC report," he wrote in an e-mail to a colleague. "I will keep them out somehow—even if we have to redefine what the peer-review literature is!"[16]

What's more, Jones, while making his climate analysis, failed to sufficiently factor in the fact that the weather stations he used to record temperature readings on earth were subject to urban heat. One reporter puts it this way: "Stations that used to be rural are now in cities. And because it is always warmer in cities than outside, the temperatures measured at these stations are bound to rise."[17] If Jones didn't get something as basic as that right, what's to say his approach to scientific discovery in other areas of this issue was not equally flawed?

Are you starting to get the picture?

This isn't science. It's an outright fraud.

Which explains why the majority of Germans who, in the past, were ardent supporters of Anthropogenic Global Warming (AGW), are now overwhelmingly saying *Auf Wiedersehn* to this myth. In April 2010, a leading German newspaper assembled one of the most comprehensive and damning indictments of AGW. The paper quotes Reinhard Hüttl, one of Germany's leading scientists, who is clearly unhappy about the blind eye some in the scientific community exhibit—as Jones has done—in the face of contrary evidence to pet theories. Hüttl said, "Scientists should never be as wedded to their theories that they are no longer capable of refuting them in the light of new findings." Hüttl adds, "Scientific research is all about results, not beliefs. Unfortunately, there are more and more scientists who want to be politicians."[18]

The evidence of this scam grows with each passing day.

When challenged about his raw data and the lack of accurate record-keeping practices, the discredited co-conspirator of Climategate, Professor Jones, made an astonishing confession: there hasn't been any "statistically significant" global warming for fifteen years![19] Talk about an earth-shattering admission. Of course, you probably didn't hear that in the news since only a handful of media outlets reported it.[20]

These revelations created the perfect storm for global warmers, and an embarrassed Al Gore had to swing into damage control mode. Utilizing mental gymnastics worthy of a North Korean peace prize recipient, he responded to the groundswell of critics with an editorial in the *Old York Times*. Gore wrote, "I, for one, genuinely wish that the climate crisis were an illusion. But unfortunately, the reality of the danger we are courting has not been changed by the discovering of at least two mistakes in the thousands of pages of careful scientific work over the last 22 years by the Intergovernmental Panel on Climate Change. In fact, the crisis is still growing . . . What is important is that the overwhelming consensus on global warming remains unchanged."[21]

What planet is this man living on?

These "mistakes" are, by the way, the same data and computer models that the U.S. Congress used in order to justify the cap-and-trade legislation. Will the fact that the data and computer models have been revealed as fraudulent halt the global warming movement via cap-and-trade? As Terrell and Hiserodt explain:

Of course not. Cap-and-trade is about raising taxes and increasing government control over our entire economy. Our socialist politicians in Washington will never stop pushing this issue, even if global-warming alarmism is disproven to the point that Hell really does freeze over. Will widespread and irrefutable knowledge of scientific fraud silence the socialist promoters of a new United Nations Climate Change protocol?

Nonsense. In the name of saving the planet, the UN Copenhagen Treaty they intend to impose on the world would help to shackle it. Specifically, their "green" agenda would impose international controls, diminish the industrial might and living standards of developed nations, and transfer wealth from rich countries to poorer ones in an emerging world government. Internationalists and socialists will not back away from their long-sought-after global designs simply because the "science" supporting runaway global warming is shown to be flawed.[22]

Speaking of the Climate Conference in Copenhagen, leave it to Doc Savage to say what nobody else has said. I want you to look at those who attended this sham. Let's start with one of the world's worst dictators, Robert Gabriel Mugabe, president of Zimbabwe, who has destroyed his nation. Why am I not surprised that Mugabe is in favor of climate control legislation? Then there's Hugo Chávez, the socialist dictator of Venezuela, who supports climate control legislation.

To me, that says it all.

What more do you need to know?

These dictators favor such a bill because it will take money from your pocket and give it to them so they can continue to oppress their own people. And yet the dunces of the West attending the Copenhagen conference were all dancing to their tune—with President Obama leading the chorus line. Obama, who probably never owned a microscope, told his fellow dictators, "We would not be here unless you, like me, were convinced that this danger is real. This is not fiction. It is science."[23]

If I had been in the room, I would have said, "Mr. Obama, I know a little bit more about science than you do. You're a politician. Science is based upon facts, not politics. To suggest that all scientists agree is unto itself a lie. When it comes to climate science, there's a great debate raging within the scientific community. This thing is far from settled." Has Obama forgotten that, as recently as 1974, *TIME* magazine warned another Ice Age was in the works?

Look at what *TIME* reported:

... when meteorologists take an average of temperatures around the globe they find that the **atmosphere has been growing gradually cooler for the past three decades. The trend shows no indication of reversing.** Climatological Cassandras are becoming increasingly apprehensive, for the weather aberrations they are studying may be the harbinger of another ice age. Telltale signs are everywhere ... the ice and snow cover [in the Northern Hemisphere] had suddenly increased by 12% in 1971 and the increase has persisted ever since. Areas of Baffin Island in the Canadian Arctic, for example, were once totally free of any snow in summer; now they are covered year round [24] [emphasis added].

So which is it? Is the world warming as Obama and Goreleoni claim? Or should we be anticipating another ice age as predicted by *TIME*?

Could both realities be true because they represent the natural course of physics? Trying to make a connection between human activities and the warming or cooling of the world is simply foolish. A writer for Accuracy in Media puts it this way: "In general terms, the Earth's climate is determined by the sun, the oceans, and other factors of such magnitude as to suggest that an ant hill poses a threat to a skyscraper." [25]

As any student in the fifth grade knows, there have been at least *five* ice ages in the history of planet Earth. At one time, ice covered the planet from the North Pole down to the Great Plains almost to the equator. And yet, somehow the ice receded long before man invented the internal combustion engine, decades before the creation of the first Model-T or even the millionth SUV hit the streets.

What's more, when compared to the number of people who inhabit the earth today, the population of humankind was rather small during the most recent ice age. So, why did the ice melt? Did man somehow create global warming to end that ice age because he rubbed a few sticks together to build his campfire?

None of this matters to President Obama.

His mind has been made up because he *wants* global warming to be true. Why? Because that will enable him to confiscate and control an even larger portion of the private sector. So, with the soaring voice of a preacher, Obama concluded his message to the delegates in Copenhagen, saying, "With courage and faith, I believe that we can meet our responsibilities to our people and the future of our planet."[26]

With "courage and faith"?

Obama went from science to faith in order to save the planet.

Thankfully, as of this writing, cap-and-trade legislation has stalled in the Congress. But don't be fooled. That setback isn't about to thwart Barack Obama in his quest for ultimate power and authority over every aspect of our lives. Indeed, one of the characteristics of Obama's governance is that he has no respect for the rule of law or for the U.S. Constitution. If he can't implement his agenda through the legislative process, he'll bypass Congress and find a way to achieve his ends regardless. He's demonstrated this particularly egregiously with regard to his energy policy agenda.

When cap-and-trade bombed out in Congress, Obama, using an ill-advised 2007 U.S. Supreme Court decision that said that the so-called "greenhouse gas" carbon dioxide was a pollutant and that the EPA had the "obligation" to regulate greenhouse gases, went ahead and empowered that government office to do what the failed legislation was designed to do.[27]

Mark my words. Just as President Obama and his gangster regime rammed a socialist healthcare plan through Congress using tactics seen in South American banana republics, he won't stop until he shoves cap-and-trade down our throats, too. If so much were at stake, upwards of $45 trillion worldwide,[28] wouldn't you at least want to hear all sides of the argument? While President Obama and many members of Congress turn a deaf ear to the emerging Climategate scandal, the middle class and the Tea Party movement are awakening to the fact their pocketbooks and wallets are about to get screwed.

Sticking It to the Middle Class: All Cost, No Benefit

The other day, I was in the supermarket picking up a few things for dinner. I was headed toward the checkout line when a woman who drove her shopping cart like a go-cart cut me off. She blazed a trail through the vegetable section in order to cut me off at the pass. I'm about to put my four items down and this clipped hair lib cuts in front. I looked at her, but didn't say anything.

As she put down her six or seven items, she started to fume. I can tell by the way she's tilting her head that she's counting the number of items of the person in front of her. She's gunning for a fight. This was the express lane after all, the one with a ten-item limit. The guy up front had eleven items. Granted, he had two bananas. The bananas were probably once together. So the lady develops an attitude. She's itching to bust him. I can tell she's dying to say, "Hey, they're not connected anymore. You took them apart." Theoretically, he could be thrown off the express lane.

Admittedly, while I didn't appreciate being cut off by her, I can understand her impatience. My patience is tried when I get stuck behind a troublemaker in a supermarket line. They know it's a checkout line for ten-items-or-less, and the sign clearly says "express," but then he pays by check! Granted, the sign doesn't say "cash only" and there's no governing legal authority to settle the matter.

Still, when they pull out their checkbook, moths fly out of the pages and I'm stuck. Slowly, they fill out the check as if they're an ancient scribe carefully transcribing the Old Testament. Meanwhile, the express line has grown until it circles back to the meat department. Now I'm fuming.

The manager sends the guy with the earrings and pierced nose to open another lane. The kid mumbles, "Next in line." Naturally, it's always the guy just behind you who didn't put the groceries down that he takes in his lane. If you were to say, "Wait a minute. I'm next," the kid suddenly thinks he's a member of the UN peacekeeper force. He says, "No, sir, next in line. You already put your groceries down."

I hate shopping for this reason. They've taken all the joy out of it.

Normally I enjoy walking down the rich aisles of America's supermarkets, particularly when I see the bountiful harvest that we have. It all dies for me at the checkout line. Here's the connection to cap-and-trade. There's one thing about shopping you *can* count on. Whether you're at the grocery store, a department store, or the gas station, when it comes to making a purchase, you *know the price* of what you're buying *before* you have to pay for it.

There's no ambiguity, no guesswork, and no costly surprises.

That's *not* the case when it comes to paying for President Obama's costly cap-and-trade scheme. If Congress buys into this unnecessary legislation and passes some version of cap-and-trade, guess what? *Nobody knows the real cost of what we're "buying"!* Although we're left to foot the bill for the rest of our lives, not one person in Congress can tell you, with precision, what you the middle-class consumer must fork over to reduce greenhouse gasses.

Did you get that?

Not one person.

Projections regarding the final cost to the taxpayer are all over the map. The *Wall Street Journal* concurs: "The reality is that cost estimates for climate legislation are as unreliable as the models predicting climate change. What comes out of the computer is a function of what politicians type in." [29] And, while cap-and-trade legislation is supposed to provide a "solution" for the threat of global warming, it's a solution to a problem that *doesn't exist.*

What's more, even if global warming wasn't an alarmist fictional invention hatched in Al Goreleoni's mind, not one politician can tell us how much CO_2 reduction will actually occur for our money. Even the corrupt Environmental Protection Agency (EPA) estimates a mere drop in global temperatures of 0.1 to 0.2 degrees Celsius by the year 2100. [30] But of course they can't say that with certainty because while America may attempt to cap carbon output, China, which is the biggest carbon polluter on the plant, "has no intention of capping greenhouse gas emissions" for the foreseeable future. [31]

Ditto for India and several other countries.

Do you know what that means?

Polluting companies in America will just move jobs offshore to China.

Let's look at a few examples of the projected price tag for this charade. The Congressional Budget Office estimated an increase of $175 a year per family for the Waxman-Markey cap-and-tax bill (which passed on June 26, 2009, by a vote of 219–212 in the House of Representatives and is pending in the Senate). [32] The Dems aren't the only ones complicit in passing this nightmare for the middle class, by the way. Eight Republican turncoats in the House of Representatives went along with this folly.

You might think, "Well, Michael, $175 doesn't sound like that much money." Let me put it to you this way. Why fork any amount of money over to the government to solve a problem that doesn't exist? Not to mention that the $175 figure doesn't factor in the decrease in gross domestic product (GDP), and higher cost of goods and services resulting from the cap.

Don't believe for one minute that cap-and-trade will cost you $175 a year.

Obama's own budget director, Peter Orszag, pegs the number much higher. He estimates the average American family will pay $1,300 per year in higher utility costs[33]—and that's supposedly buys us a mere reduction of 15 percent in CO_2 emissions, a far cry from the fanciful targeted reduction of 80 percent in carbon impact over the next number of years. To obtain that lofty goal of cap-and-trade, using Orszag's numbers, your out-of-pocket spending would ultimately be $6,933 per year by 2035.

Senator James Inhofe, one of the few outspoken global warming detractors in Congress, puts the *initial* cost of cap-and-trade at $3,200 per family per year, almost triple the figure used by Obama's budget operative. Inhofe didn't make up his numbers out of thin air—hot or otherwise. He cited several studies including those by Massachusetts Institute of Technology (MIT) and the Wharton School of Economics to arrive at this figure.

The scholars at the Heritage Foundation did a careful review of the Waxman-Markey bill with an eye on the long-term implications. They project the cost to the average family of four for cap-and-trade would rise to $6,800 by 2035. Some perspective is in order. Obama's plan will require you to shell out more than the average American family spends *annually* on clothing, shoes, furniture, appliances, and select groceries (meat, poultry, fish, eggs, dairy, fruits, and vegetables) combined![34]

You might want to read that again.

There's a dirty little secret in all of this.

As the *Wall Street Journal* points out, the Demoncats structured the Waxman-Markey cap-and-trade proposal to "water down the cap in early years to please rural Democrats, and then severely ratchet it up in later years to please liberal Democrats."[35] In other words, in order to get the thing passed with minimal resistance, they presented the proposal in the best possible light and then, years later, the most confiscatory provisions kick in which will soak the middle class with an incredible tax burden.

None of these estimates includes the cost of high gas prices at the pump—predicted to be $5 to $8 per gallon. One Harvard study reports in order to meet President Obama's goal of slashing greenhouse gas and carbon emissions from cars, Americans better get used to paying $7 a gallon.[36] The idea here is that the more you, the middle class, must pay for auto fuel, the less you'll want to drive. With fewer cars on the road, there will be fewer emissions, which will lower the impact on global warming. The other goal of high fuel costs is to drive you to spend $30,000 on an electric car with a top speed slower than a galloping horse.

What's more, there's an incredible financial burden on the middle class associated with the loss of millions of U.S. jobs that will be outsourced overseas. While pinpointing how many million jobs will be lost, or what the dollar value of those lost jobs represents is difficult, the Heritage Foundation provided this analysis. As mentioned previously, they determined that if *six hundred hurricanes slammed our shores*, they wouldn't cause as much economic damage as would the cap-and-trade legislation Congress is considering:

> In the first 20 years, Lieberman-Warner [an earlier version of a cap-and-trade bill] would have destroyed nearly 3 million jobs, caused some manufacturing sectors to cut jobs by 50% and generated up to $300 billion per year in government revenue while reducing income by nearly $5 trillion. For comparison, this is equal to the economic damage done by over 600 hurricanes . . . **and the Markey-Waxman bill is worse**[37] [emphasis added].

Are you starting to get the picture?

Cap-and-Trade is really Cap-and-TAX.

What's more, the preachers of the global warming myth are using the alleged crisis to line their pockets. Yes, this is nothing less than a massive tax on energy to enrich a handful of carbon-offset investors. We're seeing unrestrained fraud overseas where a version of cap-and-trade is already being abused by fat cats who have made millions in profits and stand to make billions. Lakshmi Mittal, the richest man in Great Britain, comes to mind.

As WorldNetDaily reports, Mittal "stands to gain a £1 billion windfall, not from the operation of his ArcelorMittal steel company, but from carbon credits given his company—at no cost—by the EU emissions trading scheme."[38]

In Europe, the top ten largest polluters on that continent reaped carbon permits in 2008 "worth 500 million euros." One report estimated these same firms "stand to collect surplus CO_2 permits that—at current market rates—could be worth 3.2 billion euros ($4.3 billion dollars) by 2012" and, making matters worse, noted "little or no actual 'effort' toward emissions reductions need have taken place, yet these companies will be able to literally bank the profits."[39]

The temptation to engage in this swindling is overwhelming, especially when $31 billion in carbon credits are being traded on the European Climate Exchange. As one columnist points out, "Unlike other commodities, like wheat or coffee, you can't ship a boxcar-load of carbon dioxide to the purchaser. The trades are done strictly on paper. The intangible nature of carbon credits provides the perfect opportunity for international fraud."[40]

Beyond the profiteering, what the sheeple seem to forget is that cap-and-trade presents a bonanza of opportunities for those in political power to court favor and extract cash from business. Even the leftist *Old York Times* admits the cap-and-trade measure "is almost perfectly designed for the buying and selling of political support through the granting of valuable emissions permits to favor specific industries and even specific Congressional districts."[41]

In spite of these abuses, in spite of the clear and mounting evidence that global warming is nothing more than an elaborate house of cards constructed out of trumped-up pseudo-science, Obama wants to increase—not decrease—spending your tax dollars! Like a drunken poker player who doesn't know when to leave the table, he's doubling down on the expansion of the federal climate science program. In 2009, the Congressional budget included $2 billion in funding for the Global Change Research Program. In 2011, Obama's federal budget calls for that figure to jump to $2.6 billion.[42]

The timing of such wasteful, unnecessary and, yes, immoral spending couldn't be worse. The middle class is already breaking under the weight of the deepest recession in their lifetime. Thanks to this lack of leadership or, should I say, because of these arrogant corrupt politicians, the very real crisis of trickle up poverty is guaranteed to mushroom. If the Senate passes the Waxman-"Malarkey" bill, millions will lose their jobs to outsourcing to countries without caps. The cost of home electricity and heating oil will skyrocket.

Prices at the pump will jump.

The hit to your pocket book is monumental and permanent.

Some rich will get richer. The middle class will get poorer.

I am angry. You should be, too.

Read My Lips: No New Taxes

President George H. W. Bush failed to be reelected largely for violating a campaign promise not to raise taxes. During his campaign for president, candidate Obama repeatedly said something strikingly similar: "But let me be perfectly clear. If your family earns less than $250,000 a year, you will not see your taxes increased a single dime. I repeat: not one single dime."[43]

That is false on so many levels it's laughable.

It's a well-known fact that the middle class pays a significantly higher *proportion* of their income on energy bills (electric, gas, oil, gasoline) than do wage earners in the upper tax brackets. For example, if your salary is $3,000 a month and your utility bill is $300, that means 10 percent of your income is used to pay for this expense. However, if your salary is $9,000 a month, then just 3.3 percent of your income goes to this expense. As such, in order to meet a government mandated cap on CO_2 emissions, the net effect of higher costs to heat and cool your home, or fuel your car, will be steeply regressive.

In other words, Obama misled the middle class when he promised not to raise their taxes "one single dime." Look at what the man predicted would happen to the price of your utility bill in light of a cap-and-trade energy tax program. Barack Obama told the *San Francisco Chronicle* in January, 2008:

> When I was asked earlier about the issue of coal, you know, under my plan of a cap and trade system, electricity rates would necessarily skyrocket. Even regardless of what I say

about whether coal is good or bad. Because I'm capping greenhouse gases, coal power plants, you know, natural gas, you name it, whatever the plants were, whatever the industry was, uh, they would have to retrofit their operations. That will cost money. They will pass that money on to consumers.[44]

He just said your electricity rates would "necessarily skyrocket."

Actually, your utility bills don't "necessarily" need to do anything if the government would stick to the things they are constitutionally mandated to do. Defending our national borders—not defending an indefensible, manufactured, straw man crisis like cap-and-trade—comes to mind.

What Obama and his cadres want you to believe is that cap-and-trade is nothing more than a "market-based approach" toward cutting back emissions. That's more than misleading. It's an outright lie. Myron Ebell, Director of Energy and Global Warming Policy at the Competitive Enterprise Institute, rightly notes, "Cap-and-trade subordinates markets to central planning. It takes the most important economic decisions out of the hands of private individuals acting in the market and puts them in the hands of government."[45]

Pause there for a moment.

Central planning?

Does that ring any bells?

Central planning was exactly what Vladimir Lenin attempted to implement when he seized control of the farming sector. And, as I've already demonstrated, the concept of Marxist-Leninist centralized planning has been a disaster everywhere it's been tried. Ebell concurs, saying, "most centrally-planned economies collapsed towards the end of the last century . . . if enacted, Title III's cap-and-trade regime would be the single largest government intervention in the economy and in people's lives since the Second World War."[46] Time will tell whether this scheme or the newly passed Obama socialist medicine bill will prove to be the greater intrusion of government into our economy and the lives of the middle class.

Enough has been said about the costs.

The fact remains, we don't know what it will cost.

What *can* be said with certainty is that cap-and-trade—or whatever Obama and his senior policy advisor David Axelrod eventually call it—is just another way for the government to trample on your freedom and further impoverish your standard of living. When did it become the role of government to legislate the kind of energy you can consume, or how much you use, or whether you want to use fluorescent or incandescent light bulbs in your closet? Is this suddenly a low watt republic?

Adding insult to injury is the fact that you and I will be forced to pay for something that we completely disagree with, something that we know to be false. That was never the intention of our Founding Fathers. In the words of President Thomas Jefferson, the principal author of the Declaration of Independence: "To compel a man to furnish contributions of money for the propagation of opinions which he disbelieves and abhors, is sinful and tyrannical." [47]

Make no mistake: Obama's energy policies are a federal tyranny.

Think about the incredible loss of personal freedom that comes when the government tells you, in effect, what size car to drive (small), what kind of food not to eat (meat from methane producing cows), or what temperature to run your heater during the winter (the lower the better). Don't you see your liberties are at risk? Can't you see that the proposed energy legislation is nothing more than a gigantic expansion of power in the marketplace? The global warming farce is nothing more than a Trojan horse for more federal regulation! In the ex-Soviet Union and currently in Cuba, electric power is only turned on twice a day.

For only a few hours.

By the central government.

While there's an abundance of electricity in America, there's a shortage of good energy policy ideas coming out of the Obama administration. Look no further than how the Waster-in-Chief blew $5 billion on an empty "stimulus" scheme to weatherize homes in 2009. What were the results of this much trumpeted, federally run, home energy-savings and stimulus plan? Disaster. According to the Associated Press:

> In Indiana, state-trained workers flubbed insulation jobs. In
> Alaska, Wyoming and the District of Columbia, the program

has yet to produce a single job or retrofit one home. And in California, a state with nearly 37 million residents, the program at last count had created 84 jobs . . . after a year, the stimulus program has retrofitted 30,250 homes—about 5% of the overall goal—and fallen well short of the 87,000 jobs that the department planned, according to the latest available figures.[48]

Talk about ineptitude. Can you name one privately owned company that would remain in business if it were run with such inefficiency? How long would any business stay open if it missed its overall goals by 95 percent as the government has done? None. What's the Waster-in-Chief's solution? Throw more of *your* tax dollars to insulate your neighbors' home and to buy them a new water heater—yet another example of Obama's spreading-the-wealth mission. This time President Weatherstrip has upped the ante with $6 billion in what some are calling a "Cash for Caulkers" rebate plan.[49] As of this writing, it's pending congressional approval.

Five *billion* dollars in 2009 for a program that was a miserable failure.

Six *billion* more dollars proposed for 2010.

Eleven *billion* dollars in just two years.

Do you understand what an enormously large sum of money $11 billion represents? Let me put it to you this way. The government could literally feed every man, woman, and child *in the world* a McDonald's double cheeseburger . . . and still have money left over to buy everyone a candy bar for dessert. That's what the Waster-in-Chief hopes to spend in the name of creating jobs while reducing America's impact on global warming.

There's a thread of good news in the midst of this.

The fog is beginning to lift among the sheeple and the Obamanics.

According to a Gallop survey in the spring of 2010, 48 percent of Americans are cooling to the global warming alarmism. They now believe the crisis is exaggerated. The pollster has conducted the Gallup Social Series Environment poll since 1997 where the number of skeptics stood at just 31 percent.[50] They note that the reversal of public opinion began in 2009, which coincides with the timing of numerous reports debunking Al Gore's premise.

I realize some have been duped because we've been living with a blend of Marxism and capitalism for sometime. After seventeen years of Clinton, Bush, and now Obama, we are fundamentally a socialist-capitalist state. And while we are already, in effect, living in a socialist-capitalist nation, that's not good enough for President Obama. The only thing that will make him happy is to move us toward a hard-core Marxist-Leninist state, which the progressives in Congress—Harry Reid, Nancy Pelosi, John Kerry and the others—demand. This explains why BO is getting so extremist, even fanatical in his efforts to pass energy legislation.

Let's remember where the word "progressive" comes from.

Mao Zedong wrote, "Communism is at once a complete system of total-itarian ideology and a new social system. It is different from any other ideo-logical and social system and is the most complete progressive revolutionary and rational system in human history." Notice Mao's choice of words. If we were to boil down his definition of communism and looked at it as a simple math formula, it would read this way:

"Totalitarian ideology" + "new social system" = "progressive revolu-tionary."

Now you know where the word progressive comes from.

Progressives want to usher in a new socialist system that gives them total control over your lives. The problem is most Americans are politically un-educated. They do not understand that *progressivism* is a new code word for Marxist-Leninism, otherwise known as communism.

Now you know who progressives really are.

Are you beginning to understand why they want more control over your life?

Muzzling the Opposition

Al Goreleoni may be the biggest liar of the century, if not one of the greatest con men in history. But he hasn't acted alone. Gore wouldn't have amassed a fortune peddling fear and apocalyptic prophecies if he hadn't received a little help from his chums in Congress. Case in point. On Friday, April 24, 2009, Big Al was scheduled to appear at a hearing on climate change before the Energy and Commerce Committee.

That's when the Demoncats circled the wagons.

To present an opposing point of view, Representative Joe Barton, the ranking member on the Energy and Commerce Committee, had invited Lord Christopher Monckton, former science adviser to Margaret Thatcher, to testify. He would be essentially going head-to-head with Goreleoni to refute Gore on Climategate. Of course, the Demoncats were afraid of Lord Monckton engaging in a scientific duel of wits with an unarmed opponent.

Upon arrival from England the day before he was to testify, moments after deplaning at the airport in Washington, D.C., Lord Monckton received a call in which he learned he was being banned from appearing in Congress! The Stalinist Democrat party under Obama put their jackboots to the throat of this respected authority. House Demoncats essentially said they didn't want Gore humiliated, and so they slammed the door of the capital in his face.

What was Lord Monckton's reaction? He said, "The Democrats have a lot to learn about the right of free speech under the U.S. Constitution. Congress-creature Henry Waxman's refusal to expose Al Gore's sci-fi comedy-horror testimony to proper, independent scrutiny by the House minority reeks of naked propaganda."[51]

Is this the America that you want to live in?

Do you want to live in a country where you cannot hear both sides of a discussion, especially when the implications directly impact your wallet? Under Obama, that is exactly what's happening. President BO could have stepped in and said, "No, let the man speak. Let's hear from this trustworthy scholar who traveled thousands of miles to make his case." That didn't happen. Far from it. Instead, Lord Monckton's scholarly views were censored from the public debate.

What was Henry Waxman, one of the authors of the Waxman-Markey bill, so afraid of? Could it be that Lord Monckton would blow the lid off his precious little power grab for more control of your income? "Waxman knows there has been no 'global warming' for at least a decade. Waxman knows there has been seven and a half years' global cooling," said Lord Monckton. "Waxman knows that, in the words of the UK High Court judge who condemned Gore's mawkish movie as materially, seriously, serially inaccurate, 'the Armageddon scenario that he depicts is not based on any scientific view.'"[52]

Lord Monckton and I share several things in common: I was banned in Britain, and he was banned from addressing Congress in the United States. Likewise, we are both experienced in the field of science. When I heard that he had been censored by our government, I immediately had him on my radio show to address the Savage Nation.

Of particular interest was his explanation why some scientists—whether on the political right or left side of the spectrum—are too afraid to come forward with a dissenting viewpoint on climate change. After all, thousands of scientists agree that global warming is a farce, the science doesn't support the theory, and the models being used to back the data were fabricated. Why, then, do scientists cower instead of speaking out? Lord Monckton said:

> Most scientists know it's rubbish. Yet very few of these scientists dare to say that it's rubbish because the Left is ruthlessly in control of the academic world and the universities. Anyone who dares to say, "Just a moment. None of this adds up. It's all nonsense," they get penalized. They get moved to ever-smaller offices with no daylight.

Which, of course, sounds like what they did in the ex-Soviet Union.

But this isn't a communist nation where dissenters are silenced—unless you hold an unpopular scientific opinion that Obama's government doesn't want you to hear. If you don't want to believe that's happening, here's one example of the censorship of true science in academia. Colorado State University professor emeritus Dr. William Gray is "often called the World's Most Famous Hurricane Expert"—according to the *Washington Post*.[53] He's been in the field of meteorology for more than half a century. He knows weather like Al Gore knows a good con.

Dr. Gray is also an outspoken critic of global warming.

Blasting Gore's theory of global warming, Dr. Gray said, "I am of the opinion that this is one of the greatest hoaxes ever perpetrated on the American people." He's basing that on personal observation of the data in the field, not some spreadsheet cooked up by a bureaucrat with a computer and an agenda. Dr. Gray said, "Few people know what I know. I've been in the tropics. I've flown in airplanes into storms. I've done studies of convection, cloud clusters and how the moist process works."[54] Because of his dissenting view, he says he's watched most of his government funding evaporate, forcing him to use personal funds of more than $100,000 to maintain his research into global warming.

I'm not surprised.

Despite all the evidence, Obama, Waxman, Gore and their cadre of "climatenazis" will not believe it. Their minds are made up. They don't want to know what Dr. Gray is reporting just as they didn't want Lord Monckton to testify in Congress. The darkness in their vacuous souls fears the light of truth. Contrary to their predictions that, for example, the levels of CO_2 in the atmosphere should be rising, Lord Monckton, had he testified, would have demonstrated that these accelerated levels are not accumulating at a rate originally forecasted by their computer models. He told my radio audience:

> The computer models say there ought to be twice as much CO_2 staying in the atmosphere as there is. But it's all being taken out. You know, it is being taken out by trees and plants. It's being taken out to form the shells of ocean creatures. It's being taken out in huge quantities by what we call the biosphere and the hydrosphere. That's why it *isn't* accumulating at the rate that the UN would like it to be accumulating—so as to justify the continued existence of its climate panel as the New World government. But the fact is that CO_2 is rising at far less—about half—the rate the UN predicted. The UN admits that it can't explain why the CO_2 isn't rising as fast as it wants it to rise.

Despite the total collapse of the credibility of the global warmist mob, despite the fraud of engineering and manipulating the scientific data, these left-wing progressive fanatics continue to tell the big lie. For example, a recent issue of a local San Francisco newspaper featured an article entitled, "The Best Argument Against Global Warming." When you read the story, the writer, who thinks he's a genius, quips, "There isn't one."[55]

That's classic liberal sophomoric stupidity.

In my day, a guy like that would be selling hotdogs at a stadium, not writing a newspaper column. How does this empty inkjet explain the fact that current temperatures in Greenland are actually *colder* there now than they were in the 1930s and 1940s?[56] You got that right—Greenland today is colder than it was seventy years ago. Empty inkjets in the media like him don't report that pesky fact, do they? Why? It flies in the face of the popular notion that the world is warming.

Likewise, if the climate is warming to dangerous levels, how does this denier of reality explain that, for the first time in fourteen years—since the winter of 1995–1996, Lake Erie was entirely frozen over?[57] How does he explain that parts of Britain were under a winter snowstorm watch *in April* while Scotland prepared for near-blizzard conditions?[58] He can't. His mind is made up—evidence be damned. He'd probably argue that, although it was colder in Britain, it was really warmer. He's probably been brainwashed by those plight-of-the-polar-bear TV commercials.

Polar Bear Propaganda

For several years, we've been barraged with images of desperate polar bears clinging to ice floes half their size, adrift helplessly at sea. Momma polar bears are struggling to feed their cubs, we've been told. And, if the press is to be believed, polar bears are dying in record numbers. One panicked newspaper headline worried, "Will polar bears make it back to shore?"[59] Beneath it was a photograph taken by a tourist, whose name is irrelevant, picturing a polar bear and cub "stranded" twelve miles out at sea.

Stranded?

The photographer was worried sick about the survival of the bears. What this dunce doesn't apparently know is that *a polar bear can swim fifty miles.* For all he knows, those bears went out for a joyride on an ice floe one sunny day. Of course, images like these are manipulated to provoke one thing: fear. Fear drives public policy. It also drives donations, which is why the World Wildlife Fund (WWF) takes advantage of the emotions such images generate to put cash for their pockets while milking global warming for all it's worth.

Here's an especially offensive bit of polar propaganda created by the

WWF. In it, we hear the voice of an actor speaking in what might be best described as manufactured caring tones on par with a seasoned mortician. Looking straight into the camera with his sad, puppy dog eyes, he gives this dire warning. (Cue the violins):

> A tragedy is unfolding in the world today. Climate change is threatening one of the most magnificent wild animals on the planet. Polar bears. They're struggling to survive. The ice is melting all around them and food is becoming harder to find as they lose their hunting grounds. Climate change. It's happening right now and it's leaving mothers weaker and unable to provide for their young and cubs dying without enough to eat.

Designed to tug at your heartstrings, video footage of a mother bear and her cub floating on a raft-sized ice chip take full screen. The pancake-faced spokesmouth continues turning up the heat with more "they're all gonna die" rhetoric:

> As the struggle and the search for food continues polar bears are hanging on for survival. Polar bears are on their way to extinction. If we don't act *now*, most will die in our children's lifetime. But you can change that. Call now and join the Wildlife Rescue Team. For just $16 a month you'll be part of the most ambitious effort to save wildlife and wild places the world has ever seen . . . If we don't act now, it could be too late . . . [pause for effect] . . . for the polar bear. It's all up to us.[60]

Nothing could be further from the truth.

The polar bears are *not* on the brink of extinction due to rising temperatures and shrinking ice caps. The exact opposite is true. Dr. Mitchell Taylor, a renowned Canadian biologist, whose work involves the hands-on study of these arctic mammals, says, "We're seeing an increase in bears that's really unprecedented . . . Of the 13 populations of polar bears in Canada, 11 are stable or increasing in number. They are not going extinct, or even appear to be affected at present. It is just silly to predict the demise of polar bears in 25 years based on media-assisted hysteria."[61]

Translation: global warming isn't about to kill off the polar bears, your SUV emissions aren't jeopardizing their habitat, nor should polar bears be put on an endangered species list, as some are attempting to do in Congress. Senator James Inhofe puts it this way:

> The bottom line is that the attempt to list the polar bear under the Endangered Species Act is not based on any evidence that the polar bear populations are declining or in trouble. It is based on computer climate models fraught with uncertainties. . . . And frankly, listing the polar bear isn't about the bear either. It is about trying to bring about climate change regulations using the most powerful development-stopping law in the land, the Endangered Species Act. Polar bears are being used to achieve long sought left-wing environmental regulatory policies.[62]

If the aforementioned actor had done his homework rather than read a script about something he doesn't understand, he might have learned the Fish and Wildlife Service estimates that "the polar bear population is 20,000 to 25,000 bears, whereas in the 1950s and 1960s, estimates were as low as 5,000–10,000 bears due to sport hunting, which has since been restricted."[63] In other words, five times the number of polar bears roams the planet today than fifty years ago.

As for those ice caps, political analyst, Jim McConalogue, of the European Foundation, put it this way: "Since the cause of global warming is mostly natural, then there is in actual fact very little we can do about it. We are still not able to control the sun."[64]

Hot Air and Scare From Hollywood Idiots

The global warming scam has all the ingredients for a blockbuster movie. Lies, deception, payoffs, backroom deals, falsification of data, record tampering, and a cast of buffoonish characters in empty suits pulling off the greatest scam of the century. Not surprisingly, Leonardo "DiCrapio," a junior member of the scare-America crowd, figured he'd cash in on the global warming scarefest with a movie of his own, *The 11th Hour.*

You probably never heard of it because it tanked at the box office.

Fashioning himself an expert on the subject, yet denying the input from any trained scientist with a different opinion,[65] DiCrapio speaks in solemn tones throughout the movie trying to sound authoritative. After all, he is convinced that global warming is "the number one environmental challenge."[66] But his narration sounds more like a junior high kid trying to muster the courage to ask a girl out on a date. Against the backdrop of earthquakes, hurricanes, and flooding, this neophyte says, "The evidence is now clear. Industrial civilization has caused irreparable damage. Our political and corporate leaders have consistently ignored the overwhelming scientific evidence."[67]

Did you see what this Al Gore–wannabe just said?

Overwhelming scientific evidence?

What universe is DiCrapio living in?

I guess he didn't bother consulting with John Coleman, founder of the Weather Channel, who amassed more than thirty thousand scientists— nine thousand with real PhD's in science—who signed up on the side of debunking the myth of global warming.[68] Coleman was one of the first in his field to challenge the "dastardly scientists with environmental and political motives" who "manipulated long term scientific data back in the late 1990's to create an allusion [sic] of rapid global warming . . . Their friends in government steered huge research grants their way to keep the movement growing."[69]

Coleman echoed something I've been saying for the last five years on radio when he said global warming "is not about environmentalism or politics. It is not a religion. It is not something you 'believe in.' It is science; the science of meteorology. This is my field of life-long expertise. And I am telling you Global Warming is a nonevent, a manufactured crisis and a total scam."[70]

Then again, DiCrapio would have difficulty entertaining such an opposing point of view. I'm sure listening to a meteorologist might be too much to ask of a kid who, by his own admission, "never went to college."[71] It's clear that educating the public with actual scientific truth wasn't his goal. When asked what he hoped the film would accomplish, DiCrapio said, "I want the public to be very scared by what they see. I want them to see a very bleak future. I want them to feel disillusioned halfway through and feel hopeless."[72]

To what end is the purpose of such fear mongering?

He wants us to embrace "green technology" and engage in a "cultural transformation" to save the planet. Let's be clear on this point. I don't oppose the overall concept of being a good steward of the world in which we live. Whether you're a liberal or conservative, each of us would do well to find ways to reduce pollution and produce energy-saving devices.

On that topic, I was collecting and studying plant life in the South Pacific (1969–1989) long before being an environmentalist was fashionable. I have two Masters degrees in anthropology and botany and I was a pioneer in the field of ethno-medicine upon which I formed the basis for my doctoral work at the University of California at Berkeley. I'm a trained scientist. I understand ecology better than this actor knows the clasps of brassieres.

Where I disagree with Leonardo DiCrapio, Al Goreleoni, and the other soothsayers, is the use of trumped up science to scare people into emptying their pockets to support radical eco-terrorist issues and causes while worshiping at the altar of environmentalism. Make no mistake about it. Adherents to this fable, having tuned out all contrary scientific data, are zealots with a capital "Z" and will say or do anything—including the manipulation of data or the suppression of facts—to advance their cause.

Case in point.

About the time DiCrapio was promoting his film, singer-songwriter Sheryl Crow teamed up with another global warming alarmist, whose name doesn't matter, to kick off a "Stop Global Warming College Tour." Her goal? She hoped to enlist thousands of college sheeple to fight the perceived threat that global warming represents. Midway through the tour, Crow actually made this suggestion to combat global warming:

I have spent the better part of this tour trying to come up with easy ways for us all to become a part of the solution to global warming. Although my ideas are in the earliest stages of development, they are,

in my mind, worth investigating. One of my favorites is in the area
of conserving trees, which we heavily rely on for oxygen.

I propose a limitation be put on how many squares of toilet paper
can be used in any one sitting. Now, I don't want to rob any law-
abiding American of his or her God-given rights, but I think we are
an industrious enough people that we can make it work with only
one square per restroom visit, except, of course, on those pesky occa-
sions where 2 to 3 could be required.[73]

While Crow actually graduated from college, unlike the aforementioned
actor, one wonders how an educated person could come up with such a
featherbrained idea. It was an absurd comment heard around the world. In
the wake of her idiotic comments, she became the laughing stock of the nation virtually overnight. The public ridicule prompted Crow to claim, "it
was a JOKE."[74]

I don't buy it.

This is a typical liberal trick. They tell us how we should live, they make
foolhardy comments, and they offer harebrained solutions and the second
someone calls them on it, they play the "it was a joke card." Remember,
Sheryl-use-one-square-Crow wasn't doing a standup comedy routine at the
time. She was in the middle of a "serious" effort to educate students about
the catastrophic implications of global warming. It wasn't the first time we
heard her say something loony. It won't be the last.

Which brings us to yet another Hollywood idiot, Danny Glover, who
forgot he's an actor, not a scientist. Let's set aside the fact that a number of
scientists are good actors. Glover, who has no training in science, is suddenly an expert on the topic. In the wake of the earthquake that hit Haiti,
here's what Glover said of the people in Haiti: "They are all in peril because
of global warming."

But wait, he envisions more damage on the horizon because of the failure of the UN Climate Summit in Copenhagen to throttle the threat of
climate change:

> I hope we seize this particular moment because the threat of
> what happened to Haiti is the threat that could happen any-

where in the Caribbean to these island nations, you know. They're all in peril because of global warming, they're all in peril because of climate change . . . When we look back at what we did at the climate summit in Copenhagen, this is the response, this is what happens, you know what I'm saying? But we have to act now.[75]

Not only are these actors ignoramuses, they're outright hypocrites.

Two examples will suffice. Compare the global warming rhetoric of Barbra "Babs" Streisand with how this singing yenta lives. On her website Babs talks about making a difference to stop global warming "by making simple, conscious decisions" to "conserve energy and help protect the environment from further deterioration." She then links to an article entitled, "Simple Things We Can All Do to Help Stop Global Warming."[76] Great. So what has this diva done to cut back on energy consumption?

Nothing.

Streisand and her husband live alone in a gated compound sporting *five* homes and a twelve-thousand-square-foot barn that's larger than Al Gore's mansion. Did I mention the barn is air-conditioned?[77] And this yenta wants you to cut back on energy usage by switching to compact fluorescent light bulbs? Let's set aside the fact that Babs once starred in a movie as a crazy person. I'm sure there was no typecasting involved. However, in real life, she must think we're nuts to take her concern about global warming seriously.

She has zero credibility.

To stop global warming, maybe she could stop singing for starters.

Take John Travolta who owns five airplanes, two of which are parked in the front yard of his home in Florida—one of which is a Boeing 707 four-engine behemoth. He owns a Lear jet and his own private runway. I have no problem with that. If he wants to double his fleet, more power to him. And yet it smacks of hypocrisy when he, like Al Goreleoni, tells us how *we* should live to minimize the impact on the environment, while ignoring his own preaching. Regarding global warming, Travolta said, "It is a very valid issue. I'm wondering if we need to think about other planets and dome cities."[78] In other words, things are getting so bad here on earth, we might need to move to another planet.

I say, be my guest.

When it comes to the Hollywood idiots, it's "Do as I say, not as I play."

I understand how easy it is to be hoodwinked by Hollywood's cheer-leaders. On the surface, they sound convincing. Their "star power" makes them seem believable. It's easy to forget that their lines have been scripted for them on the screen. In real life, they demonstrate a poverty of ideas, a poverty of values, and a poverty of integrity. If you allow their illogic to sell you on the global warming fiction, their poverty of the soul becomes yours.

Which brings me to a final story.

While working on this book, I took a break from the writing to at-tend to some other business. After driving across town, I parked my car in the underground garage of an older, towering building in San Francisco. I rang for the elevator and soon found myself standing next to three or four twenty-somethings. Each was neatly dressed, reasonably nice looking peo-ple. I punched the button for my floor, the doors closed, and up we went.

I couldn't help but notice that every one of my fellow travelers held a handheld device, maybe eight inches from their faces. They were star-ing into their little screens as though they were their personal oracle. I thought, "This is amazing. These people are completely oblivious of their surroundings."

They neither heard nor saw anybody else in the elevator.

Me? I'm looking around, thinking I might exchange a few words, you know, as people do to pass the time. Especially since this wasn't one of those supersonic elevators like the kind you'd ride up in the Willis Tower in Chicago. Sometimes I believe I could actually climb up the stairs faster than this thing was moving . . . 5th floor . . . 8th floor . . . 12th floor . . . still, not a word. As the elevator ascended, I wondered whether these people would even recognize danger when it approached them.

They didn't seem to know what world they were living in.

I'm sure the last thing on their mind would be who the president re-ally is, his Marxist-Leninist roots, or the fact that Congress was consider-ing saddling them with more taxes under the guise of preventing global warming, or how fragile life itself really is. I realized, watching them work their little wheels on their BlackBerrys without looking up once, that an evil government could literally take away their freedom and they wouldn't even know it.

That's when a chilling thought struck me: *Would they even care?*

As long as they could surf the Internet with their phone, would it matter that they were losing their fundamental freedoms? What's more, I wondered which would be worse—to know the truth but to ignore it? Or, to be *oblivious* to the truth, to be ignorant of the reality that the world is collapsing around them?

Thank God those aren't the only two choices.

Thank God some of us are still alert.

Thank God there's an awakening as the Tea Party movement demonstrates. The resistance to what this president is doing to foist trickle up poverty on the middle class via Climategate is growing.

I can only pray it's not too late to stop Obama's hate.

CHAPTER 7

The Real Cost of Legalizing Illegals—It's the Vote, Stupid!

President Obama, Broken Borders are not a laughing matter.
No one in Arizona is laughing. Do your job and secure the border.
—Advertisement by Governor Jan Brewer[1]

In the 21st century, we are defined not by our borders but by our bonds.
—President Barack Obama[2]

Entering the United States illegally has been a crime since 1929, and federal law affirms that it is a crime to be in this country illegally. In 2006, the U.S. Senate passed legislation authorizing the construction of a 700-mile fence along the Mexican border by a vote of 80 to 19. In 2010, Homeland Security Secretary Janet Napolitano announced that she was freezing funding for the Secure Border Initiative Network, effectively abdicating the primary responsibility associated with her office: securing the borders of the United States.[3]

This shouldn't come as a complete surprise. Let's set aside the fact that Napolitano is completely incompetent and should be fired. In this case, she was just reflecting the agenda of her boss, President Obama, who wants to erase the borders. That's not hyperbole, that's what Obama said to Mexican President Calderon during a Mexi-fest in the White House. Obama said, "Your business speaks to the truth of our time, in North America and the world. In the 21st Century, we are defined not by our borders but by our bonds, so I say to you and to the Mexican people, let us stand together. Let's face the future together. Let us work together."[4]

While Napolitano and Obama were busy compromising and erasing our border, Arizona residents were increasingly besieged by illegals crossing their southern border. Mexicans smuggling drugs and illegal aliens into the country were becoming more desperate and violent. Phoenix had gotten the nickname "Kidnapping Capital of the USA,"[5] and the tragic murder of Arizona rancher Robert Krentz, known as a Good Samaritan for the help he frequently gave to illegal immigrants,[6] finally brought the consequences of the growing lawlessness along the border to a head.

Tragically, after Robert Krentz was murdered, "deputies and U.S. Border Patrol agents tracked footprints from the crime scene nearly 20 miles to the Mexican line, border-policy critics concluded that the killer must be an illegal immigrant."[7] The very people he was helping appear to have been the ones who took his life. The state of Arizona, with the approval of 70 percent of its citizens, passed its own immigration enforcement law, essentially restating federal law but taking responsibility for protecting the border and monitoring the presence of illegal aliens in the state into their own hands.

The response from the left was immediate, loud, and violent.

The left has this habit of protesting common sense.

Those speaking out and demonstrating against the new law resorted to willful misrepresentations of its contents, insisting that it gave law enforcement officers the right to arbitrarily approach anyone they pleased and demand to see identification. On those grounds, the protesters called those who supported the new law racists. President Obama, as he had done on the occasion of Professor Gates' arrest, reacted intemperately. Before the bill had even been signed into law and certainly without his having read or been briefed on so much as a single word in the law, the president called it "poorly conceived" and "not the right way to go."[8]

In response to a question by Texas Republican Representative Ted Poe during a House Judiciary Committee hearing, Attorney General Eric Holder was forced to admit that he had "not had a chance" to read the bill, despite the fact that he had called it unconstitutional and vowed to sic Justice Department attorneys on the legislation to prove it.[9] Of course, the president and his leftist whiners also failed to mention that the House of Representatives had passed a bill that affirmed "the authority of state and local law enforcement officers to enforce federal immigration laws while in the course of their regular duties." [10]

In fact, the law is very straightforward.

It clearly states that those involved in, or suspected of, committing a crime can be approached by law enforcement officers. If you're suspected of having committed a crime, you'll be asked for ID. If you can't produce ID, you'll be taken to jail. If it turns out you're in the country illegally, you'll be deported. What's wrong with that? This procedure applies to both those in the country legally and those here illegally. For some reason, Obamanics can't seem to understand that the law applies to Caucasians as well as Chicanos, Jews as well as Christians, those who have jobs and those who are unemployed. It discriminates against suspected criminals if it discriminates at all. In any case, those stopped under this law are entitled to due process. Further, citizens have recourse in that they can sue the state government if they feel the measures being taken aren't aggressive enough.

The circumstances that made passage of Arizona's new illegal immigration law necessary contrast with how we often view those in the country illegally. Many Americans have a benign picture of illegal aliens. They view illegals as peacefully doing housework, gardening, and pool maintenance for well-to-do Americans in states along the U.S.-Mexico border. The problem is, while that may be true on some levels, not all illegal immigrants come to the United States to work.

Some come here to sell black tar heroin, the latest "drug of choice" being marketed to middle-class American youth in cities around the United States. Police report a nationwide network of illegal aliens selling this new potent and deadly form of heroin from Mexico. Since 1998, deaths in Ohio from heroin overdoses have tripled. The *LA Times* reports these illegals "have focused on middle- and working-class whites," [11] further burdening the middle class with a lethal addiction.

What's more, not all illegals are actually doing productive work.

In fact, a significant percentage of them are not here to work.

They're here to work the system.

They make up a "shadow economy" and they take advantage of valuable resources, including health care and financial aid, without contributing to the taxes that pay for them. In fact, even those who work cost taxpayers substantially more than a family of citizens. The Center for Immigration Studies reports, that "illegal households created a net fiscal deficit at the federal level of as much as $400 billion." [12] The middle class must pick up the tab.

Criminal aliens are increasingly becoming a burden on our Federal prison system as well, accounting for more that 29 percent of all prisoners in Federal Bureau of Prisons facilities. The percentage of all federal prison inmates is even higher.[13] The percentage of illegals in prison jumps dramatically when we focus on California: Investors Business Daily reported in 2005 that about half the prisoners in that state were illegals, adding to the financial burden average Americans are strapped with.

And despite the fact that illegal aliens take jobs from American citizens in an economy where the unemployment rate among citizens remains close to 10 percent and real unemployment is closer to 20 percent, Barack Obama is determined to create a "pathway to citizenship" for illegal aliens rather than deport them so that Americans can do the jobs they've usurped.

La Raza and MEChA:
The Subversive Base of a Chicano-Leftist Takeover

Illegal immigration, especially from Mexico and Central and South America is not a new phenomenon. In fact, as far back as the middle of the last century, Chicanos were assuming a racial and cultural identity within the United States that would become a movement which spread throughout the American southwest and California. In his 1960 novel, *The Ferguson Affair*, about southern California attorney William Gunnarson's solving a complex series of murders, author Ross MacDonald makes one of the first mentions of the term *la Raza* as a description of how Hispanics refer to themselves. Gunnarson is being lectured about his implicit racism by Detective-Lieutenant Harvey Wills, who offers this:

> You may not realize it, but you don't like cops, and you don't
> like Spanish people. If you want to practice law in this town,

do it effectively, you're going to have to get to know *la Raza,* understand 'em.

When Gunnarson asks, "What does *la Raza* mean?" Wills answers that the term is what "they call themselves. . . . It's a proud word, and they're a proud people. . . . They have a lot of ignorance, a lot of poverty, a lot of crime. But they make a contribution to this town."

Things have changed significantly in the ensuing five decades. La Raza, which is Spanish for "the race," is now an official organization, not just a nickname. The National Council for La Raza (NCLR) receives tens of millions of dollars in federal grants annually. La Raza is a subversive anti-American "Hispanic advocacy" group that is determined to, as its founding document, El Plan Espiritual de Aztlán, says, reverse the "brutal gringo invasion of our territories."[14] Its members have wormed their way into city, county, and state governments, and into schools throughout the southwestern U.S. and California, bringing with them a philosophy that promotes flouting the law in support of its goals.

The list of La Raza's subversive goals is very long.

First, they favor the abolition of the border between the United States and Mexico as one of the steps to their reclaiming portions of the American southwest and California from Americans who allegedly "stole" the territory from its rightful Hispanic owners. NCLR and its sister group, MEChA (Movimento Estudiantil Chicano de Aztlán), have expressed the intention to "liberate" the mythical territory of Aztlán, which stretches from areas occupied by pre-Columbian Indians in Mexico up into the southwestern United States and California.

Illegal immigration is part of a strategy to enable La Raza to take back territory that it feels was "stolen" from it by the United States. Aztlán is seen as the "birthplace of the Aztecs," and it includes California, Arizona, Nevada, New Mexico, and areas in Texas and Colorado. Abolishing the borders between the United States and Mexico to enable illegal immigration into the United States is one of the most effective strategies they propose to work toward that goal.[15]

Let's not mince words.

The two groups hate the United States and all that it stands for.

Antonia Darder, who teaches "cultural studies" at Claremont Graduate University, recently received a standing ovation at an annual La Raza Youth Conference held at UCLA for the purpose of promoting Aztlán culture. She said, "Capitalism is the root of domination. Racism and sexism exist because capitalism requires it. . . . We're here because U.S. foreign policy in Latin America has forced us here." [16]

The "Mechista" philosophy holds that "Aztlán belongs to indigenous people, who are sovereign and not subject to a foreign culture." The philosophy supports "Chicano nationalism" in a characteristically totalitarian way, claiming that "we must be consistent in our thinking and our actions." It makes it clear that MEChA members are "Chicanes and Chicanos of Aztlán reclaiming the land of our birth (Chicana/Chicano Nation)." [17]

Another of the critical goals of La Raza is the granting of amnesty for illegal aliens. Achieving this also means working against enforcement of laws to stop illegal immigration. Several groups, including the Red Diaper Doper Babies of the American Civil Liberties Union and La Raza, among others, have petitioned President Obama to drop Immigration and Nationality Act Section 287(g) agreements, which authorize state, county, and city law enforcement personnel to arrest illegal immigrants.

The incompetent Homeland Security Secretary Janet Napolitano is said to be working on revising the agreements to focus on arresting only illegals who are fugitives from justice. As usual, the Obama administration simply ignores the fact that being in this country illegally is a crime in itself, and our Homeland Security Secretary actively works to bypass the enforcement of federal law, to the detriment of our national security, precisely what Napolitano is charged with protecting. [18]

One of the first things the new Congress did in its first session after the election of 2008 was to prepare the way for re-introducing comprehensive immigration reform legislation. Senate bill S 9, introduced by Senate Majority Leader Harry Reid, is titled "Stronger Economy Borders Act of 2009." The problem is that it's precisely the opposite of what that title implies! Make no mistake about it. The liberals like to say one thing and do the exact opposite in order to mislead the sheeple. This bill includes language that encourages legitimizing illegal aliens in the service of improving the economy. It echoes the sentiments of Los Angeles Cardinal Roger

Mahoney, who has said, "Immigrants must be brought out of the shadows so they can fully contribute to our nation's future economic and social well-being."[19]

In addition, Barack Obama addressed a group from the National Council of La Raza in November, 2008, shortly after the election, promising amnesty to illegals. Among the things he said?

> We need to offer those who are willing to make amends a pathway to citizenship. That way, we can reconcile our values as both a nation of immigrants and a nation of laws. . . . We should require them to pay a fine, learn English, and go to the back of the line for citizenship—behind those who came here legally. But we cannot—and should not—deport 12 million people.

Obama's offering the same rhetoric that informed the ill-fated Teddy Kennedy–John McCain Comprehensive Immigration Reform Act of 2007. That bill resurfaced in March, 2010, when Obama met with his staff in order to try to jam through a new version of immigration reform with the same provisions as Kennedy-McCain before mid-term elections.[20]

What's being proposed here is nothing less than anti-American legislation that makes a mockery of the rule of law. It's also an indication that Obama is nothing less than a brazen revolutionary who will stop at nothing to ramrod his subversive agenda down our throats. The will of the people be damned! The president is beholden to NCLR, MEChA, and the American Civil Liberties Union.

And by the way, if you think Barack Obama is about to support any legislation that makes learning English mandatory for Hispanics or anyone else for that matter, then you need to readjust your thinking. In fact, promoting Spanish-English bilingual education is another of La Raza's foundation principles, despite the fact that bilingual education has done enormous harm to the prospects of Spanish-speaking children in California.

Until 1998, California's liberal educators and administrators, along with La Raza and MEChA and other Hispanic separatist activists, countermanded the wishes of 85 percent of the state's Hispanic population by perpetuating bilingual education. In effect, they were reverting to the "separate but equal" doctrine of education outlawed in the late 1950s in the United States. California Proposition 227, which passed with a landslide majority in 1998, outlawed bilingual education. By August, 2000, the average reading scores of the state's more than one million Hispanic elementary students had improved more than twenty points across the board.[21]

The Hispanic and left-liberal education segregationists were dumbfounded.

This misguided cultural vanity, which somehow sees Hispanic culture as superior to "gringo" culture, has led to the need for Hispanics to insist on pursuing yet another leftist goal: Racial and ethnic preference for Hispanics—in other words, "affirmative action"—in areas such as hiring and college admission. Even though it's clear that Hispanic students are perfectly capable of competing with their peers of any race if they're given the tools with which to compete, the champions of Hispanic separatism aren't willing to provide them with the tools.

No, they'd rather Hispanics be given a free ride, the same special treatment that has done so much harm to Blacks' ability to make real progress in the classroom and in the marketplace. Underlying this agenda item is, of course, the ultimate desire to become the dominant ethnic and cultural force in America. You can bet that La Raza wouldn't allow English to be taught in its Spanish-only classrooms.

Two other closely intertwined La Raza goals, allowing illegal aliens to get drivers' licenses and giving the right to vote to illegals, are part of a broader conspiracy to gain a permanent Democratic majority at the polls. Eleven states already issue drivers' licenses to illegals, and illegal aliens use them as "breeder documents." Once you have a driver's license you can get on an airplane, rent an apartment, and open a bank account. It's a passport to a fraudulent existence, because it makes it look as if you're legitimate. In most states, you can use a driver's license as identification when you register to vote, and so it's a free pass to cast an illegal ballot.[22]

La Raza and Racism in the Obama Administration

As its name suggests, La Raza (NCLR) is an overtly racist organization.

Its ultimate goal is to see one "race" of people (Hispanics or Chicanos) conquer another race (Caucasians) by rapidly taking over the latter's social territory. Here's one of the many ironies associated with La Raza's and MEChA's desire to take back the birthplace of the Aztecs for "Chicanos": the Aztecs were not Chicanos, of course, but Indians. What's more, the Spanish, from whom Chicanos are descended, are the original imperialists, having conquered and destroyed Central American Indian civilizations centuries ago.

Simply put, La Raza doesn't represent an ethnically pure population.

It's the conqueror calling the conqueror guilty.

Of course, La Raza and MEChA aren't going to listen to that argument. Their logic is as twisted as their goals and their methods for achieving them. Their ancestors include the Spanish conquerors who brutally decimated the Indian populations of South America in their own imperialist expansion into the new world, and NCLR members are no less tied to "European imperialism" than are the Americans from whom they seek to reclaim portions of the United States.

NCLR's best-known member is newest U.S. Supreme Court Justice Sonia Sotomayor, a dismally under-qualified, racially biased woman who insisted in a speech she gave in 2001 that "I would hope that a wise Latino woman with the richness of her experience would more often than not reach a better conclusion than a white male who hasn't lived that life." The remarks were published a year later in, appropriately enough, the *Berkeley La Raza Law Journal* of the University of California's Berkeley School of Law. Yes, the commies at California's most radical leftist university have a racist law journal.

What did you expect?

The Almanac of the Federal Judiciary cites comments by Sotomayor's peers describing her as "a terror on the bench." The Supreme Court nominee "abuses lawyers," "she really lacks judicial temperament." And finally, "she doesn't understand [lawyers'] role in the system—as adversaries who have to argue one side or the other. She will attack lawyers for making an argument she does not like."[23] She's yet another reason why I say the stench on the bench is making me clench.

Sotomayor had amassed an ugly record of judicial incompetence before she was confirmed as Supreme Court Justice. Among other things, she had her decisions reversed on appeal more than 60 percent of the time![24] Her approach to the law is at best sloppy and uninformed, and, as her testimony in her Senate confirmation hearings revealed, she's a truly second-rate intellect. Sotomayor used the phrases "imminent domain" when she meant "eminent domain" and "providence of Congress" when she meant "province of Congress."

She also referred to her "story of knowledge" when she clearly meant to say "store of knowledge." And she used the phrases "vagrancies of . . . the moment" and "the national labor relationships board," the latter possibly a dating service we're not familiar with. As "allahpundit" describes her gaffes, "she only ever claimed to be wise, not to have the vocabulary of, say, the average 10th-grader." [25]

She's the judge, by the way, whose racial and gender bias led her to rule—along with two other judges in the three-judge panel of which she was a part—against twenty New Haven firefighters, eighteen white and two Hispanic, receiving the promotions they rightfully earned in a competitive examination. Her denial of the firefighters' promotions was in response to a challenge by seven African-American firefighters who did not score high enough on the test to earn advancement to Lieutenant or Captain. Sotomayor ruled in the Blacks' favor on the grounds that they had been discriminated against on the basis of race.

The U.S. Supreme Court ruled *against* Sotomayor, saying that her ruling unfairly discriminated against the people whose performances merited promotions, two of whom were Hispanic, by the way. Sotomayor's ruling was essentially a race-based affirmative action decision, in this case one which the courts correctly reversed. In the process, though, the firefighters waited the better part of seven years, their careers on hold, for justice to be served. [26]

Most thinking Americans understand that the quality of empathy, which Barack Obama and Sonia Sotomayor value much more highly than they do true judicial temperament or respect for the U.S. Constitution, is better applied to raising one's children and giving to charity than to judicial decisions. In the current environment, empathy for anyone bent on breaking the law in order to subvert the United States is precisely what is needed from a racist judge in the continuing war against freedom, religion, and capitalism that the Obama administration is so intent on pursuing.

The real problem is that Sotomayor's racism seems to be her primary qualification for a Supreme Court judgeship in this most racist of administrations. In other words, she's the perfect choice for a judge in the American legal system, which exists, in Obama's and other leftists' eyes, as a tool for the imposition of the "politically caponized" principles on the American people. Such a court system is at the service of its administrators' political agenda, and it ridicules any attempt at impartial justice.

In addition to Obama's managing to get a highly unqualified La Raza member on to the Supreme Court, La Raza is also well-represented in the Obama administration. Cecilia Muñoz, NCLR's Senior Vice President for the Office of Research, Advocacy, and Legislation, has been appointed Director of Intergovernmental Affairs. Muñoz has been a La Raza member for eighteen years, and she's also on the boards of directors of Center for Community Change and the Open Society Institute.

In other words, she's a career activist and community organizer, not unlike the president himself. And Cid Wilson, a member of the board of directors of NLCR and the LatinoJustice PRLDEF (Puerto Rican Legal Defense and Education Fund) is an appointee to the Commission to Study the Potential Creation of a National Museum of the American Latino.[27] Obama also appointed John Trasviña to the position of Special Counsel for Immigration Related Unfair Employment Practices. Trasviña is a long-time civil rights attorney and president and general counsel for the Mexican American Defense Fund, as well as a board member of the NCLR Lawyers Association and the Latino Issues Forum.[28]

In another example of the arrogance and blindness to the wishes of the American people—not to mention the laws of the United States—that characterizes this administration, Obama appointed Maria del Carmen Aponte to the position of Ambassador to El Salvador. This despite the fact that when Bill Clinton appointed her in 1998 to be the ambassador to the Dominican Republic, the vetting process revealed that she had intimate ties with the DGI, the Cuban intelligence agency. She's a committed communist who was also a board member of NCLR, and shares its subversive goals. The nomination was withdrawn, but it stands as a marker of the arrogance and incompetence of this administration.[29]

One of the things that is clear, and one of the things that makes Barack Obama a danger to the republic, is that he seems simply to be unaware that any of the numerous subversives he's appointed to serve in his administration might be objectionable to rational, law-abiding, freedom-loving Americans. His administration is riddled with appointees who, like the *La Raza* members he's selected, have ties with any number of subversive racist, leftist, and Islamist groups.

Because of its racism, La Raza's's agenda fits perfectly with the left's overall political agenda, which includes supporting policies to pursue identity politics at every possible opportunity. If you're not a member of a minority group, you don't count. If you're a member of a racially identifiable group—Blacks, Hispanics, Native Americans—even better. There's a place for you in the big leftist tent as long as you're willing to give up your individuality and any thought of taking responsibility for your own life. And if you're a member of a racial group that has a grudge against Whitey, even better. Finally, if your chip-on-the-shoulder attitude leads you to want to help in the destruction of the United States, welcome aboard!

The USS Hate America is about to set sail.

We're all in for a very bumpy ride.

Illegal Aliens: Crimes and Consequences

In April, 2008, San Francisco launched a new ad campaign boasting that it was a "sanctuary city" for illegal immigrants. At the ceremony held to kick off the campaign, San Francisco Mayor Gavin Newsom proudly announced, "We are standing up to say to all of our residents: We don't care what your status is. We care that you, as a human being, are a resident of our city and we want you to participate in the life of our city."

On June 22, less than three months later, Edwin Ramos, an illegal immigrant from El Salvador, shot and killed forty-eight-year-old Tony Bologna and his sons, Michael, twenty, and Matthew, sixteen, in cold blood while they were in their car on a San Francisco street. Ramos apparently mistook them for rival gang members. Either that or, as several reports had it, Bologna's car temporarily blocked Ramos from making a left turn and Ramos killed him and his sons in a fit of road rage.

His weapon? An AK47 assault rifle.

When Ramos was a juvenile he had two previous felony convictions: one for assault and one for attempted robbery. He even served time in California juvenile incarceration facilities. Despite this, San Francisco juvenile authorities failed to alert federal immigration officers about Ramos' immigration status because it was against the municipality's illegal-friendly policies to do so.[30] Ramos was a member of Mara Salvatrucha, also known as MS-13, a gang of illegal aliens with ties to El Salvador.

In his post–murder spree news conference, Mayor Newsom seemed almost proud of the fact that the killings occurred on his watch, as if it somehow validated the policy that enables illegals to violate the law with impunity in *their* "city by the bay" (with profound apologies to Tony Bennett).

The whole issue of whether illegal immigrants commit more crimes than do American citizens, which leftists love to argue when they're trying to convince America to grant amnesty to illegal aliens, is moot. In the first place, someone in this country illegally *is* committing a crime. If you're an illegal alien, you're a criminal. Period. Beyond that, if you're in the country illegally *and* you commit another crime, it's a crime that could have, and should have, been prevented by more stringent enforcement of immigration laws.

It's a crime that's an affront to decent, law-abiding American citizens everywhere. The blood of the victims of these crimes is on the hands of America's elected officials, legislators, and judges. They share in the responsibility for the unnecessary death and suffering caused by the violent acts of illegal immigrants every day.

The argument that being in the country illegally is a "victimless" crime is as stupid as not recognizing that it's a crime in the first place. Every taxpayer is being victimized financially by every illegal alien in the country. It's not the same thing as being robbed at gunpoint, which so many illegals are prone to do. However, it's being robbed nonetheless. You're being robbed when the child of an illegal attends school at taxpayer expense. You're being robbed when an illegal shows up at a hospital emergency room with an injury or illness that needs to be treated and it gets charged to taxpayers. And you're being robbed when an illegal takes a job "off the books" and doesn't contribute his or her fair share of the taxes that should be levied on that person's earnings.

It's not a victimless crime.

Don't let anybody tell you it is.

Although the victims of the crime of illegals' simply being in the United States are indirect victims, illegals also commit crimes directly against American citizens, as Government Accountability Office report GAO-05-646R shows in this disturbing analysis. The report identifies more than 55,000 illegal aliens in prison at the federal, state, and local levels based on Homeland Security Department data. These prisoners have been arrested a total of 459, 614 times for more than 700,000 criminal offenses.

That's an average of eight arrests per prisoner.

That means these 55,000 illegal aliens collectively were arrested and released back into the general population of the United States more than 400,000 times. Eighty percent of the arrests occurred in California, Texas, and Arizona. Ninety-eight percent of those arrested had more than one arrest. More than a quarter of these prisoners had been arrested more than eleven times, and nearly three thousand of them had been arrested more than twenty times.

Twelve percent of the illegal aliens in American prisons have been arrested for violent offenses such as murder, robbery, assault, and sex-related crimes. That works out to more than 6,600 violent offenses, assuming no more than one arrest for a violent felony per prisoner. Given the lax attention paid to the immigration status of prisoners, though, that's not an assumption we can make.

The number is undoubtedly much higher than that.

The report notes that the 459,614 figure represents the *minimum* number of arrests for this population, since not all arrests of illegals are captured in the Homeland Security database. If we had deported these criminals after their first arrest, and if we had secured our borders so we could be even reasonably effective in keeping them in Mexico—most of the incarcerated illegals are Mexicans—we would have saved American taxpayers billions of dollars and our law enforcement officers at all levels the dangerous job of making nearly half a million arrests that shouldn't have needed to be made.

You may be thinking, "Come on, Michael, isn't that an exaggeration?"

Actually, no. According to a report by the nonpartisan Urban Institute, "Mexicans made up the largest share of illegal aliens sentenced in federal court. The second largest group was Colombians, followed by Dominicans,

Jamaicans, and Nigerians. Mexicans dominated in most of the major immigration states, but Colombians were the largest group in New York, Florida, and New Jersey."[31]

It's a travesty of justice at best.

It's a travesty this president refuses to do his job to secure the border.

The criminal activity that is most prevalent among illegal aliens is drug trafficking. According to the GAO, nearly a quarter of all arrests of illegal aliens in American prisons were for drug offenses. Drug cartels in Mexico have become so powerful that they control many of the provinces bordering the United States. More than six thousand people, including Mexican police and military personnel as well as innocent Mexican citizens, were killed in the war between the Mexican government and those engaging in illegal drug trafficking. The U.S. Department of Justice released a statement saying that drug gangs are the "biggest organized crime threat to the United States." The threat is so dire that Mexico is in danger of becoming a failed state, an event that would trigger massive floods of immigrants across the border into the U.S.[32]

The National Criminal Justice Reference Service (NCJRS), a federally funded organization that gathers information on the effects of drug use in America, cited the cost of illegal drug use in the United States in the mid-1990s at $66.9 billion as a result of increased need for healthcare interventions because of illness, injuries, and deaths; lost productivity; drug-related crime; and extra law enforcement requirements.[33]

While most of us associate Mexico and South American drug cartels with marijuana and cocaine, the latest "designer drug" being pushed by illegal aliens is black tar heroin, and its purveyors have developed a new business model for getting it into the hands and veins of America's youth. Rather than go through established gangs in larger metropolitan areas, the black tar heroin entrepreneurs are decentralized, preferring to peddle their wares in smaller American cities and suburbs where the threat of competition and takeover by rival gangs is minimal. It's a problem that hasn't received nearly the attention given to methamphetamine trafficking.

This form of heroin comes almost exclusively from a region of Mexico called Xalisco, and its purveyors have developed a distribution system in which dealers come to the customers rather than the other way around. If you're living in a small town in Ohio, for instance—one area which has been particularly devastated by this drug—you call a number and the person at the other end of the line tells you where you can meet your supplier. Then that person calls one of his drivers, and he meets you there and makes the sale.

It's much more difficult for law enforcement to shut down these operations because these dealers will meet you at shopping malls or in residential neighborhoods in the suburbs. The dealers generally carry small amounts of the drug with them at any given time, so even if they're caught they usually face only possession charges. They rarely carry guns, and they don't engage in "turf wars" with other large organizations for control of territories. Their network has expanded in the past ten years to cover virtually every state in America.

In Ohio, where the effects of black tar heroin have been particularly devastating, deaths from heroin overdose have tripled from 70 in 1998 to 229 in 2008. Similar increases in heroin-related deaths have occurred in Denver and in rust belt and Appalachian states where statistics are available. Those dying from heroin overdoses are overwhelmingly whites, since the Xalisco networks, because they avoid doing business in inner cities, do not sell to blacks and Latinos.[34]

This influx of illegal aliens selling illegal and lethal drugs must be stopped!

The Shadow Economy: How Obama Uses Illegals to Further His Attack on the Middle Class

Among the mistakes most people make when they analyze Barack Obama's policies is to assume that he's not a deceitful, power-mad subversive. That's number one. Second, they assume he wants the American economy to grow and for America's small businesses to be successful. The president pays lip service to the idea of economic recovery, but, in fact, in order to gain control over Americans' lives in a manner worthy of a third-world dictator, he's more than willing to cede global economic supremacy to China. Exploiting the shadow economy, which is fed by off-the-books illegal immigrant labor, is one of the ways he plans to realize this traitorous goal.

Ultimately, the whole process leads to the ballot box.

In order to disguise the left's true immigration agenda, *shillegals*—those people who shill for immigrants' rights—will exhort you, as Obama himself did during the presidential campaign, to think of the families you're breaking up by heartlessly sending illegal aliens back to their home countries. They'll also tell you that violence by illegal immigrant gangs is not a serious problem in U.S. cities. And they'll tell you that Americans aren't willing to do the work that illegal immigrants do.

They're wrong on all counts.

In the meantime, the underground economy in the United States, built on the backs of illegal immigrant labor, is helping to suck the American economy dry. Writing in *Barron's*, Jim McTague notes that the economic output of the shadow economy might well be over a trillion dollars a year, with estimates of lost tax revenues reaching $400 billion. And this is not to mention the tens of billions of dollars illegals send back to family members in their home countries.[35]

A study conducted by Bear Stearns found that "undocumented immigrants . . . hold approximately 12 to 15 million jobs in the United States (8% of the employed)." In addition, "four to six million jobs have shifted to the underground market, as small businesses take advantage of . . . illegal residents."[36] The enormous influx of illegals has put a severe strain on the availability of housing in many localities, driving up the cost of education, and making planning for such things as school enrollment difficult, this though only about half of illegal immigrant children attend school.

As the number of illegals entering the United States continues to rise, their presence here has increasingly disastrous economic and security consequences. In the wake of this, Obama and his shamelessly incompetent and unqualified Homeland Security Secretary, Janet Napolitano, have put on hold one of the primary tactics used by the Immigration and Customs Enforcement Agency (ICE) to thwart illegals in the workplace. Among ICE's jobs is going into businesses suspected of employing illegal aliens and checking IDs. Those who don't pass muster are removed from the workplace and detained.

But when a recent successful raid on a business in Bellingham, Washington, netted twenty-eight illegals, Napolitano stepped in to put a stop to this practice. Her reasons? In her view, immigration enforcement needed to focus not on the criminals themselves but "on employers who intentionally and knowingly exploit the illegal labor market."[37]

Of course the real reason Napolitano wants to change the rules of enforcement is that it's much tougher to prove that a business was aware that it was hiring an illegal alien than it is to prove that a person is in the country illegally. It means that ICE is likely to virtually suspend the kinds of workplace raids that might restore jobs for Americans by eliminating illegal aliens from American payrolls. When they do conduct such raids, it will be to penalize the companies themselves and not the illegals who fraudulently obtain work there.

Incidentally, the day after the story of the Bellingham raid hit the papers, hundreds of people showed up at the plant to apply for jobs. Did you really think that illegals are only doing work Americans *don't* want to do?

Let me connect the dots. As the number of American citizens who are unemployed increases, that means the number of people relying on the government for support will increase. This, of course, brings Barack Obama closer to his goal of total control. That's the Marxist-Leninist state-controlled view of America Obama envisions.

The idea is to build a large majority of potential voters who are on the dole and who are not motivated to get out and look for work. As Senator Jon Kyl pointed out in debate on the Senate floor, "continuing to pay people unemployment is a disincentive for them to seek new work." The longer they receive these benefits—they're eligible to get them for up to ninety-nine weeks in many areas now—the less motivated they are to go to work. Demoncats constantly push to extend the length of time those out of work can receive unemployment, which is one of the primary ways they try to make American citizens more and more dependent on the federal government for their livelihoods.

It shouldn't be a secret that Obama is out to hobble private business in the interest of centrally managing the economy and putting more and more power into the hands of the government. Allowing illegals to siphon off taxable income furthers that. But taking over the economy also helps him expand the Democratic voter base. Because of this, the Obama administration has a vested interest in maintaining high unemployment rates.

Anyone who believes Obama wants or needs to see unemployment rates come down to achieve his ends hasn't been paying attention. While the deaf and blind people who pass for journalists in this country wail about how Obama's policies aren't working and cite increasing joblessness as evidence, they're only demonstrating how little they understand about what this president is out to do.

It's not, and it never has been, Obama's intention to reduce unemployment.

Having an illegal do a job that rightfully belongs to a citizen is one way for Democrats to drive citizens out of the labor market and accomplish their goal of making Americans beholden to them. It also translates to more workers in the shadow economy where they don't contribute to tax revenues, thus hastening America's economic decline.

The shadow economy extends to the area of healthcare services as well. Here our population of illegal immigrants affects us economically in a number of ways. Because medical treatment is rudimentary or nonexistent in many third-world countries, including Mexico and other Central and South American countries, people entering the United States illegally carry with them diseases that have been wiped out in our country or have mutated into strains of diseases that are nearly impossible to treat. People who enter the country illegally are not screened in any way.

They're certainly not screened medically.

This is no small matter.

Take, for example, the outbreak of Dengue fever which hit Key West, Florida in August, 2009. Keep in mind Florida hasn't seen a case of Dengue since 1930. But over a nine-month period, more than several dozen cases have rocked the town. How did this happen? We know that Dengue is a viral infection that, for the most part, is transmitted by mosquito bites. However, it's also spread when illegals enter our country from Mexico or when a tourist visits Mexico, the Caribbean, and countries to the south where there have been "an estimated 4.6 million cases from 2000–2007."[38]

To be redundant, there have been zero cases in Florida for the last 80 years. But according to a report by public health officials in Florida teaming up with the Centers for Disease Control, during the last 30 years a number of "locally-acquired cases have been confirmed along the Texas-Mexico border."[39] That's code language. What they're really saying is that illegals who are breaking into our country aren't just breaking the law—they're intro-ducing a disease which has been long eradicated from this country.

I warned you about this years ago in my bestseller, *The Savage Nation*. I told you that your grandparents and great-grandparents were screened for diseases at Ellis Island on the East Coast and Angel Island on the West Coast before they were permitted to enter. If they had a disease, guess what? They were quarantined until they could recover or were even sent back to where they came from. I realize the *faaaairness* police of today wouldn't stand for that. But that policy of prevention prevented an avalanche of dis-eases from infecting our people.

Tuberculosis, for example, was almost wiped out in the United States until it was reintroduced by immigrants who were no longer screened or who entered here illegally. Left unchecked, it's possible we'll see cases of Dengue fever spread from Key West to the heartland of America. We've already learned about one woman visiting Key West who fell ill with Den-gue fever and then transported the disease to Rochester, New York.[40] That's the first domino in this deadly game of unscreened illegal immigrants and the spread of epidemics.

Many illegals carry diseases that would otherwise cause them to be de-clined entry. This means that in many areas emergency rooms and hospitals are taxed beyond their limits dealing with diseases that are resistant to con-ventional treatments. The cost of providing medical treatment in emergency rooms and at free clinics for illegals in the United States is estimated to be $4.3 billion annually. If illegal aliens were covered under Obama's health-care insurance legislation, that figure would rise to more than $30 billion annually.[41]

That ought to make you sick.

Illegals and The Vote:
How the Obama Administration Plans to Stuff Ballot Boxes

Finding ways to enable illegal aliens to vote, especially in national elections, is one of the cornerstones of Barack Obama's plan to seize total control over you and your life by the left wing of the Democrat Party. The strategy is already well-developed; we've seen evidence of it in the 2008 election, and it will only get worse as this administration further implements its voter fraud agenda. Let me illustrate with three examples.

Voter Intimidation: During the 2008 election, Attorney General Eric Holder called Americans "cowards" because they were unwilling to engage in a public debate about "race." Holder cemented his reputation as a racist when he looked the other way regarding the prosecution of members of the New Black Panther Party for voter intimidation on election day 2008 in Philadelphia. Remember that one?

The Panthers, dressed in black and wearing black berets, wielded nightsticks and shouted at potential voters approaching the polling station. A civil rights activist described the incident as "the most blatant form of voter intimidation" he had ever seen, including during the days of the voting rights movement in the 1960s. The Justice Department had won the case by default when the defendants failed to respond to the charges. And yet, despite the fact that the case had been won, Holder dismissed the charges against all but one of the miscreants. The one against who the charges remained was told, not that voter intimidation was illegal, but that he had to wait until after 2012 before brandishing a nightstick at an election site again.[42]

Holder is the Obama administration's "Bull" Connor.

Where Connor called out firemen and policemen to prevent blacks from demonstrating in Birmingham, Alabama, in 1963, Holder looked the other way when members of the New Black Panther Party brandished weapons and shouted insults at white voters, intimidating them in a way similar to that of Connor's thugs forty-five years earlier. Look for more of the same in the 2012 elections from this administration.

Buying Votes Using Stimulus Dollars: Among the most telling statistics regarding the Democrat vote-buying initiative is the way stimulus dollars are being used. According to a study conducted by the Mercatus Center at George Mason University, nearly three-quarters of all stimulus dollars spent through early 2010 had gone to Democratic congressional districts. But of course you probably don't know that because the media didn't report it.

What's more, no correlation whatsoever existed between the number of unemployed people in areas receiving stimulus dollars and the amount of money received. In other words, Democrats are rewarding their own, essentially buying votes with taxpayer dollars, arguably in violation of the very law under which the money is being distributed. In addition, significantly more stimulus money has gone to high-income areas rather than low-income areas, where it is certainly needed more.[43]

Rigging the Census: In a press release issued to Hispanic organizations, Obama's U.S. Census Director, Robert Graves, essentially says that the administration intends to count illegal aliens in the 2009 census. Ominously, the press release appeared on the website of the Service Employees International Union (SEIU), the radical leftist organization whose president, Andy Stern, should be paying rent to the White House, given the inordinate number of times he's spent the night there.

The press release reads, in part, "We have the enormous challenge of convincing everyone in the country to participate in the national count—regardless of race, ethnicity, or citizenship status. To reach the Latino community, we are counting on community-based initiatives like *ya es hora* to partner with us in spreading the word that the 2010 Census is easy, important and safe."[44]

In other words, Democrats are going to subvert the law by not arresting illegal aliens discovered by census takers in order to swell the ranks of Democratic voters. Such an initiative has the potential to see redistricting favoring Democrats on a broad scale, and it promises to channel additional federal funding to districts with large populations of Hispanic illegals.

The 2010 census questionnaire, incidentally, is the first one *not* to ask if the persons recorded on the form are citizens. While it asks questions about race and ethnicity, it fails to note citizenship. That's an outrage! In addition, several key players involved in administering the census "are part of an umbrella group called the National Hispanic Leadership Agenda, an organization that loudly advocates amnesty for millions of illegals." Of course, NCLR is at the top of that list. The group also presses to make it easier for illegal aliens to vote in this country. Nor is the census bureau screening applicants to work on the census as to whether or not they're U.S. citizens.[45]

In addition, census officials "are going to release data on prison populations to states when they redraw legislative boundaries next year." That opens the door to prisoners being counted in the areas where they're imprisoned or in their hometowns . . . or both.[46] It's obvious that the census is turning into yet another tool for Democrats to increase their constituency, the group of voters that is beholden to them.

Of course, Hispanics are already intentionally committing voter fraud on a very large scale. Southern California Democratic congressional candidate Francine Busby was caught on tape telling illegal aliens that they didn't need identification in order to vote. She explained that she was only telling her potential constituents what other Democratic candidates across the country were telling similar groups.[47]

Most voter-registration centers across the United States have very limited ability to check whether someone registering to vote is an American citizen. Often the only verification of citizenship is a question on the registration form asking whether the registrant is a citizen. In other cases, identification such as a driver's license is all that's required. For that reason, the drive by Democrats and leftists to allow illegals to obtain drivers' licenses also has implications at the ballot box. A driver's license is, as I've said, a "breeder document," and among the things it enables illegal aliens to do is register to vote . . . fraudulently.

New Jersey Republican strategist Janice Martin puts it this way: "Americans would be shocked to discover that hundreds of thousands of general election voters are illegal aliens, green-card immigrants, and criminals who've murdered, raped and robbed U.S. citizens. And guess which party benefits the most from their votes? The one that's pushing for amnesty and a bag full of free goodies."[48]

A corollary to counting illegals in the census is the drive for Universal Voter Registration. As it has done with its health care legislation, the Obama administration will try to push through "universal voter registration," possibly this year, certainly before the 2012 election. Universal voter registration essentially transfers the responsibility to register to vote from each individual citizen to the government.

As *Wall Street Journal* columnist John Fund explains, "What is universal voter registration? It means all the state laws on elections will be overridden by a federal mandate. The feds will tell the states: 'take everyone on every list of welfare that you have, take everyone on every list of unemployed you have, take everyone on every list of property owners, take everyone on every list of driver's license holders and register them to vote regardless of whether they want to be.'"[49] Of course, there will be virtually no capability to cross-check lists for duplicates, and no way to check for fraud. Essentially everyone, including illegal aliens and convicted felons, would be eligible to vote under the proposed legislation.

Conservative political strategist Michael Baker puts it succinctly: "While the liberal media and the liberal establishment ignore what is a huge scandal, American voters are having their rights violated. When an illegal alien or felon or other person prohibited by law votes, their votes cancel out those of American citizens." [50]

Finally, the Dems plan to top it off with a second comprehensive amnesty bill for illegal aliens. In addition to Senate Bill S 9, President Obama and Democrats plan to reintroduce Comprehensive Immigration Reform legislation, more popularly known as Amnesty for Illegal Aliens. [51] While the particulars of the bill have yet to be drafted, it will no doubt mirror the failed 2007 Immigration Reform bill, the one rejected out of hand by the American electorate and by legislators at the time it was introduced. At best the bill is another gift to illegal immigrants in the United States, another opportunity for Democrats to demonstrate their superiority by arrogantly forcing through legislation directly counter to the will of the American people.

Barack Obama is after nothing less than to bribe the illegal aliens in this country to vote for him and his party in perpetuity. He's about to offer them amnesty and a path to citizenship again. He's prepared to ignore the crimes they commit by refusing to deport illegals who are arrested in the United States. If you throw in free medical care and free schooling paid for by American citizens who still have jobs or are trying to run small businesses, you have a voter base of fifteen to twenty million illegal aliens, along with about the same number of out-of-work Americans who depend on unemployment and welfare to get by.

These people are not about to jump ship and vote against socialism.

These people are not about to bite the hand that feeds them.

Toss in ACORN and you have the perfect storm for a Marxist-Democrat takeover. Even though ACORN, because of the voter fraud scandals of the 2008 election, is technically not eligible for federal funds, the group will still be active in the 2010 elections. In fact, its tactics are being copied by other subversive groups participating in the census and the elections.

ACORN's strategy is built on registering Democratic voters, legal or illegal, and helping them vote, in many cases several times. The organization also tries to fraudulently register enough voters that the system for checking whether the registrations are legal is overwhelmed and brought to a standstill. ACORN's lobbying efforts target minimizing voter identification standards so that voter fraud is easier to commit. Illegal aliens and disenfranchised workers are their primary target populations.[52]

ACORN is, of course, the same corrupt bunch of redistribute-the-wealth vermin that Obama represented during his days in the mid 1990s as a community organizer in Illinois, when he was one of the attorneys who successfully argued for legislation that enabled the state's residents to register to vote at the same places where they get their drivers' licenses renewed. Our president also ran ACORN's Project Vote during his organizing days in Chicago. His purpose was simple: to rig elections by making voter fraud the norm.[53] And yet, the American sheeple fail to see the true motives and objectives of the Commander-in-Sneak.

They assume Obama wants what they want.

They assume Obama has America's best interests at heart.

They refuse to realize that Barack Obama doesn't want you to succeed in your job or your small business. He wants to see you on your knees before him. In what way do I mean that? He wants you to be dependent for your very survival on government largesse. Exploiting the illegal immigration crisis to expand the Democratic voter base is one of his signature strategies for accomplishing this. He won't stop until we boot him and the Marxist fellow travelers in his administration out of office.

Arizona Governor Jan Brewer was right when she put out this statement: "President Obama, Broken Borders are not a laughing matter. No one in Arizona is laughing. Do your job and secure the border."[54]

Illegal aliens are *illegal*.

What could be more clear than that?

CHAPTER 8

From Panthers to ACORNs— Little Dictatorships Grow

Any group that says, "I'm young, I'm Democratic, and I'm a socialist" is all right with me . . . This rise of this Tea Party so-called movement [is a] bowel movement in my estimation.

—Bertha Lewis, ACORN CEO[1]

In 2009, two young activists, filmmaker James O'Keefe and his partner in exposing crime, Hannah Giles, blew the lid off the Association of Community Organizations for Reform Now (ACORN). How? By revealing ACORN to be little more than a front organization for lawbreakers. Not just your run-of-the-mill lawbreakers, but also the kind who were perfectly willing to support the opening of houses of prostitution for underage illegal immigrant girls and human trafficking.

What's more, they had no qualms about defrauding the government in order to distribute taxpayer dollars to other undeserving degenerates. By the time O'Keefe and Giles exposed the truth, ACORN had established more than two thousand local offices around the United States and was raking in tens of millions of dollars in federal, state, and local taxpayer money to advance its corrupt leftist agenda.[2]

Whore mongering and tax evasion aren't the only things they excel at. In fact, they're just the tip of the iceberg. ACORN's stock-in-trade is election fraud. Voter registration fraud with the intent to influence elections in favor of their leftist cohorts is the group's criminal activity of choice. As of

October, 2008, ACORN election irregularities were under investigation in fourteen states.

ACORN's alleged illegal activities resulted in more than 57,000 voter registrations being thrown out as "clearly fraudulent" in Pennsylvania in 2008; five out of every six ACORN voter registrations found to be fraudulent in Virginia in 2005; and three ACORN employees pleading guilty in a voter fraud case involving more than two thousand registrations in Washington State in 2007.[3] There are dozens more investigations of voting irregularities by the group under way on the state and local levels across the United States.

Barack Obama's association with ACORN, a group that has correctly been described as the "key modern successor of the radical 1960's 'New Left,'"[4] goes back almost two decades. Toni Foulkes, a Chicago ACORN leader and National Association Board member, explains, "Obama started building the base years before [his election successes] . . . when he was organizing on the far south side of the city with the Developing Communities Project."[5]

In 1992, before he attended Harvard Law School, Obama also worked as an organizer on "Project VOTE" in Chicago, partnering directly with ACORN. His responsibilities included conducting leadership-training seminars. His work on that project helped net Carol Moseley-Braun some fifty thousand votes.[6] You can bet that Moseley-Braun's victory was largely due to the voter fraud that ACORN has become famous for—and that Obama was instrumental in engineering it. ACORN volunteers turned out in force for Obama's initial 1996 campaign for the Illinois State Senate and for his unsuccessful bid for a U.S. Senate seat in 2000, and they helped get him elected to the U.S. Senate in 2004.[7] Obama cut his teeth on corruption during the ACORN years.

ACORN, like the Obama administration, is corrupt down to its roots. If ACORN is involved, it's a virtual stone cold lock to be illegal or unethical, and it's guaranteed to be exclusively for and at the behest of Democrats. Democratic illegal activity associated with elections doesn't stop with ACORN. It extends all the way up through the branches of Obama's Department of Justice (DOJ) and to Attorney General Eric Holder. By now it should come as no surprise that the Holder DOJ, having received documented evidence of rampant voter fraud by ACORN from the organization Judicial Watch and after taking a cursory look at the overwhelming proof of "duplicates, underage, illegible and invalid addresses" in the registrations, decided to shut down its investigation, claiming "ACORN broke no laws."[8]

Holder's action is similar to one he took in another case of voting irregularities involving another leftist organization, the New Black Panther Party. Despite the fact that the Justice Department had actually won its case of voter intimidation against the organization, Holder dismissed the charges. In fact, the U.S. Commission on Civil Rights explained that the Justice Department "repeatedly refused" to provide them with information about why the case was dismissed. A letter from Commission Chairman Gerald A. Reynolds to Holder explained:

> The actual basis for the department's continued refusal to cooperate with the commission remains unclear. For example, has the president invoked executive privilege over the materials that the commission is seeking? If that is the case, the president or the attorney general must so state. The department's continued refusal to provide the requested information will lead to a conflict of interest, whereby the target of the subpoena—the department—can evade its statutory obligation to the commission by refusing to respond to or enforce the commission's subpoena.[9]

The Democratic Congress, of course, looked the other way while the Holder DOJ refused to respond to every subpoena issued by the U.S. Commission on Civil Rights, despite the fact that it is required by law to provide information sought in the subpoenas. The responses of the Holder Department of Justice "fall short of even a minimum level of cooperation" according to the commission's general counsel, David P. Blackwood.[10]

The country is, effectively, being run by leftist, racist thugs.

I put the president and his Attorney General in that group.

We're getting a taste of Marxist "justice," which really amounts to Marxist "revenge" for conditions, among blacks especially, that have largely disappeared over the past fifty years. It's the revenge of a racial-political group intent on inflicting on white people the same usurpation of freedom they, the whites, inflicted on blacks in the past. This, of course, ignores the fact that over the last half century blacks have achieved equal rights in the United States.

It's the "justice" of a group out to prove, not only that black people are not capable of running their own lives and so must have Al Sharpton and Jesse Jackson and Eric Holder and others of their ilk tell them how to do it. That's number one. They believe white people should not be given the freedom to make their own decisions either. The American people have been duped into allowing this country to come under the rule of a racist regime, one that will stop at nothing short of inflicting its tyrannical will on us. Voter fraud and intimidation are among the important ways they attempt to advance their illegal agenda.

A look at ACORN's socialist roots and its ties to other Black Muslim revolutionary groups shows just how intertwined the Obama administration is with this backward-looking movement. It also demonstrates how in tune with its utterly fatuous worldview the people currently charged with governing the United States really are. Leave it to Doc Savage to get to the root of the problem.

The Obama Administration: Where Marxism Meets Radical Islam

While its ostensible purpose was to provide aid and consultation to poor people in inner cities through "community organizing," in fact, the policies and practices that ACORN supports have done more to enslave America's inner city poor in the prison of perpetual poverty than any others since the Emancipation Proclamation. American minority populations, if they buy into the lies and disingenuous rhetoric of leftists like ACORN organizers, black power advocates, and Democratic state and federal legislators, are setting themselves up to be as dependent on outside sources for their survival as were their ancestors at the middle of the 19th century. Since then, so relentless has been the left's agenda against, particularly, American blacks, that the people—including President Obama himself—who support and perpetuate it through the work of agencies like ACORN, should have been exposed long ago.

Their intent and their practices are nothing short of criminal.

ACORN grew out of the National Welfare Rights Organization (NWRO), an organization that came into being in the mid 1960s after the passage of the so-called Great Society legislation as part of the Cloward-Piven strategy to bring down America's capitalist economy. Its leader was an alienated Chemistry Professor named George Wiley. The group was founded for the purpose of removing restrictions on eligibility requirements for people receiving welfare. It was thought that burdening the welfare system with so many new welfare recipients would bring it to a standstill. This, as the founders' reasoning went, would force "a radical reconstruction of America's unjust capitalist economy." [11]

The group was highly successful in achieving its goals. Thanks to NWRO, welfare rolls more than doubled in the decade after it initiated its strategy, but the results weren't quite what had been envisioned. The huge increase in the number of people dependent on government for their sustenance fostered dramatic increases in crime, drug abuse, and poverty among inner city poor people. It also created a backlash against welfare mothers, in no small part because of the disintegration of the family in America's inner cities that it caused.

Among other things, the NWRO's efforts contributed to a huge spike in births to unwed mothers, to the point where today more than 70 percent of all births to African-American women are born out of marriage.[12] It's managed to effect this consequence—it may well be an intended consequence—through lobbying and demonstrating on behalf of bringing increasing numbers of low-income American women onto welfare rolls.

In fact, it wasn't until the mid-1990s that welfare reform legislation reversed the trend of increasing numbers of families on welfare and brought so many formerly dependent and unproductive people back into the economic mainstream. From a peak of five million families on welfare in the mid-1900s prior to welfare reform, the number had fallen to only 1.6 million by 2009.[13] Today, though, with its return to emphasizing putting more and more people back on the dole as part of its response to the economic downturn, the Obama administration is reversing the trend again through encouraging dependency on welfare, and the number of welfare recipients is again on the rise.

While the NWRO strategy was successful in increasing welfare rolls, it didn't bankrupt the federal government. When George Wiley realized, in the 1970s, that the NWRO was not going to bring about the anti-capitalist revolution he'd envisioned, he sent Wade Rathke, an NWRO operative, to Little Rock, Arkansas, where he started the Arkansas Community Organization for Reform Now, the first chapter of what would become, after the first word in its name was changed to Association, ACORN.

Over the next thirty years, ACORN pushed a radical leftist agenda using a highly decentralized model. Rather than function as a top-down organization, the group founded relatively independent local organizations that employed its tactics in order to "improve" the lives of its constituents. The tactics favored by ACORN are described by leftist apologists John Atlas and Peter Dreier in their article, "Enraging the Right." The organization is, as they boastingly point out, "not shy about using . . . in-your-face tactics," including, in one instance in Baltimore, "[piling] garbage in front of City Hall to protest lack of services in poor neighborhoods, wield[ing] huge in-flated rubber sharks to disrupt a bankers' dinner and stag[ing] a protest in front of Mayor Martin O'Malley's home."

Furthermore, the group is described as "unapologetic about its tactics . . . because it not only helps draw public attention to neglected issues but also helps build membership." The results are frequently that "public officials who decry ACORN's tactics wind up agreeing with its agenda—or at least negotiating with its leaders to forge compromises." In sum, thanks to ACORN, the progressive tradition is alive and well, with a policy agenda "in the populist and New Deal tradition of saving unfettered capitalism from excessive greed by pushing for tenement housing reforms, workplace safety laws, the minimum wage, aid to mothers and children, Social Security, the right of workers to organize and bargain collectively for better wages and working conditions, subsidies to house the poor, and policies that encourage banks to make mortgage loans to boost homeownership."[14]

But if the Obama administration's Marxist-socialist roots were forged through Obama's long association with ACORN, his administration is guilty of ties with another, perhaps even more wrongheaded and danger-ous element of the left: the Nation of Islam. These ties were initiated in the 1960s through one of the seminal black nationalist groups, the Black

Panther Party, and continue today through the current administration's ties with that group's offspring, the New Black Panther Party.

If ACORN has been in the spotlight recently because of O'Keefe's and Giles's exposure of its absolute corruption, it is in fact only one of many such leftist organizations intent on keeping American blacks in poverty and despair for the purpose of enabling the takeover of the United States by Marxists. The New Black Panther Party, while its ostensible purpose is to free blacks through revolutionary means, is, like ACORN, perpetuating poverty and suffering among its constituents.

The most comprehensive and unapologetic history of the original Black Panther Party can be found, appropriately enough, at the website Marxists. org in a section about the history of the "workers" movement in the United States. Never mind that Huey Newton and Bobby Seale, founders of the original Black Panther Party in the 1960s, probably never worked a day in their lives but were small-time petty thugs who disguised their criminal intent behind the beard of working to "establish revolutionary socialism through organizing and community based programs." The website goes on to explain:

> from the tenets of Maoism they set the role of their Party as the vanguard of the revolution and worked to establish a united front, while from Marxism they addressed the capitalist economic system, embraced the theory of dialectical materialism, and represented the need for all workers to forcefully take over the means of production.[15]

After a tumultuous history marked by rampant criminal activities—the group sold copies of Chairman Mao's infamous Little Red Book, *Quotations from Chairman Mao Zedong*, on college campuses in order to raise money to purchase weapons—internal strife, and conflict with local and federal authorities—J. Edgar Hoover called the Panthers the "greatest threat to the internal security of the country"—the group disbanded in the early 1980s as its leaders were either imprisoned, killed, or sank into disillusionment and drug dependency.

By the early 1990s, though, the New Black Panther Party was formed to carry on the dubious work of its predecessor. The motto of the New Black Panther Party is "Freedom or Death." The lead stories in the Spring 2010 edition of the group's newspaper, *The New Black Panther*, the organization's self-described "Fastest Growing Black National Newspaper," paint a picture of the "New Black Panther Party under fire," particularly from "Congress" and the "Right Wing."[16] New Black Panther Party leader Malik Zulu Shabazz, the author of a feature article on Party founder Dr. Khallid Abdul Muhammad in "The New Black Panther," describes Muhammad in glowing terms: He stayed "true to core Black Muslim teachings, Nationalist Pan-Africanist Ideology and Revolutionary Doctrine in a time when everybody else was running for cover." The article features a picture of Muhammad brandishing an automatic rifle.[17]

Are you starting to get the picture?

It is the "core Black Muslim teachings" that Shabazz refers to that bear closer examination than American journalists have done. First, they're straight out of the 1960s radical left Muslim playbook. The Nation of Islam combines all the dangerous anti-Christian, anti-western teachings of the religion of Islam with a racist message of hate for the white man. You probably weren't aware of this, but according to the Honorable Elijah Muhammad, the founder of the Nation of Islam in America:

> The entire creation of Allah (God) is of peace, not including the devils who are not the creation of Allah (God) but a race created by an enemy (Yakub) of Allah. . . . These enemies of Allah (God) are known at the present as the white race or European race.[18]

Muhammad clarifies, explaining that the white man is "the devil."

The "Yakub" Muhammad refers to is, according to the Nation of Islam version of the history of humankind, a mad scientist, a man who, more than eight thousand years ago, "embittered of Allah. . . . decided, as revenge, to create upon the earth a devil race, a bleached-out, white race of people."[19] Mr. Yakub did that by systematically genetically engineering a new race of people. In order to further his purpose to enslave the black race, Yakub began to separate out the children.

As the Nation of Islam website explains, "We know that Mr. Yakub set up a rigorous birth control system at the beginning of his civilization, by dividing the brown babies from the black, the brown from the reds, the reds from the yellow. Now bear in mind these are only the major solutions, for there were *nine* more lighter colors that came after these."[20]

It's on this sort of perverse and distorted belief system that the Nation of Islam—whose followers call themselves Black Muslims—was built, and it's this belief system, which rests on a hatred of white people that is systematized in the beliefs and preachings of the sect's founder and in those of the Black Muslim leaders that have followed him. They form the foundation of yet another radical leftist group with direct ties to the Obama administration.

The New Black Panther Party's connections to the Obama administration are manifest in the special treatment they're receiving from Attorney General Eric Holder. They're further manifested in the administration's pursuit of the political agenda formulated and followed by the Panthers and other Marxist organizations.

The Enslaving Politics of Color

One of the most devastating effects of the activities of groups such as ACORN and the New Black Panther Party is their reduction of a racially identified group of people to the status of pawns in a leftist power play. Minorities, especially inner city blacks, have seen the individuality they had been trying to recover as they emerged from slavery systematically stripped from them as they were grouped together by the Marxist militants, with whom Barack Obama and his administration have close ties, for the purpose of advancing their leftist "causes."

This type of identity politics is rampant in the Obama administration and among black leaders in general. Although its purpose is ostensibly to promote the interests of blacks and other groups identified by race, ethnicity, or sexual orientation, in fact, the practice of separating out groups of people leads to their interests being subsumed in the greater purpose of the left: to gain power.

The 2008 presidential campaign provides the classic example of how

Democrats use identity politics as the basis for almost all their strategic decisions. One of the first things Hillary Clinton brought up when she ended her
campaign and endorsed Barack Obama for the presidency was her "gender":

> I was proud to be running as a woman, but I was running
> because I thought I would be the best president. But I am a
> woman, and like millions of women I know there are still bar-
> riers and biases out there, often unconscious, and I want to
> build an America that embraces and respects the potential of
> every last one of us. We must make sure that women and men
> alike understand the struggles of their grandmothers and their
> mothers and that women enjoy equal opportunities, equal pay
> and equal respect.[21]

But if Hillary Clinton was engaging in identity politics by playing the
gender card, *Old York Times* columnist Bob Herbert who, as a true affirmative action journalist, is always ready to remind us that he's black, was ready
with the race card. After Clinton had conceded the nomination to Obama,
Herbert referred in his "celebratory" column to Bobby Kennedy's picturing, in the late 1960s, America electing a black president within forty years:
"The fact that even a dreamer could imagine nothing shorter than a 40-year
timeline gives us a glimpse of the nightmarish depths of racial oppression
that people of goodwill have had to fight."

Herbert, like all left-leaning liberals, insists on telling us of the egregious
inequities that held at the time Kennedy made his prediction. Instead of cel-
ebrating the fact that a woman and a black man were the contenders for the
Democratic presidential nomination, he wallows in the statistical inequities
of the 1960s: "Fewer than 1% of all federal judges were women, fewer than
4% of all lawyers, and fewer than 7% of doctors."[22] Of course, the kicker is
that it wasn't Democrats or those on the left who really championed equal
rights for minorities.

Herbert, as is the tendency of Marxist sympathizers in general, is either
ignorant of history or is engaging in the common leftist practice of rewriting it. Perhaps both are true. While he cites the examples of inequity in the
'60s, what he fails to point out is that it was Republicans, and not Dem-

ocrats, who actually enabled, for instance, then-President Lyndon Johnson's Civil Rights legislation to pass. Republican Senator Everett Dirksen was called on by Johnson to lead the vote in the Senate. As a result, while twenty-one Democrats voted *against* the Civil Rights Act only six Republicans did so. Republicans did the right thing, and Democrats would have obstructed passage of the Civil Rights Act.

And Herbert conveniently manages to overlook the fact that it was a Republican, President Dwight D. Eisenhower, and not a Democrat, who mobilized federal troops in support of the integration of Little Rock, Arkansas's public schools in 1957, following the landmark 1954 *Brown v. Board of Education* decision. Without the support of Republicans, the anti-civil-rights Democrats in the Senate would have torpedoed President Johnson's Great Society legislation, which has unfortunately turned out in retrospect to be a budget-busting entitlement that has essentially created a permanent minority underclass in the United States dependent for its very survival on federal largesse.

If Republicans had not supported the bill, they'd have been branded as racists, even though not supporting it would have been the right thing for them to do. The fact that Democrats voted in large numbers against the legislation is conveniently ignored by commentators like Herbert, even though, as we look back, they were, without knowing it, voting to save blacks from the terrible fate of once again becoming slaves to their white massas. Democrats did the right thing because they were racists; Republicans did the wrong thing because they weren't. It's identity politics at its most perverse.

Always ready to pull out the club of identity politics in their search for reasons to denigrate America, leftists insist on mouthing such absurdities as this:

> No doubt there has been a decline in the overt expression of race and gender bias [in the past 40 years]. But in the most fundamental sense, in class and economic terms, America is more unequal today than at any time since the days of the Robber Barons in the late nineteenth century.
>
> The top one percent in American society controls more than 45 percent of the wealth. The top one-tenth of one percent has mo-

nopolized nearly the entire increase in national wealth over the last two decades, while the vast majority of the people have seen their living conditions deteriorate, their jobs become more precarious, their overall social position become more insecure.

For black workers and youth, the decline has been even more precipitous. It is hardly necessary to recite the well-known figures: more young black men in prison than in college, crumbling schools and other social services in the inner cities, poverty levels once again approaching those of the early 1960s, disproportionate levels of unemployment, drug abuse, violence, homelessness and other social evils.[23]

The fact is that the author of these lines is right: all those things he cites are rampant today, especially in our inner cities. But they have gotten worse not because we *didn't* try to address them through socialist, identity-politics-based legislative initiatives, but because that's the way we *did* address them. It is precisely because of policies that have their origin in the left's insistence on seeing people as members of groups rather than as individuals that these conditions have worsened. Identity politics legislation invariably brings about precisely the opposite of its stated outcomes because it subsumes the individual in the group. In denying individuality and the strength and creativity of the human spirit, it dehumanizes those it seeks to help.

Such legislative initiatives reflect a fundamental inability of those on the left to understand an important economic principle: There's not a finite and limited amount of capital that somehow needs to be "redistributed"; rather, capital is created by people and is an unlimited and unending resource through which people can lift themselves out of the prison of poverty through individual initiative. Legislation that fails to recognize the creative power of the individual spirit if it is given the freedom and the economic tools to realize its limitless potential merely creates dependency.

Identity politics insists on seeing people as caricatures, exaggerated, distorted versions of the human beings they are at heart. It insists on seeing minorities based strictly on the color of their skin and on the assumption that if they're black, they're not capable of fending for themselves and need some sort of big brother to protect them. It's precisely this soul-killing, enterprise-denying nature of leftist identity politics that makes it so dangerous and so wrong. It's precisely because it is so dangerous that the legislative initiatives of President Obama, who insists on dehumanizing so many Americans by demanding that the government interfere in every aspect of their lives, must be turned back.

The Myth of the Living Wage

Democrats seem to view the concept of wages in the same way they view the U.S. Constitution: As something "living" that they should be allowed to change at their whim. They demonstrate no understanding whatsoever of what's involved in running a business. Look no further than the makeup of Obama's advisory staff: Between 30 and 60 percent of the cabinet advisors appointed by every other president over the past century have been from the private sector, reflecting the recognition by our nation's Chief Executives that they need to get input from people who have real-world experience.

By contrast, only 8 percent of Obama's cabinet comes from the private sector, and too many of these are from a single organization, Goldman Sachs.

What's worse is that 92 percent of the president's cabinet appointees are either government flaks or "college pudding," as late Beatle John Lennon so aptly described these ivory-tower know-nothings.[24] The reason this is the case is that anyone who's had any private sector business experience knows what a sham the leftist, community-organizer agenda supported by the president is.

The "living wage" movement has been championed by radical leftist political groups such as ACORN, which founded the Living Wage campaign in 1995 in cooperation with several unions, including the United Food and Commercial Workers International Union (UFCW) and the Service Employees International Union (SEIU).[25] Both groups have been lobbying to get municipalities to pass legislation that requires employers to pay more than the federal minimum wage to their "low-income"—formerly "unskilled"—workers. The movement has been very successful, if by "success" you mean driving employers to reduce their use of unskilled labor and to move their operations out of cities that have instituted living-wage policies.

That means that in cities which have passed living-wage laws, residents now face diminishing employment opportunities and a reduced standard of living. Like the minimum wage, the so-called "living wage" requires, in cities where it is passed, that designated employers pay an hourly wage to their employees that would sustain "a family of four based on an area's cost of living"[26] if it were extended out to full-time employment. In other words, if the cost of living in a specific area were determined to be $40,000 a year for a family of four, the living wage for that area would be $20 an hour.

The living wage movement has also broadened out into other areas under the umbrella concept "sustainable economics." The socialistic policies favored under this agenda include such things as the provision of money for job training programs, so-called "socially responsible banking" (which includes making ill-advised loans to those unable to pay them back), and "environmentally friendly" projects.[27] And to the charge that the living wage movement is not a socialist movement, ACORN, failing to recognize the irony, has actually published a manual entitled "The Living Wage undercuts the incentive to privatize." It's a blatant attempt to bring more and more local, state, and, because the president is considering living wage legislation on the national level, federal contracts under government control.

Studies conducted by David Neumark of the University of California, Irvine, indicate that the effects of living wage laws are often harmful for the populations they're supposed to help. In general, even when wages are as much as 50 percent higher than the federal minimum wage, no increase in income levels is realized by those employed. Such laws also reduce unemployment among unskilled, low-income workers by only 3 to 6 percent. This despite the fact that the percentage of unemployed workers that fall into this category ranges from 15 to 25 percent depending on the area surveyed.

It's a miniscule improvement that has other consequences that are insidious, among them the fact that, because the wages they're required to pay are so high, many contractors hire skilled workers instead of unskilled labor, because skilled workers can be utilized in a number of ways, unlike unskilled workers. In addition, many potential contractors decide to opt out of such projects, meaning there's less competition in bidding for the work. This translates into higher costs for the government, which in turn manifest as greater pressure on what is required of taxpayers.[28]

The consequences of living wage legislation aren't simply measurable by statistics, though. In Oakland, California, the city invested more than $100,000 in improvements to a 3,000-square-foot restaurant location. Because the city had invested that much money in the location, this particular spot, which was being offered to restaurant companies as a location where they might open a new facility, was bound by living wage laws. Other Oakland restaurants were not operating under the same restrictions. The result?

Eight potential bidders to open a restaurant at the location decided that the additional $175,000 to $225,000 a year in operating costs that would result from their having to pay employees because of living wage laws made the project unworkable for them. Oakland's other restaurants, because city taxpayer money had not been invested in their properties, are not required to pay a "living wage" to their employees; trying to compete with other businesses not bound by the same rules is simply not feasible, and so another employment opportunity is lost to Oakland residents.[29]

One commentator describes ACORN's tactics and ties them to the financial irregularities in the group's accounting:

"In Baltimore, the group stormed banks in an effort to shut them down over foreclosures, sought to physically disrupt auctions of foreclosed homes on the steps of the courthouse and, while television cameras rolled, broke the padlock on a foreclosed home in an effort to reclaim it for its owner. Is it any wonder that its tax advice wasn't by the book?"[30]

Among other concerns that arise when living wage legislation is considered are the effects on wage-earners' eligibility to receive other benefits. The proposal to implement living wage laws in New York City brought up this possibility:

Especially in cities like New York with a high cost of living, low-wage earners and their families often depend on public support in order to get by from month to month. For example, they may receive Medicaid, food stamps, or help with rent. But these programs are only available to families with very low incomes, and so the wage hike being proposed could potentially make families ineligible for benefits that they used to receive. Moreover, higher earnings will very likely mean higher taxes, as well as lower tax credits (such as the Earned Income Tax Credit). The fear, then, is that the families we are concerned about might actually end up worse off under the living wage law.[31]

But the living wage movement also impacts the quality of life of those where such laws are in effect in other ways. One of the consequences of such legislation is that it either keeps companies such as Wal-Mart and other big box retailers out of the areas where the laws are in effect, or it drives them out after they've located there. This means that, not only are residents of such areas denied employment opportunities, they're also penalized by not having access to the low priced goods that outlets such as Wal-Mart provide. Living wage laws, which broadly apply to any companies contracting with cities to do work, also dramatically raise the cost of such contracts. Because of this, they tend to level the playing field for labor unions, making them "more competitive" with nonunion contractors.

The Obama administration isn't content to let the living wage campaign be conducted only on the local level, though. In yet another example of the president's support for radical socialist causes, there is news of "a plan taking shape in the White House to rewrite federal contracting rules to give bidding advantages to those companies that pay higher wages and offer more health and pension benefits to workers in unskilled jobs—from janitors and landscaping crews to cafeteria workers at federal facilities."[32]

In other words, the president is nationalizing what had heretofore been only local initiatives to keep, especially, inner-city minorities enslaved as members of the permanent underclass. As unproductive as the results of the campaign have been in our cities, the president is determined to nationalize yet another failed leftist agenda item.

Driving Big Box Retailers Out of Cities

In addition, though, to keeping inner-city residents on the "reservation," so to speak, the policies supported by Obama harm the chances of our nation's poorest for gainful employment that might make it possible for them to move out of the inner city or better their lives there and, as I've mentioned, also diminish their quality of life by reducing their access to low-priced goods. In the more than eighty cities that have implemented living wage laws, one of the effects has been to discourage companies such as "big box" retailers like Wal-Mart from locating stores in inner city areas.[33]

One of the ways ACORN has found to keep such retailers from locating in areas where they would compete with union shops and businesses that are required to pay a "living wage" is to stage demonstrations against them. Gregory Hession describes how ACORN manages such protests:

> ACORN partners with wealthy trade unions that pay ACORN large sums of money to organize a labor protest. ACORN, in turn, hires protestors, paying them poverty-level wages with no benefits, to agitate against Wal-Mart and other retailers for allegedly paying poor wages and no benefits. Ironically, those ACORN picketers often earn less than the ones inside the retailers that are the object of the picketing.[34]

In fact, picketers working for ACORN and other advocate groups typically earn *less* than the federal minimum wage and *less* than employees of the companies against whom they're picketing. Why am I not surprised? On one protest site in Nevada, picketers were making $6 an hour with no benefits to walk around in the blazing sun for five hours a day, with two ten-minute breaks. In the Wal-Mart against which they were picketing, workers were being paid $6.75 an hour and enjoyed air-conditioning in the workplace. ACORN "seeks exemption from paying minimum wage increases which it demands from employers it pickets, has to be forced by government to pay overtime to its employees, completely misses wage payments to many of its workers, and engages in union busting tactics against its own workers who are agitating for unions at places like Wal-Mart for sub-par wages."[35]

One of the unions that hires ACORN to do its dirty work is the United Food and Commercial Workers International Union (UFCW). In fact, the UFCW has a vendetta against Wal-Mart. The headline of a screed on its website cries, "How Much Is Wal-Mart Scamming Your State." The ironies are devastating. Even as labor unions are receiving exemptions from the so-called Cadillac Health Care Plan tax, the UFCW rails against Wal-Mart for "using tax loopholes and fancy accounting schemes" to avoid paying its fair share of taxes, this while they essentially seize dues from their members' paychecks, demanding obeisance from the workers they "represent."[36]

One commentator sums up the situation succinctly:

You can understand how living-wage legislation might seem reasonable to local legislators, so many of whom have never worked in the private economy. It puts money into the pockets of hardworking low-wage employees at no cost to the city treasury. To oppose it would make you seem like a fat-cat, top-hatted robber baron who relishes the oppression of starving workers. On the other side of the equation, how many city councilmen would understand the thick pile of studies from liberal as well as conservative economists showing conclusively that big hikes in the minimum wage ultimately kill low-wage jobs, as employers replace now-expensive receptionists with newly cost-effective voice-mail systems, say, or pile more duties onto experienced employees instead of hiring additional low-wage beginners?

And how many councilmen would understand that increasing the costs of city contractors today will require them to raise the prices they charge the city tomorrow, requiring eventual tax hikes that will drive employers—and jobs—out of town to cheaper locales, isolating the poor who are left behind?[37]

The push for so-called "living wage" legislation by ACORN and other leftist groups is a perfect example of just how fatuous and dangerous community organizer "causes" can be. That's not only for the companies and local governments they target, but for the people they're designed to help as well.

With friends like ACORN, America's minorities don't need enemies.

Democratic Voter Fraud

While ACORN is certainly the most public leftist entity implicated in voter and tax fraud, in fact, it's only part of the picture. Marxist activists have for decades been organizing and plotting a stealth overthrow of the U.S.

government, and the election of Barack Obama, which was engineered on a foundation of electoral fraud and voter intimidation was seen by the left to represent the opportunity they'd been seeking for the better part of a century.

In order to seal the deal, they needed to perpetrate election fraud far beyond merely fabricating voter registration documents, although ACORN, with the Democratic candidate's full knowledge and implicit approval, was happy to oblige with that. Barack Obama, having cut his political teeth on election fraud, was more than willing to implement many of the techniques he learned in his community organizer days to put his campaign and those of other Democrats he needed to push his agenda over the top.

In September, 2007, Obama declared, "If I am the Democratic nominee, I will aggressively pursue an agreement with the Republican nominee to preserve a publicly financed general election."[38] Earlier in the year, he'd badgered John McCain to agree to the same terms and they'd figuratively shaken hands on it.[39] In one statement, Obama explained that under his plan "both major party candidates [would] agree on a fundraising truce, return excess money from donors, and stay within the public financing system for the general election. . . . If I am the Democratic nominee, I will aggressively pursue an agreement with the Republican nominee to preserve a publicly financed general election."[40]

Of course, that was the furthest thing from Obama's true intentions.

With Obama, you have to watch what he *does*, not what he *says*.

It quickly became apparent to his campaign that to limit his fundraising to public financing would also severely limit the ways it could game the system. The Democratic candidate, as he has done so often in his political career, reneged on his pledge and went full speed ahead with a campaign finance strategy that included accepting money from "bundlers." These bundlers put together packages that included, in many cases, illegal contributions from foreign donors, and rigging credit card screening in ways that disabled the capability to check the identities of those contributing by credit card.

"Bundling," a practice perhaps unintentionally encouraged by the McCain-Feingold Campaign Finance Reform legislation in 2002, allows a single individual to collect together small donations from individual donors

and "bundle" them together in one contribution. It's the "practice of pool-
ing together a large number of contributions from PACs and individuals in
order to maximize the political influence of the bundler and the interests
they represent. Most often, the bundler is a corporate executive or lobbyist,
with expectations of something in return."[41]

In an age in which the amount of money raised often determines a candidate's political viability, bundling has become one of the chief methods
of raising cash. In the 2008 presidential election, bundling accounted for
more than 25 percent of all the money raised by Barack Obama and John
McCain. And because the names of those bundling campaign contributions
are not required to be disclosed, the process is ripe for manipulating.[42]

In one case, tens of thousands of dollars were contributed to the Obama
campaign by one Monir Edwan, a bundler from the town of Rafah in the
Gaza Strip. Monir had raised the money he sent Obama by selling Obama
T-shirts to young Arabs for the princely sum of $9 each, a great deal of
money for impoverished Gazans.[43] Although it is illegal for presidential candidates to accept contributions from foreign nationals like Monir, such support poured in to the Obama campaign from over fifty countries, often in
the form of small donations from contributors "with names such as 'Hbkjb,'
'jkbkj,' and 'Doodad.'"[44] Perhaps the contributions from those suffering
under terrorist rule in Gaza reflected their sense that the candidate they
were supporting would turn out to support their hatred of Israel and their
wish to eliminate the Jewish state.

Credit card fraud was one of the tactics of choice used by the president
to swell his campaign coffers. Not only did the Obama campaign corrupt
the system through its practice of accepting bundled contributions from
foreign donors, they also employed the tactic of disabling identity checks
on credit card donors in order to allow multiple contributions by single donors that exceeded the limits election law said they could donate. Normally,
when systems are set up to accept credit card payments, protocols are put
in place to confirm that the identity of the person making the payment
matches the one to whom the credit card is assigned.

Commentator Tom Blumer explains in the case of the Obama campaign, it's "virtually impossible that the system for accepting card contributions was inadvertently set up without adequate controls, and almost certain

that existing controls were instead deliberately disabled to create untraceability." The total amount thus collected very likely ran to tens of millions of dollars.[45]

Of course, once Obama had secured the presidency, with the help of rampant election fraud on many fronts, he needed a veto-proof majority in the Senate to enact legislation that would enable him to advance the leftist agenda. Enter Al Franken and the Democratic political thugs seasoned in stealing elections. You didn't think Al Franken's election to the U.S. Senate was in any way fair, did you?

The Secretary of State Project, a not-for-profit "527" corporation, has as one of its agenda items "putting Democrats in jobs where they can 'protect elections.' " The SOS, as it is sometimes known, was founded by MoveOn .org principal James Rucker with financial and organizational assistance from George Soros and several of his comrades. The Secretary of State Project made campaign contributions to Mark Ritchie, the Democrat who's the Secretary of State in Minnesota and who was charged with overseeing the election that ended up seating Al Franken as a U.S. Senator from that state.

Don't think for one minute that it's a coincidence that Ritchie is also an ally of ACORN.[46] Although Republican Norm Coleman won the election by 725 votes, by the time Ritchie and his cohorts finished manipulating the vote count, Franken had picked up "new" votes that totaled "more than all the changes for all the precincts in the entire state for the Presidential, Congressional and statehouse races combined (482 votes)."[47] Franken "won" the sixtieth Democratic seat, although he trailed by double digits in opinion polling just before the election.

You Don't Need an Acorn to Know Which Way the Oak Grows

Nearly two years into the Obama presidency, we're able to gather enough evidence to assess how the administration is progressing toward its goal of making all Americans subservient to its radical agenda. The news is disturbing at best. From his association with such radical leftist groups as ACORN, the SEIU and other labor unions, and the patently Islamo-fascist New Black Panther Party to his willingness to engage in the most corrupt electoral practices, the president is making clear his intent to stamp out individuality and the human spirit and replace it with an ugly repressive regime that tramples on the notion of American liberty.

From the early days of his presidential campaign, Obama made it very clear where his sympathies lay. As commentator Mike Baker puts it, "The endorsement of the New Black Panther Party was posted on Barack Obama's website. Why was this tolerated unless Barack Obama wanted their endorsement? If he does not want their endorsement, how much control over his staff is he going to have once he's elected President?"[48] Obama's Nation of Islam ties don't end with a mere website posting, though.

The former treasurer of Obama's U.S. Senate campaign, Cynthia K. Miller, is a member of the Nation of Islam, as was Obama's Director of Constituent Services, Jennifer Mason, during his time in the Senate. Obama also has close ties with Islamist Palestinian activist Ali Abunimah, who, along with the Obamas, attended a fund-raising dinner at which the keynote speaker was Edward Said, who had been an advisor to former PLO chairman Yasser Arafat.[49] And in the latest affront to America's people and their support of the struggle against Islamo-Fascism, the Obama administration allowed deported Muslim scholar Tariq Ramadan back in the country to promote his own brand of Islamism.

Ramadan's smarmy, disingenuous "hope" for America is that we won't, "in the name of [our] fear or mistrust of Muslim-majority countries, . . . end up betraying [our] own values." Ramadan's visa had been revoked in 2004 because he had contributed money to an Islamist organization that was on the U.S. terrorist list, but the ACLU sued on his behalf to have it reinstated. He was permitted to return after Hillary Clinton signed an order enabling him to re-enter the country, while doing nothing to have Michael Savage's name removed from the UK list of banned terrorists and murderers.[50]

And don't be fooled by the fact that it appears as though the efforts of O'Keefe and Giles have crippled ACORN, the Marxist component of the Marxist-Islamist thrust of the Obama administration. ACORN lives on, even if it's being forced to close many of its offices. It lives on in the practices, policies, legislative initiatives, and sympathies of the Obama administration, with its hatred of white people and its implicit commitment to the Marxist principles on which ACORN was built.

Likewise, ACORN lives on in the form of numerous ACORN affiliates and front groups, including Wake Up Wal-Mart, Wal-Mart Organizing Project, Wal-Mart Alliance for Reform Now, Site Fighters, and the Wal-Mart Workers Association, all of whom perpetuate ACORN's anti-business agenda. Add in such labor unions as SEIU and UFCW, along with the leftist Secretary of State Project, and you have the foundation for Obama's ongoing assault on free elections and free enterprise.[51]

One of the things that so many so-called analysts miss is the fact that Barack Obama, while he may not technically be a practicing Muslim—the jury is still out on that point—is very much a Muslim sympathizer. It's amazing to see pundits wonder why Obama treats Israel, one of the United States' most important allies, not just in the Middle East but in the world, so badly. When you see our president looking the other way as Iran rushes toward its goal of having nuclear missiles while he comes down hard on Israel for developing real estate in its own capital city, Jerusalem, you begin to understand what a perversely leftist moral equivalency Barack Obama created.

What is it about the fact that Obama is a Muslim sympathizer that analysts don't understand? What is it about the fact that Barack Obama is in sympathy with the radically absurd Nation of Islam version of Arabs versus Jews that is so difficult to comprehend? It's a wonder Obama hasn't referred to New York City as "hymie town," as his anti-Semite associate Jesse Jackson once did.

White people are the devil incarnate if you buy into Nation of Islam founder Elijah Muhammad's version of the evolutionary process. And Obama seems to buy into it. His sympathy for the Nation of Islam extends to include that group's hatred of Jews as he ignores Israel's plight, rudely dismisses the Israeli Prime Minister during the latter's visit to the United States, nods his approval through silence when Mahmoud Ahmadinejad threatens to drive Israel into the sea, and holds up shipments of bunker buster bombs to Israel to make sure Iran's nuclear weapons development program is not interfered with.

Barack Obama seems to harbor a deep and visceral mistrust, not to say an outright hatred, of the United States and Israel and the freedom they represent. His long associations with such radical anti-American groups as

ACORN and the New Black Panther Party reinforce that mistrust, and it is becoming institutionalized in the policies and legislative initiatives currently being pursued and enacted in the Obama administration.

From the outright disrespect he's displayed toward Israeli Prime Minister Bebe Netanyahu to his insistence that Israel is the culprit holding up the Middle East peace process and his demands that the Israelis stop building settlements in their own capital city, Obama has made a strong case that he sympathizes with the notion that Israel should not be allowed to survive. Like ACORN and the New Black Panther Party and so many other black–Black Muslim radical political groups, Obama continually demonstrates his race-based enmity toward Jews and those who support them.

Domestically, his support for policies designed to keep minorities on the dole through encouraging the re-invigoration of the welfare state demonstrates that, far from being a champion of minorities, he uses them cynically, subsidizing failure in exchange for their votes. His open calls for blacks, Hispanics, and other minorities to support the Democratic Party in the mid-term elections of 2010 reinforce the racist bias of his administration. Obama is certainly in sympathy, if not in league, with would-be revolutionaries like ACORN and the Black Muslims. His actions and policies indicate that he's committed to helping them advance their anti-American agenda.

CHAPTER 9

School Daze:
Eliminating the Propaganda Ministry

It would be good . . . if (Obama) could be dictator
for a few years because he could do a lot of good things quickly.
—Woody Allen[1]

The unofficial Obama Ministry of Propaganda has managed to adopt a disturbingly skewed, anti-capitalistic, anti-personal freedom, anti-spiritual, rule-by-the-gentility vision of what the world should be, and they're damned if they'll be stopped from trying to impose that empty, nihilistic view on the middle class. The current iteration of the U.S. Ministry of Propaganda isn't made up only of members of the press—once the fourth estate but now the fifth column—who have been in Obama's hip pocket since the presidential campaign of 2008 began. It encompasses other institutions, including American schools, that perpetuate the leftist version of "the big lie" that today threatens to turn our representative democracy into a dictatorship favored by Marxist fellow travelers like *Old York Times* columnist, Thomas L. Friedman. It includes the U.S. film industry and many Hollywood filmmakers who continue to insist on producing movies that promote a leftist agenda.

Look no further than Friedman. In an op-ed piece entitled, "Is China the Next Enron?"[2] Friedman offers an assessment of China's place in the world, one that illuminates the political left's attitudes toward America and toward representative government. It's his contention that "when [a country] is led by a reasonably enlightened group of people, as China is today, . . . that one party can just impose the politically difficult but critically important policies needed to move a society forward in the 21st century."

The policies Friedman is referring to include dictating that a society's industries pursue such technologies as "electric cars, solar power, energy efficiency, batteries, nuclear power and wind power." In other words, Friedman is ignoring the abject fiscal failures of every socialist-communist government of the past century. In fact, he's promoting for the United States precisely the same communist-style dictatorship as those who engaged in criminally negligent homicide in the name of a managed economy in Red China and the Soviet Union during that time.

Friedman goes on: "Our one-party democracy is worse." He insists that in America "only the Democrats are really playing." By "playing," he means trying to force America down the same ill-advised technology development path that China, very likely to its ultimate economic detriment, is traveling. This is 21st-century state-speak at its worst by a writer who's a member of this administration's unofficial and loosely organized Ministry of Propaganda.

It's Friedman's modus operandi to spew assertions unbuttressed by fact in his writing. The fact is that he is apparently neither intelligent enough nor informed enough to understand America's place in history and to compare it with the state-run economies of, for instance, the Soviet Union or Red China in the 20th century. Unfortunately, it's a problem he shares with so many others who have been blinded by the leftist ideology. Friedman's ersatz arguments are typical of leftists who, having been indoctrinated rather than educated, don't understand that propagandistic assertions are not the same as reasoned arguments. His insistence that tyranny is better than democracy is absurd on its face, but because so many on the left have adopted that position, it needs to be dealt with.

The fact that there has emerged a kind of loosely defined Ministry of Propaganda on the left reflects the fact that the Marxists of the last century never really went away; they only went underground.

The Obama administration is pursuing the same strategy—assertion rather than argument, bullying rather than persuading—that's been pursued by single-party regimes and their Ministries of Propaganda throughout history to enslave their people. In fact, in an important sense, Friedman is nothing more than a cog in the emerging leftist Ministry of Propaganda in the United States. It's not an official department, but because of the leftist educational hegemony and the complicity of the so-called "mainstream media" in perpetuating the left's anti-American, anti-Democratic message, it serves much the same function as such ministries served in the Soviet Union during the 20th century and in such dictatorships as that in Iran today.

With its emerging Ministry of Propaganda, America under Barack Obama is pursuing a similar course to other countries that currently have official ministries. These include those sparkling examples of democracy Egypt, Iran, Kuwait, and the United Kingdom. Iraq's Ministry of Information was disbanded after Saddam Hussein was deposed, but who can forget Muhammad Saeed al-Sahaf. Remember that piece of work? During the American invasion of Iraq, he blindly asserted before an international television audience that things were fine in Baghdad. He claimed American troops were being repulsed on every front—despite the fact that the sounds of American tanks only a few blocks away from where he was speaking could be heard in the background.

We're getting lies equivalent to that whopper out of Obama's administration and the *press corpse* daily, and the results, if those lies are allowed to go unchallenged, will be only slightly less devastating for the United States than those al-Sahaf and Friedman insist on perpetuating.

And, as was the case in more than half a century ago, when anti-Americanism threatened to overwhelm us, it might just be time for a return of the House Committee on Un-American Activities. HUAC, as it was known, unflinchingly outed suspected communists and their associates and required their testimony before Congress. What is particularly disturbing, though, is that the reason we need to bring back HUAC today is to weed out Marxists at the very top of the current federal government. It's the people running the government, from the Chief Executive on down, we should fear for their un-American propensities.

How the Obama Ministry of Progapanda Works

In many ways, what's happening in the United States today mirrors what was happening at the middle of the last century. Only then, the people who operated the communist Ministries of Propaganda were primarily in other countries. A relatively small number of communist agents were infiltrators of the U.S. Government. Of course, the *Old York Times* was always ready to answer the leftist call and promote Marxist causes. Today, though, far from being a threat from outside our country, the Ministry of Propaganda that spews leftist-slanted "news" is a functioning component of our own leftist administration, supplemented by members and supporters who work as educators and in the entertainment and communications industries in the United States.

The first decade of the 21st century has become the '50s on steroids, thanks to the proliferation and homogenization of many media outlets. Among print media, it's not just the *New York Times* that promotes the anti-American agenda, but newspapers, albeit dying newspapers, in every city that toe the administration's hate-the-U.S. line. And although spewing anti-American venom is demonstrably bad for business, most TV news outlets also ignore their plummeting ratings and continue to hew to the leftist message.

The aftermath of the Democrats' victory over the American people through their passage of healthcare legislation demonstrates several of the key ways the left gets its message out. The message in this instance is that anyone who opposed health care and didn't buckle under to political pressure is mean, nasty, and racist. One conservative columnist explains how that message gets sent, describing it this way:

> . . . the well-prepared stunt of having several members of the Congressional Black Caucus walk above ground to the Capitol on the evening of the vote, rather than through the underground tunnels. Their route took them past a noisy crowd of tea party protesters. Two members later claimed that they had run a gauntlet of ugly racial slurs. Representative John Lewis, D-Ga., said, "I haven't heard anything like this in 40, 45 years.

Since the march to Selma, really." Representative Emanuel Cleaver, D-Mo., claimed that he was spat upon. . . . Headlines were assured.[3]

Although Congressman Cleaver claimed he was spat on by a protester, video of the incident, examined frame by frame with Zapruder-worthy intensity, produced no evidence of intent to expectorate. Ignoring the fact that there were no grounds to prosecute in the first place, Cleaver magnanimously refused to press charges against his so-called "attacker."[4]

In other words, Democrats themselves typically create the situations, make the threats, or perform the acts that incite violence (throwing bricks through their own Democratic campaign office windows, for instance, or walking conspicuously past protesters just prior to a controversial vote). Then they blame conservatives, using trumped up or phantom threats or acts of violence in order to show how thuggish conservatives are. They're not above using these set-ups to raise money from Democrat supporters by playing on the fear factor they themselves have created, either.

David Axelrod, senior advisor to President Obama, explained how Democrats capitalize on such incidents. In response to questions about letters sent out to Democrats in order to raise funds based on the supposed threats that followed passage of healthcare legislation, Axelrod confirmed that such threats are "not out of bounds to use as fundraising tool."[5]

Creating an incident of violence, or even political incorrectness, against your own allies and framing the political enemy for the deed is accurately described as perpetrating a mini-Kristallnacht. The name refers to the 1938 burning of the Reichstag likely perpetrated by Nazis but blamed on their opposition. The Democratic Party's use of the method is part of the latest iteration of the tactic, and although its use by Nazis was far more brutal and far-reaching, resulting immediately in the deaths and deportation of tens of thousands of Jews and the destruction of thousands of Jewish businesses, the ultimate intent of Democrats' using the tactic is very similar: the takeover of a nation by tyrants.

The contemporary U.S. ministry of propaganda is complicit in this tactic.

They vilify conservatives and Republicans for reprehensible behavior often committed surreptitiously by Democrats' own, while ignoring precisely the same tactics committed by Democrats against Republicans, conservatives, and Tea Party members. *New York Times* columnist Paul Krugman, for instance, has no problem telling his readers to "hang Senator Joe Lieberman in effigy" for the latter's resistance to the public option in Obama's healthcare bill.[6] And writing in the *Washington ComPost*, left-liberal columnist Courtland Milloy relishes the thought of knocking "every racist and homophobic tooth out of their [Tea Party members'] Cro-Magnon heads."[7] The irony of the contrast between Milloy's acerbic words and the title of his piece, "Congressmen show grace, restraint in the face of disrespect," seems to be beyond Milloy's intellectual capacity to comprehend.

In fact, it's overwhelmingly Democrats and others on the left who perpetrate hate speech in an attempt to brand their enemies. Washington Democratic Congressman Brian Baird used the term "lynch mob tactics"— a blatantly cynical attempt to liken opponents of our black president to Ku Klux Klan members—and compared those opposed to Obama's healthcare legislation to "Timothy McVeigh" in one of his speeches.[8]

Inciting to violence has been a leftist tactic for decades, but it became especially prevalent during the presidency of George W. Bush. The vitriol spewed out at Bush was unimaginably vile and excessive, and the chance to use it without fear of retribution by a complicit journalistic corps brought radical leftists out of the woodwork. Referring to Bush as a Nazi was about as common as it was unreported. Not only wasn't it *not* news when a fraudulent idiot like the University of Colorado's Ward Churchill used the term to label the president, since most of the mainstream media couldn't find anything wrong with the practice, journalists couldn't find any grounds on which even to consider that it might be newsworthy.

Websites such as oreilly-sucks.com posted pieces with titles like "Bush is Becoming More Like Hitler Everyday."[9] British playwright Harold Pinter and decades-past-her-prime American rock diva Linda Ronstadt likened Bush to Hitler. So did Cuban dictator Fidel Castro, as did Harvey Wasserman writing in the Toronto Star. The George Soros–funded MoveOn.org was one of many left-wing websites that used the term.[10]

As to the charges that most newspapers ignore Democratic transgressions: John Hinderaker, an attendee at the 2008 Republican convention, reports that anti-Republican protesters "threw bricks through the windows of buses, sending elderly convention delegates to the hospital. They dropped bags of sand off highway overpasses onto vehicles below. Fortunately, no one was killed. . . . We haven't seen that sort of hate campaign since the Democrats went after Abraham Lincoln."[11]

Hinderaker goes on to comment on the virtual lack of press coverage of these incidents of violence. It's the Ministry of Propaganda at its willfully ignorant best, withholding reportage of newsworthy events of leftist violence in order to present the most one-sided coverage possible to a diminishing and increasingly savvy audience, one no longer willing to swallow the tainted "reportage" that passes for journalism in this country today.

Such tactics characterized "The Big Lie" in the 1930s, when the Nazi regime in Germany put it into practice. Simply put, it said that if you repeat a lie over and over, people will start to believe it. It's the favored tactic of the informal Democratic Ministry of Propaganda in contemporary America. They've used it to misinform the American public about key economy-wrecking issues such as global warming and healthcare "reform." The Big Lie incorporates the tactic of smearing your opponent in order to divert attention from the fact that you're the party actually using deceit and violence to achieve your ends.

Congressional perpetrators of the left's contemporary "big lie" abound. In an attempt to vilify conservatives and Tea Party members, South Carolina Democratic House Majority Whip James Clyburn whined after the incidents of vandalism and threats against member of Congress that ensued following passage of Obama's healthcare legislation that Republican opponents of healthcare reform were "aiding and abetting terrorism."[12] In fact, Republican leaders spoke out unanimously against the minor crimes against property—rocks had been thrown through the windows of the offices of two House members—committed in the wake of the administration's passage of healthcare legislation in defiance of the oft-expressed "will of the people."

What Clyburn failed to mention in his attempt to paint the right as violent in their reaction was that someone on the left had actually fired a gunshot through a window of the office of Virginia Republican Representative

Eric Kantor. Apparently this would be okay with Democrats, perhaps because Kantor is Jewish or just because he's a Republican. Kantor had chosen not to publicize the incident precisely because he didn't want to appear to be politicizing it, but after Clyburn's intemperate and misleading remarks, Kantor made a public statement about the incident, chastising Democrats for politicizing the issue of violence as he, like other Republicans, spoke out against it.

What Representative Clyburn also failed to mention is that it was equally likely that sympathizers with Obama's agenda threw rocks through the windows of their own congressmen and tried to blame the incidents on their opponents.

Readin', 'Ritin', and Radicalism: Education's Role in the Ministry of Propaganda

On March 30, 2010, President Obama, with a few strokes of his pen, nationalized the student loan industry. This makes the federal government the arbiter of a financial service to students that, even in the best of lights, has led to the bloated and undeserved rise in the costs of college education over the past forty years. The takeover makes the Department of Education "one of the country's largest banks—originating more than $100 billion in federal student loans each year." That's number one. It also displaces more than 35,000 workers in the financial industry, replacing them with government employees.[13]

This new government takeover was tucked away in the healthcare bill that the president rammed through Congress. What does education have to do with health care? Nothing. Why did they sneak it into the ObamaCare bill? A separate student loan bill had been passed by the House in 2009, but it was not taken up by the Senate. That's why it was tucked away in the healthcare bill, too.

But beyond the financial and employment implications of the bill, it's also likely to change the face of higher education even further, with a federal bureaucracy having a say over who gets money for college and who doesn't. The situation is ripe for the imposition of leftist political views on the process of funding higher education. So obviously, schools that adhere to the leftist party line are more likely to get federal dollars than those that don't.

What's more, we'll no doubt be seeing affirmative action standards applied where the distribution of dollars for college is concerned. They'll likely go to everyone from illegal aliens to those in selected racial and ethnic categories before they go to Caucasian Americans, for instance. And it's highly unlikely anyone will ever need to worry about paying back their college loans. The American taxpayer is, once again, on the hook for potential irresponsible behavior on the part of those who, in this case, receive college tuition guarantees.

The whole process also reeks of the potential for the same political cronyism that characterizes the distribution of stimulus dollars. By a nearly two to one margin, stimulus money has gone to Democratic recipients over Republicans. In addition, there seems to be no relationship between need and funding. Districts with high unemployment rates are not getting a proportionate share of stimulus money, with many truly needy districts receiving no funding at all.[14] There is no way the same dynamic will not be at work with the government in charge of hundreds of billions of dollars worth of education money, and there's no way the government will not use that financial clout to further contaminate educational content and freedom of expression on college campuses, pushing further and further to the left.

The Federal Government's role in underwriting student loans in order to "make college more affordable" began in 1965, with the passage of the Higher Education Act. The original act was intended to encourage "leveraging private financial markets and competing for the right to lend to students," according to the Federal Government's Student Loan Facts website. The legislation created a Fannie-Freddie-like agency, the "Federal Family Education Loan Program (FFELP), a public-private partnership of schools, students, loan providers, and the government that has financed the dreams of millions of Americans since 1965,"[15] again according to the partnership's website.

Since that time, thanks in no small part to the government's intervention in the college tuition market, the cost of attending college has skyrocketed. In 1965, tuition at the University of Pennsylvania was $1,530 per year, with room and board costing $1,000 a year.[16] Today that $1,500 annual tuition has grown to $38,970[17] Add another $7,748, the average cost of room and board at an American university during the 2009–2010 school year,[18] and you have a total of almost $47,000, a nearly 20-fold increase in the cost to get a university education for a year. And, in 1960, to cite a non-Ivy League example, the fee for tuition and room and board at the University of Oklahoma was $660 for an entire year. In 2009, that number had risen to $15,077, a greater than 2,000 percent increase.[19] The cost of attending college rose 80 percent in the first decade of this century alone.[20]

Because federal guarantees essentially cut out market forces as determinants for the cost of a college education, something akin to what has happened to healthcare costs has occurred. For, as in the healthcare industry, when you're not directly spending your money for a service, and when what you owe is guaranteed even if you default, nobody pays nearly as much attention to how much things cost as they do when they are personally the guarantors of payment. And with the federal takeover of the student loan business, conditions are now ripe for government even more closely controlling the content of educational material and the conditions under which American students will be allowed to go to college.

When you add in the Federal Textbook Act signed into law in August, 2009, by President Obama, you have another nail in the coffin of freedom of expression on the campuses of what has become the American equivalent of the Soviet gulag archipelago. That law, which is supposed to control the pricing and availability of textbooks at colleges and universities that receive federal funding, is now also seen as a vehicle to control their content. Among other things, the law requires textbook publishers to provide "a description of the substantial content revisions made between the current edition of the college textbook or supplemental material and the previous edition, if any."[21] It's another invitation to the Federal Government to take over control of our and our children's daily lives, and Barack Obama will not pass up the chance to increase his power.

The Obama administration is also moving to strengthen the hold of unions on the public education system. The appointment of Arne Duncan to the position of Secretary of Education was the first step in furthering that end. Duncan comes out of the Chicago City School system, where he was Superintendent of Schools from 2001 to 2009. By the time Duncan assumed that post, much of the damage to the city's school system had been done. The reason?

Chicago was one of the cities where outcome-based education got a firm foothold and where its principles were put into practice in the late 1970s and early '80s. As a result of the virtual collapse of Chicago's public schools that followed implementation of that leftist policy, graduation rates plummeted and literacy virtually disappeared among the city's students. In fact, nearly half of Chicago's high school students dropped out of school during the five years "mastery learning," as it was then called, was the mode of instruction in that school system.[22]

Of course the media hide such failures from the taxpayers who foot the bill.

Largely because of the abject failure of this educational approach, the overtly communistic National Education Association (NEA), the largest teachers' union in the United States, withdrew its support for "mastery learning," renamed it Outcome-Based Education, and resumed its assault on educational integrity and excellence by gradually re-implementing the methodology's principles more broadly in American schools. Bush Education Secretary Rod Paige called the NEA a "terrorist organization,"[23] largely because the results of the pedagogy they've forced on our nation's students are so disastrous.

Outcome-Based Education's methodology dictates that until all students have mastered the content in a given subject area, no students are able to advance to the next. Remediation is given to those unable to keep up, while those who have already mastered a unit's objectives on the first pass are given supplemental work to do as they wait for others to catch up. The intent with this method is to eventually wipe out the differences between high achievers and low achievers, making it possible for every student to achieve the same outcome. The real desired outcome is to stultify and suppress the achievement of the best and the brightest. In order to do this, school curricula have had to be dumbed down to such an extent that the material could not possibly be challenging to an intellectually gifted student.

While Duncan was not at the helm in Chicago during the Outcome-Based Education disaster, he's nonetheless continued his assault on excellence for American students, and he's done this overwhelmingly at the behest of the teachers' unions. Among the moves that Duncan has either initiated or condoned since he came to his current position are the withdrawal of voucher funds for Washington, D.C., students to attend the schools of their choice rather than be permanently victimized by a public school system that is one of the worst in the United States, if not the world.

This move, initiated during Obama's tenure, demonstrates that not only does the administration not have minority students' interests at heart, in fact, they're actively working to keep minority children from the chance for educational excellence, despite the fact that the voucher program has produced admirable results in the Washington, D.C., area. In addition to enabling the nineteen hundred students who received voucher money to realize gains in math and reading achievement, the program has also improved the safety of the students involved and greatly increased parental satisfaction with their children's educational progress.[24]

That would be reason enough for an administration bent on making sure that minority students are denied equal opportunity; the fact that unions gain more power when voucher money is withdrawn sealed the deal for this most racist, anti-achievement president and his Education Secretary.

Duncan has also overseen the distribution of $4.35 billion of our money under what's known as the "Race to the Top" fund.[25] Actually, he's only distributed about $600 million of the money. That's because, in selecting the recipients, Duncan insisted that "winners must garner broad support from teachers' unions and local school boards." Florida, one state that implemented many of the other changes looked-for in those getting Race-to-the-Top grants, lost out largely because it had only 8 percent approval from its teachers unions. Tennessee and Delaware, two of the states that paid obeisance to the teachers' unions, were awarded roughly $500 million and $100 million respectively.[26]

But perhaps the most damning indictment of our public school system and the abjectly criminal role the unions play in keeping our children, especially our disadvantaged children, in education hell was recently brought back to light with the death of an educational pioneer, Jaime Escalante. Escalante's enduring educational legacy, celebrated in the film "Stand and Deliver," was created when he took a group of poor inner-city students at Garfield High School in East Los Angeles and, through intensive classroom instruction, taught them advanced math skills that enabled them to score as well as, if not better than, students in much more affluent districts.

At the peak of his success, more of Escalante's students passed Advanced Placement calculus than did those at Beverly Hills High School. Because Escalante believed every student should have the opportunity to excel, he didn't limit the number of students in his classes to the teachers-union mandated thirty-five. He often had fifty or more students in his classes. This, of course, earned him the wrath of the unions. They managed to strip him of his position as chair of his school's math department, and Escalante eventually left the school.[27]

Liberals, with the support of teachers' unions, also used to protest prayer in schools. That was until students started praying to Barack Obama. Now they rejoice as second graders sing Obama's praises at B. Bernice Young Elementary School in Burlington, New Jersey, substituting Jesus' name with that of Obama.[28]

This type of indoctrination into a leftist worldview is consistent with goal number seventeen of the Communist Party as read into the Congressional Record in 1963 by Florida Congressman Albert Herlong Jr.:

> Get control of the schools. Use them as transmission belts for socialism and current Communist propaganda. Soften the curriculum. Get control of teachers' associations. Put the party line in textbooks.[29]

You'd better read that again.

Beyond the examples of the indoctrination of young minds into socialism are the efforts to undermine and erase evidence of our Judeo-Christian heritage. As Barack Obama himself has said, "Whatever we once were, we're no longer just a Christian nation." In fact, pagans following an "earth-centered religion"—such religions include Wicca and Druidism—have been granted worship space at the Air Force Academy.[30] This neopaganism is to religion as Renaissance fairs are to history. PC forces everyone, teachers and chaplains alike, to nod and go along or lose their careers.

There are glimmers of hope for our taking back the federal education system that has been so dominated by leftists for the better part of the past century. As with so many similar issues, the resistance to federal corruption must often start at the state level. While the left has overseen the rewriting of American history as taught to our children, in the spring of 2010, Texas educators are rewriting that state's textbooks to correct the misrepresentation and politicization of U.S. history that has dominated textbooks. They're explaining that, for instance, Founding Father Alexander Hamilton was not a proponent of strong central government, as the left has portrayed him, in doing so ignoring such Hamilton pronouncements as "It's not tyranny we desire; it's a just, limited, federal government."[31] They're explaining that Theodore Roosevelt was a socialist and that, far from ending the Great Depression, Franklin Delano Roosevelt's big-government policies actually caused it.[32]

Looming over all, though, is the ongoing threat posed by the teachers unions, and especially the National Education Association, which have done more to permanently diminish the achievement of American students than any other forces we could have imagined. They've perpetuated a Marxist agenda since the days of John Dewey, the so-called "father of progressive education," in the early part of the last century, and they've consistently championed policies that lead, not to educational excellence, but to the consolidation of power in their hands.

Through the centralization of education and the watering down of educational standards in order to turn those who are culturally and educationally disadvantaged into members of the permanently disadvantaged underclass in our country, they've managed to pervert one of the most sacred institutions in our country.

Hollywood, Liberal Talk Shows, and the Ministry of Propaganda

Mentioning free market capitalism in front of a leftist Democrat is analogous to holding up a cross in front of a vampire. Neither Democrats nor vampires can stand anything resembling truth, and so they shrink away from symbols that remind them of just how devoid of truth and meaning their lives and their politics are. But beyond that, nowhere does the free market render its judgment more harshly on Democrats than in the area of communications and artistic production, specifically broadcast journalism and movies. When you give an audience a choice of whether or not to subject themselves to the anti-American, anti-freedom, anti-religious messages contained in so many leftist news-talk shows and films, Americans vote with their wallets.

The votes are an almost universal collective "nay."

Like the slow dying of left-leaning newspapers across the country, the film industry is discovering that movies which perpetuate the radical left's anti-American agenda are box office poison. In the past decade, dozens of anti-American films hit the big screen across America, and they've generally all sunk like stones. *In the Valley of Elah* an anti-war film starring committed lefties Tommy Lee Jones and Susan Sarandon, is what the *Old York Times* calls a film whose "message is that the war in Iraq has damaged this country in ways we have only begun to grasp."[33]

Make no mistake: That's commie-speak for "a film that shows the United States military at its murderous and imperialist worst." The film's producers have apparently not yet "begun to grasp" the fact that Americans found the 2007 film itself to be unwatchable, as the movie's worldwide box office receipts of a mere $29.5 million attest.[34]

Other America-as-imperialist-pariah movies haven't even fared that well. Despite boasting such Marxist mega-stars as Robert Redford, Meryl Streep, and Tom Cruise, the anti-American bomb *Lions for Lambs*—which drearily summons up a fairly typical leftist assessment of the War in Iraq, college professor Redford is "fighting the good fight" against the war-mongering Bush administration; "opportunistic," "true-believing," "conniving" Republican politician Cruise is "compromised"—couldn't claw its way out of the box office basement. The film grossed only $15 million worldwide,[35] hardly enough to pay for the on-location catering during the filming of the movie.

The only Ministry of Propaganda–sanctioned film that scored at the box office was James Cameron's *Avatar,* and the reason for its success had a great deal more to do with the movie's special effects than with its message. Cameron is the director of the mega-hit *Titanic* and the mother of ugly rhetoric, including his desire to "shoot . . . those boneheads" who deny man-created global warming.

In fact, interviews with Cameron make it clear that the director's intent in making *Avatar,* in addition to trashing America, was to deliver a stinging rebuke to global warming "deniers," the people who, unlike Cameron, actually possess the intelligence and the savvy to see through the fraudulent "science" underlying Cameron's cause of choice. Reviewer John Nolte offers the following assessment: It's " 'Avatar' as 'Death Wish 5' for leftists. A simplistic, revisionist revenge fantasy . . . if you freakin' hate the bad guys (America)." [36]

But if the leftist message is bombing at the box office, it's finding even less success with its forays into broadcast media. One of the prime examples of that is the left's flagship radio talk show, Air America, or, more accurately, Hot Air Radio, although to imply that the emptiness of its content is the equivalent to playing Air Guitar is actually an insult to Air Guitar players everywhere. The perpetrators of this broadcasting embarrassment, once they'd exhausted the A-list of lefty guests—Michael Moore, Al Gore, Al Sharpton, Hillary Clinton, Chuck Schumer, Susan Sarandon, Tim Robbins, Sean Penn, Barbra Streisand, and a few dozen other celebrity airheads—had to answer the question, "Where do we go from here?"

The left couldn't produce anything remotely resembling the intellectual firepower conservatives bring to serious political issues. And even if a large *cadre* of analysts who could shed light on key political issues from a Marxist perspective were available, the hosts of Air Radio shows simply didn't have the intelligence or the integrity to delve deeply and dispassionately into the issues.

While supporters of and investors in Air Radio pushed ad nauseam the idea that there is a huge public hungry for talk radio that caters to their liberal sensibilities—in much the same way they pushed the idea that Americans were eager to see their healthcare legislation pass—America wasn't buying it. A small group of disaffected leftists does not a market make, especially when the marketers and the front people they enlist to represent them can do little more than whine about how unfair it is that conservative ideas and policies are getting so much run.

No matter how trendy and viable liberal talk radio might have seemed, no matter how urgently its "message" was pushed, in the final analysis, air was not enough. The network met its end on January 21, 2010, a victim of its own embarrassingly bad programming and the unsustainability of a message that mercilessly denigrated about 90 percent of the American people.

Left-leaning cable television news-talk network MSNBC would have met the same fate as Air Radio long ago if it weren't for the fact that it can fall back on the bankroll of its parent network, original TV broadcast behemoth, NBC. Its partner in news broadcast crime, CNN, which was founded in 1980 by one of the original liberal idiots, Ted Turner, but has since been taken over by Time Warner, survives despite ratings that reflect the emptiness of its content.

Among the reasons the ratings are so dismal are CNN's Wolf Blitzer and MSNBC's Keith Olbermann. In Blitzer's case, the problem is credibility. The CNN news anchor made the mistake of appearing as a contestant on *Celebrity Jeopardy*. He confirmed what everyone who has ever watched one of his broadcasts knows: that he's way out of his depth. Blitzer's painfully embarrassing performance—he ended up thousands of dollars in the hole as the result of being unable to answer questions such as one about where Jesus Christ was born—drew derision even from those on the left.

Long before the Jeopardy fiasco, though, Slate.com's Jack Shafer observed that "Blitzer draws on such a limited vocabulary that I predict that when he dies and the coroner cores his skull, the world will learn that he possesses a brain the size of a walnut."[37] Keith Olbermann's brain is not likely to prove much bigger. The angry misogynistic host of MSNBC's nightly show "Countdown" has alienated even the most hardened leftists with his ugly rants. By the end of 2009, his show was attracting less than 20 percent as many viewers as those who were watching his competition, and even his colleagues at the lowest-rated cable news network were wondering why management was keeping him on.[38]

One of the important things we need to take away from the fact that television news networks still survive despite ratings so dismal they would have driven unsubsidized businesses out of existence long ago is that, with liberals, what audiences think and what markets select is meaningless. The only thing important to the left is to blast its message out to the public, even if the public is, in increasing numbers, getting wise to the lies that lurk at the foundation of the message.

The left's answer to the fact that it can't compete in the marketplace is the same for broadcasting as it has been for banks, health care, and the auto industry: Try to nationalize the radio and television industries. The method they've chosen to do that is to revive the Fairness Doctrine, and although it appears to be legislatively dead in its current iteration, it lives on in the hearts and minds of free-market-hating liberals everywhere. The original Fairness Doctrine, passed in 1949, demanded that airtime must be devoted equally to both "sides" of any political issue.

In 1987, the Federal Communications Commission repealed the Fairness Doctrine on the grounds that it violated the free speech rights of broadcasters and that as a result there was less broadcast time devoted to important issues. Despite the obvious constitutional challenges a law that reintroduces the Fairness Doctrine would inevitably face, the Obama administration insists, unsuccessfully so far, on trying to bring it back through the legislative process.[39]

Among the obvious problems for the left in trying to reinstitute the fairness doctrine is that only one TV news network even comes close to presenting more than one side of any political issue today, and that's Fox News. CNN and MSNBC are radically skewed toward favoring coverage of issues only through a liberal lens and through hosting liberal guests. This is not to mention that most MSNBC broadcasts can be characterized as scurrilous and invective-intensive at best. The law's target is conservative talk radio, its intent to silence conservative talk show hosts.

Ignoring the fact that in all the media outlets they run, the left shows no signs of allowing opposing viewpoints to be heard, they continue to promote this egregious affront to true fairness, which involves allowing the people who access such services to make their own choices. Where that happens, the will of the people is clear, and Marxists are routed.

Even more serious, though, "fairness" legislation, which would be the communications equivalent of Outcome-Based Education, would put the United States on track to become what Canada has become where free speech is concerned. If you thought American college campuses were bastions of leftist hate speech and repression of any speech not in compliance with the rules of the Marxist thought police, perhaps you haven't tried to speak out in Canada.

Our neighbor to the north is one of the most repressive countries outside of the Arab world when it comes to allowing its citizens (and its visitors, for that matter) to express themselves. One conservative American writer was publicly warned before she visited the country that things she might say could be construed as "hate speech" under Canadian law and that she could well face prosecution in Ottawa, where she was scheduled to appear. She needn't have worried about being arrested for what she said, though. Several hundred people who opposed her appearance showed up brandishing rocks and sticks, and the Canadian authorities caved in and canceled the speaker's appearance, fearing for her "safety."

The questions surrounding the incident focused on whether the Canadian police, who should have dispersed the mob, were actually acting in sympathy with the political left, who favor being able to shut down such performances if they disagree with the opinions likely to be expressed.[40]

Bring Back HUAC

In addition to being pervasive in American movies, media, and classrooms, anti-Americanism has found champions throughout the Obama administration. We have elected as president a man who conspicuously bows to Islamic leaders and apologizes to Muslims for America's bad behavior. Our Commander in Chief seeks out photo ops with the likes of communist dictator Hugo Chávez while weakening our ties with our strongest and most important allies. He's alienated England and Israel by insulting their leaders and siding with a world hostile to Israel's presence in the Middle East through his insistence on preconditions that would help cripple Israel's economy as part of a deal to promote even more fruitless Israeli-Palestinian peace talks.

Much has been made of the communists and communist sympathizers in the Obama administration, and of the power given to the appropriately named "czars" the president has appointed without Congressional vetting or, apparently, without any vetting whatsoever in so many cases, to oversee everything from energy policy to executive pay. The administration's approach smacks of the same totalitarianism that Thomas Friedman seems to favor so strongly when he talks about how much better China's one-party system is than our own. Friedman is getting his wish. The United States is moving rapidly toward a one-party dictatorship in which decisions about every aspect of our lives are made centrally, in much the same way they have been in communist regimes during the last century.

Obama's left-hand man, Attorney General Eric Holder, a true coward if there ever was one, insulted a majority of Americans by calling *them* cowards for not engaging in a public debate on race, this in the only country in the history of this planet's civilizations ever to have granted full citizenship rights to a racial-ethnic group that had formerly been enslaved. Perhaps our Attorney General is unaware of the debate that raged in the mid 20th century when we created legislation that guaranteed those rights. Perhaps he's unaware of the brave people, both black and white, who stood up for human rights as our country made itself over into something more honorable, something more humane than it had been.

Holder's ignorance, or disavowal, of American history extends well beyond his inability to acknowledge the true transformation that has taken place over the last fifty years. It now encompasses—in contravention of both reason and morality—his promoting giving terrorists the same rights to protection under the law as those afforded American citizens; in keeping with his willful dismissal of all things just, he's expressed his support for prosecuting the officials in the Bush administration who lawfully did their duty in actually trying to protect America from the same terrorists Holder now openly advocates for.

By the time both Obama and Holder were of school age, but especially by the time they were in college, leftists had already substantially rewritten American history to suit their own perverse ideological requirements. The American education system was increasingly becoming the means to promulgate misrepresentations and outright lies about our country's past and about its intentions. Young, disaffected blacks were particularly vulnerable to this sort of misinformation. Many leaders of the black community preached, as they still do, the message that blacks could not get ahead without special treatment.

Even Martin Luther King Jr. expressed the need for "a Marshall Plan for aid to Negroes" that involved giving taxpayer money to blacks to make up for the economic hole their enslavement had put them in.[41] For young black males like Obama and Holder, that message got translated into one of hate for the white "oppressor," and it found expression in the increasingly Marxist-influenced American education system, centralized and dominated by unions that supported leftist policies in their efforts to control the economics of education and what was taught in the classroom.

A rationale for retribution, and not simply reparations for the suffering of their people, was what people like Obama and Holder increasingly sought in the teachers and preachers who mentored them. Equal rights, what they were offered instead, was not close to enough, and once they began to gain power, they moved quickly toward the destruction of a system and a country that they saw as the enemy.

It's un-Americanism at its ugly and uninformed worst, and if it starts with the perversion of history and education, it continues in complicit journalists' censorship of the news in the loosely knit American Ministry of Propaganda's refusal to report or offer opinions in support of anything critical of political figures with whom they're in sympathy. Such cultural influences as the content of many of the movies produced in Hollywood demonstrate the reach and power of leftist propaganda. They're among thousands of such phenomena that represent anti-Americanism run amok on the left.

Anti-Americanism is the informing sensibility of the Obama administration, and it has put our country at a crossroads very similar to the one we faced at the middle of the last century. But unlike the situation then, when we had to back down only the Soviet Union, now we face two enemies: militant Islam and Marxism. Both the political left and Islamists share a hatred of our country and what it stands for, and they've found an ally in President Obama, whose actions and policies demonstrate that he's committed to undermining the principles on which our country was founded and on which it rose to greatness, and to replacing them with something very much like Thomas Friedman recommends: a dictatorship of the leftist elite.

In fact, so un-American are the president's policies that it may well be time to revisit the 1950s again, this time to resurrect the House Un-American Activities Committee that was formed to weed out precisely the kind of purveyors of traitorism that we face today. It's time to bring back HUAC! For the many people alive today who don't remember HUAC, it was an investigative committee of the United States House of Representatives charged with uncovering subversive activity in the United States. It looked into the activities and associations of, particularly, those in the government and the entertainment industry, especially in Hollywood, who were suspected of being communists.

HUAC rooted out Soviet operative Alger Hiss, who was convicted of perjury on January 21, 1950, and it revealed the extent of the communist infiltration of the film industry, ultimately resulting in prison terms for the so-called "Hollywood Ten," people found guilty of contempt of Congress for refusing to answer questions about their communist affiliations.[42] In addition, many other Hollywood communists were blacklisted and refused employment in the film industry.

HUAC served America and protected it from what was then the most serious threat to the national security of the United States: the spread of Soviet Communism. But the generation of leftists and fellow travelers that surfaced in the 1960s and '70s began a systematic rewriting of American history, claiming that the efforts of HUAC and its most famous leader, Joseph McCarthy, had been nothing but a witch-hunt. As they continue to do today, the leftists characterized McCarthyites as persecutors.

But the evidence of history, particularly since the Venona Papers were released after the fall of the Soviet Union in the early 1990s, tells a different story. The Venona Papers were a collection of transcriptions of encoded radio messages by Soviet KGB agents in the United States to their superiors in Moscow between the years 1943 and 1948. They reveal that by the time World War II had ended, the United States government had been infiltrated at every level by Soviet agents who influenced policy and recruited others as Soviet spies. The Venona Papers revealed that HUAC's pursuit of communists was a justified attempt to identify and weed out traitors to America who had infiltrated our government and our entertainment industry.

Today, the specific threat of Soviet communism is gone. But other threats, arguably even more dangerous ones, remain. The old far-left infrastructure still exists in the form of the American Civil Liberties Union (ACLU), the National Lawyers Guild, the NEA, and other organizations that are the new enemy within. Added to the threat of communism is that of Islamist terrorism, especially that which we face from converts to Islam right here in America. This threat also implicates members of the Obama administration, including the president himself and his attorney general.

Both have clear sympathies for and, in many cases, outright ties to both Marxism and Islamic terrorism. Covington and Burling, the law firm for which Holder worked, represented or currently represents as many as eighteen detainees at Guantanamo Bay prison. The firm contributed at no charge more than three thousand hours of legal services to Gitmo detainees during 2007 alone, bringing lawsuits against the American people to try to ensure that their clients, although they were terrorists captured on the battlefield, get civilian trials in American courts.[43]

What brings the leftist and Islamist movements together is a virulent hatred of the United States, and the fact that both have gained extensive support in the Obama administration is an indicator of just how far this administration has come toward achieving its covert purpose of overthrowing the U.S. government and replacing it with a tyrannical regime. For that to be successful, Obama requires the support of people like Eric Holder and deposed green jobs czar Van Jones and manufacturing czar Ron Bloom—who concurs with former White House Communications Director Anita Dunn that "we kind of agree Mao is right"[44]—people who believe in the leftist agenda, genuinely hate America, and will enact and promote policies that put that animus into practice. Un-Americanism is the theme of the Obama presidency, and he's installed HUAC-worthy people in positions of power. It's a heretofore unimaginably pro-socialist, pro-Islamist administration.

There is not a single issue in the left's agenda that isn't characterized by outright lying and misrepresentation of fact, coupled with relentless propagandizing in order to try to persuade American citizens that the Democrats' Marxist manifesto is beneficial, that the science is decided, that whatever they do is going to save money, and that it's going to benefit Americans. It's another component of the Democratic "big lie," one of the most disturbing aspects of the leftist mentality, their penchant for arranging facts and theories to fit their politics.

Of course, that's what it takes for the left to advance their true agenda. In fact, only one thing is important to the left: the accumulation of power over the American people in the exercise of a vendetta designed to make us pay for being the most powerful, most successful, richest, most generous nation in history. Until we are all enslaved by their Marxist-Leninist totalitarian mind machine, they will not relent. And then the gulags will open to "re-educate" the former "Savages" and "Savagettes" who believe in freedom, self-determination, and God.

CHAPTER 10

Obama's War on the Military and Our National Security

When I was a boy, maybe ten or eleven years old, I loved going to the circus. Whenever the Ringling Brothers Circus came to town, I wouldn't miss it. I didn't go to see the elephants or ride the Ferris wheel, mind you. I went for the freak show in back. In those days, they had genuine freak shows. You know, the conjoined twins. The man with two faces. The bearded lady. In other words, the people of today who became politicians were, in my day, working in the back room of the circus without a Windsor knot. Or, let's say they were the same people you might find on MSNBC or CNN after some surgery.

Going to the freak show was a wonderful experience in its own way. Something about looking at these human oddities made life richer. You know, as a kid you walk around eating the popcorn, you gape at the freaks, and you thank God that you're not like them. I realize some will say that the circus was exploiting them. Not so. If you ask them, they appreciated the chance to make a living. Aside from becoming a Congressman, how else could a guy with two faces make a living?

That said, fast forward a couple months after I went to the circus.

I was working in my father's little antique store on the Lower East Side of New York. Late one afternoon, just before closing, in walks a Ringling Brothers circus performer, a guy from the freak show. I remembered seeing him. I mean, how could you forget a guy like this. He was billed as the half man/half woman. He had a breast on one side and not on the other side, and he had half a beard. Turns out the freak just so happened to live over on Long Beach Island when he wasn't traveling with the circus.

Imagine my surprise to see him in our store. So, I watch him order a couple large pieces and then ask Dad to deliver them. Like I said, Dad had a small operation—after work, my father delivered his own sales. He didn't have a delivery boy. I was the kid. I'd go along on the ride, whether it was in the Desoto or the Cadillac Series 62, with the merchandise piled in the back. My job was to lug the bronzes inside.

I'll never forget this as long as I live. We pulled up late at night because this guy didn't like to come out during the day. Doors are shut. Blinds are drawn. The porch light is off. My father rings the bell. We're standing there in the dark, waiting. He rings again.

Me? I'm wondering what his house is gonna look like inside. As a kid with a sizable imagination, my mind is churning with the possibilities. How does a freak live? What kind of bizarro stuff would we see? Did he have a three-legged dog? Was he married to one of the other freaks at the circus? More than that, was he a dangerous person? Or did he just look scary? Part of me wasn't so sure I was ready to find out.

Dad hits the buzzer a third time.

Finally, we hear "Who's there?" from behind the closed door.

Dad tells him it's us with his bronzes and, a moment later, the freak tries to open the door but he can't. He can only open it a crack. Why? Turns out there was too much stuff in the way, blocking it. So we wait some more while he moves stuff around then invites us in. Following my father's lead, I squeezed inside and saw his house was littered with art objects cast about in no particular order. I'm talking hundreds of statutes and paintings covering the floor. By the looks of it, this guy lived alone and would buy one beautiful thing after another. He just randomly put them on the floor like a giant warehouse.

That night, riding home over the empty Southern State Parkway, I couldn't help but think about my first impressions of the freak. I thought

I had him pegged based upon his public persona as one of the oddball members of the circus. But I had been wrong. Never in my wildest dreams would I have thought he would have been a collector of fine art and statues. I mean, he may have been physically hard to look at, but he wasn't an ugly person. He had a genuine appreciation for beauty and decided to surround himself with beautiful things as much as possible, even if it was in a compulsive way.

In other words, I learned *first impressions are often misleading*.

You cannot assume people are the way they're portrayed to be in public.

In the case of Barack Obama, the analogy works in the reverse. On the outside, he's a well-dressed man. There's certainly nothing freakish or sinister looking about him. But that first impression is, likewise, misleading. When you pull back the curtain and see the monstrous things Obama the Destroyer has done—and is doing—you realize this president, his agenda, and his policies are to be feared because he is putting the survival of a nation on the line.

Why do I say that?

As I'll document in a moment, Barack Hussein Obama is *dismantling*, *disarming*, and *demoralizing* our military. In this chapter, you'll see how this man is systematically dismantling our nuclear defense through an unnecessary treaty with Russia, disarming the ability of our troops to fight and win wars through a maze of politically correct rules of engagement, and demoralizing our valiant young men and women on the front lines.

No question, the troops are brave. They're doing their jobs as the best fighting force on the planet. They are not the problem. And yet, as you'll also see momentarily, they get nailed to a cross when they do their job too well. The blame for this war on the military lies with our president of unknown origin, whose loyalties—based upon his actions—don't appear to lie with the country that elected him.

I also blame Defense Secretary Robert Gates and Mike Mullen, Chairman of the Joint Chiefs of Staff, who have been reduced to empty suits. They're basically little more than a gaggle of Stepford Wives in Obama's harem, there to do his bidding. Whatever Obama says, they do—even though Obama never served in the military and it remains doubtful he has ever fired a Daisy BB gun in his life.

How else can you explain the fact that these men in tights let Obama kill production of the F-22 Raptor fighter jet, one of the best fighter planes in the Air Force's arsenal? Forget about the fact that these jets are considered to be "the most technologically advanced fighter ever made."[2] That means nothing to this president. Instead, Obama justified shooting down the jets, saying, "At a time when we're fighting two wars and facing a serious deficit, this would have been an inexcusable waste of money."[3]

Let's get this straight. President Obama is spending *trillions* of dollars on ineffective, wasteful economic stimulus packages, and *trillions* of dollars more to socialize health care, and is hoping to pass some sort of costly cap-and-trade measure, but he didn't think twice about making America more vulnerable in order to trim a relatively paltry $1.75 billion from the defense budget? How does that make any sense? Constitutionally speaking, one of the president's top priorities is to defend our country, not turn it into a socialist wealth–fare state. What's more, by scrapping the F-22's, he's saving a meager one-third of 1 percent of the 2010 defense program.[4]

This is a profound military blunder. Why?

The Heritage Foundation reports, "Russia is expanding its fighter forces more now than at any other time since the end of the Cold War. The Russians plan to field 300 Su-Fullback strike aircraft by 2022 and an additional 300 Sukhoi Pak fifth-generation fighters."[5] Likewise, China is ramping up its purchase of additional attack jets. How, then, could any American president think it was a good idea to cut our radar-evading F-22's?

What's more, we didn't hear a peep out of Gates and Mullen when Obama surrendered our anti-missile defense shield in Poland and the Czech Republic or when Congress cut back on funding for Future Combat Systems—an essential program that enables the U.S. Army to modernize its equipment and strategies. We didn't hear a word of protest from them over the recently announced "almost 20% cut in the dedicated forces they could allocate to respond to a weapon of mass destruction attack on U.S. soil."[6]

We're talking about our very survival as a nation. Why won't these men stand up to this radical president who continues to impoverish the military and compromise the ability for America to defend herself against those who would want to wipe us off the face of the earth? Make no mistake about it. The trickle up poverty here is the weakening of America's capacity to defend ourselves and the impoverishment of the fighting spirit once the centerpiece of the U.S. military—all because of the mental disorder of liberalism exhibited by the far left's influence on the top brass and Barack Hussein Obama's radical policies of appeasement.

One of the clearest examples of the Obama administration's efforts to undermine our military is the new rules of engagement, which are killing our troops in Iraq and Afghanistan—literally.

Ready, Aim, Hold Your Fire

Imagine you've voluntarily signed up for active duty in the military because you believe in defending this great country—even if it costs you the ultimate sacrifice: your life. You leave friends and family behind and subject yourself to the rigors of grueling training for weeks on end. You study the strategies of combat, you're trained in the use of the best high-tech weapons on the planet, and then you're deployed to Afghanistan to fight the Taliban.

Now, imagine you're told the following about your mission:

- No night or surprise searches.
- Villagers have to be warned prior to searches.
- The Afghan National Army (ANA) or the Afghan National Police (ANP) must accompany U.S. units on searches.
- U.S. soldiers may not fire at the enemy unless the enemy is preparing to fire first.
- U.S. forces cannot engage the enemy if civilians are present.
- Only women can search women.
- Troops can fire at an insurgent if they catch him placing an improvised explosive device (IED) but not if insurgents are walking away from an area where explosives have been laid.[7]

Nothing imaginary about those rules of engagement (ROE).

According to the *Washington Times*, that's just a partial list of what our brave service men and women actually must do while rooting out the Taliban! Tell me that's not absolute madness. Does the American military really need the ANA or the ANP babysitting our highly trained, perfectly capable troops every time they search a mud hut? How many of them are Taliban by night? What's wrong with conducting surprise searches?

Isn't the "element of surprise" key to most victories?

What's more, if our soldiers are required to go door-to-door as if they're selling Avon cosmetics, to warn villagers of a pending search, doesn't that give the enemy time to pack their explosives and slip out the back? Why aren't nighttime searches permitted? Are we afraid of interrupting a terrorist in the middle of his bomb making? Is it any wonder our troops are bogged down? Is it any wonder we're not making progress against an enemy who doesn't play by the same rules?

Army Captain Casey Thoreen is frustrated by the disadvantage these rules create for his men. "We have to follow the Karzai 12 rules," he says, referring to Afghanistan's president, Hamid Karzai. "But the Taliban has no rules. Our soldiers have to juggle all these rules and regulations and they do it without hesitation despite everything. It's not easy for anyone out here."[8] Ah, but you know that President Karzai didn't create the list of regulations hamstringing our troops? That was crafted by the commander of our forces in Afghanistan, General Stanley McChrystal.

Why did McChrystal do this to our troops?

Captain Thoreen concedes, "It's a framework to ensure cultural sensitivity in planning and executing operations. It's a set of rules and could be characterized as part of the ROE." In other words, the Obama military establishment is running a damn PR campaign, not a war! They're more concerned about cultural *seeeensitivity* than getting the job done—which is no way to win. Thoreen adds, "For our guys, it's tough. Sometimes they feel they have their hands tied behind their backs."[9]

Need proof? In an article entitled, "Strict rules slowing offensive, troops say," the reporter covering a battle in Marja, Afghanistan swerves into the ugly truth of this untenable situation:

> If a man emerges from a Taliban hideout after shooting erupts, U.S. troops say they cannot fire at him if he is not seen carrying a weapon—or if they did not personally watch him drop one. What this means, some contend, is that a militant can fire at them, then set aside his weapon and walk freely out

of a compound, possibly toward a weapons cache in another location.

Tell me that isn't crazy. Tell me that's not a formula for disaster. Why must our men hold their fire? Isn't killing the enemy the whole point? Not so, as this reporter goes on to explain:

> NATO and Afghan military officials say killing militants is not the goal of a 3-day-old attack to take control of this Taliban stronghold in southern Afghanistan. The more important focus is to win public support.[10]

If we're intent on playing with the enemy as some sort of goodwill gesture, where does that leave our troops? In short, we have a military that's about as threatening as a candy striper passing out flowers to the sick. As Captain Sam Rico, of the Division's 4–25 Field Artillery Battalion, puts it, "You get shot at but can do nothing about it. You have to see the person with the weapon. It's not enough to know which house the shooting's coming from."[11] Why must our soldiers fight with such oppressive handicaps in the heat of a battle? All in the name of winning "public support"? That's an outrage!

What's more, if our men are not permitted to search women for weapons, which is one of the Karzai ROE, that creates a dangerous Catch–22. As the *Washington Times* points out: "Because of the Karzai 12 rules, U.S. forces have had to bring in American women to conduct searches of their Afghan counterparts." I thought America had a policy forbidding women in combat? As one soldier explains, "It's OK for the insurgents to use their women to hide weapons but it's not OK for us [men] to search them. So now, we have to break our own rules and bring women into combat just so they can search the women."[12]

That's the price we're paying to fight a war according to rules laid out by college leftists on a pot high who now run the military! Instead of creating reasonable rules of engagement that protect our troops, they spend their time poring over complicated PowerPoint presentations created by independent contractors who have little or no experience facing the heat of battle.

One such convoluted PowerPoint slide—featuring hundreds of arrows in eight different colors, swirling in every direction—was designed to "inform" the top military brass about the complex relationships in Afghanistan. It was so baffling, General McChrystal said, "When we understand that slide, we'll have won the war." [13]

This complete waste of taxpayer money was created by the PA Consulting Group because the military is being run by incompetent leftists who think they are still attending college seminars and need such data. By the way, I had requested permission to reprint the diagram in my book, but they denied my request citing "client confidentiality purposes" for "any use of the diagram." I pointed out that it was already featured in newspapers around the world. That didn't matter to them. (You can view the chart at the Daily Mail online: www.dailymail.co.uk/news/worldnews/article–1269463/ Afghanistan-PowerPoint-slide-Generals-left-baffled-PowerPoint-slide.html.)

Let's set that aside.

The larger point is that these absurd rules of engagement put America's troops at war with themselves. How? If they shoot before being shot at, they risk disciplinary action. If they wait to shoot before being shot at, they risk dying. If you think this isn't happening, think again. In March, 2010, a reporter for the Associated Press, whose name is unimportant, reports:

> The number of U.S. troops killed in Afghanistan has roughly doubled in the first three months of 2010 compared to the same period last year as Washington has added tens of thousands of additional soldiers to reverse the Taliban's momentum. Those deaths have been accompanied by a dramatic spike in the number of wounded, with injuries more than tripling in the first two months of the year and trending in the same direction based on the latest available data for March.

This reporter completely misses the point. It's not the presence of additional troops—which he obviously opposes since liberals don't have a stomach for war—that accounts for the increase wounded. Rather, the spike in casualties has everything to do with the rules of engagement that make our men sitting ducks. He goes on further to misrepresent reality: "A rise in

the number of wounded—a figure that draws less attention than deaths—
shows that the Taliban remain a formidable opponent."[14] Wrong. They are
not a "formidable" foe.

No, about the only credit that can be given to the Taliban is that they're
just smart enough to use our ROE against us. Look at how blatantly the
Taliban leverages their advantage, as this editorial in the *Washington Times*
demonstrates:

> In Marjah, the enemy quickly adapted to the rules, which led
> to bizarre circumstances such as Taliban fighters throwing
> down their weapons when they were out of ammunition and
> taunting coalition troops with impunity or walking in plain
> view with women behind them carrying their weapons like
> caddies. If World War II had been fought with similar rules,
> the battles would still be raging. Paradoxically, America's most
> successful post-conflict reconstructions were in Germany and
> Japan, where enemy-occupied towns like Marjah were flattened
> without a second thought.[15]

General McChrystal thinks being *seeeeeensitive* to the locals is a strategy
worth the risk to our soldiers: "Destroying a home or property jeopardizes
the livelihood of an entire family—and creates more insurgents. We sow the
seeds of our own demise."[16] Others see things differently. Take retired Army
colonel Doug Macgregor, a military historian who sees the futility of such
actions: "You surrender whatever military advantage you have by compelling the U.S. conventional soldier or Marine to fight on terms that favor the
enemy, not the American soldier or Marine."[17]

In the end, our boys are dying unnecessarily. Do we really want more
body bags filled with American's young men because we were afraid of hurting the *feeeeelings* of the locals? I say it's time to take off the handcuffs and
let our military finish the job or get the hell out of Afghanistan. Start un-
leashing the full force and might of the American military on the Taliban,
and get the job done or leave.

In the words of General George S. Patton: "No bastard ever won a war
by dying for his country. He won it by making the other poor dumb bastard

die for his country." Patton wouldn't be playing this peek-a-boo game with the Taliban swine. He wouldn't have hesitated using air power to flatten and pulverize the rat holes where these vermin hide.

America needs more Patton . . . and less patent leather.

Obama the Destroyer

At the outset of this book, I described Barack Obama as a destructive child who, in his ignorance, takes apart a watch and cannot put it back together. With regard to his reckless dismantling of our military, there's no quick solution to rebuild it. If, and when, this child president wakes up one morning and finds America under attack, it will be too late to start rebuilding what he has torn down.

Why do I say this?

On April 8, 2010, Obama the Destroyer attacked America's sovereignty and safety by signing the Strategic Arms Reduction Treaty (START) in Prague, Czech Republic, with Russian President Medvedev. Let's not mince words. This treaty is the work of the mentally disordered Left. If the U.S. Senate ratifies the treaty, America will have to slash our nuclear arsenal by 33 percent while *cutting in half* the number of missiles, the submarine fleet, and our strategic bombers that deliver them.

You might want to read that again.

As bad as these cuts are in terms of our national security, the Obama regime has further handcuffed America's position on how we can use what few nuclear weapons we still posses. As detailed in the 2010 Nuclear Posture Review (NPR), "the United States will not use or threaten to use nuclear weapons against non-nuclear weapons states that are party to the NPT and in compliance with their nuclear non-proliferation obligations." In other words, if we're attacked with chemical or biological weapons by Russia, Obama has promised he won't retaliate with nuclear weapons as long as Russia is "in compliance" with the START treaty.

That's insane.

Likewise, as one columnist points out, "if some terrorist group linked to a Middle Eastern country murders millions of Americans by blowing up domestic nuclear power plants or through germ warfare, such as with anthrax, a nuclear retaliatory strike is off-limits."[18] Tell me Obama's reckless NPR policy won't embolden our adversaries. The president is backing America into an obscure corner rather than stepping out with strength onto the world stage. What's more, as this columnist rightly observes, "His delusions may play well with the liberal press corps. But in the real world—the world of Chinese militarism, Russian gangsterism, Iranian adventurism and Islamist imperialism—he is viewed as the caretaker of a declining hyperpower."[19]

By these rules, we would still be fighting Japan in the Pacific!

Here's what Obama the Naive has clearly forgotten.

One reason America got rid of her chemical and biological weapons is that we were told that we would always have the nuclear deterrent available. And now, thanks to this feckless president, we don't have that option. The Enemy Within is very sly. Over the years, this anti-nuke, anti-military Enemy Within has said, "Oh, you can get rid of your chemical and biological weapons, America, because you have so many nukes. You can always attack a country that attacks you with chemical and biological weapons. You don't need chemical or biological weapons yourself. You can use your nukes."

Now we find out that we can't even use our nukes because Obama the Destroyer has taken that option off the table—with the exception of North Korea and Iran. This is unsettling news to Americans, the overwhelming majority of whom believe Obama's nuclear stance is a sign of weakness and sets the stage for an attack on our soil. According to one poll taken after President Obama announced his new NPR position, "Sixty percent of Americans said they think it is likely Obama's new policy pronouncement will result in attacks on the U.S."[20]

Why am I not entirely surprised that Secretary of State Hillary Clinton takes the Obama view? Clinton praised the news as "a good day for America and our security" because "we do not need such large arsenals."[21]

We don't need such large arsenals? Nonsense!

This nuclear disarmament is on top of the fact that Obama has already put a wrecking ball to the defense budget and stopped a comprehensive missile defense system for our allies in Europe. Now, in the name of diplomacy and his race to turn us into a third-rate military power on par with Krapistan, Obama the Destroyer is destroying our nuclear capacity precisely when Iran and North Korea are building up their nuclear capabilities and China is racing to develop more advanced, nuclear-armed submarines.

While Obama is axing away at our missile defense, China is working overtime to build up its missile defense system. In January, 2010, the Chinese military conducted a successful test launch of an ABM interceptor missile. What's more, according to one report, China is working on long-range missiles capable of hitting the United States. The reporter observed, "As soon as China has its missile defense system, it will win the status of a global superpower which no one will be allowed to ignore."[22] Why is Obama ignoring this buildup? Does this seem like the right time for our president to be making cuts in this vital part of our strategic defense?

Meanwhile, restlessness resides within the European Union. Calls for a joint EU international army are being made by Italy's Foreign Minister Franco Frattini. Even though the EU is a political union, fears that America will betray its allies are in the region. I don't blame them for that considering the ways our president has snubbed a number of our long-time partners around the world, most notably Israel. Take, for instance, the time President Obama walked out of a meeting at the White House with Israel Prime Minister Benjamin Netanyahu. Remember that humiliation? An Israeli newspaper described the encounter as "a hazing in stages."[23]

Aside from the embarrassing treatment of our allies, which sends distressing signals to other allies, "experts say that the creation of the common European force is good for Russia. Russia supposedly used its friendly relations with Italy and initiated Frattini's statement to distract the EU from the USA and move forward with the implementation of Medvedev's plans connected with the creation of the European security system."[24] With such dangerous unrest in the world, America must maintain a vigorous defense.

Obama is naïve. This inexperienced man believes the START treaty will, like sprinkling pixie dust on the heart of the axis of evil, coax North Korea and Iran into discontinuing their nuclear programs. Obama actually said, "With this agreement, the United States and Russia—the two largest nuclear powers in the world—also send a clear signal that we intend to lead."[25] That's laughable. Mahmoud Ahmadinejad, the fascist dictator and Hitler of Iran, wants these weapons to intimidate the United States and to annihilate Israel.

Does Obama really think a meaningless piece of paper will stop Ah*mad*inejad who called Israel the "most cruel and repressive racist regime"?[26] Has Obama forgotten Iran's Hitler said that Israel "must be wiped out from the map of the world"?[27] How about this one from the little Iranian bully: "Anybody who recognizes Israel will burn in the fire of the Islamic nation's fury."[28] What, is Obama nuts? How can he believe that cutting our nuclear warheads will create a kinder, gentler Junior Hitler?

And what about our friends in Russia?

Anyone who believes they'll keep their word is a few fries short of a Happy Meal. Russia has a long history of reneging on agreements, including nuclear agreements. That's number one. What's more, it's impossible to verify how many they've destroyed. Toss in the fact that the Russians have already signaled that they can pull out of the agreement at any time, and you have a lose-lose situation as far as American interests are concerned.

Obama signed it anyway.

Need I point out that most of Russia's nuclear arsenal is aging and outdated? Without the treaty, the Russians would have had to spend a fortune updating their nuclear arsenal just to keep pace with us. If we didn't agree to take apart our nukes, Russia would fade as a nuclear power because it would be too costly to stay in our league. Instead, they can just scrap the most antiquated weapons in their stockpiles to meet the requirements of START. Whether or not our president wants to admit this, his nuclear agreement actually *helps* Russia because now they don't have to upgrade those useless missiles.

There's more to this madness. Obama is far from finished.

After signing the START treaty, look at what Obama the Destroyer announced to the world: "It is just one step on a longer journey. As I said last year in Prague, this treaty will set the stage for further cuts. And, going forward, we hope to pursue discussions with Russia on reducing both our strategic and tactical weapons, including non-deployed weapons."[29] Further cuts? Why? Because Obama has a long history of working to disarm America's nuclear capability. It's one of his core beliefs and lifelong aspirations.

Let me take you back to 1983.

At the time, Obama was a twenty-two-year-old college student at Columbia University. Although most of his college records and papers have been sealed, hidden or, more likely, destroyed, Obama penned an article for the campus newspaper, which has recently surfaced. In his article entitled, "Breaking the War Mentality," the young Obama sided with the anti-nuke/nuclear freeze camp and wrote of pursuing "a peace that is genuine, lasting and non-nuclear."[30] In other words, this man is a college radical who is implementing every imagined academic leftist, give-peace-a-chance experiment.

We all know that college is a season in life when kids will banter about fanciful solutions to a world they hardly understand. But it's one thing to sit around waxing eloquent about various extreme notions of pan-Leninism with your college buddies posited by your Marxist-Leninist professors. It's quite another to endanger the lives of millions of Americans and our allies around the world by pursuing such fantasies. The sandbox of the ivory tower can be a dangerous place when brought to the arena of national security.

I must ask the deeper question that nobody is asking.

We're not at war with Russia, are we?

Isn't Russia our friend?

If Russia is our friend, then why do they need us to cut our nuclear arsenal? If they're our friend, and if they have no harmful intentions toward us, why do we need to cut our nuclear arsenal to convince them that we're their friend? After all, we're trading partners with this former Cold War enemy. The Russians export oil and petroleum products, aluminum, semi-finished iron and steel, precious metals, and railway equipment among other things to us. United flies in there every day. Delta flies in there the last I checked.

Why, then, is our President suddenly signing a peace treaty with Russia when we're not at war with them?

If we had been at war and the hostilities had ceased, it would be understandable to craft some sort of postwar arrangement that included the disarming of various weapons. Remember what Germany had to do after World War I? At the Treaty of Versailles, the Germans had to abandon their Air Force. They had to shrink the size of their Navy by sinking most of their fleet. They were forbidden to have any submarines, tanks, or even armored cars. Why? Because they lost the war and those were the terms hammered out by the Allied Forces. If they hadn't lost, do you think the Germans would have laid down their weapons and compromised their defenses?

Why, then, are we disarming?

Did we just lose some war that I don't know about?

Did Obama lose a war somewhere that I missed while taking a nap?

The only explanation is that this move by Obama is a unilateral decision to demilitarize the United States of America. And in the background, while we're jettisoning our jets, missiles, subs, and nukes, the Dragon is rising. Is China cutting its nuclear arsenal? Did China agree to cut back on its launchers? Did China agree to stop developing ballistic submarines? Did China agree not to expand its Navy? I don't think so. How is Obama getting away with this?

I have to go back to my initial statement. Obama is the Destroyer.

Which is why Congress must *not* ratify START.

Yes, there is one remaining opportunity to end this radical agenda of appeasement and destruction. It resides in the U.S. Senate that, by law, must ratify it by a 67 percent majority. That means sixty-seven votes must say, "yes we agree to cut our military and our national security." Not by 51 votes, but 67 percent of the Senate has to go along with this. Obama could be stopped in the Senate. But I ask you where is the Republican opposition? Where are the Blue Dog Democrats? Each day, it's as if a hostile foreign power has taken over the United States of America and our elected officials don't have the spine to stop it.

We must remind Congress of something that should be obvious:

One nuclear bomb can ruin your whole day.

Obama the Space Cadet: Houston We Have a Problem

We know Obama is taking apart America's military infrastructure. And yet this man, who has created nothing in his life except absolute chaos, anger, divisiveness, and fear, as well as trillion dollar deficits designed to break the backs of the middle class, can't restrain himself from destroying the centerpiece of American technology and accomplishment: the NASA space program. As you'll see, dark implications for America's national security interests are beneath this move, and a troubling money trail that the Savage Spotlight will illuminate.

On April 15, 2010, Obama the Space Cadet delivered a speech at NASA's Kennedy Space Center in which he announced his plans to scrap NASA's current space exploration program. He goes to the Mecca of space travel and announces with a placid smile on his face that he's about to tear the program apart. Why would he destroy NASA? Don't we already have the best aeronautical program in the world?

We do. Do I need to point out that it's one of the few government programs with direct benefits to the taxpayer? Thanks to NASA's research and development, we now have a list of inventions that enhance and protect our lives. Among them is the TV satellite dish, fail-safe flashlights with system redundancy, shock absorbing helmets for sports and biking enthusiasts that use Temper Foam (first developed for aircraft seats), edible toothpaste, "space pens" that can be used to write upside down, cordless tools (originally developed to help Apollo astronauts drill for moon samples), smoke detectors first used in the Skylab space station, ear thermometers that don't use mercury, and joystick controllers created for the Apollo Lunar Rover.[31]

Why does Obama the Space Cadet want to fix what isn't broken?

Evidently, Obama thinks private companies can build the current space shuttle's replacement quicker and more cost-effectively than NASA. Really? So this is all about saving money? Retired astronaut John McBride points out, "Back in Apollo days our space budget for NASA was three to four percent of the federal budget. Today it's less than one percent."[32]

That doesn't sound like NASA is breaking the budget, Mr. Obama.

Let's set aside the fact that Obama dismantled the private sector healthcare system because he believes the government can do a better job, but now he thinks the private sector is suddenly better positioned to tackle space. Why the double standard? Leave it to Doc Savage to break down the truth for you. As I've often said, follow the money. To fund the civilian development of the next shuttle, Obama intends to hand $6 billion dollars to private companies to do the job instead of NASA.

Just who are these companies?

Lockheed Martin is one.

On the surface, there's nothing wrong with that pick, right? Lockheed Martin does a fantastic job building aircraft. But did you know that in 2010 they've given $800,000 in campaign contributions to Democrats? Then there's the Chicago-based Boeing Company, which, as of this writing, has already dished out $900,000 to the Demoncats in 2010. Why does any of that matter? Consider this: although Obama is increasing NASA's budget by $6 billion, most of that money will go to "seed commercial development." In other words, it will go to pay off the same companies that just contributed to Obama's friends in Congress. Are you starting to get the picture? He's using NASA to fund a massive payoff of his campaign contributors.

Give a million; get a billion.

Not a bad investment for Boeing and Lockheed Martin.

Beyond that payback scheme, Obama the Space Cadet is destroying the space program—which wasn't broken—while making us fully dependent on Russia. How so? This Space Cadet is proposing that the USA buy tickets on a *Russian* rocket to get our astronauts and cargo into space. In fact, he proposes that we buy six seats a year on Russia's Soyuz spacecraft—at $56 million per seat[33]—for however long that it takes for the private sector to build a replacement.

Am I the only one who sees a problem with that? Isn't Russia the same nation we fought for decades to win the space race? Won't this give the edge to Russia when it comes to weaponizing space? Since Russia will be providing the ride, they get to dictate the terms of what our astronauts can and cannot do, how much gear they're permitted to bring, and how much they can bring back.[34] And Russia gets to eavesdrop on their activities.

Thanks to Obama, Russia now holds all the cards in terms of space exploration. What's more, in the best-case scenario, the soonest a privately built space shuttle can be ready is 2014. In an attempt to quell criticism of this move, Obama said:

> Nobody is more committed to manned spaceflight, to human exploration of space, than me. But we have got to do it in a smart way, we can't just keep doing the same old things that we've been doing and thinking that somehow that's going to get us to where we want to go.[35]

The same old things? Look, we all know NASA has made their share of mistakes. But that's not reason enough to scrub their mission. Even a reporter for the *New York Times* was left scratching his head about Obama's decision. He writes, "In place of the Moon mission, Mr. Obama's vision offers, at least initially, nothing in terms of human exploration of the solar system. What the administration calls a 'bold new initiative' does not spell out a next destination or timetable for getting there." [36]

Meanwhile, astronauts Neil Armstrong, the first man on the moon, and Eugene Cernan, the last to set foot on its rocky soil, made a prediction about the impact of Obama's plan: "the USA is far too likely to be on a long downhill slide to mediocrity. America must decide if it wishes to remain a leader in space." [37] I couldn't agree more.

Obama doesn't want us to go to the moon.

He wants America to be damned.

Remember Reverend Wright's sermon? "Not God *Bless* America," Wright roared into the young, community activists' ears, "God DAMN America!" To put it another way, Obama clearly concurs with something his Secretary of State, Hillary Rodham Clinton, has said:

"God bless the America we are trying to create." [38]

Shooting Stars: From Leathernecks to Rubberneckers

Obama's war on the military and America's national defense continues to defy logic. Perhaps no better example exists than the treatment of our brave heroes on the front lines. The case of Captain Matthew Myers comes to mind. Myers, who won the Silver Star for bravery in action when his men were surrounded and outnumbered, was also reprimanded for not doing enough to prevent the attack! Did you hear about that one?

In the battle of Wanat, one of the deadliest to date in the Afghan theater of operations, Captain Myers and his troops were manning an outpost deep inside the enemy's position. According to a CBS News account, the Taliban had surrounded the outpost and were "shooting down on U.S. soldiers like fish in a barrel. When it was over, nine Americans lay dead." [39] It was a surprise ambush in which hundreds of Taliban fighters far outnumbered our forty-nine men assigned to the outpost.

Not only were our men outflanked, they were short on supplies, running out of water, and were without overhead surveillance when the unmanned drone providing data to the troops' position was reassigned to a different mission. CBS reports the dire straits Myers and his men found themselves in. In this exchange, Myers is talking via radio to U.S. Apache gunships calling for help:

> "Be advised, we're in a bad situation," Myers said. "Need you to come in hot immediately." The enemy was so close that Myers told the incredulous pilots to lay down fire within 10 meters of his position. "I know it's high risk, but we need to get these guys off of us," Myers said. "Ten meters," the pilot replied. "You got to be kidding me."[40]

It took over an hour before the Apache helicopters arrived to drive back the enemy. Although nine were killed and twenty-seven were wounded, Myers' leadership saved the entire fort from being overrun by a much larger enemy force. He was rightly awarded the Silver Star. So far so good.

But in the upside-down world of Obama's military, Myers was also *blamed* for not having established enough of a defense to prevent the attack—a function that wasn't even his job. It gets worse. The men whose job it was to prevent the attack were promoted up to the higher levels of command. Lieutenant Colonel William Ostlund was promoted to colonel while brigade commander Colonel Chip Preysler got a cushy job working for the Joint Staff at the Pentagon.[41]

How much crazier does it get than this? A hero who fought back the attack gets a career-ending letter while his superior gets promoted to the Joint Staff! If we had these rules of engagement in World War II, rules introduced under George Bush, now magnified under BO, and if these rules had been pro-actively applied to WWII, half the men buried in Arlington Cemetery would have to be disinterred and their medals taken away from them.

This is not the only case. Nor did this insanity start under Obama. Even George W. Bush blew it with the persecution of Marine Lieutenant Colonel Jeffrey Chessani. In this case, which dragged on for four years, the government wasted millions of taxpayers' dollars investigating and prosecuting this soldier for the "Haditha Massacre." Remember that one? Although Chessani wasn't present for the events that led to the deaths of a number of Iraqi civilians, he was charged for failing to launch an investigation.

Long before the facts were compiled, U.S. Representative John Murtha, the now deceased blowhard Demoncat, blasted our troops claiming they had "overreacted because of the pressure on them. And they killed innocent civilians in cold blood."[42] This lie was based on false reporting by *TIME* magazine's Tim McGurk. Murtha's fiery rhetoric unnecessarily ramped up hostilities in Iraq and sparked enemy retaliation.[43] In turn, Chessani became the political scapegoat. In the end, the Navy named a ship after Murtha! How's that for justice? Realizing the raw deal that Officer Chessani was getting, I took his case to the Savage Nation who, in turn, joined me in raising tens of thousands of dollars for his legal defense.

Or take the case of Army Ranger Lieutenant Michael Behenna. In short, Ali Mansur, a known terrorist member of an al-Qaeda cell, was captured by Lieutenant Behenna's platoon in Iraq an April 21, 2008. Mansur was suspected of organizing an attack that killed two U.S. soldiers from Behenna's platoon, two Iraqi citizens, and injured two more American troops. Lieutenant Behenna was personally ordered to return the terrorist to his home and release him.

Let's set aside the fact that, from a layman's point of view, it makes no sense that we'd catch and then release a known terrorist. According to Lieutenant Behenna's account, Mansur lunged for Behenna as he was being returned home and Behenna shot him in self-defense. Though an expert witness for the government supports Behenna's version of events, the government refused to hear this testimony! Now Behenna, who is rotting in a cold cell, has been sentenced by his government to serve fifteen years in prison for killing a terrorist.

Behenna's case is currently in the Army Court of Appeals.

According to his girlfriend, Shannon Wahl, Behenna remains imprisoned at Ft. Leavenworth, Kansas, with no access to the Internet or e-mail, and he is not allowed to have any phone calls or visits from anyone he didn't already know before he was jailed. Wahl told me that contact with the media could potentially get him moved to a maximum-security facility. This is the same Army that gives all the rights in the world to Major Hasan who, as I pointed out in the last chapter, murdered twelve soldiers in the Fort Hood massacre.

Meanwhile, Scott Behenna, his father, a retired Special Agent with the Oklahoma State Bureau of Investigation, and Vicki Behenna, his mother, an Assistant United States Attorney, have had to mortgage their house to save their child. Is this how we should treat an American hero who defended himself against this Iraqi terrorist who was caught planting IEDs and killed several of his men? What's more, Vicki Behenna told me something startling: more Marines who fought in Iraq and Afghanistan sit behind bars right now than those imprisoned during Vietnam and the Korean war combined!

The Marine Corp was once the proudest division in the U.S. Military. But under George Bush—and now under Barack Obama—they're sadly being reduced by the rules of non-engagement to rubberneckers, watching accidents on the side of the road. If they do fight, and if they do their job too well, they're imprisoned and tried in court.

While the U.S. Army won't do a damn thing to defend one of its own, thankfully the listeners of the Savage Nation have come to Behenna's defense. To date, my loyal audience and I have contributed nearly $150,000 for Behenna's legal expenses. I've gone to bat for a number of U.S. Marines over the years, raising hundreds of thousands of dollars for their defense.

That said, none of us is looking for a pat on the back.

We want justice for these heroic men.

We want our heroes to know America is still on their side.

Of course, that's a bit difficult for them to believe when the Commander in Chief blows off an opportunity to pay tribute to those who have paid the ultimate sacrifice on the battlefield. Case in point. In what was a stark slap in the face to both tradition and the military, Mr. Obama did not attend the ceremony honoring fallen troops at Arlington National Cemetery on Memorial Day, 2010. Rather than participate, he dispatched Vice President Joe Biden to take his place.

Barack Obama is the first U.S. President to skip this important ceremony at a time when American troops are engaged in two active wars. Making matters worse is the fact that tens of thousands of additional troops were on high alert due to threats from North Korea and Iran. None of that mattered to this president.

We all know Mr. Obama has displayed contempt for the military. He has cut them off at the knees with oppressive rules of engagement that jeopardizes their safety and the ability to complete their mission.

He has slashed away at the military budget, cutting it until it bled. His military prosecutes brave soldiers for doing their job with excellence. Now, he has thumbed his nose at the tradition of laying a wreath at the Tomb of the Unknown Soldier.

America deserves better than a President who stabs the military in the back. America deserves better than a Commander in Chief who'd rather be at a cookout in Chicago vacationing with his family than a breakfast with Gold Star families—those incredible families who suffered the loss of a loved one on the front lines. American heroes in the military need to know that while they may not have the support of President Barack, America still has their back.

School Lunchrooms: Heroes or Food Fight?

As I was working on this chapter, studying the ways Obama the Destroyer is compromising our military and national security, I was stunned to read the following headline: "First Lady Credits School Lunch Program for Bolstering National Security." That got my attention. I started scanning the article to see what possible link might exist between the cafeteria ladies who serve the junior sheeple mystery meat in middle school and our brave soldiers in the middle of combat fighting terrorism. The reporter writes:

> First lady Michelle Obama said at the School Nutrition Association Conference in Washington, D.C. on Monday that individuals who work in school cafeterias across the country not only educate and feed children, but help to strengthen national security.[44]

Help strengthen national security? Really?

Michelle Obama, who appears to be going after the cafeteria vote, said, "Whether it's national security, education or child hunger, for decades we've looked to you for help in achieving our most urgent national priorities." So, in other words your son or daughter, who may be serving as a U.S. Marine in Afghanistan or Iraq or who is a trained member of the U.S. Navy stationed at the helm of a nuclear submarine, is now equal to the cafeteria worker in your elementary school. Maybe serving nutritionally balanced meals is a form of combat, especially when you have to serve pots of boiling tomato soup to kids who can't stand the stuff.

What's next? Maybe these heroic cafeteria workers—with little white nets on their heads instead of helmets and armed with sixteen-ounce plastic ladles instead of M16 assault rifles—can qualify for burial in the Arlington National Cemetery because of their role helping defend our national security. After all, it's the least we can do for the "food workers" who are "shaping the future of this country."[45]

I knew it would be mad and bad under these radicals.

I just didn't think it would get this bad, this fast.

Ironically, three short weeks after the First Lady sang the praises of the Lunchroom Battalion, a band of retired military officers took aim at the nation's school lunch program, calling it a "national security threat." What's their beef? They cited a new study, which found "more than 9 million young adults, or 27% of all Americans ages 17 to 24, are too overweight to join the military."[46] Speaking on behalf of the officers' group, *Mission: Readiness*, retired Navy Rear Admiral James Barnett Jr. said, "When over a quarter of young adults are too fat to fight, we need to take notice."[47]

This, of course, will end badly for the students.

No doubt Michelle will tell her Kitchen Brigade to declare war on dessert.

Big Brother is *Not* Watching—And Big Sis is Amiss

On February 15, 2010, Bob Thomas and his wife Leona were taking their four-year-old son, Ryan, to Walt Disney World to celebrate his fourth birthday. Keep in mind Bob is a police officer with Camden, New Jersey's emergency crime suppression team. As they approached the Transportation Security Administration (TSA) security checkpoint at the airport, I'm sure little Ryan had visions of Mickey Mouse dancing in his head.

Fun was in the air, and this was to be his first flight.

Did I mention that Ryan cannot walk without his leg braces?

When Ryan's leg braces triggered the metal detector alarm, the TSA screener informed his parents that the young boy had to remove the braces and try again. Ryan's father explained the obvious: *Ryan needed them to walk.* That meant nothing to the stern-faced screener who repeated the demand. Ryan's mother suggested a compromise. She offered to steady Ryan as he went through the screening machine. Nope. Not good enough, said the screener with a mental capacity of a 40-watt light bulb.

The boy would have to walk unassisted.

With the line of passengers behind them growing longer by the minute, Laura passed through the metal detector first with Ryan just steps behind her. Bob followed closely behind his son in the event Ryan were to fall. While they made it through, Bob was fuming and demanded to speak to a supervisor. "I told him, 'This is overkill. He's four years old. I don't think he's a terrorist.'"[48]

That's the kind of insanity you get under Janet Napolitano's incompetent Homeland Security regime. In her world, four-year-old crippled children must walk to prove they're not armed and dangerous, while true threats to our national security breeze through the system. Remember the case of Umar Farouk Abdulmutallab, the Christmas "Underwear Bomber"? The Nigerian-born twenty-three-year-old Abdulmutallab, a Muslim whose head was filled with the explosive teachings of radical Islam, attempted to ignite a makeshift bomb in his underwear aboard Northwest Flight 253 bound for Detroit. He should never have been permitted on the flight. The warning signs were all there.

Even though he purchased his tickets in cash . . .

Even though he had no checked luggage . . .

Even though a month prior to this near-fatal incident his own father warned the U.S. Embassy in Abuja, Nigeria, that his son could pose a threat to the United States . . .

Even though the Customs and Border Protection had documentation supplied by the Department of State indicating his possible extremist ties as Napolitano later admitted.[49] Even after all those pieces of the puzzle were in place, the Christmas Crotch Bomber wasn't put on the "no-fly list."[50] If it were not for the quick and courageous actions of the adjacent passengers and crew on that flight, hundreds of Americans could have died. Rushing to the microphones after the inexcusable security breach, Big Sis Napolitano told nervous Americans that "the system worked." The Muslim fanatic smuggled explosives onto a U.S. airplane, didn't he? How was he able to do that if the system worked? When a reporter asked this homeland security genius that question, Napolitano said, "We're asking the same questions."[51]

Two days later, Big Sis was backpedaling saying, "Our system did not work in this instance."[52] Which is it? How does this amateur keep her job? After what was clearly an attempted terrorist attack on Christmas Day, and with the vacationing Obama avoiding his beloved cameras, Representative Peter King said, "We're now, what, 72 hours into this and the President's not spoken, the Vice President's not spoken, the Attorney General's not spoken and Janet Napolitano has now told two different stories in two days. First, she said everything worked; now she said it didn't."[53] And when Obama finally did address the near-fatal act of terrorism, his first reaction was to say it was the actions of "an isolated extremist."[54] Is that so?

Let's be clear: this was an act of Islamic terrorism hatched from within the bowels and terrorist training camps in Yemen. Big Sis didn't acknowledge that fact. Nor did the president. If anything, that intel was covered up. Instead, we had to discover it from the twisted mouth of Anwar al-Awlaqi, a top al-Qaeda leader and Imam of mosques in Virginia and San Diego. After the attack, he bragged that he personally trained the Underwear Bomber *and* Major Nidal Hasan—the Muslim shooter in the Fort Hood massacre. This terrorist-training Imam said, "I am proud to have been their teacher."[55]

Contrary to what the president said, the Underwear Bomber wasn't acting alone. He was an al-Qaeda operative. That's number one. Second, when it comes to the horrible, unspeakable, traitorous actions of Major Hasan, let's not mince words: Hasan didn't *slip* though the cracks—he was *pushed* through the cracks. In fact the cracks were widened by the Department of Defense. How so? By cultivating a climate within the military that bends over backward to make sure Muslim *seeennnsitivities* are not offended.

The fact is that Major Hasan, a mental case posing as a psychiatrist, was both a screw-up and a ticking time bomb. He was a keg of dynamite with a sizzling fuse. But nobody would fire him for fear of losing their jobs. They were too busy looking over their shoulder at some demented Red Diaper Doper Baby defense lawyer from NYU if they had fired Hasan for proselytizing the patients while treating them.

A columnist for the *New York Post* put it this way: "Hasan's superiors feared—correctly—that any attempt to call attention to his radicalism or to prevent his promotion would backfire on them, destroying their careers, not his."[56] What is meant by Hasan's "radicalism"? Among other things, did you know that Hasan would write "Allah be praised" on the medical reports of his patients? Imagine if a Christian doctor wrote "Jesus Saves" on a medical report—how long do you think he would have lasted in the military?

That just shows you how far we've fallen.

After the shooting, while families were grieving the unnecessary loss of their loved ones, President Obama offered this feeble comment:

> I want to begin by offering an update on the tragedy that took place at Fort Hood. This morning I met with FBI Director Mueller and the relevant agencies to discuss their ongoing investigation into **what caused one individual** to turn his gun on fellow servicemen and women. We don't know all the answers yet and I would **caution against jumping to conclusions** until we have all the facts[57] [emphasis added].

That's code language designed to mask the fact Hasan was a Muslim. That's also his way of downplaying any connection to al-Qaeda.

Regarding the possibility that Hasan was inspired by his ideological views, television talk show host Dr. Phil said, "You don't take the guy's last name and impugn the Islamic nation. Are you kidding me? . . . That is irresponsible. It is ridiculous to say."[58] Really? How else do you explain that witnesses to the massacre heard Hasan shout "Allah Akbar" before opening fire on American soldiers?[59] Why is it "ridiculous" to suggest Hasan was acting out his ideology with a gun?

Such cowardice is killing us—literally. It killed thirteen men and wounded thirty others! Which brings me to a number of difficult questions yet to be raised. Why were our men disarmed in that room? When did soldiers on military bases become disarmed? Think about it. How did Hasan get in with guns? Why was there no Sergeant at Arms at the door? Why was there a breakdown there?

A month later, a worthless hearing was held. The public wanted to know how this happened and who was behind it. One reporter timidly asked Defense Secretary Robert Gates whether this was an act of terrorism because Hasan shouted, "Allah Akbar," as he opened fire. The reporter rightly wanted to explore whether there was a tie to militant Islam. Defense Secretary Robert Gates reportedly said, "I'm not even going there."

I say Gates better start going there! Why?

Read on.

From the Gang That Couldn't Shoot Straight to the Gang That Couldn't Shoot At All

On May 1, 2010, New Yorkers dodged another terrorist attack—no thanks to the incompetence of Big Sis. The Pakistani-born, terrorist-trained, thirty-year-old Faisal Shahzad, who lied on his citizenship application to become one of us in order to kill us, parked a Pathfinder packed with explosive material and a timer in Times Square. If it were not for the quick action on the part of a street vendor who alerted police to the threat, more Americans would have died at the hands of a radical Muslim terrorist.

What is happening to the government of the United States? It seems they are unable to provide security from threats both foreign and domestic. A bomb almost goes off in Times Square and who finds it?

Not the military.

Not the FBI. Not the police.

A street vendor selling T-shirts.

Don't think that the fact a street peddler spotted this bomb was unusual. Remember the passengers on United Flight 93 who took back the plane and saved the capital? Or two tourists who tackled a gunman who was shooting at the White House several years ago? Or the Flying Dutchman who stopped the Underwear Bomber? Over and over again, individual Americans using personal initiative and good judgment have been the true First Responders that saved us from these attacks. The citizens of this country are doing their job, not the inept government hacks whose job it is to keep America safe.

What was the reaction from Big Sis when the Times Square plot was first uncovered? Janet "the system worked" Napolitano said, "We're taking this very seriously. We're treating it as if it could be a potential terrorist attack."[60] What world is she living in? How could a car bomb deliberately planted and designed to maximize casualties on the crowded streets in the heart of Manhattan *not* be an act of terror? Of course it's terrorism. The only thing scarier than her remark is that this attack SUCCEEDED in every way but one.

This radical Muslim terrorist was able to enter the U.S. on a student visa.

This radical Muslim terrorist was able to obtain a work permit.

This radical Muslim terrorist was able to romance an American woman, marry her and get a green card, then obtain American citizenship. As soon as Shahzad did, the terrorist sprang into action, returned to his native land, learned to make bombs, and then got his orders to blow up Times Square. He was able to procure all the necessary equipment, assemble it, place it in Times Square, and then escape the FBI. He was unhindered when he purchased a last-minute ticket on an airplane and then breezed through security check points while four-year-olds wearing leg braces and elderly women with walkers were scrutinized. He ultimately boarded a plane and almost got away.

This radical Muslim terrorist made one mistake.

The bomb didn't go off because he failed to set the timer properly, not because of anything we did to prevent it. He did all this without ever coming to the notice of American intelligence. How many others are following this same plan? Maybe they won't make the same mistakes. When a Republican charged that Shahzad was foiled only because of a lucky break, Missouri Demoncat Representative Ike Skelton said, "What's wrong with being lucky?"[61] There you have it. Another genius in Washington crossing his fingers hoping our "luck" in the war against terrorism holds up.

An editorial in the *Washington Times* calls this "Obama's Good Luck Terrorism Strategy." In it, they ask the questions I've been asking, such as why was Shahzad who, in 2008, was on the Department of Homeland Security's Traveler Enforcement Compliance System list, pulled from the list by the Obama administration? Why did the Obama administration tell the national Joint Terrorism Task Force, who had been tracking Shahzad's moves, to back off? The *Times* writes:

These disturbing revelations about the case of Mr. Shahzad raise pertinent questions regarding U.S. domestic security. Who gave the order to shut down surveillance of Mr. Shahzad? Who removed him from the Traveler Enforcement Compliance System list? Who else has been removed from this and other lists and why? Were they removed simply because they were Muslims and the administration believed that ipso facto they were being persecuted unfairly?[62]

For our part, I pray to God that Obama and Homeland Security stop making the willful mistake of refusing to profile those who are most likely to attack us. That goes for New York City Mayor Michael Bloomberg, who was quick to say, "I want to make clear that we will not tolerate any bias or backlash against Pakistani or Muslim New Yorkers."[63] Does a "backlash" include profiling those who are at war with us in order to prevent another attack? Radical Muslims are waging jihad around the world.

Radical Muslims are strapping bombs to their backs in Russia.

Radical Muslims are strapping bombs to their underwear in America.

Radical Muslims are strapping bombs in their SUVs in Times Square.

Radical Muslims have killed at U.S. Army bases.

But who is the Obama administration most concerned about?

Radical *Christians.*

That's right. Barack Hussein Obama is concerned about a group of nine suspects with rifles in Michigan who the FBI claims were plotting to use weapons of mass destruction against the police and the government. Of course, by weapons of mass destruction, Team Obama means improvised homemade explosives. By the way, an interesting development occurred in this case.

While the feds marched in with a heavy show of force to round up these guys with guns, the FBI wasn't quite as prepared when it came time to present their case in court. In fact, Agent Leslie Larsen, the lead FBI agent on the case, who spent two years on the undercover probe, had difficulty recalling a number of key details when confronted by the defense attorneys. The fuzzy command of the facts baffled the judge, U.S. District Judge Victoria Roberts, who said, "I share the frustrations of the defense team . . . that she doesn't know anything."[64]

Usually, the stench on the bench makes me clench. Not so in this case, at least so far. Judge Victoria Roberts, who, by the way, was a Bill Clinton appointee, after listening to two days of testimony and arguments by the lawyers involved, made an observation that agrees with the position I've maintained on my radio show. Roberts noted, "Mere presence where a crime may be planned is not a crime . . . How does this add up to seditious conspiracy?"[65] In other words, the Fed had nothing that would warrant the court to hold the accused without bail until the trial as the Fed had asked. All nine were permitted to return home.

The whole thing was a government red herring designed to fire a shot at anyone who owns a gun in America. The Obama administration wanted to cause law-abiding citizens to think twice about gun ownership. While I oppose violence and, in fact, I'm a pacifist, the fact of the matter is that the Second Amendment gives every citizen the right to bear arms.

"This is an example of radical and extremist fringe groups which can be found throughout our society," said one FBI special agent whose name isn't important.[66] Attorney General Eric Holder was quick to label it an "insidious plan."[67] Question: Why didn't the FBI or Eric Holder blast Major Hasan for his "insidious plan" that actually *did* claim the lives of thirteen troops? Why don't they label the well-known Muslim radicals living among us like Hasan as "an example of radical and extremist fringe groups"?

Speaking of this obvious double standard, for years liberals have said that someone accused of a crime is innocent until proven guilty. Did they maintain this standard with regard to the so-called Christian militia members? No. What's more, helicopters were sent out with paramilitary forces to capture the Christian militia members. Why weren't those same black helicopters sent to the homes and mosques of those plotting to blow up U.S. Military bases such as Fort Dix and Fort Hood? Why aren't paramilitary forces being commissioned to shut down the vicious and violently dangerous MS-13 gang of criminal thugs running through the streets of our cities?

After all, their motto is "rape, kill, control."[68]

The Obama administration has raided the houses of Christian militia members because they allegedly planned to use weapons against the police. And yet we have documented evidence of the MS-13 gang not threatening but actually killing people in towns from Los Angeles to Atlanta. Likewise, we hear reports of communities such as Islamberg, New York, where Muslim military-style training has been observed and, according to FOXNews, "Shoe bomber Richard Reid has been linked to the group, along with convicted D.C. sniper John Allen Muhammad."[69] Yet nothing has been done. Why not?

Unfortunately, in the modern politically correct world, certain institutions, religions, and states are more targeted for delegitimization than others. Take the Pentagon, which disinvited evangelist Reverend Franklin Graham from participating in the May 6, 2010, National Day of Prayer event. Even though the son of Billy Graham is the honorary chairman of the National Day of Prayer task force, a source at the Pentagon stated: "While we appreciate [Franklin Graham's] worldwide outreach, and his willingness to speak at this Pentagon multi-faith event, his presence would be inappropriate."[70] No explanation why his participation would be "inappropriate."

As I said, certain religions have been targeted for delegitimization. For example, Jewish nationalism is targeted, Palestinian nationalism is not. Catholic sins are frequently seen to reflect mainstream Catholicism, while Islamist violence is deemed a rare deviation from Islam, "the religion of peace." Similarly, conservative criticism of liberal critics gets labeled McCarthyism; liberal criticism of conservatives is merely free speech. The calculus of delegitimization reflects a moral hierarchy rooted in New Left sensibilities, refined in universities, spread by much of the media and now by the military.

This explains something: when radical Muslims, based upon the teachings of the Qur'an, threaten and attack us, they are ignored. And yet Obama's Homeland Insecurity Department is quick to arrest and level charges of sedition against a fringe, rag-tag "Christian" militia who are misrepresenting, at best, the teachings of the Bible.[71] Need I point out that the central message of Christianity includes these words of Jesus: "Blessed are the peacemakers, for they shall be called sons of God" (Matthew 5:9).

Let's contrast those words with the teachings of Islam in the Qur'an: "Fight and kill the disbelievers wherever you find them, take them captive, harass them, lie in wait and ambush them using every stratagem of war" (Qur'an 9:5). Or how about this one: "I will cast terror into the hearts of those who reject Me. So strike off their heads and cut off their fingers. All who oppose Me and My Prophet shall be punished severely" (Ishaq:322).[72]

What could be more clear? Obama is declaring war on the wrong religion.

Obama's Jihad on Jihad

Of course, such hatred for America exhibited by the Underwear Bomber and Major Hasan among others is consistent with what we know of militant Islam. Rather than acknowledge that we're at war with Islamo-fascism, and that the Fort Hood massacre was the most recent effort to kill the American infidel in the name of Allah, Big Sis, taking her marching orders from the Commander in Chief, has called for a jihad on the use of the word jihad! In an effort to make nice with Muslim countries, she doesn't want the government to mention any words such as "jihad" or "Islamic extremism."

In April, 2010, the Obama administration deleted those words from the U.S. National Security Strategy guidelines. Are we fighting a war on terror or not? If we are, then why aren't we allowed to name the enemy? Why is Homeland Insecurity more concerned about not offending Muslims than they are defending Americans? We don't need a public-relations stunt. At least one Senator called such verbal gymnastics nonsense. Here's what Joe Lieberman said:

> We're in a war not with some nebulous group of violent extremists. We're not in a war with environmental extremists or white extremists. We're in a war with violent Islamist extremists and terrorists. The people who attacked us on 9/11 were not just violent and extreme, they were motivated by an ideology of Islamist extremism which took the religion of Islam and essentially transformed it into a radical political ideology.
>
> And if we don't call it what it is, first off we're violating the first rule of war, know your enemy. Secondly, how do you defeat your enemy unless you describe it as what it is? And third, in many ways this is an ideological conflict between one set of values and this violent Islamist extremist ideology. Most people in the Muslim world reject this ideology. But if we don't say there's a difference between most Muslims in the world and the violent Islamist extremists and terrorists, I think we're disrespecting most of the Muslims.[73]

An editorial in the *Washington Times* rightly points out both the deeper issue and the danger here, saying, "the National Security Strategy is not some kind of outreach initiative, it is the framing document for America's global safety. The United States cannot effectively combat the root causes of Islamic extremism by ignoring them. Such sanitizing may please the White House, but it's likely to put the United States in more danger as threats that should have been detected in advance slip by because officials have been trained not to look for them."[74] Which probably explains why the 2009 Homeland Security glossary of domestic "extremist" groups omitted any Muslim groups but listed both Jewish and Christian organizations as potential threats.

Once again, they're focusing on the wrong religions.

We've been told by the government that sleeper cells are here. We've known this fact for years. Back in 2004, the FBI estimated there were al-Qaeda sleeper cells in upwards of forty states.[75] Let me ask you something: Where are these operatives congregating? Where would Muslim terrorists gather to exchange information and resources? Would they gather in the synagogues, churches, or mosques? It's not such a difficult question if you use common sense. So, where do you put your FBI agents to ferret out the vermin?

Synagogue, churches, or mosques?

But, in light of the appeasement strategy of the Obama administration, Big Sis won't do that. Because of her inaction to target the real enemies of America, the enemy is laughing at us. They're laughing at us from within the mosques here because we have college girls running America.

Worse Than Chamberlain

The world is mocking and taking advantage of President Obama's weakness. The world is laughing and exploiting President Obama's naiveté. Listen to President Mahmoud Ahmadinejad, the Hitler of Iran in elevator shoes, who flat out called Barack Obama an amateur: "Mr. Obama, you are a newcomer [to politics]. Wait until your sweat dries and get some experience."[76] Obama has traveled the world, bowing to world leaders—a number of which are communist despots. With the START treaty, he has signed away the power of the United States of America without getting anything in return. He wants to dismantle NASA, giving Russia the advantage in space. This man is weakening what was once the greatest superpower the world has ever seen at every turn.

Frankly, I'm not surprised.

Obama views America's role as a superpower with contempt. He sees our military might as a burden. Look at what he said during the closing session of a two-day nuclear security summit: "It is a vital national security interest of the United States to reduce these conflicts because whether we like it or not, we remain a dominant military superpower . . ."[77]

Pause right there. *Whether we like it or not?*

What are we to make of that comment?

What kind of Commander in Chief and leader of the free world would say such a thing? Would Obama be happier if America *wasn't* a dominant superpower? Evidently that is his position. With regard to the downside of intervening in conflicts around the world, Obama went on to say, ". . . and when conflicts break out, one way or another we get pulled into them and that ends up costing us significantly in terms of both blood and treasure."[78]

Since when is President Obama concerned about the cost of anything?

In his first eighteen months in office, he raised our national debt higher than President Bush did after an eight-year spending spree.[79] Obama's federal budget has spilled more red ink than any president in modern history. Every economist knows Obama's reckless spending is unsustainable. No, his fretting over military actions that will end up "costing us significantly" in "treasure" isn't about trimming the budget. Nor can he be sincere about the loss of "blood" by our soldiers. If he were, he'd scrap the politically correct rules of engagement, which are killing our troops.

The fact is that President Obama hasn't the first clue why America must remain strong. By contrast, in 1984, his predecessor, President Ronald Reagan, said, "There are some who've forgotten why we have a military. It's not to promote war; it's to be prepared for peace."[80] Reagan knew the value and responsibilities associated with being the world's last remaining superpower. Reagan never apologized for the role America plays to protect our national security interests both at home and abroad. Thanks to Reagan's commitment to a strong military and his hard line "peace through strength" leadership in world affairs, we watched the Berlin Wall crumble and an end to the Cold War.

While I disagree with John McCain on many things, he had the right response to Obama's lunacy: "That's one of the more incredible statements I've ever heard a president of the United States make in modern times," said McCain. "We are the dominant superpower, and we're the greatest force for good in the history of this country, and I thank God every day that we are a dominant superpower."[81]

John McCain's outrage is echoed in this "open letter" written by an ex-Navy survivor of World War II, the now ninety-five-year-old Harold B. Estes. This senior patriot, incensed over the disgraceful behavior of the Commander in Chief, addressed his letter to President Barack Obama, Representative F. Allen Boyd, Senator Bill Nelson, and Senator George LeMieux. See if his words don't resonate with you:

Dear President Obama,

I enlisted in the U.S. Navy in 1934 and served proudly before, during and after WW II retiring as a Master Chief Bos'n Mate. Now I live in a "rest home" located on the western end of Pearl Harbor, allowing me to keep alive the memories of 23 years of service to my country.

One of the benefits of my age, perhaps the only one, is to speak my mind, blunt and direct even to the head man. So here goes.

I am amazed, angry and determined not to see my country die before I do, but you seem hell bent not to grant me that wish.

Pause there for a moment. Wouldn't America be a different country if our leaders spoke with such candor? Wouldn't it be a refreshing change of pace if our congressmen and women had, like Harold, the guts to stand up to this president, speak the truth, and let the chips fall where they may? He continues:

I can't figure out what country you are the president of. You fly around the world telling our friends & enemies despicable lies like:

"We're no longer a Christian nation." "America is arrogant." (Your wife even announced to the world, "America is mean-spirited." Please tell her to try preaching that nonsense to 23 generations of our war dead buried all over the globe who died for no other reason than to free a whole lot of strangers from tyranny and hopelessness.)

I'd say shame on the both of you, but I don't think you like America, nor do I see an ounce of gratefulness in anything you do, for the obvious gifts this country has given you. To be without shame or gratefulness is a dangerous thing for a man sitting in the White House.

After 9/11 you said, "America hasn't lived up to her ideals."

Which ones did you mean? Was it the notion of personal liberty that 11,000 farmers and shopkeepers died for to win independence from the British? Or maybe the ideal that no man should be a slave to another man, that 500,000 men died for in the Civil War? I hope you didn't mean the ideal 470,000 fathers, brothers, husbands, and a lot of fellas I knew personally died for in WWII, because we felt real strongly about not letting any nation push us around, because we stand for freedom.

You can almost feel the heat and passion leap off of the page as Harold exoriates this president. But this ex-Navy man isn't finished speaking his mind. There's much more fire where that came from. Harold writes: Take a little advice from a very old geezer, young man.

Shape up and start acting like an American. If you don't, I'll do what I can to see you get shipped out of that fancy rental on Pennsylvania Avenue. You were elected to lead not to bow, apologize and kiss the hands of murderers and corrupt leaders who still treat their people like slaves.

And just who do you think you are telling the American people not to jump to conclusions and condemn that Muslim major who killed 13 of his fellow soldiers and wounded dozens more. You mean you don't want us to do what you did when that white cop used force to subdue that black college professor in Massachusetts, who was putting up a fight? You don't mind offending the police calling them stupid but you don't want us to offend Muslim fanatics by calling them what they are, terrorists.

Of course, one of the reasons why Obama is soft on terrorism is because he never had to serve in the military. He never faced the barrel of a gun or the heat of battle. He never put his life on the line to defend America. Harold has a few choice words for Obama on that score. He writes:

> You're the Commander in Chief now, son. Do your job. When your battle-hardened field General asks you for 40,000 more troops to complete the mission, give them to him. But if you're not in this fight to win, then get out. The life of one American soldier is not worth the best political strategy you're thinking of.
>
> You could be our greatest president because you face the greatest challenge ever presented to any president. You're not going to restore American greatness by bringing back our bloated economy. That's not our greatest threat. Losing the heart and soul of who we are as Americans is our big fight now. And I sure as hell don't want to think my president is the enemy in this final battle.
>
> Sincerely,
> Harold B. Estes[82]

America needs more leaders with his spunk, courage, and patriotism.

In a way, these actions of Obama are just history repeating itself.

The leaders of Great Britain in the 1920s and 1930s did the same thing. They bowed to Hitler and Mussolini. They signed documents such as the Locarno Treaty and the Munich Agreement, signed by British Prime Minister Neville Chamberlain. They gave Nazi Germany more and more power at the same time that England was cutting back on military expenditures. By the time Hitler was ready to strike, England was so anemic, it was barely able to survive the Nazi onslaught. Chamberlain, like Obama, was so afraid of the terrors of war that he forgot that a strong arsenal is the best way to prevent a war.

In 1940, the British were defeated by the Germans in Norway. Finally, the British Parliament, even the far left Labour Party and its leader Clement Atlee, realized that the pacifist Prime Minister Chamberlain had to go. They scrambled to hold a two-day debate and, at the end of it, Chamberlain was given a vote of "No Confidence." He was thrown out of power and Winston Churchill became the Prime Minister of England.

When will the establishment of America realize that Obama is demilitarizing America and move to remove him from office? Mark my words. A point in time will come when rational liberal Democrats of the current power structure will realize that their ability to stay in power and America's national survival are being threatened by Obama's weakness on the world stage. And when that time comes, Obama will be removed from office. President Obama is worse than Neville Chamberlain and he will be remembered by history as a president worse than Jimmy Carter.*

More and more, each day as I look around it's as though a hostile foreign power has taken over the nation. Let me ask you something. If China had actually taken over the United States of America and put a Chinese leader in power with a blue hat and a red star, who spoke nicely and didn't yell, and he said and did the same things that Obama has said and done by stages—which is Fabian socialism; a gradual, stage-by-stage creeping socialist revolution—could they have done anything more rapidly than what Obama is doing to disarm us?

Answer: No.

Barack Hussein Obama is following the protocols of the radical Left. He is implementing the zany theories and propaganda espoused by every pothead and crackpot college professor he's chatted with. His assurances that Russia and China and the other nuclear nations are going to play *faaaair* with us is plain nuts. So, forgive me for my skepticism about his intentions here. Forgive me for expressing my concern about his dismantling, disarming, and demoralizing our military.

The outcome here is the takeover of America just as if we had been taken over by an invading army. When you have a pacifist liberal elite running throughout the halls of Congress and in the White House, they don't have to be open traitors—they're doing the same work as traitors, that's all.

I grew up in a different generation where I understood the dangers of the world. Unfortunately, so many of the American sheeple do not understand the dangers of their world. They, like our president, live in a dream world. They have no idea of the perilous times in which they live. They're like a delicate garden plant; a plant that's comfortable living with sunlight and fresh water but oblivious to the threat that surrounds them.

Although weeds are creeping into the garden, taking over their neighbors one-by-one on a daily basis, they sit there smiling up at the sun waiting for the raindrops to fall not knowing that soon, very soon, the weeds will overtake them and they, too, will cease to exist. America is that garden. The American people need a gardener who will defend them, who will uproot the enemies of freedom and till the soil of peace.

The last thing America needs is Obama the Destroyer.

---

* Just before this book went to press, the FBI arrested 11 alleged Russian agents on our soil who had been put into place to infiltrate the policy-making circles of power in Washington. It has been established that Obama knew of the FBI operation *before* he met with Russian President Dmitry Medvedev. Some have questioned the timing. Some believe there might be a shadow government within the government—a vestige of patriots within the justice depart—who felt compelled to act to keep in check the warming of relations with Russia.

Given the radical nature of the Obama Administration, another probability is that the administration itself decided to pull the trigger on the investigation at this time to throw dust in the eyes of the American people who may be concerned about the Obama Administration's tilt toward Russia and communist China. That is, by outing the Russian spies, people might be led to believe that Obama cares about our national security and that we have nothing to fear about letting our guard down.

CHAPTER 11

The Savage Manifesto: Borders, Language, Culture, and Economics

The world is a dangerous place to live; not because of the people who are evil, but because of the people who don't do anything about it.
—Albert Einstein

The future of America hangs in the balance like a loose tooth.

The more you look at America's problems, the more it looks like Lady Liberty is suffering from terminal cancer. Patriots like you and me are oncologists. Every limb of the body politic that we explore, we see that the cancer has spread. Is that an overstatement? Far from it. Name one organ of government that isn't infected with this mad progressivism, mad-Marxism, and mad-passivism that I've dissected in this opus.

Now, more than at any time in our history, we're in danger of losing our freedom and our national identity to the gang of Marxist thugs who have taken over our government. This administration will stop at nothing to exert total control over every aspect of our lives: It promises to sentence all of us to life without parole in the cradle-to-grave prison that is Marxism.

Yes, Lady Liberty has been poisoned with the cancerous toxins of liberalism. Left unchecked, her voice will be silenced and her shining beacon of hope and freedom will be forever extinguished. And, while the country that our forefathers fought and died for may be hanging in the balance, that doesn't necessarily mean America is destined to go out with a whimper.

Can America be saved?

I believe it can. Not easily, mind you.

If we seize this moment and do the hard thing, I believe our best and brightest days are ahead of us. Why? Because American exceptionalism is hardwired into our Constitution and I believe in the resilience of our people. However, for America to survive the infestation of radical liberalism, we must turn the stethoscope on ourselves and admit that we've been apathetic when we should have been outraged.

We've been indifferent when we should have been alarmed.

We've been sluggish when vigilance was called for.

Yes, America's patriots have been complacent when we should have been on the offensive. How else can you explain that a naked Marxist sits in the Oval Office and his czars, like termites, are gnawing away at the foundations upon which this country was built? As I wrote in my bestseller *Liberalism Is a Mental Disorder*, we will not have a nation unless the sheeple awaken to the reality that America has become pacified; America has become feminized; and America is being compromised from without and within. Yes, it's time we fought back.

What's the solution?

We need a revolution at the ballot box. That's number one.

That's why the elections of 2010 and 2012 are of paramount importance. We must throw out these Marxist-Leninist betrayers as fast as possible before there's nothing left of the country. While I'm not the only voice calling for that change in political leadership, I'm the only one in talk radio who freely admits we don't need just a change of party—as some counterfeit conservatives have said. The last thing we want are the phony Republican Bush-ites who got us into this trouble to begin with.

No, we need a *conservative* revolution at the ballot box.

The question is, where will it come from?

It has to be the leaders within the Tea Party movement. They are the ones who should run for office. Likewise, when conservatives seek to represent us, they must hold fast to an agenda that limits the size and role of the government, protects America's borders, language, and culture, and remains true to the vision first cast by our Founding Fathers as elucidated in the Constitution.

The Tea Party knows that, to reverse trickle up poverty, we cannot afford to lose sight of the fact that the government works for us, not the other way around.

President Calvin Coolidge put it this way:

> I want the people of America to be able to work less for the government and more for themselves. I want them to have the rewards of their own industry. This is the chief meaning of freedom. Until we can reestablish a condition under which the earnings of the people can be kept by the people, we are bound to suffer a very severe and distinct curtailment of our liberty.[1]

While I've pointed out a number of problems in this book, every one of them is solvable. An individual still has the freedom and power to address his grievances. Don't give up just because the checked-pants Republicans aren't motivated to lead the charge. You, as an American citizen, can do much to change the future of America. And, when we band together, as the Tea Party has done, we galvanize our individual voices into a deafening roar. I commend everyone who is part of the Tea Party's effort to hold Congress accountable with its 10-point "Contract From America":

1. Protect the Constitution: Require each bill to identify the specific provision of the Constitution that gives Congress the power to do what the bill does.

2. Reject Cap and Trade: Stop costly new regulations that would increase unemployment, raise consumers prices, and weaken the nation's global competitiveness with virtually no impact on global temperatures.

3. Demand a Balanced Budget: Begin the Constitutional amendment process to require a balanced budget with a two-thirds majority needed for any tax hike.

4. Enact Fundamental Tax Reform: Adopt a simple and fair single-rate tax system by scrapping the internal revenue code and replacing it with one that is no longer than 4,543 words—the length of the original Constitution.

5. Restore Fiscal Responsibility and Constitutionally Limited Government in Washington: Create a Blue Ribbon task force that engages in a complete audit of federal agencies and programs, assessing their Constitutionality, and identifying duplication, waste, ineffectiveness, and agencies and programs better left for the states or local authorities, or ripe for wholesale reform or elimination due to our efforts to restore limited government consistent with the U.S. Constitution's meaning.

6. End Runaway Government Spending: Impose a statutory cap limiting the annual growth in total federal spending to the sum of the inflation rate plus the percentage of population growth.

7. De-Fund, Repeal, and Replace Government-Run Health Care: De-fund, repeal, and replace the recently passed government-run health care with a system that actually makes health care and insurance more affordable by enabling a competitive, open, and transparent free-market health care and health insurance system that isn't restricted by state boundaries.

8. Pass an "All-of-the-Above" Energy Policy: Authorize the exploration of proven energy reserves to reduce our dependence on foreign energy sources from unstable countries and reduce regulatory barriers to all other forms of energy creation, lowering prices and creating competition and jobs.

9. Stop the Pork: Place a moratorium on all earmarks until the budget is balanced, and then require a two-thirds majority to pass any earmark.

10. Stop the Tax Hikes: Permanently repeal all tax hikes, including those to the income, capital gains and death taxes, currently scheduled to begin in 2011.[2]

This list is a good place start. Every one of these initiatives is something we can and should get behind. But it's incomplete. In a moment, I'll offer a number of other solutions and steps that must be taken to reverse trickle up poverty and save the middle class from Obama's tyranny. Before I do, let me say that the Tea Party's call to preserve the Constitution resonates strongly with me. President Obama demonstrates a shameless disregard for that precious document and the procedures of governing that it outlines.

Speaking of a shameless disregard for the Constitution, there's no clearer example than what this member of Team Obama expressed. Regarding the passage of ObamaCare, Representative Phil Hare (D-IL) said, "I don't worry about the Constitution."[3] And you wonder why America is in trouble?

This is why I believe all candidates for public office must pledge not only to uphold the Constitution, but to demonstrate that they know what's in it!

Are you starting to get the picture?

Every time this president can't have his way through the legitimate, prescribed, constitutional process of passing laws, he bypasses it. He is not an emperor who can do whatever the hell he wants—in spite of his delusions of grandeur. Barack Obama's Marxist-Leninist view of America, his hard-left march toward socialism, his spread-the-wealth-around nonsense, and his disregard for our Constitution must be stopped. How can we keep America from becoming financially, morally, and ethically bankrupt? How do we retain our place as a shining light to the world? Conservative patriots must return America to the core principles that made this country great using both the *Contract From America* coupled with these sensible, doable solutions found in *The Savage Manifesto*:

1. English Only: Make English the official language of the United States. Require all who immigrate to our country to begin immediately to learn English as part of the requirement to qualify for the privilege of American citizenship. Likewise, require voting ballots to be written in English only.

2. Close the Borders: Use illegal aliens to build a wall between the United States and Mexico. Hire Sheriff Joe Arpaio to oversee the project. Pay the illegals for their labor in the form of a one-time worker fee. Upon finishing, repatriate them.

3. Defend the Borders: Pull the troops out of Germany and South Korea where they're doing nothing and put them on our southern border where there's a real threat to our citizens. Defending South Korea can be done with our ships and subs with their tactical nuclear weapons.

4. De-Fund and Repeal ObamaCare: Remember how the Schecter Brothers overturned FDR's socialism? Sue on the grounds of religious freedom. Use Schecter Brothers strategy from chapter five.

5. Reduce the Size and Scope of Government: The Federal Government is bloated. With the exception of the military and defense, reduce all departments in size by 4 percent each year, for a total reduction of size by 16 percent over four years. Require government employees to speak English and to have achieved at least a high school diploma.

6. Liquidate TARP: It's time to abandon and repeal the Troubled Asset Relief Program (TARP), a government bailout program used to stabilize the financial sector. Use repaid TARP funds and funds that haven't been spent to reduce the federal debt.

7. Oil for Illegals: Mexico has what we want (oil), and we have something they don't want (their unemployed citizens). To offset this alien invasion, Mexico should pay one barrel of oil per month per illegal alien that sneaks into our country. Americans are also owed tens of billions of dollars in *reparations from Mexico* for the generous free health care, welfare, and ACLU-care they've received for five decades.

8. Strike Down Anchor Babies Law: Eliminate the loophole in our law that encourages illegal immigrants to enter this country for the purpose of having "anchor babies" who are U.S. citizens simply because they happened to have been born in our hospitals.

9. Export Jailed Illegal Aliens: Our federal, state, and local jails are overcrowded with 2,396,002 inmates as of 2008.[4] Of that number, 29 percent are illegal aliens! They don't even belong here, yet we're paying an average of $29,000 per year to house, feed, clothe, and entertain them.[5] Send them back to their country of origin.

10. Fire Janet Napolitano: Pressure Janet Napolitano to be removed from office. She has demonstrated her incompetence in Homeland Security, she's failing to uphold the illegal immigration laws already on the books, and she has suspended the construction of a fence along the border—despite the fact that federal law mandates it.

11. Use Profiling to Prevent Terror Attacks: The attempted terrorist plots on our own soil follow a definite pattern. All these acts were carried out by radical Muslims. Shrewd police work requires common sense. If acts of terror repeatedly come from people who practice a certain religion, and, if all these acts are in accord with some twisted notion of their holy book, prudent police work would dictate that we immediately employ national—if not religious—profiling to stop the next terrorist before he or she succeeds.

12. Name the Enemy: Identify radical Islam as the enemy. Demand that Attorney General Eric Holder stops scrubbing federal policies and communications of truly descriptive words such as "terrorist" and "jihad" and

"Islam" and start telling it like it is. Furthermore, don't extend the rights guaranteed to American citizens to enemy combatants. Don't prosecute them in civilian courts.

13. Rewrite the Rules of Engagement: The ROE should match the real world that our troops face on the ground rather than the politically correct virtual world the bureaucrats live in with their computer models and fake war-game scenarios.

14. Save the Seals: Stop prosecuting our Navy SEALs and other military personnel for doing what needs to be done to subdue our radical Islamist enemies. You can't fight a war in ballet slippers. We must stop requiring that our soldiers do a plié before they ask the enemy if he'd consent to being handcuffed and taken away.

15. Re-Enforce the Military Infrastructure: Our brave service men and women should have the benefit of the best training and equipment not seminars on how to fight a politically correct war. Furthermore, Obama's disarmament and meeker-than-thou defense policy must stop. We need to continually renew our military infrastructure by spending the necessary dollars to upgrade and modernize equipment. We must fund the F-22 fighter jets Obama has cut from the budget and increase the number of ships, subs, and missiles.

16. Pay Raise for the Military Personnel: The support of our military must expand to include increasing pay for active duty combat troops by 10 percent.

17. Silence the Hitler of Iran: Allow no more hate speech rants on U.S. soil from Ahmadinejad; deny this junior dictator permission to enter our country. Implement strong sanctions against this rogue nation, using our military to enforce embargoes and to mine and blockade Iran's harbors so that nothing goes in and nothing comes out. Meanwhile, ship to Israel the necessary munitions, including "bunker buster" bombs that will enable them to mount a military strike on Iran if necessary.

18. Impose Tariffs on China: We must draw a line in the sand with regard to China in order to loosen their strangle hold on our economy by imposing a 20 percent tariff on all goods produced in China. That tariff should be raised by 5 percent each year that China refuses to revalue its currency.

19. Offer Health Savings Plans: Make health savings accounts the ve-

hicle of choice for "insuring" people's medical needs. These accounts would
be supplemented by smorgasbord high-deductible catastrophic health insurance policies sold by private insurance companies across state lines in open
competition. By the same token, people who are injured or become ill with
long-term conditions should not be allowed to be dropped by their insurance companies. Let the insurance companies and the market sort out how
this comes about.

20. Institute a Flat Tax: This simplifies the complex tax code and the
unfair practice of tax discrimination—since 47 percent of U.S. households
pay no federal income tax![6] All Americans above the poverty level should
pay the same percentage of income tax—a straight 15 percent across the
board for individual earners.

21. Keep the Estate Tax at Zero: George Bush was right to eliminate
the so-call "Death Tax"—the confiscatory practice of taxing the inheritance
money passed from parents to children upon the parents' death. In 2011,
this tax will jump from 0 to 55 percent on estates with assets valued between $1 million to $10 million unless the Bush tax cuts are renewed.

22. Say "NO" to the VAT Tax: The Value Added Tax is a bad idea.
This raises taxes disproportionately on those who can least afford it—the
poor and the middle class. We don't need *more* taxes, we need *less* government spending, waste, and fraud.

23. Reduce Pay and Pensions for Civil Servants: Why is New York
City paying a $242,000 tax-free disability pension per year for a former fire
chief?[7] Why do almost two thousand House of Representative staffers take
down six-figure incomes? How can forty-three of them soak the public for
$172,500, which is "three times the median U.S. household income"[8] in
this down economy? This is an outrage and must be cut to reflect current
economic realities.

24. Defend the Defense of Marriage Act (DOMA): Traditional marriage is under attack. This basic building block of society must continue to
be defined as a legal union between one man and one woman. President
Obama wants to repeal DOMA, which was signed into law in 1996 by Bill
Clinton. Don't let Obama get away with that!

25. Encourage Child Bearing among Tax-Paying Citizens: Create a
marriage incentive through lower taxes for married heterosexual couples

and a tax credit for each child conceived and carried to birth. Increase the subsidies for each year the couple remains married.

26. Make Abortions Illegal: With the exception of the physical survival of the mother—to be determined by two licensed medical doctors. Require Norplant for all women on welfare of childbearing age. At the very least, prohibit taxpayer funded abortion through organizations such as Planned Parenthood.

27. End Affirmative Action: This leftist policy of giving special advantage to certain groups has no place in America. When people of all colors and ethnicities compete equally and to the best of their abilities, the best and most qualified will rise to the top. Studies demonstrate that giving certain groups of people a leg up in competing for positions and honors actually harms them more than it benefits and leads to reverse discrimination.[9]

28. Limit Welfare Benefits: Provide welfare benefits for no longer than three years. Require able-bodied recipients of welfare to volunteer fifteen hours per week in acts of community service. America will cease to exist if we continue to steal from the "makers" and give to the "takers."

29. Voting Reform: Require a government-issued photo ID such as a driver's license at the ballot box when voting. While this doesn't provide proof of citizenship, it eliminates the ACORN-style fraud of registering dead people.

30. Boot the Czars: Require immediate Senate confirmation of each of Obama's presidential appointments, and then end the practice of appointing czars who are not first vetted by Congress.

31. Put the Brakes on GM: Demand that General Motors and Chrysler be re-privatized and that they either stand or fall on their own, without further government intervention and without pretending that they've paid back the bailout money they've received. Demand restitution of the money the federal government confiscated from GM and Chrysler stockholders and gave to labor unions as part of the takeover. Require these two companies to sever all ties and fire all government-appointed officers as part of their return to the private sector.

32. Reinstate the Glass-Steagall Act: This act instituted in 1933 required the separation of commercial and investment banks. Its repeal in

1999 was one of the key factors leading to the breakdown of the residential mortgage investment sector. Senators John McCain and Maria Cantwell are proposing to reinstate it. This needs to be done while also eliminating Fannie Mae and Freddie Mac.

33. Re-instate the Wall Street "Uptick" Rule: We saw what happened when hedge fund raiders, according to one report, manipulated and rocked the stock market on May 6, 2010, causing a thousand-point drop before recovering.[10] This is why we must end the practice of short selling. The "uptick rule" must be reinstated while putting into place trading curbs. Congress and the SEC should conduct hearings and pass new safeguards to prevent a future meltdown, although this may be just a Band-Aid that masks the crisis du jour. Wall Street firms hire some of the brightest young minds, hand them supercomputers, and then cut them loose on the exchanges. However, while they produce billions in revenue through their trading, they contribute nothing of material substance to our society. This pursuit of quick financial gain leads to artificial bubbles, inflated valuation of stocks, more crises and, in the end, the potential for widespread abuse— if not the end of the capitalist system, which enabled this country to become so great.

34. Privatize the Regulation of Wall Street: Since Congress is unlikely to look beyond the millions of campaign dollars flowing from Wall Street and enact comprehensive reform, we must privatize the regulation of the financial industry, rather than allow it to become further entangled in the corrupt web that the government oligarchy is quickly proving to be. That should include creating a private clearing house for the oversight of financial derivative debt instruments.

35. Encourage Risk Taking and Entrepreneurship: Reward those "makers" who provide the jobs that drive the economy. The unparalleled success of capitalism is built on risk taking by small businesses. Obama was right to temporarily eliminate fees charged to lenders who participate in the Small Business Administration loan program. This move should be made permanent while cutting unnecessary regulation that stifles entrepreneurial endeavors.

36. Institute Tort Reform: Tort reform must be instituted for medical malpractice to curb frivolous lawsuits by the Briefcase Mafia and stop out-of-control awards for damages. Medical liability should be capped at

$250,000 per claim. This has worked in California, where it was introduced in 1978. If passed, tort reform legislation will reduce the legal industry's inordinate influence in raising medical costs.

37. Run the Country Like a Business, Not an Empire: We cannot blame President Obama for the entire economic morass we are in. However, as any homeowner knows, if you have $100,000 in debt at the end of the year you don't eliminate that $100,000 debt by incurring $300,000 additional debt, which your children will have to pay for. Instead, you pay down that debt by cutting unnecessary expenses. Maybe you have fewer vacations, drive one car rather than two, and eat out less often. That's known as belt-tightening—a simple principle bureaucrats can't seem to grasp. As such, we must stop them from further federal bailouts and "stimulus" packages altogether.

Getting Back to Basics

In truth, this is just a place to start. Much more can and should be done. It's no secret, for example, that the secular humanism—the insistence that human beings are the center of the universe and the final arbiters of right and wrong—is the religion of choice for libs. It's a spin-off from Marxism, developed by godless communists to justify a self-centered view of the world, one where the State is God. However, if you read through the documents upon which this country was founded, and if you read the writings of the founding fathers, you'll realize that the real basis of our existence as a nation is a contract with the Judeo-Christian God.

It's time that we renew that contract.

Here's how Benjamin Franklin put it in a speech during the Constitutional Convention on June 28, 1787:

In the beginning of the contest with Britain, when we were sensible of danger, we had daily prayers in this room for the divine protection. Our prayers, Sir, were heard; and they were graciously answered. All of us, who were engaged in the struggle, must have observed frequent instances of a superintending Providence in our favor. To that kind Providence we owe this happy opportunity of consulting in peace on the means of establishing our future national felicity. And have we now forgotten that powerful friend? Or do we imagine we no longer need its assistance? I have lived, Sir, a long time; and the longer I live, the more convincing proofs I see of this truth, That God governs in the affairs of men. And if a sparrow cannot fall to the ground without his notice, is it probable that an empire can rise without his aid?[11]

It's time that we begin to revisit and reestablish the religious and moral principles that flow from the Old and New Testaments of the Bible and from the Declaration of Independence and the Constitution—principles that have enabled us to become the great nation we are today. No, I'm not suggesting we turn America into a theocracy. Rather, this means that we would do well to put our religious beliefs into practice in such a way that we cleanse our national soul of the immoral and degrading cultural practices that have done our country such enormous harm.

This is not something that can take place exclusively through legislation, although there are legislative initiatives that can help it take root and succeed. Primarily, though, it is something that each of us must begin to do in our own homes and lives. It's time to make a concerted effort to bring God back into the public discourse, not for the purpose of establishing a religious state but for the purpose of re-centering our nation, of re-alerting ourselves and our fellow Americans to what is right.

As I said at the outset of this book, this isn't a picnic.

It's a showdown.

The question remains: Whose vision of America will win the day?

Barack Hussein Obama, the reverse Robin Hood, who takes from the middle class and gives to the rich, is causing an economic poverty, as well as a poverty of the body, mind, and spirit. His radical, hard-left agenda and Marxist-Leninist worldview is impoverishing how we think, feel, and view ourselves as a people while robbing our personal freedoms and bankrupting our clout as the leader of the world.

We can and must do better.

One Day After Eating Chinese Food

The other day while working on this book, I took a break for some fresh air and a bite to eat. I'm walking along the streets of San Fransicko looking at the shops and the people milling about in the sunshine. I decide to stop in at the Chinese restaurant that I love to hate. You know how it is. You get used to certain routines and this is one of them for me. It's where I get my grease fix. I've been going for years, even though the owners don't know my name.

They just glare at me until I order.

So, I fill up on the chicken and broccoli with the pot stickers. Now I've got enough indigestion to last me for the rest of the week. Back outside, I'm moving along the sidewalk just minding my own business. I turn the corner and head toward North Beach, past the playground with kids having a ball and the steak house with the bad food. A few blocks later, I see a black man sitting at a card table with an Asian lady passing out literature. What caught my eye was the huge homemade sign: "IMPEACH OBAMA."

I'm thinking, this I gotta see.

I stop and talk and read the pamphlets. They didn't know who I was or what my political positions were. I asked them, "What's this about?" They said they were running a Democrat against Nancy Pelosi for Congress. The black man vehemently opposed Obama's policies. He called Obama and the Democrats in Congress a "pack of complete frauds" and offered his ideas of what must be done to fix things in Washington.

As I walked away, I thought about the simplicity and beauty of what I had just experienced. Sure, I may disagree with him on some of his solutions. But I identified with him on a basic level. We're both Americans. We both know the system is broken. We both love our country. And, like him, I'm one man who exercises my freedom of expression every day, giving voice to my ideas of how to fix the system. His platform was a card table on the street corner. My platform happens to be behind a microphone and in the pages of my books.

All of us have a platform.

All of us must speak out wherever that platform may be.

For you, that might be the PTA, a civic group, a gathering of home-school parents, the water cooler at work, or standing with the Tea Party movement. You don't have to be a "professional speaker," a political wonk, or a candidate running for office to make a difference. Each of us has a voice. I say, *use it or lose it*. What's more, you don't have to address all the solutions that I've proposed. This isn't an all-or-nothing strategy. Pick one or two that resonates with you.

But whatever you do, fight for the country while there's time to save it.

Frankly, I've been engaged in this fight for years.

While I wouldn't take credit for sparking the Tea Party movement, we must not forget there have been others, including myself, who were involved in conservative rallies for many years. I held mass gatherings of discontented conservatives and independents dating back to 1996. That's when I started *The Paul Revere Society* and hosted five compassionate conservative conventions in the late 1990s. I held a "Name 'em and Shame 'em" event in the 2000. In 2003, in my *New York Times* bestseller, *The Enemy Within*, I concluded by calling for a conservative revolution. And then, in 2004, I rallied conservatives at the Concord Pavilion in California.

Which is to say I'm encouraged to see fresh signs that a revolution is brewing.

No doubt the Tea Party movement of today has drawn some of its inspiration from the Boston Tea Party protest, which pre-figured the American Revolution. In my case, I drew inspiration from Paul Revere, the simple craftsman who rode through the night in 1775 to let sleeping Americans know that the British were coming. I've been warning that the enemy was coming for sixteen years, and I will continue to raise the alarm every day until this cancer has been expunged from the soul of America.

Each president puts his own stamp on the White House. This president seems to stamp on the White House!

When the natural love of country is repressed, or lost, pan-Leninism emerges. Without nationalism, pan-Leninism appears. Not a "New world order" of harmony. But a new world tyranny managed by a few invisible hands.

If I have to be the last angry man who speaks out, so be it. Then I shall go out with a roar because I will fight *against* trickle up poverty and *for* the American middle class that I represent. The America that I speak to. The America that speaks to me. The Savage Nation.

From Trickle Up Poverty to Trickle Up Oil

The left wing has turned on Barack Obama—not because of his Marxist agenda, not because of his socialist czars and advisors, not because he's causing trickle up poverty. No. The left wing has finally turned on Obama because he *failed their nature religion*.

On April 20, 2010, the Deepwater Horizon oil rig blew and spewed oil into the Gulf of Mexico. Clear thinking Americans knew that quick action was required if there would be any hope of saving 40% of America's most fragile wetlands as well as the fishing industries whose livelihood and existence were immediately threatened.

In a stunning display of ineptitude, Obama did nothing—except to go on a spring vacation to Asheville, North Carolina, even as the oil barreled into the Gulf of Mexico.

It took Obama *twelve* days before he visited the site of the worst oil spill catastrophe in our history and provided no immediate leadership or action. At first the compliant press gave him a pass—the same press which had blasted George W. Bush for waiting four days before he visited New Orleans in the aftermath of Katrina. But then Obama took a second vacation while the oil continued to destroy the environment.

That's when the Gulf oil spill became Obama's Katrina. Why?

Because Barack Obama failed his core followers in their religion of the environment. You must understand the mind of progressive socialists and many on the left. To them the environment *is* their religion. Their religion isn't that of Abraham, Moses, or Jesus Christ. Their religion is the religion of Gaia. Fundamentally, they're nature worshippers and Barack Obama was their messiah who could not only walk on water but part the Red Sea.

However, due to Obama's feckless leadership, their sacred idols—the birds, the clams, the fish, the shrimp, and every mollusk in the bay—were threatened. Many of their sacred icons were dying in record numbers because the government under Obama did nothing except play the blame game. While Obama insisted this catastrophe was BP's problem, everyone knew Obama could have immediately called on the US Army Corps of Engineers to plug the leak and contain the spill.

Making matters worse was Obama's failure to immediately authorize barrier berms to block the oil from reaching the coastline. When Louisiana officials requested permission to build them, the Obama administration was silent for weeks on end. Nor did Obama request assistance from Japan, France, Russia or China, all of whom have deep sea submarines and robots with the capacity of working as deep as a mile below the surface of the ocean.

That's when it became apparent to even the most ardent Democrat Obama worshipper that their messiah had abandoned them. The scales finally fell from their eyes and they saw that Obama was mortal. They were forced to admit there was no excuse for Obama to take thirty-eight days before making a speech regarding the biggest environmental disaster since the Three Mile Island nuclear meltdown.

That's when they attacked.

At first the backlash was contained to small newspaper columns and a few talk shows. Then, at the first news conference which the messiah had held in over ten months, as if a dam had burst, the formerly fawning press acknowledged that not only could Obama not part the Red Sea and lead them to Nirvana, but he couldn't even part the black sea of sludge that decimated hundreds of miles of the Gulf Coast and the ocean for decades to come.

You may wonder why Obama took so long to respond.

The answer is really quite simple, and it reveals much about what he thinks of middle America. The reason Obama finally called the press conference and reluctantly squeezed in a three hour visit to the state (which is less time than he spends on the golf course) wasn't because he cared about the people of Louisiana. After all, Louisiana voted for John McCain in 2008. Obama knew they didn't support his socialist policies so in his mind he had little to gain by making their plight his priority. In short, he could care less since there was nothing to gain politically.

Look at it this way. If a pregnant whale was about to give birth in San Francisco Bay and someone had spilled one gallon of used motor oil in the water, I can guarantee that there would have been hysteria in the White House. Obama would have been out there in Air Force One within several hours. He would have brought with him a specialized team from the U.S. Army Corps of Engineers to cordon off the oil spill.

There would be no way Obama would allow that one gallon of oil to either poison the whale or to wash ashore in San Francisco—the liberal Mecca of America. That's his core audience. That's the crowd he plays to. To Obama, Louisiana isn't liberal country. It's Deliverance Country. It's a bunch of toothless guys wandering around down there. Why should he bother with them?

That was a gross miscalculation on Obama's part. When the oil continued to desecrate the sacred idols of Gaia, and as he continued to betray the religion of his gullible followers, even his minions were forced to cry out against their false messiah and demand that he do something.

I believe this represents a historic turning point. The sheeple on the left and in the press are finally waking up. They're asking the hard questions and writing the probing columns which should have been done by them long before Obama was ushered into the seat of power. They're even publicly admitting that they were wrong to have backed Obama, as columnist Daniel Hannan has done. He writes:

> I was wrong . . . none of [Obama's] advantages, however, can make up for the single most important fact of Obama's presidency, namely that the federal government is 30 percent larger than it was two years ago. This is not entirely Obama's fault, of course. The credit crunch occurred during the dying days of the Bush administration, and it was the 43rd president who began the baleful policy of bail-outs and pork-barrel stimulus packages.[12]

He's right about that. I've been critical of the way Bush broke the system. That said, Bush is a piker when compared to what Obama has done—and is doing—to trash our economy. He continues:

> But it was Obama who massively extended that policy against united Republican opposition. It was he who chose, in defiance of public opinion, to establish a state-run healthcare system. It was he who presumed to tell private sector employees what they could earn, he who adopted the asinine cap-and-trade rules, and he who re-federalised social security, thereby reversing the single most beneficial reform of the Clinton years.[13]

As I said at the outset of this book, Obama is a pan-Leninist. He's operating on a global level and, as Hannan points out, the future Obama envision isn't pretty:

> These errors [by Obama] are not random. They amount to a comprehensive strategy of Europeanisation: Euro-carbon taxes, Euro-disarmament, Euro-healthcare, Euro-welfare, Euro-spending levels, Euro-tax levels and, inevitably, Euro-unemployment levels. Any American reader who wants to know where Obamification will lead should spend a week with me in the European Parliament. I'm working in your future and, believe me, you won't like it.[14]

In that respect, Obama is proving to be one of the most dangerously inexperienced presidents to occupy the Oval Office. He knew how to run a campaign, but he has no idea how to run a government. Yet his incompetence hasn't stopped—or even slowed—him from pursuing his radical agenda to fundamentally transform America. However, I believe this mishandling of the Gulf oil spill could be the downfall, not only of Obama, but the entire left wing of the Democrat party. For the sake of the country and for the benefit of the entire world, let's hope this is the beginning of the end of the reign of Obama the Destroyer.

NOTES

Author's Note

1   Barack Obama, "Obama to Mexican President: 'We Are Defined Not By Our Borders,' " Real Clear Politics Video, May 19, 2010. www.realclearpolitics.com/video/2010/05/19/obama_to_mexican_president_we_are_defined_not_by_our_borders.html

2   Anna Fifield and Alan Rappeport, "US Home Loan Foreclosures Reach Record High," *Financial Times*, February 19, 2010. www.ft.com/cms/s/0/832c383e-1d86-11df-a893-00144feab49a.html

3   Robert Barron, "Bankruptcy Filings at Record High In 2009, Despite Law Changes," The Enid News and Eagle, February 21, 2009. http://enidnews.com/localnews/x1834675010/Bankruptcy-filings-at-record-high-in-2009-despite-law-changes

4   Mike Allen and Craig Gordon, "4 million jobs—Obama ups the ante," *POLITICO*, January 11, 09. www.politico.com/news/stories/0109/17298.html

5   Patrice Hill, "American Reliance on Government at All-time High," *Washington Times*, March 1, 2010. www.washingtontimes.com/news/2010/mar/01/americans-reliance-on-government-at-all-time-high//print/

Introduction

1   "Russia Hikes Price of Rocket Rides for U.S. Astronauts to $63 Million," FoxNews.com, March 14, 2011. www.foxnews.com/scitech/2011/03/14/russia-hikes-price-rocket-rides-astronauts-63-million/

2   "Pie in the Sky," *The Economist*, September 17, 2009. www.economist.com/node/14480416

3   Brown, Peter, "Odds Improve for GOP Takeover of Congress in 2012," *Wall Street Journal*, February 23, 2011. http://blogs.wsj.com/capitaljournal/2011/02/23/odds-improve-for-gop-takeover-of-congress-in-2012/

4   Niquette, Mark, "Governors toast Kasich as one of GOP's new faces," *Columbus Dispatch,* November 18, 2010. www.dispatchpolitics.com/live/content/local_

news/stories/2010/11/18/copy/governors-toast-kasich-as-one-of-gops-new-faces
html?sid=101

5   Storey, Tim, "GOP Makes Historic State Legislative Gains in 2010," *Rasmussen Reports*, December 10, 2010. www.rasmussenreports.com/public_content/political_commentary/commentary_by_tim_storey/gop_makes_historic_state_legislative_gains_in_2010

6   "BP oil spill timeline," *The Guardian*, July 22, 2010. www.guardian.co.uk/environment/2010/jun/29/bp-oil-spill-timeline-deepwater-horizon

7   Whittington, Mark, "Obama Administration Found in Contempt of Court for Gulf Oil Drilling Ban," *Associated Content,* February 3, 2011. www.associatedcontent.com/article/7716212/obama_administration_found_in_contempt.html?cat=9

8   Calkins, Laurel Brubaker, "U.S. in Contempt Over Gulf Drill Ban, Judge Rules," *Bloomberg*, February 3, 2011. www.bloomberg.com/news/2011-02-03/u-s-administration-in-contempt-over-gulf-drill-ban-judge-rules.html

9   "EPA Head Lisa Perez Jackson's Radical Brand of Environmental Justice," *Liberty Journal*, February 18, 2010. http://thelibertyjournal.com/2010/02/18/epa-head-lisa-perez-jacksons-radical-brand-of-environmental-justice/

10   Ross, Tim, Matthew Moore, and Steven Swinford, "Egypt protests: America's secret backing for rebel leaders behind uprising," *The Telegraph,* January, 2011. www.telegraph.co.uk/news/worldnews/africaandindianocean/egypt/8289686/Egypt-protests-Americas-secret-backing-for-rebel-leaders-behind-uprising.html

11   Coker, Margaret, and Summer Said, "Muslim Group Backs Secular Struggle," *Wall Street Journal,* January 31, 2011. http://online.wsj.com/article/SB10001424052748704832704576114132934597622.html

12   Henninger, Dan, "The Collapse of Internationalism," *Wall Street Journal,* March 17, 2011. http://online.wsj.com/article/SB1000142405274870389970457620476167151805.html

13   Peterson, Hayley, "Obama wary of no-fly zone over Libya," the *Washington Examiner,* March 7, 2011. http://washingtonexaminer.com/politics/white-house/2011/03/obama-wary-no-fly-zone-over-libya

14   "Arabs Love Pax Americana," *Wall Street Journal,* March 16, 2011. http://online.wsj.com/article/SB10001424052748704893604576200910152041584.html?mod=WSJ_hps_sections_opinion)

15   "Obama press conference: Japan, Tsunami, Energy, March 11 2011 Transcript," *Chicago Sun-Times,* March 11, 2011. http://blogs.suntimes.com/sweet/2011/03/obama_press_conference_japan_t.html

16   Norman, Laurence, and Ainsley Thompson, "Europe Aids Exodus," *Wall Street Journal,* February 25, 2011. http://online.wsj.com/article/SB10001424052748703408604576163861394194324.html

17   "U.S. sends second aircraft carrier to Japan—Obama," Inquirer.net, March 12, 2011. http://newsinfo.inquirer.net/breakingnews/world/view/20110312-324913/US-sends-second-aircraft-carrier-to-JapanObama

18   Shaw, Jazz, "Obama's Curious Claims on Oil Production," Hot Air Blog, March 11, 2011. http://hotair.com/archives/2011/03/11/obamas-curious-claims/

19   "The President's Curious Claims on Oil Production," Hot Air Blog, March 11, 2011. http://hotair.com/archives/2011/03/11/obamas-curious-claims/

20   Chesser, Paul, "Obama's plan 'necessarily' skyrockets energy bills," *Washington Examiner,* April 30, 2009. http://washingtonexaminer.com/op-eds/2009/04/obama-s-plan-necessarily-skyrockets-energy-bills

21   "The President's Curious Claims on Oil Production," Hot Air Blog, March 11, 2011. http://hotair.com/archives/2011/03/11/obamas-curious-claims/

22   "Federal Defense of Marriage Act," DOMA Watch. www.domawatch.org/about/federaldoma.html

23   Savage, David, and James Oliphant, "Gay marriage: Obama administration won't defend part of marriage act," *Los Angeles Times,* February 23, 2011. www.latimes.com/news/politics/sc-dc-0224-gay-marriage-20110223,0,4559816.story?track=rss

24   D'Aprile, Shane, "Santorum, Bachmann lead way in criticizing Obama on DOMA decision," *The Hill,* February 24, 2011. http://thehill.com/blogs/ballot-box/gop-presidential-primary/145979-santorum-bachmann-lead-way-in-criticizing-obama-on-doma-decision

25   "Uptick in Violence Forces Closing of Parkland Along Mexico Border to Americans," FoxNews.com, June 16, 2010. www.foxnews.com/us/2010/06/16/closes-parkland-mexico-border-americans/

26   Krikorian, Mark, "Bringing a Bean Bag to a Gunfight," *National Review Online,* March 3, 2011. www.nationalreview.com/corner/261283/bringing-bean-bag-gunfight-mark-krikorian

27   "63% Say Border Control Is Top Immigration Priority," *Rasmussen Reports,* March 11, 2011. www.rasmussenreports.com/public_content/politics/current_events/immigration/63_say_border_control_is_top_immigration_priority

28   "Obama unveils $3.73 trillion budget for 2012," *The Telegraph,* February 14, 2011. www.thetelegraph.com/articles/budget-50517-obama-trillion.html

29   Schwartz, Stuart, "Barack Obama: Let Them Eat Tar Balls," *American Thinker,* June 7, 2010. www.americanthinker.com/2010/06/barack_obama_let_them_eat_tar.html

30   Mataconis, Doug, "Michelle Obama's $375,000 Vacation," *Outside the Beltway,* August 7, 2010. www.outsidethebeltway.com/michelle-obamas-375000-vacation/

31   Koffler, Keith, "President Obama's Trivial Pursuits," *White House Dossier,* March 15, 2011.www.whitehousedossier.com/2011/03/15/president-obamas-trivial-pursuits-2/

32   Knoller, Mark, "Obama's First Year: By the Numbers," *CBS News,* January 20, 2010. www.cbsnews.com/8301-503544_162-6119525-503544.html

33   "White House: Latin America Trip Still On Despite Turmoil," *Voice of America,* March 15, 2011. http://blogs.voanews.com/breaking-news/2011/03/15/white-house-obama-latin-america-trip-still-on-despite-turmoil/

34   "Bachmann Calls on Congress to Block $105B in Health Law Money," FoxNews.com, March 8, 2011. www.foxnews.com/politics/2011/03/08/bachmann-calls-congress-block-105-billion-health-law-money/

Chapter 1

1   Phil Rosenthal, "Rant by CNBC's Rick Santelli Puts Pundit at Odds with Obama Administration," *Chicago Tribune*, February 22, 2009. www.chicagotribune.com/business/columnists/chi-sun-phil-rosenthal-22feb22,0,7002362.column

2   Ibid.

3   "Judicial Watch Uncovers New Documents Detailing Pelosi's Use of Air Force Aircraft," Press Release, January 28, 2010. www.judicialwatch.org/news/2010/jan/judicial-watch-uncovers-new-documents-detailing-pelosis-use-air-force-aircraft

4   Ibid.

5   "Health Care Reform," Rasmussen Reports, February 23, 2010. www.rasmussenreports.com/public_content/politics/current_events/healthcare/september_2009/health_care_reform

6   Carolyn Lochhead, "Pelosi: Pole vaults and parachutes," SFGate.com, January 28, 2010. www.sfgate.com/cgi-bin/blogs/nov05election/detail?entry_id=56238

7   Jake Sherman and Alex Isenstadt, "Fraction would reelect incumbents," Politico.com, February 12, 2010. www.politico.com/news/stories/0210/32893.html

8   Mark Finkelstein, "Will MSM Ignore Michelle Obama's Anger?", NewsBusters.org, April 16, 2008. http://newsbusters.org/blogs/mark-finkelstein/2008/04/16/will-msm-ignore-michelle-obamas-anger#ixzz0gTLKz2TJ

9   Dr. Paul L. Williams, "First Lady Now Requires 26 Servants," Canada Free Press, August 17, 2010. www.canadafreepress.com/index.php/article/13827

10   Jake Tapper, "Drinks Are On the (White) House," *Political Punch*, ABC News, January 28, 2009. http://blogs.abcnews.com/politicalpunch/2009/01/drinks-are-on-t.html

11   Fred Lucas, "White House Won't Reveal How Much Michelle Obama's European Vacation Cost Taxpayers," CNSNEWS.COM, July 6, 2009. www.cnsnews.com/PUBLIC/Content/Article.aspx?rsrcid=50528

12   Drew Zahn, "Michelle Obama has Staff of 22 Assistants," WorldNetDaily/Chicago Sun Times, August 4, 2009.

13   George Stephanopoulos, "Obama Calls for 'Grand Bargain' on Economy: 'Everybody's Going to Have to Give,' " *George's Bottom Line*, ABC News, January 10, 2009. http://blogs.abcnews.com/george/2009/01/obama-calls-for.html

14   Tom Raum, "US Debt Will Keep Growing Even with Recovery," Associated Press, February 14, 2010. http://hosted.ap.org/dynamic/stories/U/US_DEFICIT_CRUNCH?SITE=AP&SECTION=HOME&TEMPLATE=DEFAULT&CTIME=2010-02-14-10-11-23

15   Edmund Conway, "US Faces one of Biggest Budget Crunches in World—IMF," The Telegraph, May 14, 2010. http://blogs.telegraph.co.uk/finance/edmundconway/100005702/us-faces-one-of-biggest-budget-crunches-in-western-world-imf/

16   Brock Vergakis, "Utah Fears Repeat of Land Grab by Feds, Wary of List of National Monument Candidates in West," Associated Press, February 24, 2010. www.washingtonexaminer.com/economy/utah-fears-repeat-of-land-grab-by-feds-wary-of-list-of-national-monument-candidates-in-west-85191592.html

17   Roger Kimball, "The Gipper vs. Obama," RealClearPolitics.com, February 15, 2009. www.realclearpolitics.com/articles/2009/02/the_gipper_vs_obama.html

18   Speech at the Virginia Convention to ratify the Federal Constitution, as listed by Wikiquote.org, June 6, 1788. http://en.wikiquote.org/wiki/James_Madison

19   Joseph Farah, "Obama's 'civilian national security force,'" WorldNetDaily.com, July 15, 2008. www.wnd.com/index.php?pageId=69601

20   Rob Bloom, "Obama's Czar Ron Bloom Agrees With Mao," Speech at Investor Conference, YouTube video clip. <<Date uncertain.>> www.youtube.com/watch?v=RCvQ8BSUv-g&feature=related

21   Andrew Malcolm and Johanna Neuman, "Murtha's unlikely political bedfellow," Los Angeles Times, February 21, 2010. http://articles.latimes.com/2010/feb/21/nation/la-na-ticket21–2010feb21

22   Eric Shawn, "Tea Party Organizer Wins New York State Assembly Seat," FOXNews.com, February 17, 2010. www.foxnews.com/politics/2010/02/17/tea-party-organizer-wins-new-york-state-assembly-race/?test=latestnews

23   Patrick J. Buchanan, "November's Consequence: A Paralyzed Government," World NetDaily.com, February 18, 2010. www.wnd.com/index.php?fa=PAGE.view&page Id=125514

24   "Steele Meets With Tea Party Leaders at RNC Headquarters," FoxNews.com, February 16, 2010. www.foxnews.com/politics/2010/02/16/steele-meet-tea-party-leaders/?test=latestnews

25   Donald W. Meyers, "Hatch: Tea Party Movement Threatening to Tear GOP Apart," Salt Lake Tribune, February 18, 2010. www.sltrib.com/news/ci_14423113

26   David A. Patten, "Tea Parties Warn of 'Coordinated Assault,'" Newsmax.com, February 19, 2010. http://newsmax.com/InsideCover/teaparty-sarahpalin-cpac-conservatives/2010/02/19/id/350393

27   Dale Robertson, "WARNING—The Tea Party Is In Danger!" CanadaFreePress.com, February 11, 2010. www.canadafreepress.com/index.php/article/19921

28   Ibid.

29   Patten, "Tea Parties Warn of 'Coordinated Assault.'"

30   Bill Dupray, "CPAC Exclusive: Utah RINO Hunter Mike Lee Tries to Unseat Sen. Robert Bennett," PatriotRoom.com, February 19, 2010. http://patriotroom.com/article/cpac-exclusive-utah-rino-hunter-mike-lee-tries-to-unseat-sen—robert-bennett

31   Cliff Kincaid, "CPAC sells out? Sodomy, the ACLU, Ron Paul and the conservative movement," WorldTribune.com, February 26, 2010. www.worldtribune.com/world tribune/WTARC/2010/ss_politics0149_02_26.asp

32   Ronald Kessler, "Tea Party Patriots Launch 'Contract From America,'" Newsmax.com, February 18, 2010. http://newsmax.com/InsideCover/tea-party-contract-from/2010/02/18/id/350236

33   Bob Unruh, "'Five pillars of Islam' taught in public school," WorldNetDaily.com, October 10, 2006. www.wnd.com/index.php?pageId=38269

34   Robert Wright, "The First Tea-Party Terrorist?" New York Times, February 23, 2010. http://opinionator.blogs.nytimes.com/2010/02/23/the-first-tea-party-terrorist/

35   David A. Patten, "Media Uses Austin IRS Terror Attack to Slam Tea Party Move-

　　　　　ment," Newsmax.com, February 18, 2010. www.newsmax.com/404?nfurl=http://
　　　　　www.newsmax.com:80/Newsfront/austin-attack-media-tea/2010/02/18/id/350266

36　　　Charles Postel, "Tea party: Dark side of conservatism," *Politico*, May 14, 2010.
　　　　　www.politico.com/news/stories/0510/37217.html

37　　　Robertson, "WARNING—The Tea Party Is In Danger!"

38　　　Robert Pear and Holli Chmela, "Thousands Attend Rally in Washington, Seeking
　　　　　Greater Power for African-Americans," *New York Times*, October 16, 2005. www
　　　　　.nytimes.com/2005/10/16/national/16rally.html?_r=1

39　　　" 'White Right' Wants Obama to Be One-Term President, Farrakhan Says," As-
　　　　　sociated Press, February 28, 2010. www.foxnews.com/politics/2010/02/28/white
　　　　　-right-wants-obama-term-president-farrakhan-says/

Chapter 2

·1　　　Michelle Malkin, "Both Parties Willing to Buy Votes," *The Sun News*, November 6,
　　　　　2008.

2　　　　Toby Harnden, "Frank Marshall Davis, Alleged Communist, Was Early Influence
　　　　　on Barack Obama," Telegraph.co.uk, August 22, 2008. www.telegraph.co.uk/news
　　　　　/worldnews/northamerica/usa/barackobama/2601914/Frank-Marshall-Davis
　　　　　-alleged-Communist-was-early-influence-on-Barack-Obama.html

3　　　　"Poet Advised Young Obama," Associated Press, August 12, 2008. www.washing
　　　　　tontimes.com/news/2008/aug/12/poet-advised-young-obama/

4　　　　Cliff Kincaid, "Obama's Communist Mentor," Accuracy in Media, February 18,
　　　　　2008. www.aim.org/aim-column/obamas-communist-mentor/

5　　　　Frank Marshall Davis, "Frank-ly Speaking," *Honolulu Record*, no 41 (May 12,
　　　　　1949): 3.

6　　　　FBI file on Frank Marshall Davis, Internal Security memo, November 13, 1950.
　　　　　PDF.

7　　　　Ibid.

8　　　　FBI file on Frank Marshall Davis, Internal Security memo, November 10,1953.
　　　　　PDF.

9　　　　Cliff Kincaid, "Obama's Communist Mentor."

10　　　Ibid.

11　　　Cliff Kincaid, "Van Jones Scandal Threatens Obama Presidency," Accuracy in
　　　　　Media, September 5, 2009. www.aim.org/aim-column/van-jones-scandal-threatens
　　　　　-obama-presidency/

12　　　Jane Chastain, "Obama's Words as Troubling as Pastor's," WorldNetDaily.com,
　　　　　March 20, 2008. www.wnd.com/index.php?fa=PAGE.printable&pageId=59340

13　　　Scott Baker and Liz Stephans interview with Dr. John Drew and The B-Cast, "Was
　　　　　Obama A Committed Marxist in College?" Breitbart.TV, February 12, 2010. www
　　　　　.breitbart.tv/the-b-cast-interview-was-obama-a-committed-marxist-in-college/

14　　　Edwin Chen and Roger Runningen, "Obama, on 100th Day, Says He Is 'Remaking
　　　　　America,'" Bloomberg.com, April 29, 2009. www.bloomberg.com/apps/news?pid=
　　　　　20601070&sid=aEOXy3xJPVoU

15   Macon Phillips, "Change has come to WhiteHouse.gov," The White House
      Blog, January 20, 2009. www.whitehouse.gov/blog/change_has_come_to_white
      house-gov/

16   Ross Goldberg, "Obama's Years at Columbia Are a Mystery," *New York Sun*, Sep-
      tember 2, 2008. www.nysun.com/new-york/obamas-years-at-columbia-are-a-mystery
      /85015/

17   Joe Conason, "Blame Wright's Enablers," *New York Observer*, April 29, 2008. www
      .observer.com/2008/blame-wright-s-enablers

18   Brian Ross and Rehab El-Buri, "Obama's Pastor: God Damn America, U.S. to
      Blame for 9/11," ABC News, March 13, 2008. http://abcnews.go.com/Blotter/
      DemocraticDebate/story?id=4443788&page=1

19   Ibid.

20   Pamela Geller, "New Controversial Video Obama's Radical Marxist Pastor: 'Land
      of the Greed and Home of the Slave,' " Atlas Shrugs, November 2, 2009. http://at
      lasshrugs2000.typepad.com/atlas_shrugs/2009/11/new-controverisal-video-obamas
      -radical-marxist-pastor-land-of-the-greed-and-home-of-the-slave.html

21   Jerome R. Corsi, "Rev. Wright: U.S. 'land of greed and home of slave,' " WorldNet
      Daily.com, November 2, 2009. www.wnd.com/?pageId=114796

22   "Obama's minister: U.S. 'No. 1 killer in the world,' " WorldNetDaily.com, March
      14, 2008. www.wnd.com/index.php?fa=PAGE.view&pageId=58928

23   Ibid.

24   Mark Finkelstein, "Obama's Spiritual Guide: 'God Damn America,' " NewsBusters,
      March 13, 2008. http://newsbusters.org/blogs/mark-finkelstein/2008/03/13/could
      -mccain-be-candidate-pastor-obamas-god-damn-america-wright

25   "Obama pastor: Not God bless, but God d- America!" WorldNetDaily.com, March
      13, 2008. www.wnd.com/index.php?fa=PAGE.view&pageId=58858

26   Finkelstein, "Obama's Spiritual Guide: 'God Damn America.' "

27   Niles Gardiner, "Top 10 Obama Apologies," Human Events, June 17, 2009. www
      .humanevents.com/article.php?id=32296

28   "All aboard! Obama pals back violent Gaza flotilla," Aaron Klein, WorldNet
      Daily.com, 5/31/2010. http://www.wnd.com/index.php?fa=PAGE.view&pageId=
      160661

29   "No Regrets for a Love Of Explosives; In a Memoir of Sorts, a War Protester Talks
      of Life With the Weathermen," Dinitia Smith, *New York Times*, 9/11/2001. http://
      www.nytimes.com/2001/09/11/books/no-regrets-for-love-explosives-memoir-sorts
      -war-protester-talks-life-with.html?pagewanted=1?pagewanted=1

30   "No Regrets for a Love Of Explosives; In a Memoir of Sorts, a War Protester Talks of
      Life With the Weathermen," Dinitia Smith, *New York Times*, 9/11/2001. http://www
      .nytimes.com/2001/09/11/books/no-regrets-for-love-explosives-memoir-sorts-war
      -protester-talks-life-with.html?pagewanted=1?pagewanted=1

31   "Amazing Ayers Audio Unearthed from Same Week Obama worked with Him!"
      NakedEmperorNews, October 19, 2008. Video at www.youtube.com/watch?v=0x
      BlTdsnOh8.

32   Tom Maguire, "Obama, Ayers, and the Annenberg Challenge Cover-Up," Pajamas

Media.com, August 22, 2008. http://pajamasmedia.com/blog/obama-ayers-and
-the-annenberg-challenge-cover-up/

33   Jack Kelly, "How Could the Obama Administration Have Hired This Guy?" *Pittsburgh Post-Gazette*, September 13, 2009; B3.

34   Glenn Beck, "Van Jones, in His Own Words," FOXNews.com, September 1, 2009, www.foxnews.com/story/0,2933,545360,00.html

35   Barack Obama, "Obama: Fundamentally Transforming the United States of America," Campaign Speech, YouTube.com, video at www.youtube.com/watch?v=xvJJP9AYgqU.

36   "The Rubber-Stamping of Radicals," *Investor's Business Daily*, September 9, 2009, A11.

37   Carrie Budoff Brown, "Van Jones 'brought down,' says Dean," Politico.com, September 2, 2009. www.politico.com/blogs/politicolive/0909/Van_Jones_brought_down_Dean_says.html

38   "NAACP to Honor Van Jones as 'American Treasure,' " FOXNews.com, February 24,2010. www.foxnews.com/politics/2010/02/23/naacp-honor-van-jones-national-treasure/

39   Ron Bloom, "Czar Ron Bloom Agrees With Mao," Address at an Investor Conference, YouTube.com, posted September 12, 2009 at www.youtube.com/watch?v=RCvQ8BSUv-g.

40   "Your World" interview with Neil Cavuto, Fox News, February 4, 2010. Video at www.youtube.com/watch?v=v9-rCui_3W4.

41   Glenn Beck, "Which Revolutionaries Should Americans Choose?: First Amendment Is Under Attack," Fox News Network, Air Date October 29, 2009.

42   Nicholas Ballasy, "Obama's Science Czar on His Past Work: 'If You Read It and You Have a Problem, You're Misreading It,' " CNSNews.com, June 14, 2010. www.cnsnews.com/news/article/67690

43   Suzanne Malveaux and Ed Homick, "Obama aide fires back at Beck over Mao remarks," CNN, October 16, 2009. www.cnn.com/2009/POLITICS/10/16/beck.dunn/index.html

44   "Top White House Official Says Obama Team 'Controlled' Media Coverage During Campaign," FOXNews.com, October 19, 2009. www.foxnews.com/politics/2009/10/19/white-house-official-says-obama-team-controlled-media-coverage-campaign/

45   Stephen Dinan, "Obama Climate Czar has Socialist Ties," *Washington Times*, January 12, 2009. www.washingtontimes.com/news/2009/jan/12/obama-climate-czar-has-socialist-ties/

46   "Browner is an Environmental Radical—and a Socialist (Seriously)," Editorial, WashingtonExaminer.com, January 8, 2009. www.washingtonexaminer.com/opinion/Browner_is_an_environmental_radical__and_a_socialist_seriously_010809.html

47   Ibid.

48   Kelley Vlahos, "Obama Regulatory Czar's Confirmation Held Up by Hunting Rights Proponent," FOXNews.com, July 22, 2009. www.foxnews.com/politics/2009/07/22/obama-regulatory-czars-confirmation-held-hunting-rights-proponent/

49   Aaron Klein, "Sunstein: America too Racist for Socialism," WorldNetDaily.com, October 7, 2009. www.wnd.com/index.php?fa=PAGE.view&pageId=112243

50   Ibid.

51   Aaron Klein, "Obama Czar's Shocking Communist Connections," WorldNetDaily.com, March 3, 2010. www.wnd.com/index.php?fa=PAGE.view&pageId=126872

52   Ibid.

53   Ibid.

54   Larrey Anderson, "Obama: Bush Made Me Do It," AmericanThinker.com, March 9,2009. http://www.americanthinker.com/blog/2009/03/obama_bush_made_me_do_it_1.html

55   Ibid.

56   Jordan Fabian, "Congressman Wants all 'Czars' to Testify," The Hill, September 9, 2009. http://thehill.com/blogs/blog-briefing-room/news/57849-congressman-wants-all-czars-to-testify

57   "Head of Marxist-led institute joins Obama team," Aaron Klein, WorldNetDaily.com, 5/28/2010. http://www.wnd.com/index.php?fa=PAGE.view&pageId=159337

58   "Head of Marxist-led institute joins Obama team," Aaron Klein, WorldNetDaily.com, 5/28/2010. http://www.wnd.com/index.php?fa=PAGE.view&pageId=159337

59   John Reed, Ten Days That Shook The World, (New York: Boni & Liveright, 1922), 371.

60   Jeffrey Lord, "The Socialist Judge: Elena Kagan and the Teachable Moment," The American Spectator, May 12, 2010. http://spectator.org/archives/2010/05/12/the-socialist-judge-elena-kaga

61   "Lecture Notes: The General Election of 1945." http://web.univ-pau.fr/~parsons/45Elections.html

62   Jack Rosenthal, "A Terrible Thing to Waste," New York Times, July 31, 2009. www.nytimes.com/2009/08/02/magazine/02FOB-onlanguage-t.html

63   Chelsea Schilling, "Obama: Where Have all his Records Gone?" WorldNetDaily.com, June 9, 2009. www.wnd.com/index.php?pageId=100613

64   Hayley Tsukayama and Liz Lucas, "Thousands Cheer Obama at Rally for Change," The Missourian, October 30, 2008. www.columbiamissourian.com/stories/2008/10/30/obama-speaks-crowd-40000/

65   Frank Newport, "Socialism Viewed Positively by 36% of Americans," GALLUP.com, February 4, 2010. www.gallup.com/poll/125645/Socialism-Viewed-Positively-Americans.aspx

66   Victor Davis Hanson, "Obama and 'Redistributive Change,'" NationalReview Online, August 26, 2009. http://article.nationalreview.com/404120/obama-and-redistributive-change/victor-davis-hanson

Chapter 3

1   George Santayana, *The Life of Reason*, Vol. 1 (New York: Prometheus Books, 1905).

2   Sangeeta Parameshwar, "Spiritual Leadership Through Ego-transcendence: Exceptional Responses to Challenging Circumstances," *The Leadership Quarterly* 16, no. 5 (October 2005): 689.

3   Karl Dannenberg, *Karl Marx: The Man and His Work* (New York: Radical Review Publishing Association, 1918), 75.

4   Mark O'Neill, "Marx Appeal Alive and Well Inside the 'Communist Plots,' " *South China Morning Post*, August 16, 2004, 12.

5   Rush Limbaugh, "One Year Later, Democrats are Desperate and Backed into Corner," RushLimbaugh.com, February 22, 2010. www.rushlimbaugh.com/home/daily/site_022210/content/01125113.guest.html

6   Jenny Marx, *Short sketch of an eventful life, Reminiscences of Marx and Engels*, Eng. Ed., (Moscow: Foreign Languages Publishing House, 1940).

7   Boris Nicolaievsky and Otto Maenchen-Helfen, *Karl Marx—Man and Fighter* (Caven Press, 2007), 239.

8   Ibid., 241.

9   Eugene Kamenka, *The Portable Karl Marx* (New York: Penguin Books, 1983), 41–42.

10 Mark O'Neill, "Marx Appeal Alive and Well Inside the 'Communist Plots.' "

11 Morgan Neill, "Cuban Leader Looks to Boost Food Production," CNN.com, April 17, 2008. http://edition.cnn.com/2008/WORLD/americas/04/16/cuba.farming/index.html

12 Ibid.

13 Eric Driggs, "Deteriorating Living Conditions in Cuba," *Focus on Cuba*, Institute for Cuban and Cuban-American Studies, University of Miami, October 14, 2004.

14 Irving Louis Horowitz, *Cuban Communism* (New Brunswick, NJ: Transaction Books, 1988), 662.

15 "Vladimir Lenin quotes," Thinkexist.com. http://thinkexist.com/quotes/vladimir_lenin/3.html

16 Trotskii, *Dnevniki i pis'ma*, 100–1, cited in Orlando Figes, *A People's Tragedy: The Russian Revolution* 1891–1924 (New York: Penguin Books, 1998), 638.

17 Ronald Clark, *Lenin: The Man Behind the Mask* (London: Faber & Faber, 1988), 456.

18 Aaron Klein, "Obama Helped Fund 'Alinsky Academy,' " WorldNetDaily.com, March 18, 2010. www.wnd.com/index.php?fa=PAGE.view&pageId=129361

19 David Kupelian, "Barack Obama and the date-rape of America," WorldNetDaily.com, March 5, 2010. www.wnd.com/index.php?fa=PAGE.view&pageId=127027

20 Aaron Klein, "Obama Helped Fund 'Alinsky Academy.' "

21 "Nation & World," *U.S. News & World Report*, June 22, 2003.

22   "Quotes Against Communism," Wikiquote.org. http://en.wikiquote.org/wiki/
Communism

23   "Nation & World."

24   Boris Brutzkus and Walter J. Roth, "Russia's Grain Exports and Their Future,"
Journal of Farm Economics 16, no. 4 (October 1934), 662–679. www.jstor.org/
pss/1231182?cookieSet=1

25   Tony Barber, "Private Farms Set to Export Russian Grain," *The Independent*, September 7, 1994. www.independent.co.uk/news/world/private-farms-set-to-export
-russian-grain-1447216.html

26   Les Blumenthal, "WTO Rules Airbus got Subsidies Illegally, Damaging Boeing,"
McClatchy Newspapers, September 4, 2009. www.mcclatchydc.com/2009/09/04/
74936/wto-rules-airbus-got-subsidies.html

27   "Quotes against Communism."

28   J. Edgar Hoover, *Masters Of Deceit: The Story of Communism in America And How to
Fight I*, (New York: Henry Holt and Company, 1958), 97.

29   "EUROPE: The Odd Renaissance of Karl Marx," Time.com, May 14, 1973. www
.time.com/time/magazine/article/0,9171,907226,00.html

30   Scott Baker and Liz Stephans "Was Obama A Committed Marxist in College?"
Interview with Dr. John Drew and The B-Cast, Breitbart.TV, February 12, 2010.
www.breitbart.tv/the-b-cast-interview-was-obama-a-committed-marxist-in-college/

31   Ronald Kessler, "Obama Espoused Radical Views in College," Newsmax.com,
February 8, 2010. www.newsmax.com/RonaldKessler/obama-college-marxism
-occidental/2010/02/08/id/349329

32   Scott Baker and Liz Stephans, "Was Obama A Committed Marxist in College?"

33   "Old friends Recall Obama's College Years," Associated Press, POLITIO.com, May
16, 2008. www.politico.com/news/stories/0508/10402.html

34   Ibid.

35   J. Edgar Hoover, *Masters of Deceit*, viii.

Chapter 4

1   Zubi Diamond, *Wizards of Wall Street* (Diamond Publishing, 2009), 57 ff.

2   Ibid.

3   Noel Sheppard, " 'I'm Having A Good Crisis': Will Soros Be Attacked For HIS
Profits?" NewsBusters.org, March 26,2009. http://newsbusters.org/blogs/noel
-sheppard/2009/03/26/having-good-crisis-will-soros-be-attacked-his-profits#ixzz
0nTyU5GUQ

4   Oxbury Research, "Cassandra John Paulson Hedge Fund Manager Makes billions
from the Financial Crisis," The Market Oracle, January 30, 2009. www.market
oracle.co.uk/Article8581.html.

5   Diamond, *Wizards of Wall Street*, 39.

6   Nelson D. Schwarta and Louise Story, "Surge of Computer Selling After Apparent Glitch Sends Stocks Plunging," *New York Times*, May 6, 2010. www.nytimes
.com/2010/05/07/business/economy/07trade.html

7   Kimberly Amadeo, "The Dow Jones Industrial Average Historical Facts," About
        .com, December 29, 2009.

8   Dave Burdick, "SEC Chairman Christopher Cox Strikes Back at McCain," Huff
        ingtonPost.com, September 18, 2008.

9   Rockefeller, David, *Memoirs* (Random House, Inc.: New York), 2002, p. 405.

10   Estulin, Daniel, *The Bilderberg Group* (Independent Publishers Group), 2005,
        p. 20.

11   "Former Nato Secretary-General Admits Bilderberg Sets Global Policy," Paul Joseph
        Watson, PrisonPlanet.com, 6/7/2010. http://www.prisonplanet.com/former-nato
        -secretary-general-admits-bilderberg-sets-global-policy.html

12   http://euro-med.dk/?p=11850

13   Watson, Paul Joseph, "Hillary & Obama in Secret Bilderberg Rendezvous,"
        InfoWars.com, June 6, 2008 (http://www.infowars.com/hillary-obama-in-secret
        -bilderberg-rendezvous/).

14   Allen H. Meltzer, "Market Failure or Government Failure?" *Wall Street Journal*,
        March 19, 2010, A19.

15   Michael De la Merced, and Andrew Ross Sorkin, "Report Details How Lehman
        Hid Its Woes as It Collapsed," *New York Times*, March 11, 2010. www.nytimes
        .com/2010/03/12/business/12lehman.html

16   "25 People to Blame for the Financial Crisis," *TIME*, February 12, 2009.

17   "Fallen Lehman Brothers Chief Executive Richard Fuld sold his $13.3 million man-
        sion to his wife for just $100 last November, according to Florida real estate records,"
        Reuters, January 15, 2009. www.reuters.com/article/idUSTRE50P04A20090126

18   Susanne Craig "Lehman Brothers' Dick Fuld Has a New Gig," *Wall Street Jour-
        nal*, Deal Journal, April 3, 2009. http://blogs.wsj.com/deals/2009/04/03/lehman
        -brothers-dick-fuld-has-a-new-gig/

19   Mike Whitney, "Lehman Died So TARP and AIG Might Live," LewRockwell.com,
        September 18, 2009.

20   Ibid.

21   Dean Baker, "Bernanke's Bad Money," CounterPunch.org, September 10, 2009.
        www.counterpunch.org/baker09102009.html

22   David Glovin and Bob Van Voris, "Federal Reserve Must Disclose Bank Bailout
        Records," Bloomberg.com, March 19, 2009. www.bloomberg.com/apps/news?pid=
        20601087&sid=a2rzjENZQV5k.

23   "A Detailed Look At TARP." www.visualeconomics.com/a-detailed-look-at-tarp/

24   "Mohegan Sun Casino Owners Received $54M in Stimulus Cash," NYPost.com, June
        17, 2010. http://www.nypost.com/p/news/local/mohegan_sun_casino_received_
        in_stimulus_RwulO6UDSkO3lPO0QRIVoJ

25   www.sigtarp.gov/reports/audit/2009/Emergency_Capital_Injections_Provided_to
        _Support_the_Viability_of_Bank_of_America . . . _100509.pdf

26   Jonathan Weisman and Joann S. Lublin, "Obama Lays Out Limits on Execu-
        tive Pay," *Wall Street Journal*, February 5, 2009. http://online.wsj.com/article/
        SB123375514020647787.html

27   Ibid.

28 "Blankfein got $9.8M," *New York Post*, March 20, 2010. www.nypost.com/p/news/business/blankfein_got_98WuC85gaHwdYQCGOtji6J

29 www.ombwatch.org/node/10724

30 Cameron Reilly, "Why Obama Is Owned by Goldman Sachs," October 23, 2009. http://gdayworld.thepodcastnetwork.com/2009/10/23/why-obama-is-owned-by-goldman-sachs/

31 Bob Ostertag, "Goldman Sachs, Obama, Money," Huffington Post, March 23, 2009. www.huffingtonpost.com/bob-ostertag/goldman-sachs-obama-money_b_177611.html

32 Daniel Golden, "Countrywide's Many 'Friends,' " Portfolio.com, June 12, 2008. www.portfolio.com/news-markets/top-5/2008/06/12/Countrywide-Loan-Scandal

33 "Sweeping Wall St. regulations may not prevent another crisis: Analysis," The Associated Press, 5/23/2010. http://www.cleveland.com/nation/index.ssf/2010/05/sweeping_wall_st_regulations_m.html

34 http://findarticles.com/p/news-articles/analyst-wire/mi_8077/is_20100422/april-22-2010-msnbc/ai_n53271996/.

35 "Sweeping Wall St. Regulations May Not Prevent Another Crisis: Analysis," The Associated Press, 5/23/2010. http://www.cleveland.com/nation/index.ssf/2010/05/sweeping_wall_st_regulations_m.html

36 "Sweeping Wall St. Regulations May Not Prevent Another Crisis: Analysis," The Associated Press, 5/23/2010. http://www.cleveland.com/nation/index.ssf/2010/05/sweeping_wall_st_regulations_m.html

37 Taylor, John B., "The Dodd-Frank Financial Fiasco," *Wall Street Journal,* July 1, 2010. http://online.wsj.com/article/SB10001424052748703426004575338732174405398.html

38 "Summary: Restoring American Financial Stability," (http://banking.senate.gov/public/_files/FinancialReformSummary231510FINAL.pdf).

39 Rasmussen Reports, May 22, 2010 (http://www.rasmussenreports.com/public_content/politics/general_politics/may_2010/72_are_not_confident_congress_knows_what_it_s_doing_when_it_comes_to_the_economy).

40 Matt Taibbi, "Obama's Big Sellout: The President has Packed his Economic Team with Wall Street Insiders Intent on Turning the Bailout into an All-out Giveaway," RollingStone.com, December 9, 2009. www.rollingstone.com/politics/story/31234647/obamas_big_!sellout/

41 www.dotpenn.com/index.php/Economy/Samurai-Trains-AIG-Executives-In-Ritual-Suicide.html.

42 John D. McKinnon and John D. Stoll, "U.S. Throws Lifeline to Detroit," *Wall Street Journal*, December 20, 2008. http://online.wsj.com/article/SB122969367595121563.html

43 David Goldman, "Auto Bailout: 78% Spent So Far," CNNMoney.com, December 10, 2009. http://money.cnn.com/2009/12/10/news/companies/automakers_tarp/index.htm?postversion=2009121016

44 http://mjperry.blogspot.com/2008/11/crippling-burden-of-legacy-costs-gm-is.html

45 "Unfunded Liabilities and the Coming Class War." http://unfundedliabilitiesandclasswar.blogspot.com/2009_09_01_archive.html

46   Carl Horowitz, "Obama Arranges Takeover of GM and Chrysler; Auto Workers Union Gets Huge Stake," National Legal and Policy Center, May 1, 2009. www .nlpc.org/stories/2009/05/01/obama-administration-arranges-takeover-gm-and -chrysler-auto-workers-union-gets-huge-stake

47   Kimberly Morin, "Obama appoints far left progressive, Andy Stern, head of SEIU, to Fiscal Commission, Boston Conservative Independent Examiner, February 28, 2010. www.examiner.com/x-9100-Boston-Conservative-Independent -Examiner-y2010m2d28-Obama-appoints-far-left-progressive-Andy-Stern-head-of -SEIU-to-Fisc a l-Commission

48   Michelle Malkin, " 'Brown Shirts' vs. Purple Shirts," Townhall.com, August 12, 2009. http://townhall.com/columnists/MichelleMalkin/2009/08/12/brown_shirts _vs_purple_shirts?

49   Morin, "Obama Appoints Far Left Progressive, Andy Stern, Head of SEIU, to Fiscal Commission."

50   John Carney, "Sorry, Taxpayers, You Aren't Getting Paid Back By Goldman Sachs," Business Insider, April 15, 2009. www.businessinsider.com/sorry-taxpayers -you-arent-getting-paid-back-by-goldman-sachs-2009-4

51   Laura Meckler, "Obama Signs Stimulus Into Law," Wall Street Journal, February 18, 2009. http://online.wsj.com/article/SB123487951033799545.html

52   Cheryl Gay Stolberg, "Democrats Threaten to Block More Bush Nominees," New York Times, March 26, 2004. www.nytimes.com/2004/03/26/politics/26CND -NOMI.html?ex=1395723600&en=75637f40aa22dd96&ei=5007&partner=USER LAND

53   Ibid.

54   Jon Ward, "Obama Rewards Unions with Key Labor Appointee," Daily Caller, March 27, 2010. http://dailycaller.com/2010/03/27/obama-appoints-union-lawyer -to-key-labor-relations-board-despite-gop-protests/

55   "Andy Stern's Go-To-Guy," Wall Street Journal, May 14, 2009. http://online.wsj .com/article/SB124226652880418035.html

56   "Craig Becker, now of NLRB, admits SEIU represents illegal aliens, opposes 'punitive sanctions' against employers," 24ahead.com. http://24ahead.com/craig -becker-now-nrlb-admits-seiu-represents-illegal-aliens

57   James R. Hagerty, and Jessica Holder, "U.S. Move to Cover Fannie, Freddie Losses Stirs Controversy," Wall Street Journal, December 28, 2009.

58   Ben Tracy, "Housing Crisis Getting Uglier in 2010," February 10, 2010. www .cbsnews.com/stories/2010/02/02/eveningnews/main6167610.shtml

59   "Geithner Claims Mortgage Modifications a Success Despite House Probe," Uppi-tyBanker.com. http://uppitybanker.com/2010/02/

60   http://blogs.abcnews.com/politicalpunch/2008/10/spread-the-weal.html

61   Rea Hederman Jr. and Patrick Tyrrell, "European Levels of Taxation: Barack Obama's Tax Plan," American Heritage Foundation, June 26, 2008. www.heritage.org/ Research/Reports/2008/06/European-Levels-of-Taxation-Barack-Obamas-Tax-Plan

62   Charlie Curnow, "Are Public Employees Bankrupting the Nation?" Advisor Per-

spectives, April 13, 2010. www.advisorperspectives.com/newsletters10/Are_Public_Employees_Bankrupting_the_Nation.php

63   Dennis Cauchon, "For Feds, more get 6-figure salaries," *USA Today*, December 11, 2009. www.usatoday.com/news/washington/2009-12-10-federal-pay-salaries_N.htm

64   www.lonelyconservative.com/2010/03/20/video-dem-rep-alcee-hastings-there-are-no-rules-we-make-em-up-as-we-go-along/

65   Amity Shlaes, "Republicans Should Blow Up Party, Not Marriages," Bloomberg.com, June 30, 2009. www.bloomberg.com/apps/news?pid=20601039&sid=aEdjk7naC.zY

66   Pamela Villareal, "Social Security and Medicare Projections: 2009," National Center For Policy Analysis, June 11, 2009. www.ncpa.org/pub/ba662

67   "Senate Health Bill Would Up Costs for millions in Middle Class, Analysis Finds." www.foxnews.com/politics/2010/03/11/senate-health-care-raises-taxes-middleclass-analysis-finds/

68   Dana Blanton, "Fox News Poll: 79% Say U.S. Economy Could Collapse," FoxNews.com, March 23, 2010. www.foxnews.com/politics/2010/03/23/fox-news-poll-say-economy-collapse/

69   "Obama to Wall Street: I Do Think At A Certain Point You've Made Enough Money," Real Clear Politics, April 28, 2010. www.realclearpolitics.com/video/2010/04/28/obama_to_wall_street_i_do_think_at_a_certain_point_youve_made_enough_money.html

Chapter 5

1   Jeff Poor, "Al Sharpton: 'The American Public Overwhelmingly Voted for Socialism When They Elected President Obama,'" NewsBusters.org, March 22, 2010. http://newsbusters.org/blogs/jeff-poor/2010/03/22/al-sharpton-american-public-overwhelmingly-socialism-when-they-elected-pr

2   Peter Barry Chowka, "Rep. Dingell: It's Taken a Long Time to 'Control the People,'" American Thinker, March 24, 2010. www.americanthinker.com/blog/2010/03/rep_dingell_its_taken_a_long_t.html

3   Jonathan Mann, "Can the U.S. afford health care reform?" CNNPolitics.com, July 14, 2009. www.cnn.com/2009/POLITICS/07/14/health.reform/index.html

4   "Health Care Reform," RasmussenReports.com, March 21, 2010. www.rasmussenreports.com/public_content/politics/current_events/healthcare/september_2009/health_care_reform

5   Emily Yehle, "Phone Calls Continue to Batter Congress," Roll Call, March 18, 2010. www.rollcall.com/news/44382-1.html?type=aggregate_friendly

6   Jeffrey H. Anderson, "CBO: Obamacare Would Cost Over $2 trillion," *Weekly Standard*, March 18, 2010. www.weeklystandard.com/blogs/cbo-obamacare-would-cost-over-2-trillion

7   Ibid.

8   Mark Hemingway, "Read the Bill: ObamaCare Socks Middle Class with $3.9 Billion
        Tax Increase," *The Washington Examiner*, April 12, 2010. www.washingtonexaminer
        .com/opinion/blogs/beltway-confidential/read-the-bill-obamacare-socks-middle
        class-with-39-billion-tax-increase.html

9   Carla K. Johnson, "Health premiums may rise 17% for young adults buying own in-
        surance," Associated Press, March 29, 2010. www.usatoday.com/news/health/2010
        -03-29-insurance-premiums_N.htm

10   "Young to Pay Higher Health Insurance Premiums," The Heritage Foundation,
        March 30, 2010. http://blog.heritage.org/2010/03/30/side-effects-young-to-pay
        -higher-health-insurance-premiums/

11   "The Wrong Prescription: Democrats' Health Overhaul Dangerously Expands IRS
        Authority," Committee on Ways and Means Republican Report, prepared for Dave
        Camp and Charles Boustany, U.S. House of Representatives, March 18, 2010, 8.
        Available via PDF download at brown-waite.house.gov/UploadedFiles/IRS_Power_
        Report.pdf.

12   Ibid.

13   Ibid.

14   Chris McGreal, "US Healthcare Bill Leaves Illegal Immigrants Excluded," *The
        Guardian*, March 22, 2010. www.guardian.co.uk/world/2010/mar/22/us-healthcare
        -bill-illegal-immigrants

15   "The Wrong Prescription."

16   IRC sec. 6055(b)(2), as added by H.R. 3590, sec. 1502(a).

17   "The Wrong Prescription."

18   "Price: Obamacare Means 159 New Gov't Agencies," Newsmax.com, March 20,
        2010. http://newsmax.com/InsideCover/tom-price-healthcare-democrats/2010/03/
        20/id/353358

19   "Civil Service Appointments," U.S. Food and Drug Administration, November 24,
        2009. www.fda.gov/AboutFDA/WorkingatFDA/ucm110027.htm

20   "Establishing a Ready Reserve Corps," Section 5210 of HR 3590 (a)(1).

21   Tim Townsend, "ACLU program will protect Muslims in FBI questioning,"
        St. Louis Post-Dispatch, April 1, 2010. http://www.stltoday.com/stltoday/
        news/stories.nsf/religion/story/392EC8E5A63A468F862576F8000070D0?Open
        Document

22   "ACLU New York Times Ad Today Calls On President Obama Not To Back Down
        On 9/11 Civilian Trials," ACLU press release, March 7, 2010. www.aclu.org/
        national-security/aclu-new-york-times-ad-today-calls-president-obama-not-back
        -down-911-civilian-tria

23   Barack Obama, speech during the campaign of 2008. Video retrieved April 2, 2010.
        www.youtube.com/watch?v=xvJJP9AYgqU

24   "Pelosi Remarks at the 2010 Legislative Conference for National Association of
        Counties," Press Release, Speaker Nancy Pelosi Newsroom, March 9, 2010. www
        .speaker.gov/newsroom/pressreleases?id=1576

25   Gordon Lubold, "Obama Looks For Ways to Pay For Healthcare," *Christian Sci-*

ence Monitor, June 13, 2009. www.csmonitor.com/USA/Politics/2009/0613/obama-looks-for-ways-to-pay-for-healthcare

26   Robert Pear, "Health Care Spending Disparities Stir a Fight," *New York Times,* June 8, 2009. www.nytimes.com/2009/06/09/us/politics/09health.html

27   Richard Poe, "Obamacare to be 1 big 'death panel,' ", WorldNetDaily.com, August 20, 2009. www.wnd.com/index.php?fa=PAGE.view&pageId=107403

28   Ibid.

29   Ibid.

30   Peter Nicholas, "Obama Discusses Deathbed Measures," *Los Angeles Times,* June 25, 2009. http://articles.latimes.com/2009/jun/25/nation/na-health25

31   "Obama's Health Future," *Wall Street Journal,* June 29, 2009. http://online.wsj.com/article/SB124597492337757443.html

32   Poe, "Obamacare to be 1 Big 'Death Panel.' "

33   Hans Nichols, "Obama Says Grandmother's Hip Replacement Raises Cost Questions," Bloomberg.com, April 29, 2009. www.bloomberg.com/apps/news?pid=2060 1070&sid=aGrKbfWkzTqc

34   David Leonhardt, "After the Great Recession," *New York Times,* March 28, 2009. www.nytimes.com/2009/05/03/magazine/03Obama-t.html?pagewanted=5

35   "Obama's Health Care Rationing," Editorial, *Washington Times,* May 1, 2009. www.washingtontimes.com/news/2009/may/01/obamas-health-care-rationing/

36   "Congressional Performance," Rasmussen Reports, March 22, 2010. www.rasmussen reports.com/public_content/politics/mood_of_america/congressional_performance

37   "Obama's health care rationing."

38   Dr. James Dobson, "Bringing up Boys," WorldNetDaily.com, March 19, 2002. www.wnd.com/news/article.asp?ARTICLE_ID=26878

39   David Leonhardt, "After the Great Recession," *New York Times,* March 28, 2009. www.nytimes.com/2009/05/03/magazine/03Obama-t.html?pagewanted=5

40   "Obama's health care rationing."

41   Paul Krugman, "Republican Death Trip," *New York Times,* August 13, 2009. www.nytimes.com/2009/08/14/opinion/14krugman.html?_r=1

42   Paul Krugman, "Tidings of Comfort," *New York Times,* August 20, 2009. www.nytimes.com/2009/12/25/opinion/25krugman.html

43   Bob Unruh, "N.Y. Times columnist: Death panels will save 'a lot of money,' " WorldNetDaily.com, March 30, 2010. www.wnd.com/index.php?fa=PAGE.view& pageId=134401

44   Miguel A. Faria Jr., MD, "Getting US in Line for ObamaCare and Medical Rationing," GOPUSA, March 18, 2010. www.gopusa.com/commentary/guest/2010/mf_0318p.shtml

45   Steven Hayward and Erik Peterson, "The Medicare Monster," Reason.com, January 1, 1993. http://reason.com/archives/1993/01/01/the-medicare-monster

46   Peter Suderman, "Obama Says Health-Care Reform Won't Cut Medicare Benefits. CBO Disagrees," Reason.com, September 23, 2009. See video at http://reason.com/blog/2009/09/23/obama-says-health-care-reform.

47   Alan Silverleib, "House Passes Health Care Bill on 219-212 Vote," CNN.com, March 22, 2010. www.cnn.com/2010/POLITICS/03/21/health.care.main/index.html

48   Ibid.

49   Matt Cover, "CBO Testimony Echoes Insurers' Claims About Cuts to Medicare Advantage Program," CNSNews.com, September 24, 2009. www.cnsnews.com/news/print/54515

50   Paul Ryan, "Health Care Overhaul Plan Breaks Promises to Seniors," Heartland Institute, November 6, 2009. www.heartland.org/full/26322/Health_Care_Over haul_Plan_Breaks_Promise s_to_Seniors.html

51   Robert Bernstein, "Census Bureau Estimates Number of Children and Adults in the States and Puerto Rico," U.S. Census Bureau, March 102005. www.census.gov/Press-Release/www/releases/archives/population/004083.html

52   Macon Phillips, "Change has Come to WhiteHouse.gov," WhiteHouse.Gov, January 20, 2009. www.whitehouse.gov/blog/change_has_come_to_whitehouse-gov/

53   Paul Ryan, "Health Care Overhaul Plan Breaks Promise to Seniors."

54   Ibid.

55   Betsy McCaughey, "O's Radical Pick for Medicare," NYPost.com, June 16, 2010, www.nypost.com/f/print/news/opinion/opedcolumnists/radical_pick_for_medicare_mv32rWv9ka3kByU8H9sxBK.

56   Fred Lucas, "Health Law Bans New Doctor-Owned Hospitals, Blocks Expansion of Existing Ones," CNSNews.com, April 12, 2010. www.cnsnews.com/news/article/64034

57   Shawn Tully, "5 Painful Health-care Lessons From Massachusetts," *FORTUNE*, June 16, 2010. http://money.cnn.com/2010/06/15/news/economy/massachusetts_healthcare_reform.fortune/index.htm

58   Shawn Tully, "5 Painful Health-care Lessons From Massachusetts."

59   Shawn Tully, "5 Painful Health-care Lessons From Massachusetts."

60   Shawn Tully, "5 Painful Health-care Lessons From Massachusetts."

61   Ricardo Alonso-Zaldivar, "Gap in Health Care Law's Protection for Children," Associated Press, March 24, 2010. http://finance.yahoo.com/news/Gap-in-health-care-laws-apf-4272209396.html?x=0&.v=1

62   John Boehner, "President Obama's new health care law will cost N.C. jobs," *Charlotte Observer*, April 6, 2010. www.charlotteobserver.com/2010/04/02/1350534/president-obamas-new-health-care.html

63   Dave Camp, "The Democrats' Health Bill Does What? Eleven Alarming Tax Issues," Press Release, Committee on Ways and Means Republicans, March 20, 2010.

64   David Hogberg, "20 Ways ObamaCare Will Take Away Freedoms," *Investor's Business Daily*, March 25, 2010. www.investors.com/NewsAndAnalysis/Article.aspx?id=528137

65   Suzanne Sataline and Shirley S. Wang, "Medical Schools Can't Keep Up," *Wall Street Journal*, April 12, 2010. http://online.wsj.com/article/SB1000142405270230 4506904575180331528424238.html?mod=WSJ_hpp_MIDDLENexttoWhatsNews Second

66   Ibid.

67   "Obama Mocks Journalists for Touting Polls Showing Nation Still Divided Over Healthcare," BreitbartTV.com, April 1, 2010. www.breitbart.tv/obama-mocks-jour nalists-for-touting-polls-showing-nation-still-divided-over-obamacare/

68   Bryon York, "Democrats threaten companies hit hard by health care bill," *Washington Examiner*, March 28, 2010. www.washingtonexaminer.com/politics/Demo crats-threaten-companies-hit-hard-by-health-care-bill-89347127.html

69   Steven Greenhouse, "300 Companies Push to Repeal Provision of Health Law," *New York Times*, March 29, 2010. www.nytimes.com/2010/03/30/business/30subsidy .html

70   Ibid.

71   "Democrats Threaten Companies Hit Hard by Health Care Bill."

72   Ibid.

73   Mike Lillis, "White House Moves to Keep Employers From Dropping Insurance," TheHill.com, June 14, 2010. http://thehill.com/business-a-lobbying/103131-white -house-unveils-rules

74   Steven Ertelt, "Pelosi Calls on Catholic Saint to Pass Pro-Abortion Health Care Bill, Flubs Date," Lifenews.com, March 19, 2010. www.lifenews.com/nat6152.html

75   Alan Silverleib, "House Passes Health Care Bill on 219-212 Vote," CNN.com, March 22, 2010. www.cnn.com/2010/POLITICS/03/21/health.care.main/index.html

76   Patricia Murphy, "Ben Nelson on 'Cornhusker Kickback': I Never Asked for Just Nebraska," The Capitolist, March 25, 2010. www.politicsdaily.com/2010/03/25/ ben-nelson-on-the-cornhusker-kickback-i-never-asked-for-just/

77   Scott Whitlock, "ABC's Bill Weir: Voters Sent Senator Landrieu to Washington to 'Get as Much Sausage' as Possible," Newsbusters.org, November 23, 2009. http://newsbusters.org/blogs/scott-whitlock/2009/11/23/abc-s-bill-weir-voters-sent -senator-landrieu-washington-get-much-sau

78   "Massa: Rahm Emanuel 'Would Sell His Own Mother' For Votes," Real Clear Politics, March 8, 2010. www.realclearpolitics.com/video/2010/03/08/massa_rahm_ emanuel_would_sell_his_own_mother_for_votes.html

79   www.malcolm-x.org/quotes.htm

80   Bob Cusack and Molly K. Hooper, "Rep. Kucinich to Vote Yes on Healthcare Bill, Giving Needed Boost to Democrats," The Hill, March 17, 2010. http://thehill.com/ homenews/house/87295-kucinich-to-vote-yes-on-healthcare-giving-a-boost-to-demo crats?page=3

81   Ibid.

82   Sheldon Alberts, "Obama Praises Canada's Health-care System," CalgaryHerald.com, March 9, 2010. www.calgaryherald.com/health/Obama+praises+Canada+health+ care+system/2660133/story.html#ixzz0jsdwuFuu

83   Ibid.

84   Alan Keyes, "Is Health Care a 'Human Right'?" WorldNetDaily.com, March 5, 2010. www.wnd.com/index.php?pageId=126922

85   Ezra Levant, "PM proves health care not equal for all Canadians," *The Calgary Herald*, January 15, 2002. http://ezralevant.com/2010/02/danny-williams-flies-to-us -hea.html

86   "Democratic Senator: Health Care Law to Address 'Mal-Distribution of In-
      come,' " FOXNews.com, March 27, 2010. www.foxnews.com/politics/2010/03/26/
      democratic-senator-health-care-law-address-mal-distribution-income/

87   Byron York, "What Was Obamacare Really About?" Townhall.com, April 5, 2010.
      http://townhall.com/Common/PrintPage.aspx?g=c1b47a1e-55a5-47dd-983a-d6549
      cdec6b2&t=c

88   David Leonhardt, "In Health Bill, Obama Attacks Wealth Inequality," *New York
      Times*, March 23, 2010. www.nytimes.com/2010/03/24/business/24leonhardt
      .html

89   Curtis Dubay, "Fairness is in the Eye of the Beholder Vice President Biden,"
      Heritage.org, April 1, 2010. http://blog.heritage.org/2010/04/01/fairness-is-in-the
      -eye-of-the-beholder-vice-president-biden/

90   Ibid.

91   Scott A. Hodge, "Tax Burder of Top 1% Now Exceeds That of Bottom 95%," Tax
      Foundation, June 29, 2009. www.taxfoundation.org/blog/show/24944.html

92   "Biden: Health care is fairness, not redistribution of income," USATODAY.com,
      March 30, 2010. http://content.usatoday.com/communities/theoval/post/2010/03/
      biden-health-care-is-fairness-not-redistribution-of-income/1

93   Edward Glaeser, "The End of the New Deal," *New York Sun*, June 13, 2007. www
      .nysun.com/arts/end-of-the-new-deal/56458/

94   Ibid.

95   Amity Shlaes, *The Forgotten Man: A New History of the Great Depression* (New York:
      HarperCollins, 2007), 216.

96   Charles R. Geisst, *Monopolies in America* (New York: Oxford University Press,
      2000), 143.

97   "Support for Repeal of Health Care Plan Up To 58%," Rasmussenreports.com,
      April 12, 2010. www.rasmussenreports.com/public_content/politics/current_events
      /healthcare/march_2010/health_care_law

98   "GOP Sees Risks in Push to Repeal Health Law," Associated Press, March 31,
      2010. www.foxnews.com/politics/2010/03/31/gop-wary-health-law-repeal-push
      -fall/?test=latestnews

99   "Quality, Affordable Health Care for All Americans," H.R. 3590, Section 1402,
      Subpart B, 274.

100   Marc Heller, "Amish Families Exempt From Insurance Mandate," *Watertown Daily
      Times*, January 9, 2010. www.watertowndailytimes.com/article/20100109/NEWS
      02/301099964

Chapter 6

1   Barack Obama, "Remarks by the President at the Morning Plenary Session of the
      United Nations Climate Change Conference," White House Press Release, Decem-
      ber 18, 2009. www.whitehouse.gov/the-press-office/remarks-president-morning
      -plenary-session-united-nations-climate-change-conference

2   "O'Reilly compared Moore, Franken to Goebbels; compared Hollywood celebs to

Nazi faithful," MediaMatters.org, June 14, 2004. http://mediamatters.org/research/200406140007

3   Wesley Pruden, "The Red-hot Scam Unravels," *Washington Times*, February 16, 2010. www.washingtontimes.com/news/2010/feb/16/pruden-the-red-hot-scam-begins-to-unravel/

4   "Al Gore Could Become World's First Carbon Billionaire," Telegraph.co.uk, November 3, 2009. www.telegraph.co.uk/earth/energy/6491195/Al-Gore-could-become-worlds-first-carbon-billionaire.html

5   Richard Gray and Rebecca Lefort, "UN Climate Change Panel Based Claims on Student Dissertation and Magazine Article," Telegraph.co.uk, January 30, 2010. www.telegraph.co.uk/earth/environment/climatechange/7111525/UN-climate-change-panel-based-claims-on-student-dissertation-and-magazine-article.html

6   "Rebuttal: News Plays Fast and Loose With the Facts," Stephen H. Schneider, *Detroit News*, 12/5/1989, p. 10A. Retrieved PDF at:

7   Rory Cooper, "Cap and Trade Is A Tax and It's a Great Big One," Heritage Foundation, May 1, 2009. http://blog.heritage.org/2009/05/01/cap-and-trade-is-a-tax-and-its-a-great-big-one/

8   John M. Broder, " 'Cap and Trade' Loses Its Standing as Energy Policy of Choice," *New York Times*, March 25, 2010. www.nytimes.com/2010/03/26/science/earth/26climate.html?hpw

9   Gene J. Koprowski, "Global Warming Advocates Threaten Blizzard of Lawsuits," FOXNews.com, March 29, 2010. www.foxnews.com/scitech/2010/03/29/global-warming-advocates-threaten-blizzard-lawsuits/

10   Ibid.

11   Juliet Eilperin and Steven Mufson, "Senators to propose abandoning cap-and-trade," *Washington Post*, February 27, 2010. www.washingtonpost.com/wp-dyn/content/article/2010/02/26/AR2010022606084.html

12   Ibid.

13   Kim Strassel, " 'Cap and Trade Is Dead,' " *Wall Street Journal*, November 26, 2009. http://online.wsj.com/article/SB10001424052748703499404574558070997168360.html

14   Mike Allen, "President Obama to take strong hand with Congress," POLITICO.com, March 28, 2010. www.politico.com/news/stories/0310/35116.html

15   Barack Obama, "Transcript of President Obama's Address to the Nation on the BP Oil Spill," MyFoxDC.com, June 15, 2010. www.myfoxdc.com/dpp/news/transcript-of-president-obamas-address-to-the-nation-on-the-bp-oil-spill-061510

16   Rebecca Terrell and Ed Hiserodt, "IPCC Officials Admit Global Warming Fraud," *New American*, November 23, 2009. www.thenewamerican.com/index.php/tech-mainmenu-30/environment/2377-ipcc-researchers-admit-global-warming-fraud

17   Marco Evers, Olaf Stampf, and Gerald Traufetter, "A Superstorm for Global Warming Research," Spiegel Online International, April 1, 2010. www.spiegel.de/international/world/0,1518,686697,00.html

18   Ibid.

19   Jonathan Petre, "Climategate U-turn as scientist at centre of row admits: There has

been no global warming since 1995," *Daily Mail*, February 15, 2010. www.daily
mail.co.uk/news/article-1250872/Climategate-U-turn-Astonishment-scientist
-centre-global-warming-email-row-admits-data-organised.html

20   Marc Sheppard, "Media Not Covering Climatefraud," *American Thinker*, February
16, 2010. www.americanthinker.com/blog/2010/02/evidence_of_climate_fraud_
grow.html

21   Al Gore, "We Can't Wish Away Climate Change," *New York Times*, February 27,
2010. www.nytimes.com/2010/02/28/opinion/28gore.html

22   Terrell and Hiserodt, "IPCC Officials Admit Global Warming Fraud."

23   Obama, "Remarks by the President."

24   "Another Ice Age?" *TIME*, June 24, 1974. www.time.com/time/magazine/article
/0,9171,944914,00.html

25   Alan Caruba, "Time Magazine Has a Problem with the Truth about Global Warming," Accuracy in Media, February 5, 2010. www.aim.org/guest-column/time
-magazine-has-a-problem-with-the-truth-about-global-warming/

26   Obama, "Remarks by the President."

27   **Steven** Mufson and David A. Farenthold, "EPA is preparing to regulate emissions
in Congress's stead," *Washington Post*, December 8, 2009. www.washingtonpost
.com/wp-dyn/content/article/2009/12/07/AR2009120701645.html

28   Gerald Warner, "Copenhagen Climate Summit: 'Most ImportantPaper in the World'
is a Glorified UN Press Release," Telegraph.co.uk, December 18, 2009. http://blogs
.telegraph.co.uk/news/geraldwarner/100020279/copenhagen-climate-summit-most
-important-paper-in-the-world-is-a-glorified-un-press-release/

29   "The Cap and Tax Fiction," *Wall Street Journal*, A12, June 26, 2009. http://online
.wsj.com/article/SB124588837560750781.html

30   Cooper, "Cap and Trade Is A Tax and It's a Great Big One."

31   "China Says No Emissions Cap For Now," AFP news, February 25, 2010. http://news
.yahoo.com/s/afp/20100225/sc_afp/unclimatewarmingchina_20100225070304

32   "The Cap and Tax Fiction."

33   Rep. Steve Scalise, "Cap and Trade Will Cost American Families Thousands in
New Taxes and millions of Jobs," Townhall.com, April 23, 2009. http://townhall
.com/blog/g/3e59448a-4e66-495f-bb4e-9e07cbc3349b

34   Cooper, "Cap and Trade Is A Tax and It's a Great Big One."

35   "The Cap and Tax Fiction."

36   Sindya N. Bhanoo, "Fuel Taxes Must Rise, Harvard Researchers Say," NYTimes
.com, March 2, 2010. http://dotearth.blogs.nytimes.com/2010/03/02/fuel-taxes
-must-rise-harvard-researchers-say/

37   Cooper, "Cap and Trade Is A Tax and It's a Great Big One."

38   Jerome R. Corsi, "Businesses Hold World Hostage Over Carbon Credits," WorldNet
Daily.com, December 13, 2009. www.wnd.com/index.php/index.php?pageId=
118953

39   "EU's 'Carbon Fat Cats' Get Rich Off Trading Scheme: Study," Breitbart.com,
March 5, 2010. www.breitbart.com/article.php?id=CNG.6a237570be4660439e37
1341ae8452d5.a41&show_article=1

40   Dexter Wright, "Climategate: Is it Criminal?" *American Thinker*, February 5, 2010. www.americanthinker.com/2010/02/climategate_is_it_criminal_1.html

41   John M. Broder, "From a Theory to a Consensus on Emissions," *New York Times*, May 16, 2009. www.nytimes.com/2009/05/17/us/politics/17cap.html

42   Gene J. Koprowski, "Global Warming Skeptics Lambaste Plan to Increase Funding for Climate Change Research," FOXNews.com, February 14, 2010. www.foxnews .com/scitech/2010/02/11/obama-spending-increase-global-warming-research/

43   "Ensign Aims to Prevent Tax Hike on Low and Middle Class Families," Press Release, U.S. Senator John Ensign, April 1, 2009. http://ensign.senate.gov/public/ index.cfm?FuseAction=Media.PressReleases&ContentRecord_id=6357d5e4-95a7 -a482-c827-2e7f745c134a

44   Barack Obama, "Obama Vows Electricity Rates Would 'Necessarily Skyrocket' Under His Plan," Breitbart.tv, interview with San Francisco Chronicle. www.breitbart .tv/?p=211663

45   Testimony before the U.S. House of Representatives Committee on Energy and Commerce on the draft "American Clean Energy and Security Act," Myron Ebell, Transcript of speech, provided by Competitive Enterprise Institute, April 22, 2009. Available via PDF.

46   Ibid.

47   John P. Foley, ed., *The Jeffersonian Cyclopedia* (New York: Funk & Wagnells Company, 1900), 663.

48   Garance Burke, "Stimulus Watch: Weatherizing program slow to start," Associated Press, March 27, 2010. http://apnews.myway.com/article/20100328/D9 END8UO0.html

49   Michael A. Fletcher, "Obama to announce details of 'cash for caulkers' program during visit to Savannah," *Washington Post*, March 2, 2010. http://voices.washing tonpost.com/44/2010/03/bama-to-announce-details-of-ca.html

50   Frank Newport, "Americans' Global Warming Concerns Continue to Drop," Gallup .com, March 11, 2010. www.gallup.com/poll/126560/Americans-Global-Warming -Concerns-Continue-Drop.aspx

51   Marc Morano, "Flashback April 2009: Democrats Refuse to Allow Skeptic to Testify Alongside Gore At Congressional Hearing," Climate Depot, April 23, 2009. www.climatedepot.com/a/429/undefined/

52   Ibid.

53   Joel Achenbach, "The Tempest," *Washington Post*, May 28, 2006. www.washington post.com/wp-dyn/content/article/2006/05/23/AR2006052301305_pf.html

54   Ibid.

55   Dr. Peter Gleick, "The Best Argument Against Global Warming," SFGate.com, March 11, 2010. www.sfgate.com/cgi-bin/blogs/gleick/detail?entry_id=58962&tsp=1

56   Sen. James Inhofe, "2007: Global Warming Alarmism Reaches A 'Tipping Point,' " Speech on the Floor of the Senate, October 26, 2007. http://epw.senate.gov/public/ index.cfm?FuseAction=Minority.Speeches&ContentRecord_id=dceb518c-802a -23ad-45bf-894a13435a08&Region_id=&Issue_id=

57   Gina Cherundolo, "Lake Erie Freezes over," StarTribune.com, February 15, 2010.

www.startribune.com/weather/84400142.html?elr=KArks:DCiUBDEaLDyUiacy
KUnciatkEP7DhU

58   "Start of British Summer Time? Forget it and prepare for ANOTHER wintry blast
      as snow and freezing temperatures return," Daily Mail Reporter, DailyMail.co.uk,
      March 28, 2010. www.dailymail.co.uk/news/article-1261336/British-Summer-Time
      -Forget-prepare-ANOTHER-wintry-blast-snow-freezing-conditions-return.html

59   Louise Gray, "Will polar bears make it back to shore?" Telegraph.co.uk, March 2,
      2010.   www.telegraph.co.uk/earth/earthnews/7078673/Will-polar-bears-make-it
      -back-to-shore.html

60   "Noah Wyle PSA Polar Bears." Video retrieved March 22, 2010 at www.youtube
      .com/watch?v=l3UkwAXWBYc.

61   William F. Jasper, "Polar Bears Thrive, Contrary to WWF Claims," TheNewAmer-
      ican.com, January 13, 2009. http://www.thenewamerican.com/tech-mainmenu-30/
      environment/675

62   Ibid.

63   Senator James Inhofe, "The Polarizing Politics of the Polar Bear," Speech on the Floor
      of the Senate, January 4, 2007. http://epw.senate.gov/public/index.cfm?FuseAction=
      PressRoom.Speeches&ContentRecord_id=EF3AD1FF-802A-23AD-496D-DC3B
      128DB3CE

64   Martyn Brown, "100 Reasons why Global Warming is Natural," DailyExpress
      .co.uk, December 15, 2009. www.dailyexpress.co.uk/posts/view/146139

65   Inhofe, "2007: Global Warming Alarmism Reaches A 'Tipping Point.' "

66   Cari-Lynn Clough, "Off-Screen Hero," UKULA TRAVEL, retrieved March 16,
      2010.   www.ukula.com/TorontoArticle.aspx?SectionID=5&ObjectID=1779&City
      ID=3

67   Leonardo DiCaprio, Excerpt from The 11th Hour, Warner Independent Pictures,
      October 10, 2007.

68   "Al Gore sued by over 30,000 Scientists for Global Warming Fraud/John Cole-
      man," interview with Greg Gutfeld on Red Eye at FoxNews.com. Video available at
      www.youtube.com/watch?v=FfHW7KR33IQ

69   Joe D'Aleo, "Weather Channel Founder: Global Warming 'Greatest Scam in
      History,' " Mensnewsdaily.com, December 4, 2009. http://mensnewsdaily.com/
      sexandmetro/2009/12/04/weather-channel-founder-global-warming-greatest-scam
      -in-history/

70   Ibid.

71   "Making Films Is Leonardo DiCaprio's 'College,' " Interview with Leonardo
      DiCaprio, Starplus.com, January 9, 2007. www.starpulse.com/news/index.php/
      2007/01/09/making_films_is_leonardo_dicaprio_s_coll

72   Scott Roxborough, "DiCaprio sheds light on '11th Hour,' " Hollywood Reporter, May
      20, 2007. www.hollywoodreporter.com/hr/content_display/film/news/e3i1f890f6
      25ffdd1903ee8bde055a360d1

73   Eric Fleming, "Sheryl Crow Says: One Square of Toilet Paper Only!" Associated
      Content, April 23, 2007. www.associatedcontent.com/article/223399/sheryl_crow_
      says_one_square_of_toilet.html?cat=7

74   Laurie David and Sheryl Crow, "Let's Wrap it Up," Huffington Post, April 23, 2007.
       www.huffingtonpost.com/laurie-david-and-sheryl-crow/lets-wrap-it-up_b_46620
       .html

75   Brent Baker, "Actor Danny Glover Blames Global Warming for Haiti Earth-
       quake," NewsBusters.com, January 16, 2010. http://newsbusters.org/blogs/brent
       -baker/2010/01/16/actor-danny-glover-blames-global-warming-earthquake-haiti

76   "Simple Things We Can All Do to Help Stop Global Warming," retrieved from Bar-
       bara Streisand's website, March 22, 2010. www.barbrastreisand.com/us/statement
       /simple-things-we-can-all-do-help-stop-global-warming

77   "Name the Liberal Hypocrite" Quiz, taken from Peter Schweizer, *Do As I say
       (Not as I Do): Profiles in Liberal Hypocrisy* (New York: Doubleday, 2005). Avail-
       able via PDF at http://docs.google.com/viewer?a=v&q=cache:C78UVWHl2XQJ:
       www.randomhouse.com/doubleday/doasisay/quiz.pdf+streisand+12,000+square+
       foot+air+conditioned+barn&hl=en&gl=us&pid=bl&srcid=ADGEESgXbPv_kFO
       4no2nvir_SDsLlVtUvdMRpBwXqATukDEi7RHUEIrduwHsJuzeBf8wwzf-4mm5
       Zpgweu3DzG9USYkjaEy638MtJlY-cO3Q680RIlrC9X5bImnRFD9FIa0yqwt_Go
       CA&sig=AHIEtbSLe1gH2iJwR7-KxUNwSRr09qmXSA.

78   "With five private jets, Travolta still lectures on global warming," London Evening
       Standard, March 30, 2007. www.thisislondon.co.uk/showbiz/article-23390848
       -with-five-private- jets-travolta-still-lectures-on-global-warming.do

Chapter 7

1   "President Obama, No One in Arizona is Laughing," Paid advertisement by Gover-
       nor Jan Brewer, YouTube, previewed May 10, 2010. Available at www.youtube.com/
       watch?v=NLgZ1LWLlko&feature=player_embedded.

2   Barack Obama, "Obama To Mexican President: 'We Are Defined Not By Our Bor-
       ders,' " Real Clear Politics Video, May 19, 2010. www.realclearpolitics.com/video/
       2010/05/19/obama_to_mexican_president_we_are_defined_not_by_our_borders
       .html

3   "After squandering $700 million Janet Napolitano freezes funds for virtual fence,"
       Seeing Red AZ. http://seeingredaz.wordpress.com/2010/03/16/after-squandering
       -700-million-janet-napolitano-freezes-funds-for-virtual-fence

4   Obama, "Obama To Mexican President: 'We Are Defined Not By Our
       Borders.' "

5   Brian Ross, Richard Esposito, and Asa Eslocker, "Kidnapping Capital of the U.S.A.,"
       ABC News, February 11, 2009. http://abcnews.go.com/Blotter/story?id=6848672
       &page=1

6   William La Jeunesse, "Illegal Immigrant Suspected in Murder of Arizona Rancher,"
       FoxNews.com, March 30, 2010. http://www.foxnews.com/us/2010/03/30/illegal
       -immigrant-suspected-murder-arizona-rancher/

7   Dennis Wagner, "Rancher's murder fuels firestorm," *The Arizona Republic*, March
       30, 2010. www.azcentral.com/news/articles/2010/03/30/20100330krentz.html

8   Stephen Kaufman, "Obama Calls Arizona Immigration Law 'Poorly Conceived,' "

America.gov, April 29, 2010. www.america.gov/st/democracyhr-english/2010/April
/20100429125217esnamfuak$.6293146.html?CP.rss=true

9   Noel Sheppard, "Attorney General Holder Admits He's Never Read Arizona's
       Immigration Law," Newsbusters, May 13, 2010. http://newsbusters.org/blogs/
       noel-sheppard/2010/05/13/attorney-general-holder-admits-never-reading-arizonas
       -immigration-law

10   "80,000 violent felons run free on U.S. streets," WorldNetDaily.com, September
       22, 2006. www.wnd.com/news/article.asp?ARTICLE_ID=52091

11   Sam Quinones, "A lethal business model targets Middle America," *Los Angeles Times*,
       February 14, 2010. http://articles.latimes.com/2010/feb/14/local/la-me-blacktar
       14-2010feb14/2

12   Jim McTague, "The Underground Economy," *Barron's*, January 6, 2005. www.fair
       tax.org/site/News2?page=NewsArticle&id=9317

13   "Criminal Aliens," Federation for American Immigration Reform. www.fairus.org/
       site/PageServer?pagename=iic_immigrationissuecenters0b9c

14   Ben Shapiro, "Paying Off La Raza," HumanEvents.com, December 17, 2009. www
       .humanevents.com/article.php?id=34861

15   "What Is MEChA," Mayorno.com. www.mayorno.com/WhoIsMecha.html

16   Stephen Lemons, "What is RAZA," phoenixnewtimes.com, May 29, 2009.

17   calstatela.edu/orgs/mecha/planphilmecha.htm.

18   Mike Sunnucks, "La Raza, unions ask Obama to scrap immigration pacts with local
       cops," *Phoenix Business Journal*, August 27, 2009. www.bizjournals.com/phoenix/
       stories/2009/08/24/daily69.html

19   "Amnesty Remains a Priority for Senate Democrats, New Congress," Federation For
       Immigration Reform, January 12, 2009. www.fairus.org/site/News2?page=News
       Article&id=19721&security=1601&news_iv_ctrl=1721

20   Peter Nicholas, "Obama looking to give new life to immigration reform," latimes
       .com, March 4, 2010. http://articles.latimes.com/2010/mar/04/nation/la-na-immi
       gration5-2010mar05

21   Heather MacDonald, "The Bilingual Ban That Worked," freedompolitics.com,
       December 18, 2009. http://articles.latimes.com/2010/mar/04/nation/la-na-immi
       gration5-2010mar05

22   Kathy McKee, "Myths and Lies of Illegal Immigration," *Sonoran News*, January 4,
       2004. www.theamericanresistance.com/articles/art2004jan04.html

23   Tom LoBianco, "Lawyers Tag Nominee as 'Terror on the Bench,'" *Washington
       Times*, May 29, 2009. www.washingtontimes.com/news/2009/may/29/lawyers-tag
       -sotomayor-as-terror-on-the-bench/

24   Rick Moran, "Sotomayor Overturned 60% of the Time by Supremes," American
       Thinker.com, May 27, 2009. www.americanthinker.com/blog/2009/05/sotomayor
       _overturned_60_of_the.html

25   "Good news: Sotomayor confuses 'eminent' with 'imminent'—twice," HotAir.com,
       July 15, 2009. http://hotair.com/archives/2009/07/15/good-news-sotomayor
       -confuses-eminent-with-imminent-twice/

26   Suzanne Sataline, Jess Bravin, and Nathan Koppel, "A Sotomayor Ruling Gets

Scrutiny," *Wall Street Journal*, May 29, 2009. http://online.wsj.com/article/SB124 354041637563491.html

27   "LLANJ Board of Delegates: Cid Wilson," Latino Leadership Alliance of New Jersey. www.llanj.org/Cid-Wilson.php

28   www.disasterhousing.gov/offices/fheo/Assistant-Secretary/index.cfm.

29   Joe Wolverton, II, "Obama Nominates La Raza Activist as Ambassador," The NewAmerican.com, December 19, 2009. www.thenewamerican.com/index.php/ usnews/politics/2595-obama-nominates-la-raza-activist-as-ambassador

30   Jaxon Van Derbeken, "Slaying suspect once found sanctuary in S.F.," *San Francisco Chronicle*, July 20, 2008. http://articles.sfgate.com/2008-07-20/news/ 17173999_1_immigration-status-el-salvador-illegal-immigrant

31   Rebecca L. Clark and Scott A. Anderson, "Illegal Aliens in Federal, State, and Local Criminal Justice Systems Summary," The Urban Institute, June 30, 2000. www .urban.org/publications/410366.html

32   David Luhnow and Jose de Cordoba, "The Perilous State of Mexico," *Wall Street Journal*, February 21, 2009. http://online.wsj.com/article/SB123518102536038463 .html

33   "America's Drug Abuse Profile," ncjrs.gov/htm/chapter2.htm.

34   Quinones, "A Lethal Business Model Targets America."

35   Jim McTague, "Going Underground: America's Shadow Economy," *Barron's*, January 6, 2005. http://97.74.65.51/readArticle.aspx?ARTID=10024

36   Robert Justich and Betty Ng, CFA, "The Underground Labor Force Is Rising To The Surface," January 3, 2005. www.bearstearns.com/bscportal/pdfs/underground .pdf

37   Lornet Turnbull, "Napolitano Demands Review of ICE Raid at Bellingham Plant," *Seattle Times*, February 26, 2009. http://seattletimes.nwsource.com/html/local news/2008787533_raid26m.html

38   "Dengue Fever Hits Key West," John Gever, ABCNews, 5/20/2010. http://abcnews .go.com/print?id=10703442

39   "Dengue Fever Hits Key West," John Gever, ABCNews, 5/20/2010. http://abcnews .go.com/print?id=10703442

40   "Dengue Fever Hits Key West," John Gever, ABCNews, 5/20/2010. http://abcnews.go .com/print?id=10703442

41   Steven A. Camarota, "Illegal Immigrants and HR 3200: Estimate of Potential Costs to Taxpayers," Center For Immigration Studies, September 2009. http://cis .org/IllegalsAndHealthCareHR3200

42   "Career Lawyers Overruled in Voting Case," *Washington Times*, May 29, 2009. www.washingtontimes.com/news/2009/may/29/career-lawyers-overruled-on-voting -case/

43   Drew Zahn, "Is Obama's $789 Billion Buying Votes Instead of Jobs?" WorldNet Daily.com, December 19, 2009. www.wnd.com/index.php?pageId=119441

44   Warner Todd Houston, "Census Bureau To Count Illegal Aliens in Census?" Stop The ACLU, October 12, 2009. stoptheaclu.com/2009/10/12/obama_to_count_ illegal_aliens_in_census

45   Kerry Pickett, "2010 Census Lacks Citizenship Question," *Washington Times*, January 11, 2010. www.washingtontimes.com/weblogs/watercooler/2010/jan/11/no-question-birthplace-asked-census/

46   Hope Yen, "States Get New Leeway to Tally Prisoners in Census," NYC Wire, February 11, 2010. www.breitbart.com/article.php?id=D9DPP7L80&show_article=1

47   Jim Kouri, "Rampant Voter Fraud by Illegal Aliens Ignored by Government and Media," Examiner.com, July 6, 2009. www.renewamerica.com/columns/kouri/080810

48   Ibid.

49   James Simpson, "What the Dems Know: Universal Voter Registration," American Thinker.com, January 6, 2010. www.americanthinker.com/2010/01/what_the_dems_know_universal_v.html

50   Kouri, "Rampant Voter Fraud by Illegal Aliens Ignored by Government and Media."

51   J. D. Longstreet, "Democrats Set to Reintroduce Amnesty for Illegal Aliens," Right SideNews.com, January 18, 2010. http://newsbyus.com/index.php/article/2969

52   James Simpson, "Barack Obama and the Strategy of Manufactured Crisis," American Thinker.com, September 28, 2008. www.americanthinker.com/2008/09/barack_obama_and_the_strategy.html

53   Abdon M.Pallasch, "Strong, Silent Type," *Chicago Sun Times*, December 17, 2007. www.suntimes.com/news/politics/obama/700499,CST-NWS-Obama-law17.article

54   "President Obama, No One in Arizona is Laughing," Paid advertisement by Governor Jan Brewer, YouTube, previewed May 10, 2010. Available at www.youtube.com/watch?v=NLgZ1LWLlko&feature=player_embedded

Chapter 8

1   "ACORN CEO: Tea Parties a 'Bowel Movement,' Future Will Be Worse Than Segregation," FOXNews.com, April 22, 2010. www.foxnews.com/politics/2010/04/22/acorn-ceo-socialists-persecution-dwarf-segregation-tea-parties-racist/

2   Sol Stern, "ACORN's Nutty Regime for Cities," *City Journal*, Spring 2003. www.city-journal.org/html/13_2_acorns_nutty_regime.html

3   "Complete List of ACORN Misdeeds," www.tigerdroppings.com/rant/message topic.asp?p=15240392.

4   Sol Stern, "Inside Obama's ACORN," National Review Online, May 29, 2008. http://article.nationalreview.com/358910/inside-obamas-acorn/stanley-kurtz

5   Toni Foulkes, "Case Study: Chicago—The Barack Obama Campaign," *Social Policy* 34, no. 2 (Winter 2003): 49. http://econopundit.com/toni.pdf

6   Ibid., 50.

7   Stanley Kurtz, "Inside Obama's Acorn," National Review Online, May 29, 2008. http://article.nationalreview.com/358910/inside-obamas-acorn/stanley-kurtz

8   Mark Hemingway, "Obama Justice Dept. shut down FBI's ACORN investigation," *Washington Examiner*, March 11, 2010. www.washingtonexaminer.com/opinion/blogs/beltway-confidential/Obama-Justice-Dept-shut-down-ACORN-investigation-87360097.html

9   Jerry Seper, "Panel: Justice Stonewalling on Panthers," *Washington Times*, April 5, 2010. www.washingtontimes.com/news/2010/apr/05/rights-panel-justice-stone walling-on-panthers/

10   "EDITORIAL: Congress is Derelict on Black Panther Case," *Washington Times*, April 9, 2010. www.washingtontimes.com/news/2010/apr/09/congress-is-derelict -on-black-panther-case/

11   Jim Simpson, "Conspiracy of the Lemmings: Barack Obama and the Radical Left's Strategy of Manufactured Crisis," Worldview Weekend, March 9, 2009. www .worldviewweekend.com/worldview-times/article.php?articleid=4695

12   "Births to Unmarried Mothers Exceed 40 percent; White Fertility Low," The Thinking Housewife. www.thinkinghousewife.com/wp/2010/04/unmarried-births -exceed-40-percent-white-fertility-remains-low/

13   Sara Murray, "Numbers on Welfare See Sharp Increase," *Wall Street Journal*, June 22, 2009. http://online.wsj.com/article/SB124562449457235503.html

14   John Atlas and Peter Dreier, "Enraging the Right," National Housing Institute, Issue 129, May/June 2003. www.nhi.org/online/issues/129/ACORN.html

15   "The Black Panther Party," Marxists.org. www.marxists.org/history/usa/workers/ black-panthers/

16   www.newblackpanther.com/.

17   Atty. Shabazz, "The Value of Dr. Khallid Abdul Muhammad," *The New Black Panther*, Spring 2010, 12. www.newblackpanther.com/NBPP%20Newspaper%20 Spring%20Edition%202010.pdf

18   Elijah Muhammad, Message to the Blackman in America (Chicago: Muhammad Mosque of Islam, No. 2, 1965), 12.

19   Alex Haley, *The Autobiography of Malcolm X* (New York: Bantam, 1965), 168.

20   "YAKUB," www.thenationofislam.org/yakubabraham.html.

21   Patrick Martin, "Obama, Clinton and identity politics," World Socialist Web Site, June 9, 2008. www.wsws.org/articles/2008/jun2008/elec-j09.shtml

22   Bob Herbert, "Savor the Moment," *New York Times*, June 7, 2008. www.nytimes .com/2008/06/07/opinion/07herbert.html

23   Martin, "Obama, Clinton and identity politics."

24   Ed Lasky, "A Dearth of Private Sector Experience in Obama's Cabinet," American Thinker.com, November 29, 2009. www.americanthinker.com/blog/2009/11/a_ dearth_of_private_sector_exp.html

25   Steven Malanga, "White House Goes National With Living Wages," Real Clear Markets, March 3, 2010. www.realclearmarkets.com/articles/2010/03/03/white_ house_goes_national_with_living_wages_98366.html

26   Malanga, "White House Goes National With Living Wages."

27   Steven Malanga, "Living Wage Is Socialism," *New York Sun*, January 30, 2003. www.manhattan-institute.org/cgi-bin/apMI/print.cgi

28   David Neumark, "The Effects of Living Wage Laws: Evidence from Failed and Derailed Living Wage Campaigns," Institute for the Study of Labor (IZA): IZA Discussion Papers, Number 1566. http://ideas.repec.org/p/iza/izadps/dp1566 .html

29   Sarah Duxbury, "Living Wage Crimps Oakland Restaurant Plan," Free Republic, November 28, 2008. www.freerepublic.com/focus/f-news/2140672/posts

30   Andy Green, "Good riddance, ACORN," Baltimore Sun, March 16, 2010. http://weblogs.baltimoresun.com/news/opinion/2010/03/good_riddance_acorn.html

31   Annette D. Bernhardt Scott Schell, and Paul K. Sonn, "Making Every Dollar Count: A Targeted Proposal to Help Working New Yorkers While Protecting the Budget," Brennan Center for Justice at NYU School of Law, April 23, 2002. http://brennan.3cdn.net/215b719a6e9538e17a_55m6b1vqr.pdf

32   Malanga, "White House Goes National With Living Wages."

33   Steven Malanga, "How the 'Living Wage' Sneaks Socialism Into Cities," City Journal, Winter 2003. www.city-journal.org/html/13_1_how_the_living_wage.html

34   Gregory Hession, "ACORN: War On the Poor," New American, October 31, 2008. www.thenewamerican.com/usnews/election/466

35   Ibid.

36   "How Much Is Wal-Mart Scamming Your State," UFCW: A Voice For Working America. www.ufcw.org/

37   Stern, "ACORN's Nutty Regime for Cities."

38   Michael Dobbs, "Obama Reneges on Public Financing," Washington Post. http://blog.washingtonpost.com/fact-checker/2008/06/obama_reneges_on_public_financ.html

39   David D. Kirkpatrick, "McCain and Obama In Deal on Public Financing," New York Times, March 2, 2007. www.nytimes.com/2007/03/02/us/politics/02fec.html?_r=1

40   Dobbs, "Obama Reneges on Public Financing."

41   "Bundling Contributions for Favors," Public Citizen. www.whitehouseforsale.org/documents/bundling_2.pdf

42   Sam Smith, "Bundling Becomes Major Corrupt Game of Campaign," Undernews, November 26, 2007. http://prorev.com/2007/11/bundling-becomes-major-corrupt-game-of.html

43   Pamela Geller, "Call for an Audit of Obama's Campaign Finances," Andrew Breitbart's Big Government, January 25, 2010. http://biggovernment.com/pgeller/2010/01/25/call-for-an-audit-of-obamas-campaign-finances/

44   Ibid.

45   Tom Blumer, "The Obama Campaign's Credit Card Crack-up," Pajamas Media, November 2, 2008. http://pajamasmedia.com/blog/the-obama-campaigns-credit-card-crack-up/

46   "Mischief in Minnesota? Al Franken's recount isn't funny," Wall Street Journal, November 12, 2008. http://online.wsj.com/article/SB122644940271419147.html

47   Ibid.

48   Jim Kouri, "Talk Show Host Reveals Obama Connection to Terrorists," NewsWithViews.com, March 22, 2008. www.newswithviews.com/BreakingNews/breaking55.htm

49   Debbie Schlussel, "Obama's Nation of Islam Staffers, Edward Said & 'Inflexible Jews' Causing Mid-East Conflict: An Obama Insider Reveals the Real Barack

Obama," DebbieSchlussel.com, January 30, 2008. www.debbieschlussel.com/3356/
exclusive-obamas-nation-of-islam-staffers-edward-said-inflexible-jews-causing-mid
-east-conflict-an-obama-insider-reveals-the-real-barack/

50   Larry Neumeister, "Once-banned Muslim Scholar Arrives in NY for Forum," Associated Press, April 7, 2010. www.washingtonpost.com/wp-dyn/content/article/
2010/04/07/AR2010040704429.html

51   Gregory Hession, "ACORN: War On the Poor," *New American*, October 31, 2008.
www.thenewamerican.com/usnews/election/466

Chapter 9

1   Andrew Malcolm, "Top Political Strategist Woody Allen Thinks Obama Would
Get Much More Done as Dictator; No, *Really*," *Los Angeles Times*, May 18, 2010.
http://latimesblogs.latimes.com/washington/2010/05/woody-allen-obama.html

2   Thomas Friedman, "Is China the Next Enron?" *New York Times*, January 13, 2010.
www.nytimes.com/2010/01/13/opinion/13friedman.html

3   Mona Charen, "Dems Lose Argument—Win Dirty," Townhall.com, March 30,
2010. http://townhall.com/columnists/MonaCharen/2010/03/30/dems_lose_argu
ment_—_win_dirty?

4   Paul Kane, " 'Tea Party' Protesters Accused of Spitting on Lawmaker, Using Slurs,"
Washington Post, March 20, 2010. www.washingtonpost.com/wp-dyn/content/
article/2010/03/20/AR2010032002556.html

5   Martina Stewart, "Axelrod Weighs in on Dem Fundraising Appeals Related to Threats,"
CNN Politics, March 28, 2010. http://politicalticker.blogs.cnn.com/2010/03/28/
axelrod-weighs-in-on-dem-fundraising-appeals-related-to-threats/?fbid=eeNdYSB0
ajb

6   Paul Krugman, "Pass the Bill," *New York Times*, December 17, 2009. www.nytimes
.com/2009/12/18/opinion/18krugman.html

7   Courtland Milloy, "Congressmen show grace, restraint in the face of disrespect,"
Washington Times, March 24, 2010. www.washingtonpost.com/wp-dyn/content/
article/2010/03/23/AR2010032304018.html

8   "Rep. Baird Retreats From Living Room Meet," Clark County Conservative, August 30, 2009. http://lewwaters.wordpress.com/2009/08/

9   www.oreilly-sucks.com/hitlerbush.htm

10   http://semiskimmed.net/bushhitler.html#adamengel

11   John Hinderaker, "Thoughts On Liberal Political Violence," PowerLine, March 27,
2010. www.powerlineblog.com/archives/2010/03/025942.php

12   Brent Bozell, "Nets Lead with 'Ugly' and 'Menacing' ObamaCare Opponents Fu-
eled by Palin's Violent Words and Imagery," Media Research Center, March 25,
2010. www.mrc.org/biasalert/2010/20100325100739.aspx

13   Don Brunell, "Washington View: Federal Programs With Good Intentions Create
Uncertainty," The Columbian, March 30, 2010. www.columbian.com/news/2010/
mar/30/federal-programs-with-good-intentions-create-uncer/

14   Veronique de Rugy, "Politics: Democratic Stimulus Haul is Almost Double Repub-

licans," Big Government, March 26, 2010. http://biggovernment.com/vderugy/
2010/03/26/politics-democratic-stimulus-haul-is-almost-double-republicans/

15 www.studentloanfacts.org/whoweare/

16 University Archives and Records Center, University of Pennsylvania. www.archives
.upenn.edu/histy/features/tuition/1960.html

17 *U.S. News & World Report*, National University Rankings. http://colleges.usnews
.rankingsandreviews.com/best-colleges/national-universities-rankings).

18 Campus Grotto. www.campusgrotto.com/most-expensive-college-dorms.html

19 www.ou.edu/admissions/home/resources/cost_estimate.html

20 Mary Pilon, "Bank of Mom and Dad Shuts Amid White-Collar Struggle," *Wall
Street Journal*, April 4, 2010. http://online.wsj.com/article/SB10001424052748704
207504575130171387740744.html?KEYWORDS=bank+of+mom+and+dad#

21 Warner Todd Huston, "Obama To Take Over Control of College Textbooks?"
Canadian Free Press, March 31, 2010. www.canadafreepress.com/index.php/
article/21533

22 Ann Wilson, "Outcome-Based Education—Questions Demanding Answers,"
www.sntp.net/education/OBE_1.htm

23 Greg Toppo, "Education Chief Calls Teachers Union 'Terrorist Organization,' " *USA
Today*, February 24, 2004. www.usatoday.com/news/washington/2004-02-23-paige
-remarks_x.htm

24 Shanea Watkins, "Safer Kids, Better Test Scores: The D.C. Voucher Program
Works," Heritage Foundation, June 20, 2008. www.heritage.org/Research/Reports/
2008/06/Safer-Kids-Better-Test-Scores-The-DC-Voucher-Program-Works

25 U.S. Department of Education, "The Race to the Top Begins—Remarks by
Secretary Arne Duncan," July 24, 2009. www2.ed.gov/news/speeches/2009/07/
07242009.html

26 Neil King Jr., "Only Two States Win Race to Top," *Wall Street Journal*, March 29,
2010. http://online.wsj.com/article/SB100014240527023043703045751516824578
97668.html?mod=WSJ_WSJ_US_PoliticsNCampaign_4

27 Andrew J. Coulson, "Escalante Stood and Delivered. It's Our Turn," *Wall Street
Journal*, April 2, 2010. http://online.wsj.com/article/SB10001424052702304252704
575156154196626406.html?mod=WSJ_Opinion_LEFTTopOpinion

28 "Review ordered of Video Showing Students Singing Praises of President Obama,"
FoxNews.com. www.foxnews.com/politics/2009/09/24/review-ordered-video
-showing-students-singing-praises-president-obama/

29 www.communistgoals.com/goals/goals.htm

30 Joseph Abrams, "Neo-Pagans Get Worship Circle at Air Force Academy,"
FoxNews.com, February 2, 2010. www.foxnews.com/us/2010/02/02/neo-pagans
-worship-circle-air-force-academy/

31 "Alexander Hamilton," Quotes Daddy. www.quotesdaddy.com/author/Alexander
+Hamilton

32 Steven Thomma, "Not Satisfied With U.S. History, Some Conservatives are Rewriting It," McClatchy Newspapers, April 3, 2010. www.mcclatchydc.com/2010/04/
01/91478/some-conservatives-rewrite-history.html

33   A. O. Scott, "Seeking Clues to a Son's Death and a War's Meaning," *New York Times*, March 31, 2010. (http://movies.nytimes.com/2007/09/14/movies/14elah .html

34   www.worldwideboxoffice.com/index.cgi?order=worldwide&start=1900&finish= 2010

35   Ibid.

36   John Nolte, " 'Avatar' Is a Big, Dull, America-Hating PC Revenge Fantasy," Big Hollywood. http://bighollywood.breitbart.com/jjmnolte/2009/12/11/review -camerons-avatar-is-a-big-dull-america-hating-pc-revenge-fantasy/

37   Jack Shafer, "Wolf Blitzer is 'Watching Very Closely': A Crash Course in Blitzer-ese," Slate.com, November 4, 2008. http://www.slate.com/id/2203844/

38   Stuart Schwartz, "The Fat Lady Sings for Keith Olbermann," *American Thinker*, February 2, 2010. www.americanthinker.com/2010/02/the_fat_lady_sings_for_ keith_o.html

39   Kathleen Ann Ruane, "Fairness Doctrine: History and Constitutional Issues," Con-gressional Research Service, March 11, 2009. www.fas.org/sgp/crs/misc/R40009 .pdf

40   Mark Whittington, "Ann Coulter Canada Speech Cancelled By Angry Mob, Skit-tish Police," Associated Content, March 24, 2010. www.associatedcontent.com/ article/2821184/ann_coulter_canada_speech_cancelled.html

41   Susannah Heschel, "Praying with their Feet: Remembering Abraham Joshua Hes-chel and Martin Luther King," PeaceWork, January 2007. www.peaceworkmagazine .org/praying-their-feet-remembering-abraham-joshua-heschel-and-martin-luther -king

42   "Hollywood Ten," Spartacus Educational. www.spartacus.schoolnet.co.uk/USA hollywood10.htm

43   Andrew McCarthy, "Justice Delayed," National Review Online, November 17, 2009 .http://article.nationalreview.com/414647/justice-delayed/andrew-c-mccarthy

44   www.youtube.com/watch?v=27cXXirAIw4

Chapter 10

1   Andrew Sullivan, "Idiocy of the week," Salon.com, January 15, 2003. www.salon .com/news/opinion/sullivan/2003/01/15/crow

2   August Cole, "Senate Kills Funds for F-22 Fighters," *Wall Street Journal*, July 22, 2009. http://online.wsj.com/article/SB124818597270968593.html

3   Andrew Sullivan, "Senate votes to stop production of F-22 jet," *Reuters*, July 21, 2009. www.reuters.com/article/idUSTRE56K4KN20090721

4   "Grounding the F-22," *Wall Street Journal*, July 22, 2009. http://online.wsj.com/ article/SB10001424052970203946904574302511270077996.html

5   Conn Carroll, "Obama Just Made Us More Vulnerable . . . Again," Heritage Foun-dation, July 22,2009. http://blog.heritage.org/2009/07/22/morning-bell-obama -just-made-us-more-vulnerable-again/?utm_source=Newsletter&utm_medium= Email&utm_campaign=Morning%2BBell

6   "Whether We Like it or Not, We Remain a Dominant Military Superpower," Heritage Foundation, *The Hawai'i Free Press*, May 16, 2010. www.hawaiifreepress.com/main/ArticlesMain/tabid/56/articleType/ArticleView/articleId/1998/Obama-ldquoWhether-we-like-it-or-not-we-remain-a-dominant-military-superpowerrdquo.aspx

7   Sara A. Carter, "U.S. Troops battle both Taliban and their own rules," *Washington Times*, November 16, 2009. www.washingtontimes.com/news/2009/nov/16/us-troops-battle-taliban-afghan-rules/

8   Ibid.

9   Ibid.

10   Alfred de Montesquiou, "Strict Rules Slowing Offensive, Troops Say," Associated Press, February 16, 2010. www.boston.com/news/world/asia/articles/2010/02/16/strict_war_rules_slow_afghan_offensive_troops_say/

11   Martin Fletcher, "American Troops in Afghanistan Losing Heart, Says Army Chaplains," *London Times*, October 8, 2009. www.timesonline.co.uk/tol/news/world/Afghanistan/article6865359.ece

12   Carter, "U.S. troops battle both Taliban and their own rules,"

13   " 'When we Understand That Slide, We'll Have Won the War:' US generals given baffling PowerPoint presentation to try to explain Afghanistan mess," Daily Mail, April 28, 2010. www.dailymail.co.uk/news/worldnews/article-1269463/Afghanistan-PowerPoint-slide-Generals-left-baffled-PowerPoint-slide.html

14   Sebastian Abbot, "US Deaths Double in Afghanistan as Troops Pour In," Associated Press, March 27, 2010. www.google.com/hostednews/ap/article/ALeqM5ihcYrdxHyEs5g09fIPeMNJh0b6mQD9END6400

15   "Ready, Aim, Hold Your Fire," Editorial, *Washington Times*, March 6, 2010. www.washingtontimes.com/news/2010/mar/06/ready-aim-hold-your-fire/

16   Jim Michaels, "Airstrikes in Afghanistan Drop by Almost Half," *USA TODAY*, September 8, 2009. www.usatoday.com/news/military/2009-09-08-airstrikes_N.htm

17   Ibid.

18   Jeffrey T. Kuhner, "Does nonproliferation equal capitulation?" *Washington Times*, April 9, 2010. www.washingtontimes.com/news/2010/apr/09/does-nonproliferation-equal-capitulation/

19   Ibid.

20   Bob Unruh, "Overwhelmingly, Americas See Obama Inviting Attack," World NetDaily.com, April 21, 2010. www.wnd.com/index.php?fa=PAGE.view&pageId=143673

21   Brian Montopoli, "Obama Announces Nuclear Weapons Reduction Treaty With Russian," CBS News, March 26,2010. www.cbsnews.com/8301-503544_162-20001246-503544.html

22   Vadim Trukhachev, "China's ABM Interceptor Missiles Frighten USA," Pravda.ru January 13, 2010. http://english.pravda.ru/world/asia/111639-0/

23   "Reports: Netanyahu 'Humiliated' by Obama Snub," FOXNews.com, March 26, 2010. www.foxnews.com/politics/2010/03/25/president-allegedly-dumps-israeli-prime-minister-dinner/

24   Natalia Serova, "Europe Needs to Cast USA Aside Before It Is Too Late," Pravda.ru,
       November 27, 2009. http://english.pravda.ru/world/europe/110792-0/

25   Montopoli, "Obama Announces Nuclear Weapons Reduction Treaty With
       Russian."

26   Chip Cummins and Charles Forelle, "Ahmadinejad Calls Israel 'Racist' in U.N.
       Rant," *Wall Street Journal*, April 21, 2009. http://online.wsj.com/article/SB12402
       1935702234443.html

27   Shirzad Bozorghmehr, "Iranian leader: Wipe out Israel," CNN.com, November 27,
       2005. www.cnn.com/2005/WORLD/meast/10/26/ahmadinejad/index.html

28   Nazila Fathi, "Wipe Israel 'off the map' Iranian says," *New York Times*, November
       27, 2005. www.nytimes.com/2005/10/26/world/africa/26iht-iran.html

29   Jonathan Weisman, "After Arms Pact, a Push to Ratify," *Wall Street Journal*, April
       9, 2010. http://online.wsj.com/article/SB10001424052702304198004575171203 22
       3830386.html

30   Barack Obama, "Breaking the War Mentality," *Sundial*, March 10,1983,5. Avail-
       able via PDF download at www.americanthinker.com/2010/04/the_president
       _who_wont_grow_up.html.

31   "Inventions from Space," NASA, 9/8/2005. http://spaceplace.nasa.gov/en/kids/
       spinoffs2.shtml

32   "Barack Obama Ends NASA Space Race With Slow Road to Mars," *The TimesOnline*,
       April 16, 2010. www.timesonline.co.uk/tol/news/science/space/article7099244.ece

33   Todd Halvorson, "After Shuttle, NASA to Pay Russia $56m a Seat For Rocket
       Rides," *Florida Today*, April 7, 2010. www.floridatoday.com/article/20100407/
       NEWS02/4070341/After-shuttle-NASA-to-pay-Russia-56M-a-seat-for-rocket-rides

34   Ibid.

35   "Barack Obama Ends NASA Space Race With Slow Road to Mars."

36   Kenneth Chang, "Obama Calls for End to NASA's Moon Program," *New York
       Times*, February 1, 2010. www.nytimes.com/2010/02/02/science/02nasa.html

37   "Obama outlines new NASA strategy for deep space exploration," CNN, April 15,
       2010. http://www.cnn.com/2010/POLITICS/04/15/obama.space/index.html

38   Ted Rueter, *449 Stupid Things Democrats Have Said* (Kansas City, MS: Andrews
       McMeel Publishing, 2004), 3.

39   David Martin, "War Hero Gets Career-Ending Reprimand," CBS News, March 11,
       2010. www.cbsnews.com/stories/2010/03/11/eveningnews/main6290133.shtml?tag
       =strip

40   Ibid.

41   Luis Martinez, "Silver Star Winner Reprimanded for Afghan Battle," ABC News,
       3/12/2010. http://abcnews.go.com/Politics/Afghanistan/silver-star-winner-capt
       -matthew-myer-reprimanded-attack/story?id=10080860

42   Jim Miklaszewski and Mike Viqueira, "Lawmaker: Marines killed Iraqis 'in cold
       blood,' " NBC News, May 17, 2006. www.msnbc.msn.com/id/12838343/

43   "Critics Slam Decision to Name Navy Ship for John Murtha," FOXNews.com, April
       15, 2010. www.foxnews.com/politics/2010/04/15/navy-ship-named-late-rep-murtha
       -draws-criticism/

44   Penny Starr, "First Lady Credits School Lunch Program for Bolstering National Se-
      curity," CNSNews.com, March 1, 2010. www.cnsnews.com/news/article/62104

45   Ibid.

46   Mary Clare Jalonick, "School Lunches Called a National Security Threat," Associated
      Press, April 20, 2010. www.msnbc.msn.com/id/36664612/ns/health-diet_and_
      nutrition/

47   Ibid.

48   Daniel Rubin, "Another case of TSA overkill," *Philadelphia Inquirer*, February 15,
      2010. www.philly.com/inquirer/home_region/20100215_Daniel_Rubin__Another
      _case_of_TSA_overkill.html

49   Jim Kouri, "Napolitano Admits: U.S. Government Knew 'Underwear Bomber'
      Was an Extremist," Examiner.com, 1/22/2010. www.examiner.com/x-2684-Law
      -Enforcement-Examiner-y2010m1d22-Napolitano-admits-US-government—knew
      -Underwear-Bomber-was-an-extremist

50   Pamela Hess and Matthew Lee, "Father Of Would-Be Bomber, Abdulmutallab,
      Warned U.S. About Son," Associated Press, December 26, 2009. www.huffington
      post.com/2009/12/26/father-of-wouldbe-bomber-_n_404046.html

51   Jonathan Martin, "Napolitano: 'The system worked,' " Politico.com, December 27,
      2009. www.politico.com/blogs/politicolive/1209/Napolitano_The_system_worked
      .html

52   Peter Baker and Scott Shane, "Obama Seeks to Reassure U.S. After Bombing At-
      tempt," *New York Times*, December 28, 2009. www.nytimes.com/2009/12/29/us/
      29terror.html

53   Ibid.

54   "Cheney Says Obama Initially Said Christmas Day Bomber Was an 'Isolated
      Extremist,' " *St. Petersburg Times*, February 15, 2010. www.politifact.com/truth-o
      -meter/statements/2010/feb/15/dick-cheney/cheney-says-obama-initially-said
      -christmas-day-bom/

55   "Al Qaeda Trained US Major, Nigerian Bomber," Yahoo.com, April 27, 2010. http://
      in.news.yahoo.com/43/20100427/896/twl-al-qaeda-trained-us-major-nigerian-b_1
      .html

56   Ralph Peters, "Hood Massacre Report Gutless and Shameful," *New York Post*,
      January 16, 2010. www.nypost.com/p/news/opinion/opedcolumnists/hood_mas
      sacre_report_gutless_and_yaUphSPCoMs8ux4lQdtyGM

57   Frank James, "Obama On Ft. Hood Cautions Against 'Jumping To Conclusions,"
      NPR, November 6, 2009. www.npr.org/blogs/thetwo-way/2009/11/obama_on_ft
      _hood_cautions_agai.html

58   "Shoshanna Johnson Calls Out JAG Tom Kenniff For 'Dangerous' Assumptions
      on Fort Hood Shootings," exchange on the Larry King Show, Crooksandliars.com,
      November 6, 2009. http://videocafe.crooksandliars.com/node/32557/print

59   " 'Allahu Akbar': Ft. Hood General Says Hasan Shouted 'God Is Great!' Before
      Shooting," Associated Press, November 6, 2009. www.huffingtonpost.com/2009/
      11/06/robert-cone-nidal-malik-h_n_348145.html

60   Alison Gendar, Rocco Parascandola, Kevin Deutsch, and Samuel Goldsmith, "Time Square car bomb: Cops evacuate heart of NYC after 'potential terrorist attack,'" NYDailyNews.com, May 1, 2010. www.nydailynews.com/news/ny_crime/2010/05/01/2010-05-01_times_square_evacuated_after_smoking_vehicle_sparks_emergency_ probe.html

61   "Obama's Good Luck Terrorism Strategy," Editorial, *Washington Times*, May 10, 2010. http://www.washingtontimes.com/news/2010/may/10/obamas-good-luck-terrorism-strategy/

62   Ibid.

63   "Mayor Bloomberg Addresses Media; Arrest Made in Time Square Bombing Attempt," Brooke Baldwin host, CNN News, May 4, 2010. http://edition.cnn.com/TRANSCRIPTS/1005/04/cnr.02.html

64   "FBI Agent Short on Details on Militia Inquiry," Associated Press, April 28, 2010. http://www.toledoblade.com/article/20100428/NEWS02/4280343/-1/rss

65   Ed White, "Judge Asks Feds to Show Militia Did More Than Talk," Associated Press, April 29, 2010. http://apnews.myway.com/article/20100429/D9FCD8I00.html

66   Nick Bunkley and Charlie Savage, "Militia Charged With Plotting to Murder Officers," *New York Times*, March 29, 2010. http://www.nytimes.com/2010/03/30/us/30militia.html

67   Ibid.

68   Bill Torpy and Bill Rankin, "It's a Dead End in MS-13," *Atlanta Journal-Constitution*, April 4, 2010. www.ajc.com/news/its-a-dead-end-433983.html

69   Rick Leventhal, "Quiet Muslim-Only Town in N.Y. Founded by Alleged Terrorist," FOXNews.com, 3/23/2009. www.foxnews.com/story/0,2933,510218,00.html

70   David A. Patten, "Pentagon Widens Christian Ban; Graham Says It's Anti-Religion," Newsmax.com, April 26, 2010. http://newsmax.com/InsideCover/graham-islam-pentagon-prayer/2010/04/26/id/356950

71   Carlin DeGuerin Miller, "Christian Militia Members Charged with Sedition in Alleged Plot to Kill Police," CBSNews.com, March 29, 2010. www.cbsnews.com/8301-504083_162-20001341-504083.html

72   "Muhammad's Own Words," Prophet Of Doom, retrieved April 28, 2010. www.prophetofdoom.net/quotes1.html#terrorism

73   Jim Meyers, "Lieberman: U.S. Should Attack Iran's Nuclear Program If All Else Fails," Newsmax.com, April 12, 2010. www.newsmax.com/Headline/lieberman-iran-nuclear-attack/2010/04/12/id/355512

74   "Obama's Jihad on Jihad," *Washington Times*, April 8, 2010. www.washingtontimes.com/news/2010/apr/08/obamas-jihad-on-jihad/

75   Jerome Corsi, "Sleeper cells in America," WorldNetDaily.com, April 18, 2005. www.wnd.com/news/article.asp?ARTICLE_ID=43815

76   Ali Akbar Dareini and George Jahn, "Iran derides Obama's 'cowboy' nuclear stance," *Washington Times*, April 8, 2010. www.washingtontimes.com/news/2010/apr/08/iran-derides-obamas-cowboy-nuclear-stance/

77   "Obama: America a Superpower 'Whether We Like It or Not,' " FOXNews.com, 4/15/2010. www.foxnews.com/politics/2010/04/15/obama-america-superpower -like/

78   Ibid.

79   "Bush Deficit vs. Obama Deficit in Pictures," Heritage Foundation, March 24, 2009. http://blog.heritage.org/2009/03/24/bush-deficit-vs-obama-deficit-in-pictures/

80   Conn Carroll, "Obama Just Made Us More Vulnerable . . . Again," Heritage Foundation, July 22, 2009. http://blog.heritage.org/2009/07/22/morning-bell -obama-just-made-us-more-vulnerable-again/?utm_source=Newsletter&utm_ medium=Emai l&ut m_campaign=Morning%2BBell

81   "Obama: America a Superpower 'Whether We Like It or Not.' "

82   Harold Estes, "Do Your Job," Congress.org, November 20,2009. www.congress .org/congressorg/bio/userletter/?id=10892&letter_id=4287614061

Chapter 11

1   Available at http://webcache.googleusercontent.com/search?q=cache:PW-X9EGqUp 4J:founderswisdom.wordpress.com/category/calvin-coolidge/+this+is+the+chief+ meaning+of+freedom+calvin+coolidge&cd=3&hl=en&ct=clnk&gl=us&client= firefox-a

2   Teddy Davis, "Tea Party Activists Unveil 'Contract from America," ABCNews.com, April 15, 2010. http://abcnews.go.com/Politics/tea-party-activists-unveil-contract -america/story?id=10376437

3   "Rep. Phil Hare (D-IL): 'I Don't Worry About the Constitution,' " Publius, Big Government.com, April 1, 2010. http://biggovernment.com/publius/2010/04/01/ rep-phil-hare-d-il-i-dont-worry-about-the-constitution/

4   Total Correctional Population, Bureau of Justice Statistics, retrieved May 5, 2010. http://bjs.ojp.usdoj.gov/index.cfm?ty=tp&tid=11

5   Gerald McLeod, "U.S. Prison Population is the Largest on Earth," Associated Content, March 10, 2009. www.associatedcontent.com/article/1529685/us_prison_ population_is_the_largest_pg2.html?cat=9

6   Mark Steyn, "Sweet Licks For Tax Lovers," Washington Times, April 9, 2010. www .washingtontimes.com/news/2010/apr/09/sweet-licks-for-tax-lovers/

7   Philip Messing, "FDNY No. 2 to Pull in $242G a Year Pension," New York Post, March 29, 2010. www.nypost.com/p/news/local/golden_fire_exit_Xgr8HobTyGE 09gtAHLZLtM

8   Erika Lovely, "2,000 House Staffers Make Six Figures," Politico, March 26, 2010. www.politico.com/news/stories/0310/35050.html

9   Gail Heriot, "Affirmative Action Backfires," Wall Street Journal, August 26, 2007. www.opinionjournal.com/editorial/feature.html?id=110010522

10   Cliff Kincaid, "Hedge Fund Manipulation, Not Error, Was Behind Market Plunge," CanadaFreePress.com, May 7, 2010. www.canadafreepress.com/index.php/article/ 22894

11 "Prayer in Congress," Congressional Prayer Caucus, retrieved May 6, 2010. www
    .house.gov/forbes/prayer/prayerincongress.htm

12 Daniel Hannan, "I Admit It: I Was Wrong to Have Supported Barack Obama,"
    Telegraph.co.uk, June 14, 2010. http://blogs.telegraph.co.uk/news/danielhannan/
    100043479/i-admit-it-i-was-wrong-to-have-supported-barack-obama/

13 Daniel Hannan, Ibid.

14 Daniel Hannan, Ibid.

ACKNOWLEDGMENTS

I want to acknowledge Bob DeMoss for helping make this the book that it is; Matthew Benjamin, my editor at HarperCollins, for knowing when to say "No"; Greg Lewis for his insights and research regarding the Wall Street mess; and Ian Kleinert, my literary agent with Objective Entertainment, for bringing together all the working elements.

INDEX